THE MIDDLE INCLUDED

SERIES EDITOR

John Russon

REREADING ANCIENT PHILOSOPHY

THE MIDDLE INCLUDED

Logos in Aristotle

ÖMER AYGÜN

NORTHWESTERN UNIVERSITY PRESS • EVANSTON, ILLINOIS

Northwestern University Press
www.nupress.northwestern.edu

Printed in the United States of America

10 9 8 7 6 5 4 3 2 1

Library of Congress Cataloging-in-Publication Data

Names: Aygün, Ömer, 1975–
Title: The middle included : logos in Aristotle / Ömer Aygün.
Other titles: Rereading ancient philosophy.
Description: Evanston, Illinois : Northwestern University Press, 2016. | Series: Rereading ancient philosophy | Based on the author's dissertation (Pennsylvania State University, 2007)
Identifiers: LCCN 2016034273 | ISBN 9780810134003 (pbk. : alk. paper) | ISBN 9780810134010 (cloth : alk. paper) | ISBN 9780810134027 (e-book)
Subjects: LCSH: Aristotle. | Logos (Philosophy)
Classification: LCC B491.L64 A94 2016 | DDC 185—dc23
LC record available at https://lccn.loc.gov/2016034273

Canım annemle babam Güzin ve Birol Aygün'e

CONTENTS

Acknowledgments ix

Abbreviations xi

Preface xiii

Introduction: The Question and the Method 3

Chapter 1: Being (*Logos* in the *Categories*) 23

1. Homonymy 23

2. Synonymy 30

3. Recapitulation and Reorientation 40

Chapter 2: Potentiality (*Logos* in *On Interpretation*) 43

1. The Inherence of *Logos* 43

2. Potentiality 51

3. Recapitulation and Reorientation 61

Chapter 3: Natural Motion (*Logos* in the *Physics*) 63

1. The Natural 63

2. The Organic 75

3. Recapitulation and Reorientation 86

Chapter 4: Animal Motion (*Logos* in *On the Soul*) 89

1. Sensation 90

2. Locomotion 101

3. Recapitulation and Reorientation 110

Chapter 5: Action (*Logos* in the *Nicomachean Ethics*) 113

1. Habit 114

2. Positive State 123

3. Character 130

4. Recapitulation and Reorientation 142

Chapter 6: Speech (*Logos* in the *Politics*) 145

1. Animal Communication 146

2. Human Speech: From "Letters" to "Words" 155

3. Human Speech: From "Words" to "Sentences" 168

4. *Logoi*: Definition, Account, and Law 178

Conclusion 189

1. Overview 189

2. The Human Condition: The Cycloptic and the Oedipal 194

3. *Nous* 208

Notes 211

Bibliography 249

General Index 261

Index Locorum 267

ACKNOWLEDGMENTS

I would like to thank the Department of Philosophy at Pennsylvania State University, which provided me an educational and therefore philosophical environment between 2001 and 2005, the Fulbright Foundation which granted me optimum work conditions for research in 2005–6, and the Projects of Scientific Research at Galatasaray University which enabled me to turn my dissertation into this book.

I am deeply grateful to Robert D. Metcalf and Eli Diamond for their detailed notes and fair criticisms concerning the text in its manuscript form; to the members of the committee of my dissertation on which this book is based, Daniel Conway, Veronique Fóti, Christopher P. Long, and Mark Munn, for their suggestions and encouragement after reading the earliest version of this book; and also to Rémi Brague, Pierre Pellegrin, Jean-Louis Labarrière, and Annick Jaulin for their insightful remarks during my presentations of parts of it. I am also very much indebted to my friends, Katherine Loewy, Eric Sanday, Hakan Yücefer, Sean D. Kirkland, David Bronstein, Gregory Recco, William Harwood, Refik Güremen, Ali Çakır, and Michael Schleeter, for their companionship and challenges.

I cannot express enough my indebtedness to John Russon who directed my dissertation with immense philosophical motivation and genuine friendship, and honored my work by including it in its present form in the series "Rereading Ancient Philosophy" at Northwestern University Press. I am also grateful to Maggie Grossman, Henry Lowell Carrigan, Anne E. Gendler, and Nathan MacBrien at the Northwestern University Press for their help during the editorial preparation of the book in its published form.

Finally, I am most indebted to my wife, Ayşenur Nuhoğlu, for the constant support and diligent criticism she brought to these pages. Indeed, none of the above is to be held responsible for any shortcomings in the following, but the rest of it could not be written without them.

ABBREVIATIONS

Works by Aristotle (for complete bibliographic information, see pages 249–52)

APo.	*Posterior Analytics*
APr.	*Prior Analytics*
Cael.	*De Caelo, On the Heavens*
Cat.	*Categories*
DA	*De Anima, On the Soul*
De sensu	*On Sense and Sensible Objects*
EE	*Eudemian Ethics*
GA	*Generation of Animals*
GC	*On Generation and Corruption*
HA	*History of Animals*
MA	*On the Movement of Animals*
Metaph.	*Metaphysics*
Mete.	*Meteorology*
NE	*Nicomachean Ethics*
On Int.	*On Interpretation*
PA	*Parts of Animals*
Ph.	*Physics*
Po.	*Poetics*
Pol.	*Politics*
Prob.	*Problems*
Protrep.	*Protrepticus*
Rh.	*Rhetoric*
SE	*Sophistici Elenchi, Sophistical Refutations*
Top.	*Topics*

Secondary Works

DK	Diels and Kranz, 1956
KRS	Kirk, Raven, and Schofield, 1983
LSJ	Liddell, Scott, and Jones, 1996

PREFACE

The project of this book originated from my fascination with quite a humble natural phenomenon. I will explore this issue at length in chapter 6, but let me briefly talk about it just so that the reader may have an idea about where this book came from.

A scout honeybee sees flowers to exploit in a certain field. She returns to the hive, and describes her firsthand experience of the location and quality of the bounty to the other bees. Of course, these bees understand the message, since they will fly off to the exact location and exploit the field. And indeed, when they return to the hive, they too can convey their new firsthand experience to still others. But before they have this firsthand experience, they do not or cannot relay to others what for them is *not* a firsthand experience.

Honeybees seem capable of *understanding* what is for them a non-firsthand experience, but not of *relaying* it. There are indeed animal species that are capable of *relaying* non-firsthand experience, especially animals that imitate. But while these species are capable of *relaying* this non-firsthand experience, they seem to do so without *understanding* it.[1]

Is there an animal species that has the capacity for both *understanding* and *relaying* non-firsthand experiences? Of course. We, humans, indulge in this capacity. We *understand* non-firsthand experience as honeybees do, but we can also *relay* it. We *relay* non-firsthand experience like, say, imitating bird species do, but we do so while *understanding* that of which we never had, do not have, or may never have, a firsthand experience. A sentence like "I feel great today" is comparable to the message the scout honeybee conveyed to the other bees: I convey my firsthand experience to you who are capable of understanding what, for you, is not a firsthand experience. But when you say to others, "Ömer is feeling great today," something different is happening: like honeybees and unlike imitating birds, you are *understanding* a non-firsthand experience, but, like those bird species and unlike honeybees, you are also *relaying* that content to others. Since your audience may also relay the same information to still others, this capacity boosts the speed with which information is propagated. As there is no relay among honeybees, only the scout honeybee can inform other bees. Hence, the rate of propagation of that information will follow a *linear growth*. Among humans in everyday life, however, since the receiver *can* in turn relay the message to still others without having to undergo the experience firsthand, the propagation of information can grow *exponentially*.

But this capacity is not only ubiquitous in our everyday exchanges. It also sheds light on significant aspects of human experience. For it is this capacity that enables me to communicate, not only that I feel great today, but also that Socrates was executed in 399, that there are igneous rocks on the surface of the moon, and that the form "circle" can be instantiated in an infinite number of cases. I had understood these messages, as you just did, without ever needing to have a firsthand experience of Socrates's death, of the surface of the moon, or, indeed, of the infinite instantiations of the form "circle."

Actually, almost all science, all fiction, all history, all news media, all education, all propaganda, all gossip, all utopian fiction, all sophistry as well as all philosophy structurally require that the message relayed be such that its content was not, is not, or even cannot be, experienced firsthand. Yet indeed, when I speak, I may be expressing my firsthand experience, but I may also be lying, I may be relaying something I heard from someone else who has heard it who knows where. Further, *you* may further propagate this dubious message without having to check its truthfulness. So I am exercising this capacity not only when I say that Socrates was executed in 399, but also when I say that Socrates was *not* executed in 399. Again, I am drawing on the same capacity when I say, regardless of their actual or potential truth-value, that Athenians will regret their execution of Socrates, or that his execution was ordained by fate, that he will converse with great poets in the afterlife, or that he will be resurrected. So, besides our everyday communications, it is the major human institutions and traditions that require this capacity for both understanding and relaying non-firsthand experience. And once the communicating parties possess this capacity, there is no preestablished control over the truthfulness of the messages. This capacity pervades our experience. And with it, truth, for us, becomes less a given than a task.

As I shall argue in chapters 5 and 6 of this book, when Aristotle famously says that humans are the only animal species having *logos*, he is referring to *this* capacity of understanding and relaying non-firsthand experience along with firsthand experience. But while developing this claim, I noticed how ubiquitous and polysemic the word *logos* was in the Aristotelian corpus. It meant "standard," "ratio," "reason," and "speech," among other things. As I found no survey of the meanings of *logos* in Aristotle either in his own texts or in his posterity, I undertook the project myself and devised this book.

Thus, specifically, this book is about one of the most important words in all philosophy and science, *logos*, as it was used by one of the greatest figures in these fields: Aristotle. It is an argumentative survey of the four fundamental meanings of this word, "standard," "ratio," "reason," and "speech," as they appear in Aristotle's logic, philosophy of nature, and ethics and politics.

On a more general level, however, I consider this book to be about rationality. From this point of view, chapters 1 and 2 deal with the inner structure or requirements of rationality by means of an analysis of the sense of *logos* as "standard" in Aristotle's logical works. In chapters 3 and 4, I move on to rationality *in nature*. There I offer an analysis of natural motion, life forms, organisms, animal perception and behavior, by turning to the sense of *logos* as "ratio" in Aristotle's philosophy of nature. Finally, in chapters 5 and 6, I offer an account of *our* rationality and use of language as humans, by elaborating, in Aristotle's ethics and politics, the last two fundamental senses of *logos*: "reason," and "speech."

In short, this book is about the meanings of *logos* in Aristotle and the relation between them, with a view to, and a claim about, the specificity of human language.

THE MIDDLE INCLUDED

INTRODUCTION

The Question and the Method

Logos is said in many ways. Yet the meanings of *logos* in Aristotle have not been submitted to a thorough philosophical survey, either in the philosopher's work or in his posterity. Once we conduct this survey here in this book, Aristotle's traditional image as the father of formal logic, of classificatory or taxonomic thinking, of the principles of the excluded middle and of non-contradiction, will yield to a more accurate image of him as a thinker of inclusion. For, I shall argue, such a survey reveals that all meanings of *logos* in his works refer to a fundamental meaning, namely "relation," "comprehensiveness," or "inclusiveness." More specifically, as suggested by the etymological meaning of *logos* as "gathering," "laying," and "collecting," this "relation" holds its terms together in their difference instead of collapsing one to the other, or keeping them in indifference.[1] So *logos* involves different terms—typically ones that appear incompatible, contrary, or contradictory in light of a simply exclusive, formal version of the principle of non-contradiction or of the excluded middle. What *logos* does is to hold these terms together in a comprehensive way that was previously unnoticed or simply ruled out.

Let me offer some examples to illustrate this fundamental meaning of *logos* as an inclusive relation. First, in its simplest form, *logos* means "ratio." Take the ratio 4 to 7. *Logos* here *relates* two numbers in such a way that it neither collapses their difference as addition does (4 + 7), nor leaves them in indifference as does the set {4, 7}.

Second, let us take an example from "physics." In Fragment 51, Heraclitus says: "They do not understand how that which is disrupted has the same *logos* as itself: a back-stretched harmony as in the bow and the lyre."[2] So two contrary motions, such as an upward motion and a downward motion, can be comprehended within a single stable framework as in a bow or the lyre. If the cord is not to break off or stay loose, the upward and downward forces must be exerted according to a *logos*, that is, within a certain range outside of which the tension is dissolved. Once again, *logos* names the appropriate relation between the two opposite poles.

Third, an example from "psychology." What is it like to feel the warmth of a radiator? The sensation of warmth on my hand can be explained neither as an activity of my hand, since it is distinct from *heating*, nor as a mere passivity, since it is not reducible to *being* heated either. Thus, an account of sensation must overcome the dilemma between activity and passivity, or the dichotomy between subject and object, and admit both that I *receive* the warmth but also that I am not simply *becoming* warm—we shall see in chapter 4 that Aristotle's word of this middle way is again *logos*. Feeling the warmth of the radiator requires that I hold together *and thereby distinguish* my hand and the radiator.

Fourth example: the desire to eat and the desire to lose weight may seem incompatible. Yet a healthy diet and the very concept of health require a third option between anorexia and gluttony, a way that is neither asceticism nor indulgence, a previously unnoticed middle ground delineated by *logos* this time in the sense of "reason." *Logos* relates the seemingly contrary desires of eating and of losing weight without yielding or suppressing any one at the expense of the other.

Finally, let me illustrate *logos* in the uniquely human sense of "speech." My firsthand immediate experience of the world seems to be exclusively and eminently *mine*—whether it be my feeling great today, the experience of seeing just *this* shade of blue, of feeling a toothache, or of listening to music. These experiences are private and unrepeatable, despite my facial expression, my clenched fist, or my ecstatic smile. Nevertheless I can claim to express my experience to somebody who is, by definition, *not* the one who had it. Beside private experience, and not at the expense of private firsthand experience, we also must have some access to non-firsthand experience given that we have history, science, law, philosophy, and sophistry as part of our lives. *Logos* as "speech" is precisely the human capacity for understanding and relaying firsthand experiences *not at the expense* of experiences we never had, *may* never have, or *cannot* ever have firsthand.

As to the overall structure of this book, it takes the hybrid form of what I may call an argumentative survey. For, on the one hand, its six chapters survey the various functions of *logos* by a cross-reading of central passages respectively from Aristotle's logic, physics, and ethics.[3] On the other hand, the book presents an overall argument about the fundamental meaning of *logos* in Aristotle and also about its specifically human meaning as "speech." So the argumentative aspect of the book is well-suited to the reader who wishes to read the book from cover to cover, while the surveying aspect accommodates the reader preferring to pick out and read isolated chapters. To this end, each part opens first with a road map for the overarching argument, but then with a fresh introduction specifically designed for the topic of that chapter. Similarly, each chapter closes with a recapitulation for that individual chapter followed by a reorientation for the reader who wishes to move on to the next one.

In this introduction, let me first present the main question of the book, then offer a brief review of Aristotle's method in order, then, to argue for our own method in this book and give an outline of the overall argument.

The Question

> There is a story that a man and not a man
> Saw and did not see a bird and not a bird
> Perched on a branch and not a branch
> And hit him and did not hit him with a rock and not a rock.[4]

This riddle illustrates two requirements for riddles in general: their terms should be at once familiar to their listeners, and ambiguous enough to keep them guessing. For a riddle is never an unknown out of nothing, but always an unknown carved from out of the bulk of what is already known. Further, this ignorance should be overcome neither by acquiring a hitherto unknown piece of information, nor by making calculations, nor by multiplying blind guesses in order to approximate the correct answer by trial and error. The solution of a riddle requires that one look for that which was purposefully designed to be overlooked, and recognize the twist at the heart of the riddle. One must understand what the words "man," "bird," and "rock" mean. But one must also notice the way in which these words were deliberately designed in the riddle to have more than one straightforward meaning. Only then can one properly solve the riddle: "A eunuch threw a bit of pumice to a bat perched on a fennel plant, but missed." All riddles are subtended by this tension between familiarity and ambiguity.[5]

So is *logos*. This word is both extremely familiar in Ancient Greek and highly ambiguous.[6] In fact, the ten major senses listed in Liddell-Scott and Jones's *Greek-English Lexicon* range from mere "reckoning" all the way to the "Word of God."[7] And this is without even speaking about the amazing number and significance of its senses in the later Stoic, Gnostic, and Christian traditions.[8] Equally extensive and equivocal is Aristotle's own use of *logos*.[9] Bonitz reduces this ambiguity to a fourfold distinction which I shall roughly adopt without following its order: "standard," "ratio," "reason," and "speech."[10] Yet Aristotle never offers an analysis of this ambiguity. Actually, besides the fact that Aristotle's traditional corpus opens with a discussion of the ambiguity of words, since he insistently demands the dialectician to disambiguate such terms, and accordingly analyzes the ambiguity of fundamental philosophical terms, it is puzzling to see that he does not even mention that *logos* is used in many ways.[11]

Thus, just like the terms of the riddle above, the word *logos* in the Aristotelian corpus is as familiar as it is ambiguous. *Logos* is not that which Aristotle did not think of. Indeed, far from it. *Logos* is rather a word that Aristotle persistently used without ever explaining or even thematizing it—a "Purloined Letter," a blind spot, in his thought as well as in his vast posterity, ancient[12] and contemporary.[13] This, then, is the question: What does *logos* mean in Aristotle, and how are we to make sense of these meanings? It is this unexplored question emerging out of terms most familiar to readers of Aristotle that we shall attempt to answer in this book.

Aristotle's Method

Dialectic Explicit in Aristotle

I must touch upon the thorny subject of Aristotelian dialectic if only because it will provide justification for my own procedure in this book.[14] In what follows, I shall claim that Aristotle's method in most of his extant works can be best characterized as dialectical. In support of this claim, I shall turn, first, to some of Aristotle's *explicit* statements about dialectic and his own typical procedure, and then to his *implicit* use of dialectical method in his logic, his physics, and his ethics. Finally I shall claim that our method in this book should also be dialectical.

For Aristotle, dialectic is a kind of *syllogismos* in the loose sense of "reasoning." Syllogism in the strict sense is a *logos* in which "certain things having been put, something else necessarily follows through them" (*Top.* I, 1, 100a25–27; *APr.* I, 1, 24b19–21). A dialectical syllogism, on the other hand, is one that starts from *endoxa*, from widespread opinions, opinions accepted by everyone or by the majority or by the wise (*Top.* I, 1, 100a30–b21). Unlike syllogism in the strict sense, dialectic then begins, not by positing primary and true things, but by assuming a receptive stance, by an "induction" (*epagôgê*) or even a "perception" in the sense of a recognition of what is "out there" in the form of opinions, utterances, and appearances.[15] Yet dialectic begins by taking these for granted only in order to then return upon them with a critical evaluation and an argumentative account.[16] Starting out with an "induction," dialectic typically *uses* deductions in order to follow up or push through the implications of those opinions or appearances into eventual impasses.[17] For, as Aristotle says in resonance with Socratic elenchus, Plato's aporetic dialogues, and even the Cave Story, "it is not possible to resolve anything if you do not see how you are bound" (*Metaph.* III, 1, 995a29).[18] Thus dialectic is characterized less by its starting point than by its commitment to critically return there, to create and sustain opposition and tension. This function of dialectic is precisely that which a syllogism in the strict sense cannot do, and indeed is not intended to do.[19]

Hence, besides the gymnastic function of dialectic, Aristotle states two other uses which are both critical:

> [Dialectic] is useful for philosophical sciences because, if we are able to question both [sides of a question], we shall more easily discern truth and falsehood at each point.[20] But further, [it is useful] in connection with the first principles in each science, for it is impossible to say something about them on the basis of the principles peculiar to the science in question, since principles are prior to everything else, which is why it is necessary to deal with them through the widespread opinions on each point. This belongs characteristically or most appropriately to dialectic: for, as it is investigative, it lies along the principles of all methods. (*Top.* I, 2, 101a35–101b4)[21]

Dialectic starts out with what is already "out there," what is already known by us, already familiar, obvious, clear, and distinct for us, in order then to reach a point from which we can and must freely and critically evaluate it.[22] In this sense, dialectic is typically equipped with some sort of "principle of charity," and is in close affinity to democracy and freedom of thought and expression.[23] In this light, Aristotelian dialectic appears to be an inheritance of what Socrates says about dialectic and hypotheses in distinction from mathematics in Plato's *Republic*:

> [In dialectic, the soul] makes its way to a principle that is free from hypotheses; starting out from hypothesis and without the images used in the other part, by means of forms themselves it makes its inquiry through them . . . The argument itself grasps [the highest segment of the intelligible] with the power of dialectic, making hypotheses not principles but hypotheses—that is, steppingstones and springboards—in order to reach what is free from hypothesis at the beginning of the whole. (VI, 510b5–8, 511b3–5)[24]

We shall shortly see affinities between Aristotelian method and two other Socratic-Platonic methodological concepts: maieutics and elenchus.[25]

Aristotle's explicit remarks on dialectic seem to resonate with his avowed procedure at the opening of a great number of his central works: to proceed from what is clear and known to us, toward what is clear and known simply or by nature.[26] This procedure is clearly closer to dialectic proper than to either demonstration or gymnastic dialectic. For, first, neither demonstration nor gymnastic dialectic *begins with* "what is clear to us": demonstration begins with what is true and primary, while gymnastic dialectic can begin anywhere. Dialectic proper, however, begins with the *endoxa*, whether it be widespread opinions or perceptions. Second, neither demonstration nor gymnastic dialectic *leads us toward* "what is clear by nature": for, demonstration is a way down from the true and primary toward what is implied therein, while the goal of gymnastic dialectic is victory, as rhetoric's goal is persuasion. Dialectic proper, on the other hand, being "inquisitive" (*peirastikê*),[27] "investigative (*exetastikê*),[28] or "questioning" (*erôtêtikê*),[29] is committed to truth.[30] In a word, gymnastic dialectic can start anywhere, but is not supposed to lead us *to truth*; demonstration can only start with what is established as true and primary, and thus cannot *lead us* to truth either.

To illustrate the claim that typical Aristotelian method proceeds dialectically from what is known and already clear "to us" toward what is most knowable and clearest "according to nature,"[31] let us now turn to Aristotle's implicit use of this procedure in his logic, his physics, and his ethics.[32]

Dialectic Implicit in Aristotle's Logic

Inasmuch as we know a language, an immense range of things is "clear to us." We are immersed in a first "domain of obviousness": phonetics, vocabulary, grammar, syntax, text forms, expressions, proverbs, jokes, riddles, songs, and so on. A language is not only a tool for acquiring or exchanging information, nor simply a set of rules to which we constantly and anxiously obey. It is also such a seminal paradigm in our "outlook" on the world that it tends to be, and must be, "overlooked." Language speakers "get" a language to such a degree that they necessarily "forget" that it was acquired in the first place and is not exempt from examination. Our mother tongue is precisely developed enough to become a possible object of questioning with regard to the categories, the distinctions and conflations it instills. And it is precisely as speakers familiarized in a particular language that we may demand more rigor or justification than that language presently offers.

No wonder Aristotle often starts out in his works with an analysis of the obvious meanings of common words, and ends up challenging the status quo of his own language by introducing unnoticed distinctions or by canceling redundant ones.[33] In fact, the very opening of the traditional corpus, the beginning of the *Categories*, abruptly introduces the distinction between homonymy and synonymy, suggesting that he takes for granted that homonymy is possible as a mismatch between words and things[34]—an inescapable ambiguity in words taken by themselves.[35] It should not be far-fetched to say that Aristotle's logic addresses various levels of linguistic and mental operations dialectically first by observation and then by problematization.[36] That Aristotle's starting point is our preliminary familiarity with our mother tongue can also be expressed by the fact that, although he is arguably the first to formalize linguistic structures in logic, he seems to be tempted neither by the idea of an Adamic language, nor by the typically early modern project of an artificially engineered "perfect language."[37] So, far from naively imposing the categories of the Ancient Greek language onto things, far from being tempted by the dream of a perfectly rational artificial or natural language, Aristotle's dialogue within language is oriented from what was already clear to Ancient Greek speakers of his time, toward what is clear in itself or "according to nature."[38]

Aristotle's logic then is dialectical at least in the sense that it can be seen to be performing a dialogue of language with itself on various levels. One could even argue that this dialogue takes an essentially Socratic form, in that he openly follows up and critically pushes the claims inherent to native language speakers including himself.[39] In this sense, Aristotle's logic is not only a dialogue with and within language, but also a "maieutics" of language, in that he assists language to "give birth" to the implicit significance with which it is pregnant.[40]

Dialectic Implicit in Aristotle's Physics

But there is at least a second "domain of obviousness." For we know a lot more than words, meanings, grammatical rules, and constructions: first of all, our body, our health, our needs, and further the weather, day and night, animals, plants, motions and changes. In life, there is an obvious and unproblematic character to what all these are, how they work and especially how and when they do not work. The wildest of fantasies and the most awesome miracles precisely presuppose this practical familiarity we have with nature. This familiarity, however, is once again preliminary and far from offering us, and is not expected to offer us, say, an explicit definition of time, motion, or void. Although much is apparent to us "out there" in nature, most of it is barely sufficient to even let us ask what is going on "in there."

Similarly, Aristotle's method in his philosophy of nature is neither deductive nor simply inductive, but once again mostly dialectic.[41] First, as is obvious from any short glance at the *History of Animals* or the *Generation of Animals*,

Aristotle's extensive work on nature obviously stands on a wealth of eager investigation and direct exploration, on secondhand accounts of the experience of hunters, physicians, fishermen, farmers, beekeepers, travelers, and indeed also on the various accounts of nature by his contemporaries and predecessors.[42] But anyone who has read any part of the *Physics*, *Parts of Animals*, or *On Generation and Corruption* would know equally well that his philosophy of nature is not reducible to this minute and extensive work of recording and collectorship. If Aristotle begins as a spectator or listener of natural phenomena, he does so as one who wants to understand as much as to know, one fascinated by the concrete plurality of natural phenomena, with all its deviations, exceptions, and monstrosities, as well as by the relations and regularities embedded in nature. Whereas investigation and exploration constitute the first moment of his philosophy of nature, they are in fact meant to provide material for comparison, interpretation, specification, and generalization, in order to subject natural phenomena to an internal critique, to become informed by life forms, to access the "logic" Aristotle claims his "interlocutor," nature, to have.[43]

Just as Aristotle's logic can be seen as a gradually expanding dialogue of language with itself, reminiscent of Socratic maieutics, his philosophy of nature can be considered as equally dialogical. For it indistinguishably involves a patient and systematic listening to natural phenomena, followed by a critical challenge and cross-examination quite in line with Socratic elenchus.[44]

Dialectic Implicit in Aristotle's Ethics

Finally, we also know much, and perhaps most, about ourselves and about others, our desires, our thoughts, our goals, about our personal history and about the communities we live in. All these are out there in the form of discourse, gestures, reactions, customs, conventions, and artifacts. This clarity is what makes us able to navigate in everyday social life with a relative amount of comfort in so far as we do so. If so, then the realm of human significations and institutions may be said to constitute a third "domain of obviousness."

And yet, indeed, as our acquaintance with human meanings and institutions is the closest, strongest, and oldest kind of familiarity, it is also the hardest and most crucial kind of knowledge to critically examine. Most often this "knowledge" does not exempt us from, but rather obligates us to, much reflection and long hesitation when it comes to bearing undeserved pain, to making decisions for us and for others, to figuring out what is going on "in there" as we listen to someone or even to ourselves, to discussing what is meant by "freedom," "democracy," "terrorism," "violence," and "justice," or what Aristotle means by *logos* for that matter.

Along similar lines, Aristotle sketches a twofold program in the *Nicomachean Ethics*: an extensive review of his predecessors' opinions on political constitutions, and then an evaluation of them on the basis of his collection of constitutions of Greek city-states (X, 9, 1181b16ff.). To this extent at least, his ethics and politics follow the same dialectical pattern as his logic and physics: a gathering of a great amount of research beyond firsthand or even secondhand experiences, and then a subsequent critical discussion of them and with them.[45] The *Nicomachean Ethics* goes as far as to claim that ethics does not start from a clean slate, but requires preliminary experience (I, 3, 1094b28–1095a8; II, 4, 1105b9–18). Further, the *Ethics* can be seen to proceed dialectically, and to offer a view of individual human beings and of their political life as itself dialogical all the way down. For, according to the *Ethics*, the human soul is structured as an environment of "dialogue" between the desiring part of the soul and the rational part, comparable to one's listening to "both one's father and friends" (I, 13, 1102b29–1103a4). In fact, the *Politics* further elaborates a dialogue that is no longer metaphorical, but literal, between the two "interlocutors" just mentioned: one's growth, education, and decision-making, both within the familial environment, and within the larger political community.[46] Thus Aristotle's ethical and political philosophy can be seen as not only proceeding dialectically, but also as thematizing "dialogue" as constitutive of the individual and social life of human beings.[47]

The Modality of Aristotle's Dialectic

For these reasons, dialectic seems to characterize Aristotle's typical method quite well, especially when he investigates earthly phenomena and the human world,[48] by its procedure from what is "clear to us" toward what is "clear according to nature," that is, from the pre-given widespread opinions, habits, and perceptions toward principles.[49] But what do these starting points look like, these opinions or perceptions that are "clear to us" before being exposed to dialectical scrutiny? More importantly, what do these "principles" look like? What form does Aristotle's procession toward them take? Are we not far off from the traditional view that for Aristotle knowledge is of universals and science is demonstrative and hence from his general "theory of science" in the *Analytics*?[50]

These questions call for two distinctions. The first one is between research and exposition—a distinction perhaps effaced by a traditional reading of the *Posterior Analytics* as a theory of scientific methodology.[51] Indeed, some of Aristotle's works are *expositions* starting out with definitions and gradually exposing the results of earlier research:[52] the *Poetics*, the *Categories*, the *Sophistical Refutations*, the *Prior Analytics*, to a certain degree, some of the

Parva Naturalia, the *Rhetoric*, and *On the Heavens*.[53] On the other hand, in many of his central works, Aristotle explicitly presents the problems at hand, and proceeds to *search* for answers through a critical discussion of his predecessors' views. Among such works are the *Metaphysics*,[54] the *Physics*,[55] the *Nicomachean Ethics*,[56] *On the Soul*, and the *Posterior Analytics*.[57] So there are some Aristotelian works where Aristotle exhibits his doctrine, and in these works his procedure is not dialectical. Yet the other works, which are marked less by exhibition than by research and inquiry, are dialectical.

Secondly, in order to grasp Aristotle's procedure, one must recognize the crucial cosmological distinction he makes between the supralunar realm, marked by the perfect regularity and eternity of the heavenly bodies beyond the Moon's sphere, and the sublunar realm characterized by the relative irregularity and temporariness of earthly phenomena.[58] The modality required by the sublunar realm is irreducible to the apodictic principles of the supralunar or mathematical, and its rigor falls between pure necessity and pure contingency.[59] This modality is expressed by Aristotle in the recurrent phrase *hôs epi to polu*, often translated as "for the most part," "usually," "to a large extent," or "generally."[60] Despite appearances, this phrase is not strictly speaking a quantifier. It is rather a modifier that governs conclusions and principles typically concerning the sublunar realm.[61]

For instance, the proposition "For the most part, sheep have four legs" is, strictly speaking, neither a universal nor an existential. It differs from the existential proposition "At least one sheep has four legs" in that it presents a level of generality that may be necessary for even recognizing "at least one sheep" in the first place. It also differs from the universal proposition "All sheep have four legs" in that its truth would not be refuted in a situation where *not all* sheep would have four legs.[62] Sheep having four legs is neither apodictically necessary nor a mere eventuality on a par with them having none or seventeen. If the only options of scientific method were pure deduction and pure induction, if the only logical modalities of propositions were the universal and the existential, there would be no knowledge of the living beings on earth. So sheep having four legs can be established neither through an abstract, all-encompassing principle, nor through existential propositions concerning particulars, but by means of an inquiry into what it is *for the being at hand* to be—in this case, into the mode of sheep locomotion, its diet, its environment, and so on. Thus here the adequate method of inquiry is neither deduction nor induction alone, but dialectic, and its propositions must hold true neither universally nor existentially, but "for the most part."

Let us see another example of Aristotle's use of this phrase, "for the most part," this time from his ethics. According to Aristotle, although there are many incompatible opinions concerning the supreme human good, something is clear to all humans: the supreme human good is "happiness" (*NE* I, 4, 1095a14–21).[63] This is where the dialectical process begins, for this is what is clear to us, what is obvious, the common opinion or common sense. But what do the majority or the wise exactly mean by "human happiness"? And do their views hold up?[64] Aristotle scrutinizes the view that happiness basically means, say, honor, fame, or recognition. He does not object to this view; he simply questions it in a clearly Socratic fashion: First, if one prioritizes fame and recognition in life, *who* exactly would one want to be recognized by? Why would one prefer to be recognized by *some people* rather than by others? What is it about *those people* that makes their recognition worthy of being identified with the supreme human good? Secondly, what would one want to be famous or recognized *for*? For one's looks, for one's talent, for one's wealth? Aristotle simply observes that the answers to both of these questions converge on the idea of "virtue": people want recognition and honor, but actually they pick and choose, for they want recognition *precisely* from people who they believe to have some sort of excellence or distinction, and they want recognition *precisely* for what they believe to be their own excellence or distinction. In this way, Aristotle dialectically eliminates, conflates, disambiguates, or nuances a number of candidates (pleasure, honor, money, etc.), gathers what is left from, and common to, his criticisms and distinctions, and defines "human happiness":[65] "the actuality of the soul according to virtue" (*NE* I, 7,1098a3–5, 17–19).[66] Thus the opening dialectical discussion of the *Nicomachean Ethics* leads to a principle.[67] Because of the very subject matter at hand, this principle is neither necessary in the way a geometrical principle would be, nor is it on a par with *any* proposition, for instance, its negation (*NE* I, 7, 1098a21–1098b8). The logical modality of "for the most part" thus secures a level of generality, characteristic of the sublunar region, which allows the validity of the conclusion that human happiness requires the virtuous work of one's soul *not at the expense* of the fact that some virtuous people are unhappy. If happiness is so "for the most part," then one must inquire further into the human soul, habits, and virtues, and the external conditions of happiness—which is what Aristotle does in the rest of the *Ethics* and indeed in the *Politics*.[68]

To sum up, then, as his explicit procedure from "what is known and already clear to us" toward "what is most knowable and clearest according to nature," Aristotle's dialectical method stands midway between induction and deduction. The specific modality of his statements, "for the most part," occupies a middle ground between necessity and mere accidents or chance (*APo.* I, 30, 87b19–21). Hence Aristotle tries to distinguish incidental being not only from necessary being, but also from that which happens "for the most part."[69] This is why it is difficult to locate Aristotle's discourse within the dilemma of prescription and description, or within the divide between "is" and "ought." In each of these cases, there are two terms that we typically take to be mutually exclusive and jointly exhaustive, in accordance with the principles of non-contradiction and of the excluded middle, whereas Aristotle's method is precisely to seek a middle path that seemed ruled out.[70]

I already suggested that Aristotle's method *perpetuates* the Platonic, and especially Socratic, notions of dialectic, elenchus, and even maieutics.[71] I may even argue that Aristotle diversifies, extends, and even radicalizes Socratic dialectic. For, besides "conversing with his own soul"[72] and with others, as Socrates does,[73] Aristotle also believes, unlike Socrates, that "the countryside and the trees" can teach him as much as "the people of the city," his contemporaries or his predecessors.[74] But then wouldn't Aristotle be abusing, violating, or overstretching the Socratic method, at least in his investigation of nature? Here we should remember that, before Socrates "called philosophy down from heaven, and placed it in cities, and introduced it even in homes,"[75] there was a younger Socrates, an almost Milesian Socrates, who, according to the *Phaedo*, was "wonderously eager for the kind of wisdom called the investigation of nature" (96A), and who investigated the "cause of generation and corruption" (95E)—a Socrates who, lacking "natural gift" (96C), had to turn away from nature, for fear of being blinded by it, and to "have recourse to *logoi*" as a "second sailing" (99D-E).[76] If so, Aristotle, it would seem, took up where young Socrates left off.[77]

Our Method

Our method in this book must also be dialectical for the same reasons. Reading, understanding, and interpreting Aristotelian texts are not much different than the above-mentioned human undertakings and reasonings, irreducible to both chance and necessity, and impracticable by either deduction or induction alone. Our opting for a dialectical method itself can be substantiated dialectically by taking up and internally criticizing two possible opposite procedures: induction and deduction.[78]

The First Impasse: Inductive Method

So we are to begin a philosophical survey of the meanings of *logos* in Aristotle. Where are we to begin? There is a corpus of writings in Ancient Greek which is called "Aristotle's work" with more or less rigor. This is apparent to us not through reasoning, but already from our acquaintance with the world and its history. So we may simply open up "his books," note the occurrences of the word *logos* and make a generalization: "if *logos* means this here, and that over there, and so on, *then* the meanings of *logos* in Aristotle are such and such." This inductive-statistical approach of matching and counting seems to yield at least a clean-cut starting point by answering the question: "Does it exist?"[79]

> Induction [*epagôgê*] is the forward way from particulars to universals. For instance, if the skilled pilot is the best pilot and the skilled charioteer the best charioteer, in general the skilled person too is the best in each case. Induction is more convincing, clearer and more easily knowable by perception, and is shared by many, whereas syllogism is more cogent and more efficacious against objections. (*Top.* I, 12, 105a13–19)

So we may tentatively adopt this convincing, clear, and straightforward strategy of looking for particulars and of inferring general rules.

But first, what exactly are we to look for? The word "*logos*," of course. But what about its declinations and compounds, and its root, the verb *legein*? This method can provide us with more statistics concerning these "relatives" of *logos* such as *logismos*, *physiologos*, *dialegesthai*, and so on. It may even map out the words that are often coupled with *logos*, its "neighbors," so to speak, such as *ergon*, *mythos*, *ekhein*, *onoma*, or *ousia*. Still, the true weakness of the inductive method becomes clear as soon as one tries to understand, interpret, or translate even one occurrence of *logos*. For instance, take the famous line of the *Politics*: "*logon de monon anthrôpos ekhei tôn zôiôn*," translated by Rackham as: "and man alone of the animals possesses speech" (*Pol.* I, 1, 1253a9–10). The inductive method can provide more information about the verb *ekhein* which neighbors *logos* in this sentence. But even if in an ideal situation *logos* turns out to be always followed by *ekhein* throughout the corpus, how does this give us any insight into the meaning of *that* particular occurrence? To answer this, we are rather led to the question of what *ekhein* means and thus we fall into infinite regress.

From the viewpoint of a strictly statistical-inductive method, a single occurrence of *logos* can mean anything, and this is indeed expectable at the beginning; but it can *equally* mean anything however often it is used, however much it is explained by Aristotle. Statistical information defers the task of understanding because it is a preparation for that task. It is a material, in the sense in which, in dialectic, knowledge "draws its material" from common opinion.[80] It provides us namesakes ("homonyms") and cognates ("paronyms"), none of which guarantee the unity of meaning ("synonymy"). It processes words so as to provide more words, but does not supply any insight into the "*logos* of being" of what is being sought (*Cat.* I, 1a1–12). While it provides a potentially infinite list of the "relatives" and "neighbors" of *logos*, it remains incapable of detecting its "friends," that is, terms that are neither etymologically related, nor textually adjacent, but conceptually connected to it, such as *meson*, *êthos*, *mixis*, *physis*, or *eidos*. The statistical-inductive method then turns out to be fundamentally inadequate for moving from premises to any conclusion. Employing a rigorously statistical-inductive method for our task cannot supply a satisfying answer to the question: what exactly are we to look for?

Besides, where exactly are we to conduct our search for whatever it is we are looking for? Of course we can always choose a certain edition or manuscript—but not by using an inductive-statistical method. Editors and philologists typically warn us that a lot of *choices* are already made in the process of editing or translating an Aristotelian text.[81] So the strictly statistical method will have no resource for justifiably evaluating the potentially infinite possible readings from which it must choose, and is fundamentally inadequate, not only for enabling us to draw any inference, but even for delimiting the premises from which we wish to draw a conclusion in our task.

The Second Impasse: Deductive Method

If the statistical method pulverizes the question of *what* is to be sought, and unjustifiably picks *where* to conduct the research, one may well think of solving the first problem by simply consulting a reliable dictionary, and the second by using the most authoritative or most recent edition of the Aristotelian corpus. Besides the wealth of available resources in our subject, anyone more or less acquainted with philosophy has already some general ideas about Aristotle's thought from which one can also infer the meanings of *logos* in Aristotle's philosophy. Thus, we can conduct the research by thinking in the following way: "*Since* we already know that Aristotle's philosophy is such and such, and *since* this authoritative translator or commentator understands *logos* as that and that, *therefore logos* means such and such."

But *how* exactly are we to qualify Aristotle's philosophy in our first premise? What exactly is "clear to us" such that it may provide our much-needed starting point? Besides their unwarranted character, our preconceptions are no more consistent than dictionaries, editions, and translations we shall draw upon in our second premise. Which preconception are we to start out with? With Aristotle the empiricist or Aristotle the rationalist?[82] With the naturalist or the theologian? With the universalist or the particularist? With the "young zealous Platonist" or with the "mature virulent critique of the Academy"? Even assuming that we have clear-cut answers to these questions, these clear-cut answers or our adoption of *the* authoritative commentator or most prestigious translations exempt us from appealing to Aristotle's own text at all. For instance, we will simply repeat that the specifically human meaning of *logos* means "speech," "reason" or "rationality."[83] Using a strictly deductive method, we will then end up investigating not the meanings of *logos* in Aristotle, but the meaning of, say, "reason" in the work of the translator or commentator. Hence this task also leads to infinite regress.[84]

Similar reservations apply to philosophical inferences made from secondary sources, from biographers and from biographical indications.[85] For instance, most significantly, Aristotle has been undoubtedly influenced by Plato, and he does argue for and against him, but it is the Aristotelian corpus itself that tells us why this is so, and not mere biographical incidents reported from yet other, often much later, sources which may themselves be no less subject to suspicion.[86] So, does Aristotle's leaving Athens after Plato's death mean that he turned or would turn away from Plato's thought—assuming that he did leave Athens at that time?[87] Or does it rather mean that he would cling on to Plato ever more fervently with a stronger sense of duty, extolling him as "the man whom it is not lawful for bad men even to praise"?[88] Either way, this will not help us understand *why* Aristotle reacted the way he did. Further, it seems far-fetched to explain Aristotle's dynamic development by appealing to such a static and unitary view of Plato's philosophy, and to such a rigid dilemma of either supporting or rejecting it. To say the least, we cannot *begin* by reducing Plato's philosophy to a "Theory of Ideas," and Aristotle's career to an adherence and a subsequent reaction to that doctrine.[89] But, as we already suggested, we may well *end up* drawing conclusions that may shed light on Aristotle's relation to Plato, concerning the way he radicalizes the Platonic and/or Socratic undertaking of *logos*, but also concerning the way he perpetuates the "dialectic road" toward the intelligible in the divided line from Plato's *Republic*, and thereby answers Socrates's question: "And do you call that man dialectical who grasps the *logos* of being of each thing?" (VII, 533d7–534a8; 534b3–4).[90]

Just as the strictly inductive method turned out to be unable to move away from premises to any conclusion in the argumentative survey we are about to conduct, a purely deductive method is bound to question-begging. Just as a merely inductive method falls into infinite regress for lack of a critical distance from the texts, the exclusive adoption of a purely deductive method will do so by moving us further and further away from them. In the first case, we are stuck with "what is clear to us" without any access to "what is clear in Aristotle himself."[91] In the second case, we start out with what is supposedly clear in Aristotle, with imported "principles," but we are deprived from resources for questioning, criticizing, evaluating, or justifying them, for arriving at them. In short, while pure induction disables us from *interpreting* anything in the Aristotelian texts, pure deduction relieves us of the task of interpreting anything *in the Aristotelian texts*.[92]

Our Method

So we want a procedure that *starts out* with what is clear to us and that argues its way *to* principles. If our starting point does not reflect the whole truth, as it most probably and hopefully does not, then we want to be able to return there with an evaluation of its shortcomings and overstatements. Returning to *where we were*, our procedure must directly involve *us* at each stage, and this return should take the form neither of *petitio principii* nor of tabula rasa, but of self-criticism. This is why our method must be dialectical.

More concretely, what are we to do? First, we have occurrences of *logos* in the Aristotelian corpus, along with dictionaries, indexes, commentaries, translations, and preconceptions of our own. Since our book is not on a specific Aristotelian text, we shall go directly to the very first lines of the traditional corpus, the distinction at the opening of the *Categories* between homonymy and synonymy by the criterion of a common "*logos* of being." This distinction not only opens the traditional Aristotelian corpus, but it also opens up our problem. For, in these opening lines, synonymy is distinguished from homonymy by entailing a commonality of the "*logos* of being" of two beings in addition to the commonality of their names. Thus, these opening lines abruptly problematize the relation between beings and words by means of the concept *logos*. They designate our problem without thematizing it. It is this question of the meaning of the phrase "*logos* of being" in the *Categories* that shall drive this book as a whole by unfolding from logical and metaphysical questions into Aristotle's accounts of nature and human life in every following chapter.

Outline

Our attempt to solve the question of *logos* in Aristotle's philosophy shall cross six chapters: the first two on his logical works (*Categories*, *On Interpretation*), the third and fourth on his work of philosophy of nature (*Physics* and *On the Soul*), and the fifth and sixth on his ethical-political works (*Nicomachean Ethics* and *Politics*).[93]

Let me give a more concrete outline of the book. In chapter 1, "Being," we will discuss the function of *logos* in Aristotle's *Categories*. At the very inception of the *Categories*, *logos* distinguishes homonymy and synonymy by providing an answer to the question: "What is it for this being to be?" (*Cat.* 1, 1a2ff.). Through a discussion of the questions emerging from its context, I will argue that *logos* here must mean something like "standard." For, without this standard, the commonality between an ox and a human being as "animals" will be reduced to a relation between mere namesakes like a "spelling bee" and a "honey bee." Thus, *logos* in the sense of "standard" requires a relation between a being and "what it is *for it* to be." That a being has such a standard means that it holds on at once to its own being and to its claim concerning what it is for itself to be, without letting one yield, or remain indifferent, to the other. Yet what would such a standard mean if it is not truly inherent to the being in question, but arbitrarily imposed from without? How are we to warrant that a standard is in fact inherent to the being at hand?

Chapter 2, "Potentiality," deals with *On Interpretation* and elaborates this question of the inherence of *logos* as standard. For a being to have an inherent standard implies that it is neither indifferent nor identical to that standard and that its meeting the standard is neither merely necessary nor an eventuality on a par with an infinite number of others. So, to have a "*logos* of being" means to hold one's actual state and one's inherent potentiality together without letting one yield to the other (*On Int.* 9; 13). This actuality of a potential as such is precisely Aristotle's definition of "motion." Thus, the inherence of this standard shall be exhibited first in inherently motivated motions, that is, in natural motions, and secondly in human action as emerging from a "potentiality with *logos*," from a potentiality for two contrary outcomes without one outplaying or remaining indifferent to the other (*On Int.* 13, 23a1). In our research into the first major meaning of *logos*, namely "standard," we are thus led to the two following questions: How does natural motion instantiate the inherence of the "*logos* of being"? And how does human action do so?

Chapter 3, "Natural Motion," offers an answer to the first question. If nature is an inherent source of motion and the "form according to *logos*" in the *Physics* (II, 1, 193a30–31), then natural beings shall exhibit *logos* as their *inherent* standard by means of internally motivated motions, namely reproduction, nutrition, sensation, and locomotion (192b8–16). While a natural element, although capable of locomotion under compulsion, is indifferent to its likes and inimical to others' difference, living beings further instantiate *logos* in reproducing and self-nourishing by others in a "ratio": a reproducing being holds contrary elements together by integrating them to its own "form according to *logos*" in another body, while the self-nourishing being does so in its own body (*DA* II, 4, 416a10–18; *On Breath* 9, 485b18). This part of the book thereby introduces the second major meaning of *logos*: ratio.

Chapter 4, "Animal Motion," goes further into *On the Soul*. Unlike reproduction and nutrition, the "ratio" involved in sensation, which is the defining feature of animal life, does not destroy other forms according to their own *logos*. "Sensation is a *logos*" in that it holds together the state of the organ and that of the object in their very difference instead of being indifferent to or overtaking one another (*DA* III, 2, 426b7–8; II, 12, 424a25–28). As to the second characteristic animal motion, namely locomotion, Aristotle also analyzes it in the "logical" form of the immediate conclusion in the "practical syllogism": unlike the univocal "universal" motion of elements, animal locomotion happens when the animal holds both the universal premise "spoken" by desire and the particular premise "spoken" in sensation (*MA* 7, 701a32–33; *DA* III, 11, 434a17–22).[94] Then, the "*logos* of being" in the *Categories* means the inherent standard of a being as exhibited here in Aristotle's philosophy of nature by the being's natural motions. Each of these motions involves a rationing or a proportioning: reproduction, nutrition, sensation, and locomotion.

Chapter 5, "Action," then turns to our second question: how does *human action*, and not motion as such, instantiate the inherence of the "*logos* of being"? This discussion leads us to yet another major sense of *logos*: "reason." Having two-sided potentialities, namely "potentialities with *logos*," a human being is able to hold two contradictory options open at once without letting one yield to the other. This precisely complicates the immediacy of the "practical syllogism": the particular premise is no longer provided by immediate sensation, but rather reelaborated by positive states (*hexeis*) (*NE* II, 5). Specifically human potentialities do not exist at the expense of a contrary eventual potentiality. Thus, on the one hand, intellectual virtues such as art, science, and prudence, all positive states with *logos*, presuppose "potentialities with *logos*" (*NE* VI). Virtues of character, on the other hand, are positive states *according* to *logos*, and they involve the desiring part of the human soul. A courageous citizen is intellectually but also emotionally apt at deliberating well concerning matters involving fear, that is, he keeps open the possibility that a particular situation may call for retreat instead of attack for the action to be courageous. Positive states according to *logos* hold contrary interpretations of particular sensibles in so far as the latter are objects of desire: "The desiring part in general somehow partakes [in *logos*] insofar as it listens to and can obey it in the sense in which we say 'taking account [*ekhein logon*] of both one's father and one's friends'" (*NE* I, 13, 1102b31–1103a3).[95] Just as the human being is not a member of a family at the expense of being a citizen, she is not bound by habituation at the exclusion of acquiring positive states. The *Politics* takes this metaphor of an inner dialogue within one's soul quite literally, and claims that *logos*, this time finally as "speech," establishes both the household and the city (*Pol.* I, 1, 1253a8–18).[96]

So in chapter 6, "Speech," I shall develop an Aristotelian account of "speech" as the fourth and last major meaning of *logos*. I shall argue that speech is the human capacity to both understand and relay not only firsthand experiences, but also experiences which are not and even *cannot* be made firsthand.[97] This meaning of *logos* shares the same structure as all the previous ones: just like *logos* as "speech" breaks down the boundary between what one has experienced and what one has not, human beings are able to understand and relay firsthand experiences *not at the expense of non-firsthand experiences*.[98] This meaning of *logos* founds both the household and the city, and provides a necessary condition for historiography, myth, politics, science, sophistry, and philosophy. It also made our inquiry since chapter 1 possible, since it enabled us to ask the question of the "*logos* of being," namely what it is to be *for an ox*, that is, for a being whose experience we can never have firsthand.

Hence we shall have come full circle back to the question we started out with in the context of the *Categories*. At the term of our lengthy pursuit of answers to the question of what a being should be like if it is to have anything like a *logos* of being, we shall also reach an answer to the question as to what *we* should have been like all along if we even came up with such a question, that is, the question concerning the *logos* of being of something we are not. The question of the "*logos* of being" presents itself only to a "being having *logos*."

So the overall thesis of this book is the following:

All the senses of *logos* in Aristotle, "standard," "ratio," "reason," and "speech," refer to the same fundamental meaning: they are all relations that do not let their different terms yield or lay indifferent to one another. Propelled by the principle of non-contradiction along with this relational structure of *logos*, Aristotle's philosophy presents itself as a Heraclitean attempt to "understand how that which is disrupted has the same *logos* as itself: a back-stretched harmony as in the bow and the lyre" (Fr. 51).[99] For each of the various meanings of *logos* names a comprehensive grasp of an unforeseen common ground between seemingly disjunctive terms, an inclusive counterpart to unduly formal versions of the principles of non-contradiction and of the excluded middle. *Logos* refers to a mediation or a synthesis in all of its meanings without exception, and never to anything simple, pure, or immediate. In this sense, *logos* may be contrasted with *nous* as I shall do at the very end of this book. Further, in its specifically human sense, *logos* as "speech" or even "reason" is never associated with any animal nor with anything divine. It is strictly and rigorously secular, mundane, full of wonder, but not mystical. This may be fruitfully contrasted with the Stoic, Gnostic, and Christian uses of the word.[100] Finally, perhaps precisely because it refers to something humble, prosaic, or at least lacking purity and divinity, this ambiguous but common word has remained unthematized, hidden in plain sight, and riddle-like, both in Aristotle and in his posterity.

Hence, the project of this book.

CHAPTER 1

Being

Logos *in the* Categories

The focus of this chapter is the meaning of *logos* in the *Categories*. More specifically, here I shall elaborate the expression "*logos* of being" which appears at the very opening of the traditional Aristotelian corpus.[1] Since this expression distinguishes synonymy from homonymy, I shall study "homonymy" in section 1 below, and then "synonymy" in section 2, by drawing out an experiential stance, a governing principle, and an example for each of the two. In section 3, by the comparison of synonymy and homonymy, I shall basically claim that *logos* here means "standard." But, as I shall show in our discussion of the Cartesian concept of "substance," if *logos* is to distinguish synonymy from homonymy, this "standard" must be *inherent* to the being at hand. Thus, the question of this chapter extends into a discussion of *On Interpretation*, the focal text of the next chapter of this book.

1. Homonymy

Words are conventional signs for things according to Aristotle.[2] The Atlantic Ocean *has* a name in a weaker sense than the sense in which we *have* a name for it. At this level, language seems to be the realm of an inadequacy or distortion, but this inadequacy entails an unlimited indifference, disregard, and freedom: the freedom of naming things, calling them as we wish, and articulating those words, forming higher units even more loosely related to things themselves. This freedom is indeed at the level of language or thought, indeed it does not *touch* the world—and that is precisely its virtue. This freedom, this infinite malleability of anything by means of language makes it possible to consider the world as wide open to *our* conventions, *our* interpretations, *our* projects, *our* retrospective distortions, *our* capricious manipulations and arrangements. Hence the acquisition of language is the acquisition of an immense power which may well provoke the fantasy of a world presented *to* us instead of standing *outside* us, *around* us, and often *against* us: the fantasy of an undetermined, infinitely determinable world.

And yet, for the most part, we do not live in a world that appears to be waiting *for us* to be shaped all along, preparing treasures or traps *for us*. We also live in a world *we* await and adapt to. The world is less a candidate for answering our own demands than a question we are answerable to. But how, if at all, can, and indeed does, the world divert us from this tendency to interpret it in terms of our own control and egocentrism? What, if any, are the powers of the world for dissuading us from the capricious significations we may give it? These are the questions in the background of this first chapter.

Aspect

What does *logos* mean in the *Categories*? Since we are investigating the functions of *logos* in Aristotle's philosophy, it may be reasonable to begin our investigation with one of his logical works, the *Categories*, insofar as logic already seems to promise us at least something relating to *logos*.[3] Hence, in the *Categories*, there is a clearly philosophical and yet cursory remark concerning the priority of things themselves to *logos* (*Cat.* 12, 14b15–20).[4] Apart from this, there is one use of *logos* in the *Categories* that seems to be philosophically loaded and extensively employed in the text. This usage of *logos* appears in the very first sentence of the *Categories* within the phrase "*logos* of being":

> Those whose names[5] only are common, but whose *logos* of being according to this name is different, are called homonyms, such as "animal" for both the human being and the representation;[6] for if one supplies what is it for each of them to be animal, one will supply a particular *logos* for each. Those whose names are common and whose *logos* of being according to this name[7] are also common, are called synonyms, such as "animal" for both the human being and the ox; for each of these are addressed [*prosagoreuetai*] with the common name "animal" and their *logos* of being is the same. For if one supplies the *logos* of what it is for each to be animal, one will supply the same *logos*. (*Cat.* 1, 1a1–13)[8]

We may understandably call both a human being and her picture an "animal," and to this extent they are homonyms. In Aristotle's work, homonymy can designate the relation between a representation and a thing represented as in this example.[9] But it may equally refer to a number of other relations: the relation between *leukon* as color ("white") and *leukon* as sound ("clear") (*Top.* I, 15, 106b6–10); the relation between a particular circle and "circle said simply" (*Metaph.* VII, 10, 1035b1–2), between a hand of a living being and a wooden hand or the hand of a corpse (*PA* I, 1, 641a1), between a part and a whole (*PA* II, 1, 647b18), and even between a species and its genus (*Top.* IV, 3, 123a27).[10] Besides this wide range of relations, two random namesakes in English such as a "latch" (a collarbone) and a "latch" (a kind of lock) are no less homonyms (*NE* V, 1, 1129a29–31).[11] Further, given that the relation between beings and words is not natural for Aristotle, we may call any two beings by the same name and thus make them homonyms.[12] Moreover, homonyms need not share a name uttered, but simply a way of being "addressed." As his examples suggest, such as the hand of a statue being a hand in name only, even one being can be "addressed" homonymously as long as it is addressed regardless of what it is *for it* to be, as long as its *logos* of being is disregarded.[13] If language is conventional, we may designate two things with any word, and a fortiori we may designate any one thing any way we want.

What then is there in a being that is apart from its *logos* of being, such that it can be addressed homonymously? We encounter a conceptualization and an example of this in section 2. I shall quote extensively for later reference:

> Of beings some are said of some underlying thing but are not in an underlying thing, for instance human being is said of some underlying human being, but is in no underlying thing. Then some are in an underlying thing but are not said of an underlying thing (by "in an underlying thing" I am not saying that which is present in something as a part, but that for which it is impossible to be apart from that in which it is), for instance grammar is in an underlying soul, but is not said of any underlying thing, or the "a certain whiteness" is in an underlying body (for all color is in a body), but is not said of any underlying body. Then some are both said of an underlying thing and in an underlying thing, for instance knowledge is in the underlying soul and is said of the underlying grammar. Then some are neither in an underlying thing nor said of an underlying thing, for instance this human being or this horse. (*Cat.* 2, 1a20–b5)

Aristotle's fourfold distinction here is made along two criteria: (1) being in or not being in an underlying thing, and (2) being said of or not being said of an underlying thing. "Being in an underlying thing" (*en hypokeimenôi einai*) here is used, not in the sense that a man *is in* a house or my wallet *is in* my pocket, but rather broadly in the sense that grammar *is in* a soul and all whiteness *is in* a body. On the other hand, the second criterion of Aristotle's fourfold distinction here, "being said of some underlying thing" (*kath' hypokeimenou tinos legesthai*), is used very narrowly in the sense that animal *is said of* a human being and knowledge *is said of* grammar, but whiteness *is not said of* a body. In order to address a being homonymously, in order to address it while disregarding its *logos* of being, one then may address it merely with respect to that which *is in* it—not, Aristotle emphasizes, as that which is present in something as a part, but as that which cannot be apart from that *in* which it *is*. Thus, to consider an ox not as an ox per se, but as meat, or as a mascot, is to address it homonymously.[14] Similarly, a book may be used as a fan, a person as a corpse, a bottle as a weapon, a key as a saw, or perhaps most simply as something right here (*tode ti*). The easiest and safest way to avoid addressing a being in its *logos* of being is to address it in the most immediate way possible, as "just this right now." For this homonymous appearance, for this appearance of that which *is in* an underlying being and yet is not considered in its *logos* of being, I shall use the term "aspect."

Aspects of Somnolence

The wide range of homonymy is irreducible to a lexicological class of namesakes; it rather implies a certain experiential stance, a corresponding understanding of the relation between aspects and, most importantly, an understanding of being. To get a more firm hold on homonymy and on what is implied by its disregard for the "*logos* of being," let us first elaborate it in its experiential form.

The homonymous way of viewing things as aspects, however abstract, is not foreign to routine everyday experience. Waiting for a bus, one is not really thinking of the bus. One is rather thinking of "all sorts of things." If interrupted and interrogated about what exactly was on one's mind, one may say: "I was just thinking . . ." If insisted, one may say: "A yellow blur, a rattling, then something said yesterday, then something a little bit far away . . ." All this adding up to: "Nothing really." The content of thought here is a sequence of free-floating aspects as in daydreaming. A similar loose texture shows itself in casual conversions where people engage in small talk, "just talking," where they talk about "this and that," about "nothing really." And indeed the world is such that it can be treated in this way: to the daydreamer waiting for a bus, it offers at all times a yellow blur, a rattling, things said yesterday, then something a little bit far away, and so on; to people chatting, it always supplies a "just this now" and then a "just that." In everyday life, experience often takes the form of a sequence of aspects that do not, and are not expected to, add up to anything—aspects of "nothing really."

To be exact, however, we must acknowledge that there is something fundamentally inaccurate about our enumerations of aspects: a yellow blur, a rattling, and so on. For, first of all, they are made after the fact, from our sober analytical viewpoint. Hence, once enumerated, each aspect comes to mean more than it in fact did. These *enumerations* fail to reflect the way in which these aspects precisely do not *count*, the way in which their flow adds up to "nothing really." To be more precise, we may say that these aspects were less aspects of *nothing really* than they were simply not aspects *of*. The experiential form of these discreet homonymous aspects is comparable to somnolence.

An Exclusive Version of the Principle of Non-Contradiction

However inadequate our sober analytical perspective may be when it comes to thematizing this somnolence, we may say in retrospect that these free-floating aspects are detached from one another. Each aspect is just what it is, no more or less. That is why it defies description. It either is or is not. Aspects do not imply one another. They are not *of* one another or *of* anything else. They are so isolated that they cannot explicitly oppose or reject one another either. If there is anything regulating these disparate aspects, it is a broad or formal version of the "principle of non-contradiction," formulated as a negated conjunction: ~ (p & ~p), and its complement, the "principle of the excluded middle," formulated as an exclusive disjunction: p v ~p. Since this version of the principle of non-contradiction excludes an aspect from anything other than itself, it may be called the *exclusive* version of the principle of non-contradiction.[15]

It is indeed Aristotle himself who first formulated both the "principle of the excluded middle" and the "principle of non-contradiction" in this exclusive form as "most certain" and "most familiar" (*On Int.* 9; *Metaph.* III, 1, 996b26–30; IV, 7, 1011b26–27; 3, 1005b10, 13). This he did in explicit opposition to what Heraclitus supposedly says: "it is impossible for anyone to suppose the same to be and not be, as some think Heraclitus says" (*Metaph.* IV, 3, 1005b23–25).[16] A reformulation later in the same chapter of *Metaphysics* IV underlines a temporal qualification: "it is clear that it is impossible for the same to be and not be the same at the same time" (*Metaph.* IV, 3, 1005b30–32).[17] Thus, as each aspect is present to the exclusion of all others, the only relation between aspects is a formal, temporal one: pure succession. A yellow blur, *then* a rattling, *then* something said yesterday, and so on.

"Underlying Thing"

But is there any constant underlying being in which these homonymous aspects inhere temporarily in pure succession? If so, what is it? What might this being be that keeps receiving aspects *at different times*, although never at the same time?

According to chapter 5 of the *Categories*, there is indeed something of which it is "most characteristic" to admit contraries. It is called *ousia*, which we shall translate as "being": "Most characteristic of being seems to be that, while the same and numerically one, it admits contraries, in such a way that one cannot show anything else which is not a being that, while numerically one, admits contraries" (4a10–13).[18] Admitting contraries without itself becoming a contrary is what is most characteristic of being and unique to it. So a being is somehow uniquely capable of being now white and later not white while remaining the same being it is. A being cannot be and fail to be at the same time any more than an aspect can, and a being cannot present this aspect and another aspect at the same time either; but unlike anything else, there is a being which can present this aspect *at one time* and that aspect *at another*, without itself ceasing to be (2b5–6). What is being, as both detached from and implied by the somnolent flow of homonymous aspects? Aristotle says: an "underlying thing."

But how is this underlying thing not just another aspect? What is this underlying thing which admits and subtends different qualities that *are in* it at different times? One may think: that which remains constant after the abstraction of aspects. If it is true that aspects are abstractions, then being turns out to be the abstraction of those abstractions.

An Example

Descartes's famous wax example may be of some assistance in clarifying this conception of being. As it is well known, the "Second Meditation" engages in such a systematic abstraction of sensuous aspects in order to prove that the underlying thing is perceived by the mind alone and that the mind is therefore better known than the body.

> Let us take, as an example of the thing [*causa*], this piece of wax. It has been taken recently from the honeycomb; it has not yet lost all the honey flavor. It retains some of the scent of the flowers from which it was collected. Its color, shape, and size are manifest. It is hard and cold; it is easy to touch. If you rap on it with your knuckle, it will emit a sound. In short, everything *is present in* it that appears needed to enable a body to be known as distinctly as possible. (AT, VII, 30; AT IX, 23; emphasis is ours)

Descartes's emphasis that the characteristics of all five senses "are present in" (*adsunt*) the piece of wax translates literally the way Aristotle says that color "is in" (*en esti*) an underlying being. Descartes thinks that, in order to prove that the mind is better known than the body, the sensuous characteristics in the piece of wax must turn out to be less known than the mind. So, in order to demonstrate this, he burns the piece of wax and observes that the aspects of hardness, whiteness, or coldness vanish, and are replaced by softness, darkness, and heat. For, indeed, contraries cannot coexist. The crucial question is whether anything remains throughout the experiment: "Does the wax still remain? I must confess that it does; no one denies it; no one thinks otherwise" (AT VII, 30; AT IX, 24). Descartes thus infers that there is something unchanged although all sensuous characteristics have changed. He then asks: "So what was there in the wax that was so distinctly grasped?" The answer is: something extended, flexible, and mutable.

But isn't this alleged "underlying thing" simply just another aspect like others, albeit relatively more constant? No. For, as Descartes acutely emphasizes, unlike any actual aspect whatsoever, the underlying thing is neither flexed nor unflexed, but *flexible*. The underlying thing is neither mutated nor unmutated, but *mutable*. It is not even simply extended: "What is it to be extended? Is this thing's extension also unknown? For it becomes greater in wax beginning to melt, greater in boiling wax, and greater still as the heat is increased" (AT VII, 31; AT IX, 24). Properly speaking, then, that which underlies the change of aspects is a thing minimally extended and further extendable or retractable, flexible and mutable. As it is precisely not determined by any *actual* magnitude or shape, the underlying thing can neither be seen, nor heard, nor smelled, since all sensation is of something actually exhibiting the sensuous characteristic it has; nor can it be an object of imagination, since one can imagine only one of a finite number of *actually* flexed and mutated things each time, whereas the underlying thing is infinitely *flexible*, *mutable*, and, perhaps, *extendable*. Thus, Descartes claims, the only possibility is that the underlying thing is inspected by the mind alone, free from both sensation and imagination—and this essentially distinguishes the "underlying thing" from any aspect whatsoever. The underlying thing *can* be anything, but by itself it is pure indeterminacy, a "just this," an *x*. Further, according to Descartes's argument, being purely extendable, flexible and mutable, it reflects that which may change it. In other words, being purely indeterminate, it simply reflects the mind's power of determination, the mind's power of judgment asserting: this *is such and such*. It indeed reflects the power of judgment regardless of the truth and falsity of the judgment: as the object of a true *or* false judgment, the underlying thing attests the very existence of the mental act of judgment. Descartes concludes that the mind is clearly and distinctly known to itself as giving a judgment, regardless of the correctness of this judgment. To return to our initial question, then: what is this underlying thing admitting and subsisting different aspects that *are in* it at different times? Descartes's answer is the following: something infinitely indeterminate.

In our task of understanding the *logos* of being as the differentia between homonymy and synonymy, here we come to the end of our brief elaboration of homonymy. Homonymy is a way of addressing beings in mere aspects; its experiential form is a kind of somnolence where the relationship between aspects is nothing more than pure succession, a relationship governed alone by an exclusive version of the principle of non-contradiction; and finally, the understanding of being implied in this stance is that of a purely indeterminate substratum—Cartesian *substantia.*

2. Synonymy

Seen from a somnolent viewpoint, "being" in Aristotle is not different from Cartesian *substantia.* This can be seen from Aristotle's discussion with his predecessors about the number of the "sources" in the first book of the *Physics.* There he starts by asserting that the source is either one or many (185a5):[19] in a dialectical procedure, first he takes up the Parmenidean hypothesis that the source is one (184b15ff.), criticizes it for implying the impossibility of motion, change, and nature as such (184b27–185a1),[20] and gradually picks from this hypothesis the term "underlying thing" (*hypokeimenon*) (185a32);[21] then he takes up the hypothesis of the "Physicists" according to which the sources are many, and specifies it by claiming that in one way or another all take contraries to be sources (*Ph.* I, 4, 187a12; I, 5). In a word, Aristotle there takes both the term "underlying thing" and the contraries from both sides of the argument concerning the number of sources. What does Aristotle do with this underlying thing and the contraries? He simply puts the underlying thing beneath both contraries to ensure the transition from one to the other.[22] Aristotle even calls this underlying thing an "underlying nature" (*hypokeimenê physis*) and his examples are akin to Descartes's wax example:

> The underlying nature is knowable through analogy: as bronze is in relation to a statue, or as wood is in relation to a bed, or as the formless is before taking on its form in relation to any of the other things that have form, so is this [underlying nature] in relation to a being [*ousia*] or to the "this" [*to tode ti*] or to that which is [*to on*]. (*Ph.* I, 7, 191a7–12)

Thus, here at least Aristotle is clearly not at odds with the idea that transient sensuous aspects inhere in something constant that is indifferent and irreducible to them.[23] Even if it is clearly true that Aristotle does not connect this constant being with the "subjectivity" of the thinker as Descartes does, both the idea and the Latin word *subiectum* translate, or at least are derived from, Aristotelian *hypokeimenon*.

This being said, the concept of being implied in homonymy as indeterminate stuff is Descartes's conclusion, not in Aristotle's. To be the underlying being in which aspects inhere is only half of the account of "being" in Aristotle, and we must return to the first chapter of the *Categories* in order to see what is left out: the *logos* of being.

Logos of Being

Homonyms have their names in common, not their *logos* of being. Synonyms, however, have both in common,[24] which is why they are key to our investigation of the first meaning of *logos*:

> Those whose names are common, and whose *logos* of being according to this name are also common, are called synonyms, such as "animal" for both the human being and the ox; for each of these are addressed with the common name "animal" and their *logos* of being is the same. For if one supplies the *logos* of what it is for each to be animal, one will supply the same *logos*. (*Cat.* 1, 1a6–13)

Just as homonyms, synonyms too seem to at first come in pairs: a human being and an ox, as "animal," are synonymous, because what it is for them to be animal is the same, their *logos* of being is the same, unlike that of homonyms. My calling a cloud "a whale" is due to *my* association; but the commonality between an ox and a human being as both "animals" is *their* commonality, since *they* nourish themselves, *they* perceive, *they* move, *they* desire. Thus a being can be addressed synonymously on its own as well: if one can address an ox and a human being not as "white" or "powerful," but as "animal," one already has in view the *logos* of being of each, and can address them one by one on their own.

Note that the unlimited possibilities of homonymous designations are here suddenly limited by a condition not emerging from language or thought, but from the thing at hand: what it is *for it* to be. Simultaneously, the power of naming the aspects that *are in* an underlying being is limited by that which *is said of* it. According to Aristotle's examples, the difference between homonymy and synonymy is the difference between the way a representation of a human being is an "animal" and the way a human being is an "animal." Thus, despite our analyses in the last section, being is not only that *in* which all others are, but also that *of* which they *are said*: "All others are either *said of* these underlying beings or *are in* them" (*Cat.* 5, 2b5–6).

What is the implication? The implication is that the world is not simply made out of underlying beings and whatever is *in* or *on* it. Being is not simply an underlying thing similar to Anaximander's *apeiron*, in which determinations come and go while it remains undetermined. The world is neither mere stuff, nor some stuff *plus* external determinations. Being, in turn, is no more a purely indeterminate being than it is a mere aspect. It has a particular determination that is irreducible to an aspect, but it also does not survive the coming to be and passing away of any determination. Birth and death are not simply changes. Then not all motion and change occur *in* and *out* of beings; there are beings that come to be and pass away *themselves*.[25] They have a limit which binds them and, if transgressed, leads to their destruction. Indeed, it is "most characteristic" of being to admit contraries, yet being is not defined as that which underlies simply any change from one contrary to the other. Aristotelian being is not infinitely indeterminate and determinable as such, but already has determination. For a being, to be is not to be anything in any way, but to be something in a certain way.

This is the second half of the account of being we find not in Descartes, but in Aristotle.

A Kind of Waking

Everyday life is not exhausted by examples of somnolence where one is "*just* thinking" or "*just* talking," where homonymous aspects parade while adding up to "nothing really." Thought also seems capable of some kind of waking. To take up our previous examples, then, a daydreaming while waiting for a bus may be disturbed by an event, an accident, an object, or a memory. A chat may be interrupted by the emergence of an issue, the telling of a story, or a discussion. In Latin, such a matter for speech and deliberation is called a *causa* as a cause one is engaged in or as a case debated in court.[26] It is also called *res*, as has been suggested by the answer of the daydreamer saying he was thinking of "nothing *really*."[27] There is then something "real" about this waking stance, in the sense that it is concentrated around an issue.[28] This does not imply that there is something necessarily serious, truthful, and objective about this stance or that the matter at hand is important, but it does imply that, once awake, the somnolent thinker is no longer at the center of the world. Instead of being the pivot of disparate transient aspects, experience now gravitates around an "issue," a "case," "something real."

Already, when one interrupts a daydreamer and asks what she was thinking, one is operating in a waking stance, and there is already something at issue. It is indeed from a waking stance that somnolence can be thematized and analyzed, and indeed this thematization will be made after the fact and will remain inaccurate to that extent. This waking stance is obvious from our present argument as well, since here we are not thinking or speaking about "just this" and we hope that all that we say does not add up to "nothing really." Although somnolence can be thematized only in retrospect, the advantage of a sober stance is that it can keep in mind this inappropriateness and recognize that neither thought nor the world are exhausted by somnolence.

Indeed, the world is such that it offers "something real," instead of aspects that add up to "nothing really." Instead of "just something bulky" *or* "just something warm" *or* "just something moving," what appears now is a living being, say, an ox: the ox is bulky *and* warm, he is laying down on the grass *and* he is moving his tail *and* digesting food *and* he is turning to look at me. He is where his tail is *and* where his horns point *and* where his chest lays *and* wherein his eyeballs revolve. It is however only in comparison to the somnolent viewpoint that we may remark that these aspects are no longer simply exclusive of one another and constitute an aggregate. From a properly sober standpoint, we should rather say that the sober appearance is less a conjunction of formerly disparate aspects than the appearance of a *standard.* Aspects have not vanished here, but they appear as aspects *according to* this standard, that is, aspects *of* something. In a way, what distinguishes synonymy from homonymy, or sobriety from somnolence, is this simple conjunction: *of.* A selfsame aspect *of* "nothing really" is open to infinite manipulation because its only "demand" is to be clearly and distinctly selfsame, to be *just* "this"—which it actually is anyway. But the sober world offers something that is not infinitely malleable, something that has a demand, or better, something that *is* such a demand: to be an ox is to be what it is *for an ox* to be so.

Similarly, the small talk that could go in any direction is now interrupted by something to attend to: a story that organizes characters, actions, and circumstances, a topic of discussion that articulates different aspects of an issue, a suggestion that demands responsiveness. Note that this demand may well be rejected, the ox may well be seen as a lump of meat or a mascot, and one may well refuse to attend to an issue raised in a conversation. Nevertheless such a rejection will never make it as if the demand has *never* been made. A somnolent stance is conceivable only in reference to, and as a departure from, the sober world. "Nothing" as an answer almost always means "Nothing really." Hence Aristotle's definition of the "fictitious" (*plasmatôdes*) necessarily involves not pure creation out of nothing, but compulsion, a counterforce exerted against a preexisting force resisting it: "By 'fictitious' I mean 'forced in [*bebiasmenon*] for the sake of a hypothesis'" (*Metaph.* XIII, 7, 1082b3).[29] The rejection or dismissal of this demand will turn the demand into a *rejected* one, and to that extent will affirm its having been. *Logos* of being means this *standard* of being.

An Inclusive Version of the Principle of Non-Contradiction

Every extended being has magnitude. So every extended being is at once "here" and also "elsewhere." Similarly, the ox occupies some stretch of space. But further, the motion of his tail depends on the fact that it moves in certain ways while his body remains still. The motion of the tail *of* the ox depends on *his* somehow being at once "here" and "elsewhere." The head *of* the ox is cooler, harder, and more silent than *his* stomach. This "*of*" does not simply tack on different aspects, it does not just connect the formerly disjoined coldness and hardness and heat. The word "*of*" refers to an original that organizes, hierarchizes, and defines aspects according to something that is not an aspect. Aspects here are no longer simply subject to the exclusive version of the principle of non-contradiction. The motion and rest of the ox's tail is far from excluding the motion and rest of all its other parts. In short, here the principle of non-contradiction works no longer as a formal law of disjunction and exclusion, but as an original demand of inclusion. The principle here can no longer simply preclude the cohabitation of contraries at the same time; it must also proclaim that contraries *can and are typically meant to* belong to the same at the same time—but *in different respects*.[30]

Aristotle's discussion of the principle of non-contradiction seems to have its roots in the fourth book of Plato's *Republic*. In the passage from the *Republic*, while discussing the unity of the soul, Socrates suggests to Glaucon that "it is clear that the same will not be willing to do or undergo opposites at the same time in the same respect [*kata tauton*] and in relation to the same [*pros tauton*]" (IV, 436b8–c1). Later, Socrates shifts this emphasis from the *unwillingness* of being toward *impossibility* (436c5–6). After considering the examples of a man moving his arms and a spinning top, to which we shall return shortly, he modifies his first statement:

> Then the saying of such things will neither scare us nor persuade us that something, being the same, would ever suffer, be, or do opposites at the same time, in the same respect [*kata to auto*] and in relation to the same [*pros to auto*]. (436e8–437a2)

Here then Socrates states at least a qualified version of the exclusive principle of non-contradiction: the exclusive version holds *in the same respect* and in relation to the same, thereby implying that it would not necessarily apply if different respects were involved. Simply put, he draws our attention to the respects in which contraries are not disjoined, but conjoined. Let us call this version the "inclusive principle of non-contradiction." Then, while it is true that a top either moves or does not move absolutely, it may well be, and in fact *must* be, moving and not moving in different respects—in this instance, with respect to its different parts—according to the inclusive version.

In fact, Aristotle's statement of the principle in the *Metaphysics* takes into account these respects in which it *is* possible for the same to be and not be the same at the same time: "it is impossible for the same to belong and not belong to the same at the same time in the same respect [*kata to auto*]" (IV, 1005b19–20).[31] Although Aristotle's version of the exclusive principle of non-contradiction was formulated precisely in opposition to "what Heraclitus is supposed to have said," here, on the contrary, Aristotle joins Heraclitus in recognizing the need to modify the exclusive version and, as Heraclitus says, to "understand how that which is disrupted has the same *logos* as itself: a back-stretched harmony as in the bow and the lyre" (Fr. 51). In fact, precisely in order to reject the absolute disjunction or conjunction between being and non-being, Aristotle appeals to these respects or ways:

> In one way they [those who simply conjoin being and non-being] speak correctly, in another way they do not know. For, being [*to on*] is said in two ways so that in a way being can come into being out of non-being, in another way it cannot. And the same can at once be and not be, but not in the same respect [*all' ou kata tauto*]. (*Metaph.* IV, 5, 1009a32–35)

This passage is a major part of our textual evidence for claiming that Aristotle is a thinker of inclusion and that the recognition of this depends on the central notion of *logos*. Hence, the inclusive version of the principle of non-contradiction will inform us more about "what it is *for this being* to be" than the exclusive version: where the latter will compellingly show that the same thing cannot be both white and not-white, moving and not-moving at the same time, the former will add that this is true *not absolutely*, but only as long as we are considering the same respect. The latter will view the motion of the tail of an ox as simply moving, while the former will illuminate the interconnection between the motion of the tail and the stillness of the spine of the ox, and agree with Heraclitus that "changing, it is at rest" (Fragment 84).[32]

Aristotle then has both the exclusive and the inclusive versions of the principle of non-contradiction. Without the inclusive version, one cannot draw the difference between homonymy and synonymy, between free-floating aspects and beings having a *logos* of being in their own right, a standard of being. *Logos* here means "standard."

Another Sense of "Underlying Thing"

Let us briefly return to Socrates's examples in the *Republic* in order to see how *logos* mediates respects that previously were mutually exclusive. Socrates's first example is of a man standing still while moving his arms and head. The example may seem to present us with a trunk standing still, an arm and a head in motion. A surgeon or a beauty contest jury member may well give judgments and advice from this stance, focusing on each part of the human body in isolation from the others. A gym teacher, a coach, or a dance teacher may well approach the human body in this way, having different diagnoses and exercises for each of its parts. For, as the exclusive principle of non-contradiction dictates, his arms cannot be moving and not moving at the same time, no more than his head or his trunk.

But Socrates's example is not about a trunk and two arms and a head, *but about a man.* The motion *of his* arms and *of his* head, as well as the stability *of his* trunk, are not random aspects of his motion and rest. They are not *aspects*, they are rather *respects* precisely regulated by a standard, by the man's *logos* of being, by what it is *for him* to be (*Metaph.* VIII, 6, 1045a14ff). To be a human being is to be a living body, and to be a living body is to be the natural demand that one's motion and rest originate in oneself, the demand to articulate motion and rest in such a way that the body can find in itself both a stable ground and a joint around which motion is possible (*Ph.* II, 1, 192b8–23; *MA* 1–2). However different and contrary the possible motions of his arms may seem, they do remain specific in comparison to all possible motions as such. For they make up, or take part in, a certain species-character of a being. Even further, the motion of a living body is a demand not only to orchestrate its internal parts, but also to adapt itself to the system between the organism and its environment: the earth underneath, the water, the air, the heat of the sun, and ultimately the celestial spheres.[33] Briefly put, to move his arms and head while standing still is not a challenge to the selfsameness and unity of the man's body and life; it is precisely an indispensable part of what it is *for him* to be, of what it is *for him* to be human, of his *logos* of being.

Socrates's second example is a top which is spinning, that is, moving with respect to its periphery but not with respect to its axis. Again, this motion and rest are not primarily exclusive aspects in their own right, but rather respects precisely regulated by what it is *for a top* to be, since to be a top is to be the very conjunction of peripheral motion and axial rest.[34] Once this conjunction is disrupted, once this demand is rejected, one has a top in name only. For if the axis cannot stand still vertically while spinning, one has a wheel. And if the axis cannot stand still in any respect, then one has a ball.[35] Either way one does not have a top that is adequate to what it is *for a top* to be. Aristotle would say "one has a top *only homonymously*." In this case as well as in the previous one, the principle of non-contradiction is at work not by simply excluding different aspects, but by offering different respects in which the same can conjoin contraries and in fact demands this conjunction according to what it is for it to be—according to its *logos* of being.

Here, then, we find out that being is not simply that *in which* determinations are indifferently applied, but also that which has an inherent standard, a claim or a "say" on its being. Here, then, we find Aristotle much closer to the Heraclitean "*logos* of being" than to Cartesian *substantia*. To go back to Heraclitus's examples, both the bow and the lyre require that the cord be pulled in two opposite directions, that it be stretched within a certain range, according to a ratio or a standard. In fact, the notes of the lyre and the accuracy of the bow depend on how *well* their cords are thus stretched. Requiring that their cord be pulled in two opposite directions, they also require a stable frame to hold the tension together without one pull yielding to the other. One would disrupt what it is for a bow to be not by *establishing* such an opposition, but by *removing* it, for instance by pulling the cord too hard or by burning it like Descartes did to the piece of wax.

Return to the Example

If it is true that the regard for *logos* of being that we find in Aristotle and Heraclitus is the second half of our story, how are we to modify our previous treatment of the famous wax example? After all, wasn't it true that the wax survived the alteration of all its sensuous aspects under fire, and that its true nature was to be pure indeterminacy, that is, pure possibility?

There is something one-sided about Descartes's argument. Now that we have a better understanding of *logos* of being, we can shed light on what it is. First, one may ask: Why does Descartes take *a piece of wax* as his most crucial example? Because, as he says, it exhibits various sensuous aspects? Or because the "demand" of the piece of wax as a thing is almost unapparent and thus already seems to be immediately reducible to infinite possibilities of manipulation—which will be Descartes's conclusion? In other words, suspiciously, the piece of wax *seems to be* a thing that is not a *res* or a *causa* at all, an object that only minimally makes a *case* on its own.[36] Descartes does not take an ox, a country, or an artwork, but a piece of wax as his example. The wax is thus an almost perfect example for muffling the *logos* of being and for thereby reducing all synonymy to homonymy, all inherent determinacy to plasticity, all waking to somnolence. Perhaps it is no coincidence that Descartes grants the possibility that he is at sleep throughout the *Meditationes*, and makes recurrent references to his own sleepiness. In fact, his argument against skepticism draws much of its power from his noncommittal stance as to whether he is awake or not. As Heraclitus puts it in his first fragment: "Of the *logos* of being, humans are always uncomprehending . . . they forget what they do when awake as they forget [what they do] in sleep." Descartes's meditations as well as his wax example are excellent descriptions of somnolence, but not of the piece of wax as having a "*logos* of being."

For it is true that the sweetness, the scent of flowers, and the whiteness *were in* the wax and that after being heated these properties were replaced by other properties. As we have said, Aristotle's exposition and criticism of his predecessors in the first book of the *Physics* often suggests this structure of an underlying thing which remains constant throughout the transition from some property to its contrary. But, to return to the language of *Categories*, everything other than beings is either in them *or they are said of them.*[37] Descartes's reasoning omits the question as to whether anything is *said of* beings, suppresses the fact that, however unthingly, the wax is a thing, it is a *res* and a *causa*. There are not only things that *are in* the wax, but also things that *are said of* it.

What then *is said of* the wax? In the *History of Animals*, one finds an elaborate account of the various functions of wax and hence the corresponding kinds of material used in its production:

> After the hive has been handed over to them clean, they build the wax combs, bringing the drops from the flowers and especially from the trees, from willow and elm and others that are very gummy. With this they also smear the floor against the other creatures; the bee-keepers call this dusting. They also build up the entrances if they are wide. They fashion first the combs in which these bees themselves are produced, then those in which the so-called kings and the drones are produced. (*HA* IX, 40, 623b27–34ff.)[38]

As the rest of the passage makes abundantly clear, for Aristotle wax is a substance taken from flowers and trees by bees for the sake of building honeycombs and other complex structures. However muffled, wax does seem to exhibit a standard: just like the bow requires that the cord be tended neither too much nor too little, and in both directions, the piece of wax must have the appropriate consistency for building a honeycomb, the right dosage of softness and hardness, of cold and heat, of dry and wet. It seems then that wax does have an "essential formula," a *logos* of being, a standard stating *of it* what it is *for it* to be wax. One can always reject, dismiss, or omit this demand, deform this specific form, as Descartes does, but one can do so precisely because there is already something to reject, dismiss, or omit to begin with. Indeed, the wax can be seen as something infinitely malleable, but it will not survive all manipulation *as the wax it is*. Turning from sweet to not-sweet and from white to not-white, the wax is perhaps still what it is for it to be so; but the piece of wax is no longer what it is for it to be itself when it is heated and loses the consistency that is required for the construction of a honeycomb.

For Descartes, if it is true that the wax remains throughout the transformations of all its sensuous aspects, then it validly follows that the wax was nothing but pure extension to begin with—an object of the mind alone. Thus, Descartes asked the crucial question: "Does the wax still remain?" Then he immediately gave a strong, straightforward answer: "I must confess that it does." Although he was alone in his meditation, he added: "No one denies it; no one thinks otherwise." Why *must* he confess that the wax remains? Who is there to deny it? Who are these others that "do not think otherwise"? (AT VII, 30; AT IX, 24) It seems as if Aristotle, for one, would think otherwise, claiming that after the heating the wax remains *only homonymously*, and not synonymously, because the fire *did* disrupt its *logos* of being as wax. Before the experiment, Descartes seems to have already assumed that the wax would remain independently from its properties and to have simply inferred that the wax is indeed pure extension. Descartes's reasoning may appear to be a *petitio principii*. It is not true that the wax remains throughout the experiment, unless homonymously, thus it does not follow that the mind perceived the same piece of wax all along and was thereby confirmed in its own existence. Did anything remain constant throughout the experiment, if not the wax? Perhaps only a purely indeterminate thing, a "just this," an *x*. But the piece of wax did not remain as a piece of wax that it was.

Note that Aristotle was not unaware of philosophers who reduced the *logos* of beings to incidental properties, and all being to indeterminacy—precisely the ones who deny the principle of non-contradiction:

> In general those who say this [those who deny the principle of non-contradiction] do away with being and what it is for something to be. For it is necessary for them to say that all things are incidental [*symbebêkenai*] and that there is no such thing as the very thing it is to be human or animal. (*Metaph.* IV, 4, 1007a20–23)[39]

In order to demonstrate that the mind is better known than the body, Descartes picks up a most "unthingly" thing as a paradigm for all extended beings, treats it as indifferent to all of its aspects. He thereby spreads a waxy texture to all things, as it were, and tailors sober experience on the model of somnolence. He reduces all synonymy to homonymy and brackets the possibility for beings to have a *logos* of being, and the possibility for other beings to attend to that *logos*.

3. Recapitulation and Reorientation

What then does *logos* mean in the *Categories*? It means *standard*. In general, it is what it is to be *for the being at hand*; in the case of an ox or a human being, this means at least what it is for each of them to be an animal. The emphasis here is not so much on "being x" or "being y" as it is on the phrase "for each of them" (*autôn hekaterôi*). The question "What is 'being x'?" can be investigated from the perspective of the interested being itself only if synonymy is distinguished from homonymy. One may well designate a representation and a human being homonymously as "animals." But what is overviewed here is not the question "What is being animal?" itself, since a detailed representation of a human being may well be more "informative" than a blurred perception of one, but rather what being animal has to do *with the being at hand*.[40] By distinguishing synonymy from homonymy at the very opening of the *Categories*, Aristotle suggests that it is possible to address, and equally to fail to address, beings from the perspective of their being, and not simply in the aspects that appear to us. *Logos* articulates the way in which a being presents one aspect not at the expense of another or of an underlying thing. *Logos* means the standard that articulates the being at hand in the manifold of its aspects.

Logos is a promise to provide us something no sculpture, representation, impression, or name necessarily does: the way of being for the very thing at hand. To address an ox as an animal is to consider it with respect to what it is for it to be: to address it not only as something here, something there, something now, something then, something brown or black, but as a being that grows, desires, perceives, and moves. *Logos* captures a being from within the perspective of that being, that is, in its temporal stability, in its spatial spread, and in its inherent manifoldness. *Logos* captures the "extendedness" of beings with a crucial connotation of "stretch" that will pervade the rest of this book. Unlike Nietzsche who thinks that Aristotle simply accuses Heraclitus of contradicting the principle of non-contradiction, Aristotle's seminal use of *logos* at the opening of the corpus is a retrieval of the Heraclitean effort to "understand how that which is disrupted has the same *logos* as itself: a back-stretched harmony, as in the bow and the lyre."[41]

Logos means "standard" in the *Categories*: a being's holding on both to its being and to what it is for it to be, without letting one yield to the other. There remains an essential question: even though things may seem to be irreducible to free-floating aspects, is it true that a piece of wax, a spinning top, a bow, or a lyre has *itself* a *logos* of being? Aren't we speaking loosely or metaphorically when we claim that being a "substance taken from flowers by bees for the sake of building a honeycomb" is what it is *for the piece of wax* to be? Shouldn't *logos* be imputed not to the piece of wax, but to us or to bees, and interpreted accordingly as a result of a mental synthesis carried out by *us*, in *us* and for *us*, instead of taking place "in the world," in and for the beings themselves, within and for the piece of wax? Even though we have seen how synonymy cannot be reduced to homonymy in the *Categories*, we need to make a dialectical step back in our argument in order to pursue the meaning of *logos* in Aristotle's philosophy: what warrants for the *inherence* of the standard we concluded *logos* in the *Categories* to be?

CHAPTER 2

Potentiality

Logos *in* On Interpretation

We tried to show that "*logos* of being" means the "standard" of a being at the opening distinction between synonymy and homonymy in the *Categories*. Yet this does not mean much unless this supposed "standard" is shown to be *inherent* to the being at hand. How can we make sure that the "*logos* of being" is not an external imposition on our part? In this chapter we shall thus pursue this question by focusing on the next text in Aristotle's corpus: *On Interpretation*. In section 1, we shall first develop the problem and return to Aristotle's own examples from the previous chapter. This shall lead us, in section 2, to a discussion of his distinction between necessity and possibility or potentiality. From this, we shall conclude that having an *inherent* standard requires that the being somehow be at once actually and potentially. We close the chapter with the conclusion that the inherent character of *logos* as the standard of being can be demonstrated either in natural and animal motion, the topic of chapters 3 and 4, and in human action and speech, the topic of chapters 5 and 6. So the rest of this book is the development of this chapter's conclusion.

1. The Inherence of *Logos*

"Being is said in many ways"—the leitmotif of Aristotle's *Metaphysics*. Before we enter our discussion of *On Interpretation*, let us make a preliminary reflection on the relevance of the multivocity of being. And let us do this in the form of a reductio ad absurdum, that is, by thinking on what the univocity of being would entail.[1] So what would the world look like, assuming that there are not different and irreducible *ways* of being, but only being as such? There would be nobody *capable* of building a house without necessarily building one in actuality, nobody *capable* of seeing who is not constantly seeing, no sens*ibles* other than the ones actually sensed, no habits, no arts, no education, no memory, in extremis no coming to be.[2] A realm of eternity, necessity, pure actuality, a realm with no shade, nor depth. In a way, this world is a dream world, at least a world we humans can logically conceive and aspire to, a world involving no second thoughts, no decision-making, no responsibility.

For Aristotle, however, such a world is *not* a dream world; there *is* such a realm of eternity and necessity: the supralunar realm.[3] Our sublunar world, however, is the world of finitude, of limitation, of materiality, of potentialities with all that it entails: precisely a world of growth, decay, natural capacities, fulfilled and unexplored potentials, habits and arts. And yet, despite its sharp distinction from the serene supralunar realm, this world of finitude is not reducible to a world of random events: although being finite and lacking immediate actuality, the world of finitude exhibits forms and events that are neither absolutely necessary nor merely contingent. Much of Aristotle's work instills a wonder, not only in front of the realm of eternity and transparency which we do not inhabit, but also in front of the humble, hesitant, and yet multifarious beings among which we belong and find ourselves. In other words, the claim that being is said in many ways precludes the collapse of the distinction between actuality and potentiality, and inspires a sense of curiosity in front of the internal logic of sublunar beings, their *logos*—if, indeed, there is such an *inherent* standard, which is the problematic of this chapter.[4]

Trouble

We attempted to develop the philosophical meaning of *logos* in the *Categories*. There it appeared in the phrase "*logos* of being" and was employed to distinguish synonymy from homonymy. We discussed two different versions of the principle of non-contradiction; we developed two corresponding conceptions of "being" operative in homonymy and synonymy; we offered two approaches to Descartes's wax example; thereby we concluded that *logos* in the *Categories* means "standard". At the very end of chapter 1, however, we remarked that this conclusion can only be temporary because, being the exposition it is, the *Categories* does not supply us a justification for the fact that this standard is an *inherent* one as it must be. But how can one establish that the standard of being of something is *inherent* to it? How can one find warrant for the claim that the "*logos* of being" is truly *of that being*?

In distinguishing the wax from its homonymous aspects, for instance, we claimed that its "*logos* of being" is to be a substance produced by bees from flowers for the sake of building a honeycomb, that wax itself is not an indeterminate underlying being that is indifferent to its properties, and therefore that it cannot survive all imaginable modifications without giving up the very claim that we said it is. In a word, we claimed that wax was inherently determined and thus was destroyed when it was burnt for the sake of Descartes's example. In the same line of thought, we treated our other examples as if they themselves demanded their properties to harmonize with their *logos* of being. We spoke as if a bow itself had its own standard and that a top made a claim for its own being.

Even if we were right that these beings were neither free-floating aspects nor a pure underlying substance nor a conjunction of the two, we were speaking inadequately or only metaphorically in talking about *their logos* of being. For the standard of wax is set not by the wax itself, but precisely by bees, the bow's standard by a bow-maker, a top's by the toy-maker. To claim that the piece of wax is *concerned* about whether or not it is hot, white, liquid or solid, is not to attend to its *logos* of being, but precisely to fail to attune oneself to what it is to be *for the piece of wax*. The bees view the wax as material for building the honeycomb, but it is *precisely* them who "build the honey comb by bringing drops from the flowers and especially from trees" (*HA* IX, 40, 623b27–28). Just like the bees use these drops *as wax* for building their combs, a human being may view the wax as a material for sealing envelops or as an example in a meditation on the immortality of the soul. Similarly with the examples we imported from Heraclitus, and from Plato's *Republic*. The top, the bow, and the lyre are *themselves* indifferent to the properties they can and cannot have if they are to be at all. Strictly speaking, it does not make sense to say that a lyre's existence, production, and quality are an *issue* for the lyre itself. These are of concern not for the lyre itself, whatever that means, but for the craftsman, for his customers, for lyre-players, for the lyre-players' audience, for the political community, and even ultimately for humanity as such.[5] Thus, if *logos* is a standard, as we claimed, its inherent character remains metaphorical or figurative, and therefore in need of philosophical rigor.

So, isn't all addressing ultimately homonymous? Aren't beings palimpsests, or precisely wax tablets, receptive to all inscription and manipulation? Isn't all "standard" externally imposed according to the interpretation, imagination, skill, and power of the viewer? If beings have no specific powers already inherent in them, aren't they potentially anything? What a being can or cannot undergo or do while remaining the very being it is—isn't this question always settled from without, that is, from the perspective of a human being, a bee, or a flower, and not from within the piece of wax? Aren't all possibilities mere possibilities of a purely extend*able*, mut*able*, and flex*ible* substance devoid of inherent determinacy? Aren't we thus back to the Cartesian position according to which, on the one hand, there is a minimally determined substance with infinite plasticity, a *res extensa*, and on the other hand a purely active mind, the *res cogitans*? Aren't we back to the exclusive options of pure potentiality, and a mind fully at work in pure actuality? What warrants for the inherence of the "*logos* of being"? How are we to establish that there is something like synonymy, and that *logos* is not yet one external imposition among others?

Return to Aristotle's Example: A Matter of Life and Death

Something went wrong. As we read the opening of Aristotle's *Categories*, we thought the "*logos* of being" meant "standard," and had to be something ontologically determining enough to distinguish synonymy from homonymy. Yet our examples did not live up to this task. The Cartesian example of the piece of wax, the Heraclitean examples of the lyre and the bow, and the Platonic/Socratic example of the spinning top did not reveal any *inherent* standard of being, but rather perspectival "aspects," not issuing from the wax, the top, or the lyre, but from anything that had the power to impose external determination of these "things."

It is time to remember that none of these were Aristotle's examples, and it is time to return to his own examples. Aristotle's examples in the opening of the *Categories* were an ox and a human being.[6] If we return to Aristotle's examples, we may well find a way to fruitfully pursue our investigation of the meaning of *logos* as "standard" in the phrase "*logos* of being."[7] Is the *logos* of being of a human and an ox, namely "being an animal," a contingent, accidental, and arbitrary aspect *for them* as the color or temperature of the piece of wax is *for it*?

Take Socrates for example. Socrates can become handsome or cultured without ceasing to be. He is also famous for being able to endure cold weather and to handle much wine (Plato, *Symposium*, 214A). In these respects, Socrates then resembles the Cartesian substance subtending and surviving changes. However, Socrates is also known to have *not* survived his drinking of the hemlock. What was Socrates such that, when he drinks the hemlock, he no longer underlies change as a *res extensa*, but *passes away*, and becomes a human being "only homonymously"? Plato's *Phaedo* offers us an almost forensic account of Socrates's death, a perfect example of both the incremental progression and the sudden breaking point of his demise:

> He walked around and when he said that his legs had gotten heavy, he laid down on his back. For the man told him to do so. And with that, the one who had given him the potion laid hold of him and, after letting some time elapse, examined his feet and legs, and then gave his foot a hard pinch and asked whether he felt it; he said no; and after this, his thighs; and going upward in this way, he showed us that he was growing cold and stiff. And he touched himself and said that when it reached his heart, then he'd be gone. At that time

> the chill was around his groin; and uncovering himself—since he had been covered—he said what was his last utterance: "Crito, he said, we owe a cock to Aesclepius. Pay it and don't be careless." "That," said Crito, "will be done; but see if you have anything else to say." He did not answer this question, but after a little while he moved [*ekinêthê*] and the man uncovered him and his eyes stood still [*estêsen*]. Seeing this, Crito closed his mouth and eyes. (117e–118a)[8]

This passage first describes Socrates performing all sorts of motions and undergoing many changes. As the exclusive principle of non-contradiction would forbid, Socrates cannot be walking around and lying down *at once*, but he can lie down *after* walking while remaining the same. Further, as the inclusive version of the principle would allow, he can be at once cold and stiff *with respect to* his legs and yet still warm and flexible *with respect to* his upper body. Here he seems as determin*able* as Cartesian substance. None of these motions and changes *really* change him. After speaking to Crito, the latter asks him: Do you have anything else to say? Socrates does not respond. If he heard the question, did he have something to say and could not because he passively lost his ability to speak? Or did he *actively* choose to remain silent and thereby answer the question with the negative—very much like he *actively* refrained from fleeing prison despite Crito's insistence in the *Crito*?[9]

A similar ambiguity shows up in the subsequent phrase: "after a while he moved," "*ekinêthê*." This verb, *kineô* in the aorist indicative passive, does not clarify whether Socrates is actively moving as a living being (the sense indicated in B.4. in the LSJ article for *kineô*), being moved emotionally by something (B.2), or being moved passively as an inanimate object by the attendant (B.1.). In short, this ambiguous verb seems to mark a threshold by sharing both in Socrates's previous deliberate acts and in the subsequent passivity of the corpse. Before *ekinêthê*, Socrates *acts and moves*, is called to move and rest, uncovers himself, accepts, refuses, or fails to move, and undergoes changes, is touched and addressed as a living being. After *ekinêthê*, the attendant covers him and Crito closes his eyes and mouth. Before, he was listened and questioned. After, he was recounted and mourned. In the middle, *ekinêthê* stands as a boundary stone, a *herma*.

The reason we are focusing on the text here is because this text provides us something Descartes's meditations on the same subject, namely the immortality of the soul, passed over: life *and therefore* death. Despite the "proofs" of the immortality of the soul that occupy the previous discussion, the Platonic text shows that here a threshold has been crossed in Socrates's case. After burning the wax, Descartes asked: "Does the wax still remain? I must confess that it does; no one denies it; no one thinks otherwise" (VII, 29.11–18; AT IX, 24). In Socrates's example, however, the mourners would clearly think otherwise, and deny that Socrates remains intact. Being alive or not for Socrates is fundamentally different from what being cold or not was for the piece of wax. And, as the text shows, being cold or being hot is not unrelated to being alive, it is a condition, a symptom, a manifestation of life and death. No longer being alive, Socrates is fundamentally violated in his "*logos* of being," in what it is *for him* to be, so much so that we cannot really say that Socrates undergoes or underlies the process like the wax. For that is not the kind of underlying being Socrates is (*GC* I, 4, 319b6ff).

Our argument about the *logos* of being may then survive, provided we can uphold the fundamental difference between Socrates's drinking of the hemlock and the burning of the wax. If so, "being alive" may well be an inherent determination of Socrates's being. In that case, there may be an inherent standard, a *logos* of being of Socrates, and thus a fundamental difference between homonymy and synonymy. How are we to reformulate our question concerning the *inherence* of *logos*?

Return to *Logos*

Apparently, life is not an external determination or a simple aspect of Socrates, but is part of his *logos* of being.[10] Cartesian *substantia* is pure possibility somehow facing a pure mind which is fully and actually at work beyond all interference from imagination and sensation. Socrates, however, is not pure possibility, since there is at least something *inherently impossible* for him: to exist without being alive. Furthermore, even supposing that the wax is determined externally under the influence of fire, under the manipulation of bees building hives, or under the experimentation of meditating human beings, still the question remains whether the fire itself, the bees, and this experimenter themselves are equally determined from without.

Now that we have left aside non-Aristotelian examples and turned to Aristotle's own examples, we may have some hope of fruitfully pursuing the inherence of *logos*. To do so, we must now conceptualize a position between infinite possibility and pure actuality—not a stage indifferently squeezed between the two, but a phenomenon that stretches between them, includes them, holds them together. To take up Heraclitus's fragment 51, quoted in chapter 1, we must "understand how that which is disrupted has the same *logos* as itself," "a back-stretched harmony," but this time, not exactly "as in the bow and the lyre," but as in a human being and an ox.

The true mistake, committed here by us and by Descartes, was that we took up beings as individuals of one *kind*, namely "being," and thereby allowed ourselves to reflect on solely one example in order to draw conclusions concerning all beings. And yet, for Aristotle, if being is said in many ways, this is because not all beings are of one *kind*, their being does not take the same *form*, they do not exhibit a similar *logic*. Other than *kinds* or *forms* of being, there are *ways* of being. This is why there is something dramatic in the story of the ugly duckling: ducks and swans are synonymous with respect to being "animals" and even "birds." Yet a baby swan is a duckling "only homonymously." And the story would lose the recognition (*anagnôrsis*) and the reversal (*peripeteia*) that give it its dramatic power if the baby swan were always what it was for her to be in full actuality, and also if she never fully became what it was for her to be. The story is dramatic, riddle-like, and ambiguous, precisely to the extent that it is possible to make a fundamentally *false* assumption about the swan egg and to come to see this mistake. This is enabled by the tension between familiarity and ambiguity. No "stuff" is capable of such *fundamental* falsity—which is precisely why Descartes takes "stuff" as his object in his search for certainty.

In short, we were mistaken in assuming that the examples taken for "being" are neutral. The implications of some examples are incompatible with those of others. Since there seems to be no way of settling the question of the "*logos* of being" from without, it must be filtered through the plurality of irreducible *ways* of being.

Return of *Logos*

What are these *ways* of being then? We have already seen one way of being in chapter 1, that of an aspect: of just not being what one is not, of being determined solely in terms of self-identity, contrariety, and exclusion. To this seems to correspond in Aristotle the two pairs of contrary properties such as *the* hot and *the* cold, *the* wet and *the* dry (*GC* II, 2, 329b7ff.). These four are precisely defined according to the exclusive version of the principle of noncontradiction as two pairs whose terms exclude one another absolutely. Just as aspects, these properties are unitary and pure. They are precisely *not* things. These four properties do differ, however, from aspects in that each aspect *is* only at the expense of any other, whereas *the* hot, while excluding *the* cold, is indifferent to *the* dry and *the* wet. The relations between these properties are minimally more specific than those between free-floating, all-excluding aspects. Thus, these contrary properties exhibit a first way of being that is slightly but crucially distinct from that of aspects.

The distinction is important precisely because, unlike aspects, *the* hot, while excluding *the* cold, in fact can combine with *the* dry or *the* wet. Thereby a second way of being comes into play, beyond the aspect-like way of being: a bodily way of being. It is by means of the four possible combinations of these two irreducible pairs of contraries (hot and cold, wet and dry) that Aristotle analyzes the "simple bodies" (*GC* II, 2, 330a25–29).

No wonder it is at this first level of inclusion, of holding together, of comprehension or combination that the term *logos* returns:

> [These contraries] have attached themselves to the apparently simple bodies, fire, air, water and earth, according to a *logos*; for fire is hot and dry, air is hot and moist (as vapor is air), water is cold and wet, and earth is cold and dry, so that it is reasonable that the differences be distributed to primary bodies and the amount of these be according to a *logos*. (*GC* II, 2, 330b3–8)

A *logos* then is involved in this way of being which is primary at least in the context of perceptible beings (*GC* II, 5, 332a27–28). Whereas the way of being of *the* hot is simply *not* being cold, fire *is* according to a *logos* in that it necessarily holds together one term from both pairs of contraries—the hot *and* the dry. The simple bodies exhibit a *logos* of being, an inherent standard: they have a way of being by means of holding onto two aspects together without letting one yield to the other (otherwise, say, fire would turn back into the hot or the dry) and without letting one lay aside the other (otherwise there would be no fire, but the hot *right next to* or *after* the dry). Thus, *logos* reassumes the meaning of a being's holding on to the spatiotemporal manifold of its aspects without letting one yield to the other: unlike Cartesian *substantia*, a fire can be extinguished, just as Socrates can die as much an ox.

Whereas at the level of mere aspects *the* hot merely excluded *the* cold and was indifferent to *the* wet and *the* dry without any common denominator, here fire excludes water but preserves its affinity to earth by means of the dry, and to air by means of the hot. Aspects here no longer exist in isolation from everything else, but serve as media or common denominators between simple bodies: instead of simply being a property abstracted from concrete beings, *the* hot is the middle term of two bodies, the articulation of fire (dry and hot) and air (wet and hot). Each of these simple bodies also has a place *in* the cosmos as distinct from the aspects that simply are *away* from their contrary: "Being four, the simple bodies make up two pairs belonging to two places: for fire and air are carried toward the limit [of the cosmos], while earth and water are so toward the center" (*GC* II, 3, 330b31–33; *Cael.* IV, 1, 308a14ff.).

The transition from the two basic pairs of contraries to the four simple bodies is developed by more complex formations: just as *the* hot, while excluding *the* cold, combined with *the* dry in fire according to a certain *logos*, now it is fire which is combined with air and earth in a certain *logos* in the form of composite bodies (*GC* II, 3, 331a2–4).

> As for hardness, softness, toughness, brittleness and the rest of such qualities which belong to the parts that have Soul in them—heat and cold may very well produce these, but they certainly do not produce the *logos* in direct consequence of which one thing is flesh and another bone. (*GA* II, 1, 734b31–34)

This is the point we wish to close this section with: unlike our and Descartes's assumption that being is an overarching kind with an underlying homogenous structure and superficial modifications, there is a capital asymmetry between the divisibility of composite beings *into* simple bodies and the possibility of their generation *out of* them.[11] There *is* something called generation and corruption in a strong sense. Unlike aspects that simply negate their contrary in all senses, and unlike contrary properties (*the* hot, *the* wet, etc.) which negate one another and remain indifferent to other pairs of contraries, composite bodies exhibit a third way of being that is irreducible to the previous two.[12] Their destruction is such a fundamental violation that it is not on a par with the changing of one of their aspects, just like Socrates's body temperature was not. They are the beings that reveal the inherence of their *logos* of being, the standard of "what it is *for them* to be."

2. Potentiality

We are still trying to justify that *logos* means inherent standard. A standard is necessarily distinct from a state of affairs for the latter to meet or not meet the former. There cannot be any standard in a strict monism, as there can be no *logos*.[13] An *inherent* standard, further, is one that is not imposed on, or externally set before, a state of affairs. If *logos* is to be an inherent standard, then there must be a way of being that is not simply and purely an actuality; there must be a specific way of being in potentiality which is fundamentally different from mere flexibility, malleability, and extendibility. If there are beings that have an inherent standard, they must be neither determined *in no way* as the Cartesian *res cogitans* is, nor determinable *in any way* like *res extensa*.

Are there such beings? We saw above that even simple bodies are among them: fire *is* fire at work, but also it *may* be extinguished by water. A more explicit answer is found in *On Interpretation*:

> It is clear from what has been said that the necessary is actual, such that if the eternal beings are prior, then actuality also is prior to potentiality; and some are actual without potentiality, such as the first beings, and some are with potentiality; these are prior with respect to nature, but posterior in time; and some are never in actuality, but potentiality only. (*On Int.* 13, 23a21–26)

If the task of proving the existence of an inherent standard necessitates a way in which this standard should be different from, but internally connected to, the state of affairs, then it is neither fully actual beings, nor only potential beings, but beings that are actually at work *with* some potentiality that will warrant for the inherence of *logos* as standard.

A Trivial Concept of Potentiality

Actuality seems to be experientially the most available way of being of things in everyday life: we seem to feel *the* hot, we seem to see the fire, we seem to be actually surrounded by present, available, and ready things. Given its relatively obvious character, actuality or being-at-work (*energeia*) takes its explanatory force from its distinction from potentiality (*dynamis*), which is ontologically secondary, but also less obvious to our everyday stance. Thus when Aristotle engages in a discussion of actuality and potentiality, it is the latter that seems to him to be the real topic of debate. But potentiality is said in many ways:[14]

> Some potentialities are homonymous. For "possible" [*dynaton*] is not said simply; [it is said], on the one hand, due to being true as an actuality, for instance, "it is possible for someone to walk because one is walking," and in general something is said to be possible because it is already in actuality; on the other hand, ["possible" is said] because it might be actualized, for instance "it is possible for someone to walk because one might walk." (*On Int.* 13, 23b7–13)

Something already actually at work has a potentiality only in a trivial sense. While walking I may say a fortiori that I can walk; I may say that it is possible for a white door to be white. All these would be, not untrue, but trivially true, and in fact homonymously true. For these trivial statements use the word "can," but efface its "*logos* of being," that is, its distinction and relation to actuality. Let us call this meaning of potentiality as simply inferred from an actuality a "trivial potentiality."[15]

A Temporal Concept of Potentiality

Trivial potentiality indeed defers the question of potentiality. Looking at a man who has already recovered from a disease, one would hardly say "it is possible for him to recover." For this would rather suggest that he has *not* recovered, that *actually* he is *not* healthy. While addressing a present actuality, it is trivial to infer the present possibility and more reasonable to infer a past possibility: "So, it *was* possible for him to recover after all!" Thus even everyday speech understands the ambiguous character of trivial potentiality and tends to correct it by expressing it in the past tense. Put in another way, a trivial potentiality is discovered retrospectively and analytically without any need for a connection or a *logos*: if the event is happening *now*, then by necessity it *was* possible.

However, this temporal conception of potentiality as a past state of affairs inferred from the present, a conception suggested by Aristotle's own words, conceals a distinction which will be the object of his next step in the argument: the distinction between the modal concept of potentiality and the temporal concept. Hence, there is a sense of potentiality that is neither trivial nor temporal. It is this modal concept of potentiality that will enable us to construe *logos* as inherent standard.

If *logos* is an inherent standard, there must be a certain "distance" between the standard itself and that of which it is the standard. Here we are indeed using the word "distance" metaphorically, since the distinction we are after is not a spatial or positional one. In fact, temporal dimensions are more promising than spatial ones in understanding potentiality. And the very discussion of potentiality arises from Aristotle's discussion of the principle of non-contradiction in terms of the dimensions of time in *On Interpretation*: he argues that positive and negative statements concerning the present and the past are necessarily either true or false.[16] This indeed follows from the principle of non-contradiction: if it is impossible for an event to be and not be at the same time in the same respect, and if the truth and falsity of a statement concerning the event depends on the event itself (*SE* 1, 165a6–14), then by necessity the statement will either hold true or be false. So much for statements about present and past events.

The Modal Concept of Potentiality

Statements concerning particulars *in the future*, however, are *not* necessarily true or false according to Aristotle. In order to prove this, he embarks upon a reductio ad absurdum in *On Interpretation*, 9, where he hypothesizes that statements concerning particulars in the future *are* now necessarily true or false. This hypothetical position is also known as necessitarianism: if it were true that contradictory statements concerning a particular future event necessarily excluded each other, *until the event* we would have to deny both its occurrence and its nonoccurrence, "but it cannot be said that neither is true, for instance that it will neither be nor not be. For, first, while the affirmation is false, the negation is not true; and while the negation is false, the affirmation happens to be not true" (*On Int.* 9, 18b17–20). So, according to necessitarianism, just as it is now either true or false that it rained yesterday, it is now either true or false that it will rain tomorrow. But then, is it now true that it will rain? No. Is it false? It is not false either. Both horns of the dilemma lead from the present denial of contradictory particular future events to the present assertion of contradictories. We are bound to affirm that it will rain (since it is not true that it will not rain) and that it will not rain (since it is not true that it will rain). This is the contradiction that allows Aristotle to infer the untenability of the necessitarian hypothesis and indeed a formal version of the law of the excluded middle:

> If it is true to say that it is white and black,[17] both must be; if both will be tomorrow, both will be tomorrow. If it will neither be nor not be tomorrow, there *would* be no contingency [*to hopoter' etukhen*]; for instance, a sea-battle. For the sea-battle *would* have to neither happen nor not happen. (*On Int.* 9, 18b20–25; emphasis is ours)

Under the necessitarian assumption, one cannot affirm the event of a future sea-battle, but one cannot deny it either. Thus, since any middle or third option is excluded, one must respectively deny and affirm its future occurrence in the same respect, which is absurd.

One possible reply to Aristotle's refutation of necessitarianism is an appeal to a view of events sub specie aeternitatis, an appeal to the standpoint of an eternal spectator. All events are necessary from the point of view of a spectator situated in eternity; indeed, pretty much as the past is irrevocable for us, it is neither true nor false that a sea-battle *will* happen tomorrow, but simply it is neither true nor false *yet*, that is, it is true or false in the eyes of a being not confined to temporal distinctions such as past, present, and future. To that being, the sea-battle tomorrow *is* at least as unalterable, irreversible, and actually accomplished as the sea-battle of yesterday is for us now. Thus necessitarianism, the denial of all possibility and potentiality, may be saved by assuming the point of view of a spectator the day after tomorrow—a point of view of which we never had any firsthand experience.[18]

But besides the problems involved in positing and justifying the point of view of such an eternal spectator, this attempt to save necessitarianism defers the problem: if one now admits that one does not know whether or not a sea-battle will happen tomorrow, how can one now know whether or not the eternal spectator *will* be right tomorrow? Instead of asking "Will the sea-battle happen tomorrow?", necessitarianism simply raises a new question: "Will the eternal spectator be right tomorrow?" Then one might supply yet another omniscient spectator to warrant for the other, and so on. As long as we are confined to the options of mere being and mere nonbeing, to the options of necessary affirmation and negation, to a formal version of the principle of the excluded middle, the denied affirmation will contradict the denied negation, and we will hit upon a contradiction.

As a result, necessitarianism seems less to solve the problem of future contingencies than to defer it. Note further that the contingency of particular future events immediately contaminates the apparent necessity of the past and present state of affairs. For, applied to the past and the present, the very same question takes the following form: "Could a sea-battle have not happened yesterday?" or "Could a sea-battle have not happened today?" Thus, contingency ends up affecting all dimensions of time. Although it appears most clearly in relation to the future, contingency is not a dimension of time. The fact that a sea-battle happened, is happening, or will happen is strictly distinct from the *possibility* that it may not have happened, may not be happening, or may not happen. In other words, Aristotle's argument is not intended to clarify a feature of the future as distinct from the past and present. The argument is rather intended to clarify contingency, which as a modality may apply to all three dimensions of time.

> It is not necessary that all affirmation and negation of contraries be either true or false; for, the case for those that have the potentiality of being and of not being is not the same as for those that are and are not. (*On Int.* 9, 19b1–4)

As distinct both from trivial potentiality inferred retrospectively from a present actuality, and from a potentiality which is inferred retrospectively from an actuality seen sub specie aeternitatis, potentiality presents a modal character. If *logos* is an inherent standard, it must show itself neither in actual being as such, nor in being at a certain time, but in actually being in a certain way. In what way?

Motion

"Then we do not destroy the [principle] that everything either is or is not . . . but one can say these according to potentiality or according to actuality"

(*Ph.* I, 8, 191b27–29). The beings that exhibit the inherence of *logos* will then be understandable not in terms of the option of being and nonbeing, but in terms of both *being* and *having a standard*. Their actuality will be exactly the actuality of *a particular potentiality*. In a word, these beings will move.

> There is, on the one hand, that which is actual only, and that which is in potential *and* actual . . . A distinction having been made with respect to each kind[19] between the actuality and the potentiality, motion is the actuality of that which is potentially just as such. (*Ph.* III, 1, 200b26–28; 201a10–12, 28–30)

Moving beings will exhibit *logos* as the very articulation of their actuality *with* their potentiality. Unlike a *res extensa*, they will be in actuality; but, unlike a *res cogitans*, their potentiality will be neither trivial nor temporal. They will exhibit their potentiality modally, that is, *as potentiality*.

Motion then may attest and exhibit the inherence of *logos*. What kind of motion can do so? In other words, aside from its trivial and temporal versions, what is a potentiality, and what is the specific kind of potentiality whose actuality exhibits the inherence of *logos*? According to Aristotle's compact definition, a potentiality is "the source of change in another or [in itself] as another" (*Metaph.* IX, 1, 1046a11; V, 12). Let us think about the first part—namely potentiality being the source of change in another thing. To use Aristotle's example, the potentiality of building a house is a source of change in another, in the material: bricks, stones, and so on. Similarly, we already saw how bees had a potentiality for preparing wax—they had a source of change in the "drops from the flowers and especially from the trees" (*HA* IX, 40, 623b28). But, as we have also seen, being used for building honeycombs is *not* the inherent standard of being of wax, it is a function externally imposed on a material by bees, just as bricks and stones have the potential of being a house from the viewpoint and initiative of the builder. Thus, a potentiality as a source of change *in another* cannot help us find anything like an inherent standard.

What about the second half of the definition of potentiality? What about potentiality as a source of change not *in another*, but *in itself as another*? Here the mover and the moved are no longer separate as in the case of the builder and the house, or bees and wax. For now they happen to be the same thing. The classical example of this kind of potentiality is the case of the physician who heals himself. He is the source of change as having the art of medicine, and he also happens to be the one who is being cured. Sure enough, this kind of potentiality seems inherent to be being that is undergoing the change, unlike the piece of wax which was turned into building material by bees or used for a thought experiment by Descartes. And yet, here it is only by coincidence that actuality and potentiality, "fact" and "standard," are in the same being. In other words, it is not *as a patient* that the person heals himself, but only as happening to have acquired the art of medicine. There is no inherent connection between this person's being sick and his medical intervention. Thus, a potentiality as source of change *in the changing being itself as another* cannot help us either in finding an inherent standard. For, if the inherence of *logos* is to show itself, it can only be in a potentiality as a source of change in the changing being itself *as itself*, and not *as another*, and in a motion as the actuality of this kind of potentiality as such.

Is there such a potentiality? Is there such a source of change in the thing itself *as itself*? There is a third option:

> By "potentiality" I mean not only that which we have defined as "a source of change in another or [in itself] as another," but all source of motion or rest. Nature too is in the same genus as potentiality,[20] for it is a source of motion, but not in another, but in itself as itself. (*Metaph.* IX, 8, 1049b5–10)

It is here that actuality and potentiality, "standard" and "fact," *logos* and being, finally manifest themselves in one and the same being in a non-accidental way. Here the moving being, being the source of change in itself, will precisely exhibit the inherence of its standard of being. That it has an *inherent* standard will be apparent by its having an *inherent* source of motion. It is not the wax that we must focus on for finding the source of the process, for finding the *logos* of being, but bees. By preparing wax for honeycombs and by building them, it is not the *wax*, but the *bees* that exhibit their way of being, what it is for them to be, their "*logos* of being" as inherent standard. So the *logos* of being shall exhibit its inherent, non-external and non-coincidental, character in potentialities as sources of motion or change in the moving or changing being itself *as itself*.

What is this source of change that lies within the changing being as itself? Aristotle already said it. Nature is exactly such a source: "Nature is a source and cause of moving and resting in that which it is primarily by itself and not coincidentally" (*Ph.* II, 1, 192b21–23). We now know what this latter specification means: a man may *happen to* be a doctor and heal himself, but the source we are searching does not *happen to* be inherent, but *is* inherent. We are looking for a healing that does take place not because the patient *happens* to have learned the medical art and to operate on himself. *Logos* will exhibit its inherence not only by any moving being, but by *natural* moving beings, because only the latter contain within themselves the source of their motion, and not coincidentally. This is what we mean by saying that the living body *heals* itself, and not as a physician heals his patient—regardless of whether the patient happens to be himself or not. Further, it is because healing is a natural process exhibiting the *logos* of the being involved, that Socrates's drinking of the hemlock is a violation of his *logos* of being. Thus, if we are seeking concrete manifestations of *logos* as inherent standard, we must look at natural motions. So this is what we shall do in chapters 3 and 4.

Action

And yet, Socrates does not simply die after drinking the hemlock. His death is not just a motion or a change, a natural occurrence. The debate about immortality is not just strategic ethical consolation as for the young Pythagoreans around him. As he himself emphasizes in the *Phaedo* (98C–D), his death at the end of that dialogue is the result of a very conscious and sincere decision, whose story is told in the *Apology*, and of a resoluteness, attested in the *Crito*.

Similarly, *On Interpretation* does not simply distinguish the modal concept of potentiality from the trivial and temporal ones. It also draws a crucial distinction within the modal concept of potentiality itself. Potentiality is not only at the basis of Aristotle's concept of motion, but also of action. Hence, if rhetoric is "concerned with things about which we deliberate," and if "no one deliberates about things which cannot become, be, or hold otherwise," and if, as we saw, all dimensions of time are in a way subject to contingency, and therefore some kind of deliberation, then rhetoric is used with respect to all dimensions of time (*Rh.* I, 2, 1357a). In fact, the kinds of rhetoric map onto the three dimensions of time: "a member of the assembly judges about things to come, the dicast about things past, and the spectator about the ability [of the speaker]; so that necessarily rhetorical *logoi* will be three in kind: deliberative, forensic and epideictic" (*Rh.* I, 3, 1358b). Therefore Aristotle's *Rhetoric* develops the modal concept of potentiality into all three temporal dimensions.

Our reference to Socrates and rhetoric here is not incidental. For Aristotle himself supplies his reductio ad absurdum argument against necessitarianism with such empirical remarks: if necessitarianism were true, "it would not be necessary either to deliberate [*bouleuesthai*] or to take pains [*pragmateuesthai*] by saying that 'if we will do so and so, then this will be; but if we will not do it, it will not be'" (*On Int.* 9, 18b31–33). Here Aristotle attacks necessitarianism first by stating that contingency exists by necessity, and secondly by pointing to the empirical existence of "deliberation" and "taking pains": "We see that a source of that which will be depends also on deliberating and on some acting [*praxai ti*] . . ." (19a7–9). Aristotle here substitutes the earlier *pragmateuesthai* with *praxai*. Although the two are etymologically related, the meanings of *pragmateuesthai* are roughly "to busy oneself," "to be engaged in business," "to take in hand," "to elaborate," while *praxai* is the aorist infinitive of the broader verb *prassein*: to pass over, to accomplish, to effect an object, to make, to have to do, be busy with, to manage state affairs, take part in the government, to transact, to practice. In a word, Aristotle seems to have broadened the scope of what he takes to be a "source of that which will be" so as to include not only natural processes, but also personal business and interpersonal undertakings.[21]

True, acts, decisions, and events can always be interpreted sub specie aeternitatis, from the viewpoint of an eternal spectator. Perhaps this was what early ancient Greeks meant by *anagkê* and what we call "fate" or "destiny." In light of the eternal spectator's perspective, this interpretation must declare illusory all human processes of projection, anticipation, deliberation, hesitation, and trial and error with regard to things that, "supposedly," could have been, could be, and can be *otherwise than they are*. Humans are factually able to degrade their powers as finite and illusory in light of an eternal spectator of which they have no firsthand experience. Yet, in doing this, humans must also be overrating their powers in claiming to know what an eternal spectator knows or would know. If a person claims his ignorance about the event of a sea-battle tomorrow, he must a fortiori claim his ignorance about the existence of an eternal spectator who is right about all future occurrences. In arguing against necessitarianism, Aristotle thus seems to side with Socrates who, in the *Apology*, claims to have a wisdom that is on a par neither with any human opinion nor with divine wisdom. Indeed, humans are able to always *imagine* the future as that which will have happened anyway, or as that about which what is claimed will turn out to be either true or false. And yet this interpretation presupposes what the "source of that which will be," instead of explaining it. It conceals the distinction between the actual and the possible—whether in the future, past or present. In the introduction of chapter 4, we shall touch upon the human ability to articulate a world where all human freedom, deliberation, decision, and responsibility are deferred; in in section 3 of chapter 6, we shall offer an explanation of how humans are even capable of construing such an interpretation of the world.

So far as this chapter of the book is concerned, potentiality is a necessary concept for understanding *logos* as inherent standard because standard and fact are neither identical (as assumed in the trivial concept of potentiality) nor simply temporally successive (as assumed by the temporal concept of potentiality in necessitarianism). Potentiality grounds human action and deliberation for the very same reasons. Socrates's death is not a simple change. It is an action. It is a performance.

It is curious that potentiality grounds both *logos* as inherent standard, and action. Is this a coincidence?

> We see that a source of that which will be depends also on deliberating and on some acting, and that to be possible and not to be possible are in those that are not always actually at work, which do admit both being and not being, becoming and not becoming. (*On Int.* 9, 19a7–11)

Aristotle clearly states his previous point about potentiality:

> On the one hand, both [contradictories] admit of happening; on the other hand, whenever one of them is, then the other will not be true. For at the same time it has the potentiality of being and not-being. But if it necessarily is or is not, then both will not be possible. (*On Int.* 13, 22b18–23)

For action, what is needed is the simultaneous, inclusive, or comprehensive availability of both contraries, a relation that holds on to contraries without letting one be reduced or indifferent to the other:

> It also appears that not all that has the potentiality of being or walking have the contrary potentiality, but there are some for which this [i.e., not having both potentialities] is not true: first, on the one hand, this applies to those that are possible not with respect to *logos*, for instance fire has the potentiality of heating, a potentiality without *logos*; but, then, the potentialities with *logos* are potentialities of many and of opposites, whereas the ones without *logos* are not all like this; as we said, fire does not have the potentiality of heating and of not heating; but those that are always actual do not have this either. However some potentialities without *logos* have the opposite possibilities at the same time. But this is said for the sake of the following: that, even when they are said in accordance with the same meaning [*kata to auto eidos*], not all potentialities involve opposites. (*On Int.* 13, 22b36–23a6)

Potentialities with *logos* are open to opposite outcomes.[22] However, there is something intriguing about Aristotle's distinctions here: although all potentialities with *logos* involve opposites, not all potentialities involving opposites are with *logos*. And this is why the two distinctions do not overlap: Aristotle explicitly leaves room for potentialities that, although without *logos*, do involve opposites. In other words, although he does divide beings into those that admit opposite potentialities and those that do not, this divide does not map onto the one between "rational" and "irrational" beings. He does not divide the world into spontaneously acting free rational beings and irrational beings bound up by necessity. Here, in *On Interpretation*, Aristotle simply mentions the existence of this grey area without giving any example.

This grey area also appears in an even more covert way in the famous discussion of potentiality in the *Metaphysics*: "All [potentialities] with *logos* involve opposites, but those without *logos* involve one [of the opposites]" (*Metaph.* IX, 2, 1046b5–6). This quotation and its context consistently generalize the fact that potentialities with *logos* involve opposites by the adjective "all" (*pasa*), but do not do so for the claim that potentialities without *logos* do *not* involve opposites. Does Aristotle have in mind the grey area more explicitly indicated in *On Interpretation*? We will return to this grey area between *alogos* and *logos* in our discussion of the human soul in our chapter 5 on the *Nicomachean Ethics*.

However, the discussion in the *Metaphysics* does not simply problematize the distinctions in *On Interpretation*, but also sheds light on its context:

> Since some of these sources [i.e., potentialities] are inherent in beings with soul, some in ensouled beings and in the part of the soul that has *logos*, it is clear that some of the potentialities will be without *logos*, and some with *logos*. (*Metaph.* IX, 2, 1046a36–1046b3)

The context of the *Metaphysics* clearly points to something that was implicit in our discussion of *logos* from the beginning. In chapers 3 and 4, we shall see that natural motion exhibits how *logos* is an inherent standard holding on to the spatiotemporal manifold of the aspects of a being without letting one yield to the other. Then, in chapters 5 and 6, we shall see that human action exhibits how *logos* is an inherent openness to opposites in human action as we saw in this section.

3. Recapitulation and Reorientation

In this chapter of the book, we saw dialectic at work. We received the conclusion of our previous chapter 1 ("*logos* means standard") as an *endoxa* or a "tradition." Through a discussion of examples, we challenged this conclusion by showing that it must live up to assuming the predicate of *inherence.* Thus, we asked: how can we claim that a certain *logos*, understood as "standard," belongs to a being unless this standard is inherent to it? Returning from the non-Aristotelian example of artifacts to Aristotle's own examples, natural beings, we gathered an attestation of an inherent standard precisely in its violation: that Socrates *dies* means that *he himself* no longer changes or even undergoes change. *On Interpretation* allowed us to refine our understanding of *logos* as inherent standard: if a being is to have an inherent *logos*, it must hold on to potentiality in its very actuality. After distinguishing the modal concept of potentiality from the trivial and temporal concepts of potentiality by refuting necessitarianism, we inferred that this modal concept is nothing but an expression of Aristotle's concept of motion. So, we concluded, *logos* will prove itself to be an inherent standard only by means of inherently motivated, that is, natural, motions. This shall be the topic of chapters 3 and 4. Yet, *On Interpretation* also drew a distinction within the modal concept of potentiality itself: potentialities with *logos* and those without *logos*—with an ambiguous grey area in between. The examples of the potentialities with *logos* were taken from human action and deliberation. Thus *logos* will prove itself to be inherent if some actions turn out to be inherently motivated. This is the topic of chapters 5 and 6.

As to the overall project of this book, until now we saw *logos* in the sense of "inherent standard": an inherent relation between the fully realized, actual existence of a being and its having a claim, a potentiality *for* its being, without letting one yield to or overtake the other.

So how does *logos* exhibit its inherence, first, in natural motion, and secondly, in human action?

CHAPTER 3

Natural Motion

Logos *in the* Physics

We are still trying to get a firm hold on the meaning of the phrase "*logos* of being" in Aristotle's *Categories*. In chapter 1, we argued that there *logos* means "standard"; in chapter 2, we noticed that this standard must be inherent and exhibit this inherence in the interrelation of actuality and potentiality, that is, in internally motivated beings, in natural beings. Thus we are now led to investigate Aristotle's philosophy of nature. In section 1 we elaborate the Aristotelian notion of a "theoretical" natural scientist and of a correspondingly "spectacular" nature that exhibits the inherent character of its *logos* in motion. In section 2 we focus on living beings and their motions: nutrition and reproduction. We shall see that these two motions introduce a new meaning of *logos*: since they involve the integration of matter into the "form according to *logos*" within the living being's body (in nutrition) or outside it (in reproduction), this new meaning of *logos* can roughly be expressed by "ratio." But, in section 3, we shall note that not all meanings of *logos* denote the integration of matter according to Aristotle, and thus we shall set the stage for the elaboration of two other kinds of natural motion in chapter 4 on animal life: sensation and locomotion.

1. The Natural

What does *logos* have to do with nature?

"Nature loves to hide itself," says Heraclitus in fragment 123. When we are bitten by a dog, when an earthquake destroys houses and crushes thousands of lives, when we are struck by a virus, when we imagine a meteor hitting the Earth, it seems like all this happens on the background of the terrifying and yet essential ambient silence of the forces of nature. We may well speak about nature, translate, interpret, or represent it, voice its claims and defend or subjugate it. But it seems that, however much we try, we will always be the ones who lend voice to it, who discuss our own interpretation and understanding of it, who defend or reject one another's claim *about* that demand. Aristotle himself most famously proclaims: "Of animals, only the human being possesses *logos*" (*Pol.* I, 1, 1253a10–11). So, this seems to be the dilemma of human alienation from nature: either we dominate nature and control a servant indifferent to our command, the blind force of nature, or else we are subjected to a deaf master that does not and even cannot ask for our obedience. How can we ever approach nature *neither* as the compliant or resistant, but in any case blind, material of human undertakings, *nor* as the merciless and yet irrational avenger of the hubris of us mortals? How can we ever approach nature beyond categories of subjugation and use, *neither* as master *nor* as our servant? This is our first question.

Logos is said in many ways. But if there is anything common to these various meanings, it may be that all may denote something "unnatural." We are not unfamiliar with thinking that nature is fundamentally *alogos* unless *we* find a certain logic to it, unless *we* understand it, unless *we* give some form, voice, and meaning to it. In fact, the specifically human vocation may well be thought to be this imposition of meaning on the meaningless. Hence our second question: how are we to make sense of Aristotle's definition of nature precisely in terms of *logos*?

This chapter of the book proposes to offer a solution to both of the questions above. In this chapter, we shall work out two major occurrences of *logos* in Aristotle's philosophy of nature: first, *logos* in Aristotle's definition of nature as "form according to *logos*" in *Physics* II, 1, 193a31 and 193b3, and secondly *logos* in his understanding of *organic* nature, that is, living beings, as a *logos* of growth, in *On the Soul* II, 4, 416a10ff.[1] We shall show how and why nature is defined in terms of *logos* for Aristotle, and argue that, according to him, natural beings stretch out to put up their own show and to express their "logic."[2]

> In laws, legislators unduly forbid children from stretching and crying, for these are useful for growth since in this way a bodily exercise happens; because holding breath produces strength against hardships, which is what happens to children when they stretch themselves. (*Pol.* VII, 15, 1336a34–39)

According to Aristotle, natural beings are essentially "spectacular" before being the dull and malleable material of human impositions or our sublime but silent retaliator. Accordingly, Aristotle's natural scientist is neither a voyeur watching nature through a keyhole, nor a colonizer in search of natural resources, nor a crafty experimenter settled in a laboratory registering results.

He is rather a theoretical person—more precisely, a *theôros*, an envoy sent out of his city to consult an oracle, to ask for a *logos* and to watch rituals, games, or tragedies.[3] Overall, we wish to awaken a sense of the natural scientist as a "theorist" and a listener attentive and responsive to the "spectacular" character of vociferating natural beings.[4]

Nature

In order to do this, we must try to momentarily bracket dualities that set up nature against something else such as "human beings," "history," "culture," or "nurture," simply because we do not find such dualities in Aristotle.[5] For, according to him, nature itself is not a section of beings as opposed to another. Nature is not a *pragma*, it is not even a being (*on*) or a "substance" (*ousia*) in the sense of an individual thing (*tode ti*).[6] To put it in terms foreign to Aristotle, nature is much less a being than the being of beings.[7] Nature is not even a general name for the totality of natural beings. If nature appears at all, there is something "else" that appears "besides" nature. Perhaps this is the sense in which it "loves to hide itself" according to Heraclitus. "Every thing that has a nature is a being, since it is something that underlies, and nature is always in an underlying being" (*Ph.* II, 1, 192b33–34).[8] Then nature is never clear and distinct in the sense of being separated, isolated, or even isolatable. Nature is never over against, but under. Or rather, it is always *in* something (*en hypokeimenôi*), is essentially responsible *for* something (*aition*) or the source *of* something (*arkhê*).

These emphatic "*in*,""*for*," and "*of*" all appear in the major Aristotelian definition of nature: "Nature is a source *of* and cause *for* being moved and coming to rest *in* that to which it belongs primarily" (*Ph.* II, 1, 192b21–23; emphasis is ours). Nature is the source *of* and cause *for* motion *in* moving beings. Natural beings, instead of constituting the realm of nature, are *by* nature and *according to* nature:

> *According to* nature [*kata physin*] are both these things [an underlying thing and a being] and as many things as belong to these in virtue of themselves, just as being carried up belongs to fire. For this is not a nature, nor does it have a nature, but is *by* nature [*physei*] and *according to* nature [*kata physin*]. (*Ph.* II, 1, 192b35–193a2; emphases are ours)[9]

Aristotle systematically and emphatically distinguishes nature itself from natural beings or naturally oriented processes, without suggesting that nature is apart and away from them. Whatever the true meaning of this distinction between nature and natural beings, his examples for natural beings are "animals and their parts, plants, and the simple bodies (like earth, fire, air, and water)" (*Ph.* II, 1, 192b9–11).

Aristotle defines nature not in terms of life and soul, but in terms of motion and rest. If it is possible at all to talk about *logos* in nature, we then must get a hold of Aristotle's understanding of motion. Motion is not only among the few central concepts in Aristotle's philosophy, it is the Aristotelian concept that has been fundamentally modified, if not altogether rejected and abandoned, by early modern science. However counterintuitive it might seem, in order to grasp Aristotle's concept of motion, we must first clarify and undo both post-Aristotelian and anti-Aristotelian conceptions of motion.[10] But we cannot simply do away with them, we must understand how they are *post*-Aristotelian and *anti*-Aristotelian. More exactly, we must be able to have a sense of the historical sedimentation of the concept of motion in order to work our way through the early modern rejection of Aristotelian cosmology towards that which they rejected. Since this is a task we cannot even claim to attempt in the context of this book, what follows is a very rough attempt to undo four interconnected reductions made in the early modern era precisely against the Aristotelianism of that time: (a) the reduction of causality to material causation, (b) the reduction of *hylê* to matter, (c) the reduction of motion to locomotion, and (d) the reduction of *kosmos* to infinite space.[11] Thus, we shall be able to recover Aristotle's concept of motion, grasp his definition of nature, and understand the function of *logos* therein.

Undoing Physics

A. The Reduction of Causality to Material Causation. To begin with, Aristotle's word for "cause," *aition*, comes from *aitia,* which means "responsibility": it means "guilt, blame, charge, fault" in a bad sense, and in a good sense "credit" or even "reputation."[12] Pretty much like the term *pragma* mentioned in the previous chapters, *aitia* is also used in the sense of "case in dispute," and in the dative it means "for the sake of something." The word *aitia* itself comes from the verb *aitiaomai,* which again highlights the pejorative: "to accuse." In light of this partial semantic field, all our mechanical cause-effect relationships appear faceless, impersonal, and irresponsible. *Aition* in Ancient Greek has clear ethical-political connotations and brings to mind the idea of a definite agent who has committed a certain act, an agent who had an intention and who now has a certain face and a name.

The reason why *aition* in Ancient Greek appears much more human, ethical, legal, conscious, or responsible than what we understand by the word "cause" is that early modern philosophy has precisely criticized, reduced, and finally rejected this anthropomorphism. It is precisely by making the concept of "cause" less personal, less idiosyncratic, less capricious, less singular, and less interested, and more impersonal, more "objective," formal, universal, and quantitative, that early modern philosophers hoped to make causality a realm of better prediction and higher precision. Schematically speaking, there are four kinds of causes in Aristotle: firstly "matter" (*hylê*), secondly "the first beginning of motion" (*protê arkhê kinêseôs*), thirdly "form" (*eidos*), and fourthly the "end" (*telos*) (*Ph.* II, 3; *Metaph.* V, 2). Again schematically speaking, modern science seems to have rejected the latter two. Thus, by reducing causality to a relationship of matter in motion, early modern physics deprived causality of the face it had, of the name it bore, and of the intention that subtended it.

B. The Reduction of *Hylê* to "Matter." Deprived of "form" and "end," both "matter" and "source of motion" come to be fundamentally modified. For instance, in Homer (*Odyssey* V, 257), *hylê* meant less mere "stuff" than "the stuff *of which a thing is made*," that is, a material *for* a chair, *of* a spear, *in* a bird nest.[13] Hence *hylê* often meant a definite kind of material: "wood," "timber," or "forest trees" in distinction from *dendra*, "fruit trees," as can be seen in the English word "xylophone."[14] But *hylê* also came to mean something in direct opposition to timber trees prepared for the carpenter: "copse," "brushwood," "undergrowth." Finally, already in Homer again, *hylê* meant "forest" (*Iliad* XI, 115; *Odyssey* XVII, 316).

Just as the meaning of *aitia* grounds our conception of cause, but is significantly larger, more concrete, and more personal, *hylê* too offers a wider range of senses than our concept of "matter." For Aristotle "even *hylê* is a source" (*Metaph.* IX, 1, 1046a24). Even *hylê* generates and governs beings, and is responsible for some beings. It is their source just like nature is. Just as nature is responsible *for* something, *hylê* is material *for* something. As "undergrowth," *hylê* is not indeterminate stuff, a pure *res extensa*, but is determined as falling short of an inherent standard of growth because it is thought in terms of growth. *Hylê* means under*growth*, but also *under*growth.[15]

In short, early modern philosophy understood matter as deprived of form and end, and thus as homogenous. For Descartes, matter is *res extensa*. The *substantia* of his famous piece of wax is not an *under*growth at all; it does not quite have a name, it does not *grow* and is not to have any face itself, but rather, being receptive to *all* possible faces and conventional names, is exposed to the inspection of the mind alone. Once reduced to matter and deprived of form and end, *hylê* is no longer seen or even imagined, but simply *in*spected without having any look to offer itself. To use the terminology of Hobbes, who literally follows the basic meaning of the Ancient Greek *eidos* and the Latin *species*, once reduced to matter, *hylê* offers no "visible shew."[16]

C. The Reduction of Motion to Locomotion. It is but reasonable that early modern physics understands motion as motion of this matter deprived of form (*eidos*) and end (*telos*). Schematically speaking, we find four kinds of motion in Aristotle: change with respect to being, change of quality, change of quantity, and change with respect to place (*Ph.* III, 1, 200b33–34).[17] In early modern science, however, we see that the reduction of causality and matter entails a reduction of these four kinds of motion. Let us touch upon each of the four.

First, deprived of form and end, matter can no longer change with respect to its being. For matter as the eternal underlying thing is neither generated nor perishable.[18] Although this idea had a history before Aristotle, going back to the Atomists and perhaps to Parmenides, its posterity has proven even more fecund: the Democritean idea of the permanence of matter was extremely influential, via Lucretius, on early modern rationalism and materialism as well as on early modern physics, and even on the tenets of nascent thermodynamics and chemistry.[19]

Secondly, this matter, ungenerated and imperishable, deprived of form and end, can no longer change with respect to quality either. For it is not and cannot be *in*formed, but only shaped, and this shape can have no intrinsic unity because, being homogenous, the "parts" of matter are indifferent to one another. There is no intrinsic difference between one cubical body and many bodies happening to *form* together a cube.

Thirdly, the motion of a piece of matter cannot be a change with respect to quantity for the same reason. For again there is no intrinsic difference between a body of a certain magnitude and a certain number of different bodies adding up to the same magnitude. The only thing that counts for this body is its mass, but even so, there is no intrinsic difference between one body weighing three kilos and three bodies weighing one kilo each. The difference that counts for early modern physics is, say, between *one* body weighing one kilo and *one* weighing three kilos. But what does "one" mean here, if not an arbitrary imposition of the subject?[20] Qualitatively and quantitatively, the whole is nothing more than the sum of its parts—except our own externally imposed arbitrary conceptions.

Thus, finally, no longer being generated or destroyed, no longer *really* changing with respect to quality or quantity, homogenous matter can only undergo a change with respect to place. And indeed, together with mass, typical Newtonian physics is solely concerned with distance, that is, distance between "places," *topoi*. But although Aristotle himself proclaims that change with respect to place is the most prominent kind of motion (*Ph.* IV, 14, 223b21–22; VII, 2, 243a11; VIII, 7), the early modern notion of "place" looks extremely different than Aristotelian *topos*.[21] For it is not "measured" according to itself, but with respect to its distance to other "places" which are in fact no more "measured" according to themselves.

D. The Reduction of *Kosmos* to Infinite Space. Then we must turn to the reduction of *topos*. Early modern physics, and especially the Cartesian coordinate system, replace the Aristotelian concept of "place"[22] with "position" or "location," because here "places" are no longer contained within a finite universe (*to pan*) having a certain order (*kosmos*).[23] All "places" are instead distributed throughout an "infinite" environment and thus are determined only relatively, that is, with respect to other positions.[24] Position and location are truly adequate terms to be contrasted with the Ancient Greek *topos* and the Latin *locus* in so far as the former two emphasize the subjective activity of *locating*, *positing* according to its own relative *locatedness* or *positedness*.

Thus, as motion is reduced to locomotion in early modern science, the loci of this locomotion are also made strictly homogenous. Hence, according to what will be known as the "law of inertia," a moving body would move indefinitely in the same direction *simply because it is already moving in that direction*. Matter has no intrinsic "inclination" (*hormê*, as in *Ph.* II, 1, 192b18) with respect to its position, location, or direction.[25] Just as a body is not intrinsically related to its own parts in early modern mechanistic physics, it is also indifferent to its environment. Homogenous matter moves in a homogenous environment with no "center," no "periphery," no "up," no "down," no "limit," and no "threshold." This infinite environment of matter in motion is indeed not a universe or an "all" (*to pan*) in the sense of a finite and ordered whole (*kosmos*),[26] but is something that is by definition never an "all."[27] Thus such an environment is altogether foreign to Aristotelian physics and is designated with a term that has no equivalent there: "space."[28]

So if we are to understand motion in Aristotle and thereby find an answer to our question, that is, the inherence of *logos* in natural motion, we must recall a sense of *aition* as a "responsible" having a certain look (*eidos*) and being motivated by an "intention" (*telos*), we must think of *hylê* as having a certain "directionality" as *under*growth. Thus we must see motion and change not as the transitory external modifications of an intrinsically homogenous eternal underlying matter, but as something happening *to* something, something suffering *under* something, and even something done *by* something *to* itself.[29] We must reinstate matter, mortality, earthliness, and finitude in the Aristotelian sublunar nature. Finally, we must somehow picture a differentiated, multiple, and heterogeneous universe where bodies are in places *not* simply *because* they are actually there, where bodies are *not* absent from places simply *because* they actually are *not* there. As prefigured in our two previous discussions, we shall see a sense of "stretch" and "tension" become more and more concrete in this chapter of the book, and more and more diverse in the following ones.

For Aristotle, nature as *aition* or *arkhê* is then not an initial push or stimulation; it is comparable to a stretch that from the end (*telos*) of a process reaches back to its beginning and permeates and informs the whole change; matter is stretched out toward the mature, multiple, and settled life of a forest, as fire is stretched away from the center of the universe towards its place. In short, while elaborating Aristotle's concept of nature, we must keep in mind that an inherent back-turning stretch pervades nature, and that, according to him, "place has some power" (*Ph.* IV, 1, 208b10–11).[30]

Everyday "Physics"

If we are to employ Aristotle's typical procedure from what is clear to us, we may ask what is clear to us in the context of causality, matter, motion, and spatiality.[31] Perhaps dismantling the early modern reductions brings us less to an even more remote era of history than to what is already clear to us as living beings and involved human agents. Perhaps as *theôroi* who have left our town, each and every day we *are* in touch with an experiential sense of motion that lies beneath the way motion is taught in high school, measured and calculated from a third-person perspective. Indeed, scientific technical concepts such as cause, motion, matter, mass, and space have been historically derived from more concrete human experiences, as can be seen sometimes from their etymology, and yet this means that becoming aware of these formalizations and abstractions does not simply lead us further away from our time back to the primitive and prescientific, but also that such an awareness brings us critically back to our concrete human experience.[32]

What then is our experiential sense of causality, matter, motion, and spatiality? We are beings who cause change in the world and who move all our life or who assume to be doing so. When we move around or cause changes in the world, we very often do so with a certain purpose in mind. When we ask a question such as "Why is the coffee maker in the bathroom?" the kind of explanation we expect is *not*: "Because that is exactly where it is located" or "Because it has been put there." Such answers are uninformative, if not redundant, and hence would be immediately followed by another question: "*Who* put it there? *Why*?" In this process of asking, we are seeking neither an account of the beginning of motion in the universe as a whole, nor the very last proximate force that finally pushed or pulled the coffee maker to where it is now. Rather, we are after the "whole point" or the "overarching story" that we assume to be subtending the situation, we are trying to see the face of the disfigured state of affairs, we are trying to recognize what is going on. We are familiar with both the bathroom and the coffee maker, but the meaning of their relationship is riddlesome. Something seems out of place.

Thus, we can keep asking questions, and as long as the answers we get give us more proximate causes of motion, we will be unsatisfied, for "it must stop somewhere" (*Metaph.* XII, 3, 1070a4). If our interlocutor is expounding on the respective positions of the coffee maker in space, we are getting some answers, but no account, explanation, or justification—no *logos* in the sense of the relation holding together the formerly disparate terms. We are lacking a middle term between the bathroom and the coffee maker. When asking about the cause of the coffee maker's being in the bathroom, we are not seeking information, we are trying to understand. We are looking not for another "cause" than the ones we are getting, but for another *kind* of cause.

What we seek in our question is the final or formal cause (*telos* or *eidos*), while our reticent interlocutor keeps giving an impoverished version of the Aristotelian efficient cause.[33] If one is asking "Why is the coffee maker in the bathroom?" then one clearly already knows what a coffee maker and a bathroom are, and thus sees the coffee maker in the bathroom as *out of place*. This is evident from the words we are using: a word like "bathroom" does not supply us spatial coordinates, it does not designate an indefinite anonymous *Raum* or space, nor is it a certain space *plus* certain objects such as a faucet, a tub, towels . . . A bathroom is rather precisely a room *for* something, obviously *for* taking a bath. It is the activity of taking a bath that first gives all the previous details a unified aspect or look, because it supplies the connections between them, it provides the lines of force between them, it connects the points that turn out *not* to be points, it sheds light on them no longer as loose objects that have happened to fall together instantly, but as stretched toward one another all along. Perhaps it is in this sense that place has, for Aristotle, "a certain power." Thus, the *eidos* or *telos* is not "news." While "out of place," we notice the coffee maker almost caught red-handed in the bathroom; there it does not have a show, it is not part of that show, but of another: to "make coffee."

This "experiential logic" of everyday life not only brings us closer to Aristotle's *Physics*, but even foreshadows, perhaps, the most formal parts of the corpus, namely his syllogistic. For the connection between the disparate elements of our everyday understanding of a bathroom, the "stretch" between the objects, corresponds to the Aristotelian "middle term" (*to meson*): it is the connection that makes us understand the two other terms.[34] And while an unacquainted view of the bathroom may be seen to correspond to the dogmatic universal statement "All towels stay in the bathroom," our everyday implicit understanding is mediated: "Towels are used for taking a bath, and we take baths in the bathroom, *so that's why* they stay in the bathroom." Of course, houses and objects are organized in different ways in different cultures and according to different people's taste. Yet, the point here is not that human places are organized specifically *in this or that way* and by means of *this or that object*, but precisely that human places are *organized*. And it is only as *organized* places that different spatialities in different cultures and in different experiences come to be apparent in their very difference.

Nature at Work

So Aristotle attempts to view causality and motion, as it were, "from within."[35] Here cause looks less like an external stimulus or a push than like something "responsible" or "accountable." Places here look less like locations with definable coordinates, than like homes, hives, nests, territories, rooms, hideouts, yards, roads, detours, and resting points. Motion looks less like happenings, incidences, or occurrences than activities, undergoings, or even undertakings. This is exactly reflected in the way we would ask in English: "What is the coffee maker *doing* in the bathroom?" To draw from the senses of *pragmateuesthai* mentioned earlier in chapter 2, motion takes the form of concern, labor, and care. Hence, for Aristotle, motion is grounded on the idea of work (*ergon*) and of an end of that work (*telos*): "Motion is the actuality [*entelekheia*] of that which is potentially just as such" (*Ph.* III, 1, 201a11–12). If Aristotle defines nature in terms of motion, he defines motion in terms of actuality: "being-at-work" (*en-ergeia*) or "being-at-the-point-of-completion" (*en-telekheia*).

We are not unaware that natural beings fundamentally differ from artifacts like coffee makers, and that natural places differ from human space. However, one must not exaggerate this difference; in fact, Aristotle emphasizes more the parallelism between nature and art than their mutual exclusiveness:

> Each being comes to be from a synonym—natural beings as well as the others; for a being is generated either by art, by nature, by fortune or by chance. Then art is a source in another whereas nature is a source in [the being] itself. (*Metaph.* XII, 3, 1070a4–8)

As we have seen in chapter 2, the source of motion in natural beings is inherent to them, unlike that of the coffee maker and other artifacts. Natural beings move not only because of something they may happen to become, but because of something they already are. If we clarify the meaning of the verb "being" here, we may get a hold of what is "spectacular" about natural beings, and of its relation to *logos*.

What are composite natural beings? Form and matter. Which one gives us a better grip on their nature, according to Aristotle? After defining nature as a source or cause of motion and rest in that to which it belongs primarily in *Physics* II, 1, 192b21–24, Aristotle first takes up the view of nature as the "first underlying *hylê*" (193a28–29). According to this view, nature is that which a being boils down to. Aristotle presents Antiphon's argument: the nature of a bed is wood, for, if it is buried under the earth for some time, wood remains even after it loses its shape as a bed. Note how similar this argument is to Descartes's wax example: just as the *substantia* of the wax was some indeterminate eternal stuff underlying transient sensory aspects, Antiphon takes nature to be an unarranged (*arrythmiston*) underlying being that remains continuous (*diamenei . . . synekhôs*) and eternal (*aidion*) beneath momentary attributes or affections, states, and dispositions (*pathê . . . kai hexeis kai diatheseis*). What Antiphon and Descartes abstract is one aspect of their own interest in the thought experiment: wood cannot be the nature of bed for a viewer who is about to sleep, and extension cannot be the essence of the piece of wax for bees. Both experiment and both displace things in their experiment and thus fail to watch what nature may show. Whereas Descartes famously claims that man is "maître et possesseur de la nature,"[36] Aristotle claims:

> If human being is the best of all animals, this makes no difference, for there are many other things that are more divine than human being, for instance, the most apparent one, those out of which the *kosmos* is composed. (*NE* VI, 7, 1141b1–1141b3)[37]

Thus if "*logos* of being" is a standard inherent to the being at hand, if it truly is what it is *for that being* to be, proof of this will be provided by motion, by natural motion, that is, by motions whose motive force lies within the moving being.

Logos and Nature

Hence, Aristotle responds to Antiphon's "downward" account of nature as *hylê* in the following way: "What is potentially flesh or bone does not yet have its own nature . . ." (*Ph.* II, 1, 193b1–2). Before we read the rest of the passage, note that Aristotle is here reversing Antiphon's and Descartes's perspective: that which *can* be anything is something that is *not* according to nature. Seen "downwardly" as something unarranged that *can* be arranged in any way, the buried bed indeed has no nature. Aristotle seems to invite Antiphon to watch the spectacle a bit longer: in fact, when the bed is buried, it turns not into indeterminate stuff; having lost its "shape," it does not return to unarranged (*arrythmiston*) disorder, but precisely to another order, its *own* order, its *own* "rhythm," its inherent determination, its "form according to *logos*" (*eidos to kata ton logon*).

Now we can read the whole sentence we partly quoted above:

> What is potentially flesh or bone does not yet have its own nature, until it takes the *eidos kata ton logon*—that by means of which, in defining, we say what flesh or bone is; and [what is potentially flesh or bone] is not according to nature. (*Ph.* 193b1–4)

When the bed is buried and the wood starts to sprout, it takes up its own true face, it shows its look (*eidos*), it puts up its own show instead of that imposed by the carpenter. Buried, the wood is destroyed only in the aspect which interests one who needs a bed. Seen from the perspective of its inherent *logos*, it is not destroyed, but rather allowed to be on its own, to put on its own show. As quickly as Socrates's body returned to its elements, the piece of wood sprouts and stretches out toward the look of an oak tree. Even further, it is less the wood that now reaches ahead to the look of an oak, than it is the show of the oak that is at last allowed to stretch back toward *hylê* and take hold of the undergrowth. The awkwardness of our terms may also be found in Aristotle's central statement in *Physics* II, 1: "What, then, is it that grows? Not the from-which, but the to-which" (193b18–19).[38] This tension or backward stretch starting from the to-which back to the from-which is indeed the link that keeps apart and holds together potentiality and actuality. "Just as teachers think they deliver up the end when they have exhibited a student at work, so too is nature" (*Metaph.* IX, 8, 1050a18–19). Instead of burying the bed like Antiphon or burning the piece of wax like Descartes, instead of first stripping beings down or displacing them, Aristotle in a way makes himself a *theôros* by displacing *himself* in order to consult nature, to ask for a *logos*, to watch the spectacle of nature.

To recapitulate, for Aristotle nature is primarily an inherent source of motion—inherent not in the Anaximandrean way the unarranged (*arrythmiston*) lies beneath *rhythmos*, or in the way the faceless disorder lies deep beneath superficial order.[39] Rather, nature is inherent as a face waiting to be allowed to appear, as a show waiting for patience, interest, attention, and silence from the audience. We add ". . . and some silence" because just as natural beings are spectacular, their show is not a pantomime, but the articulation of their proper logic, the expression of what it is *for them* to be. Their face is "the *logos* of what it is for [them] to be" (*Ph.* II, 3, 194b27–28). It is in this sense that the *inherently* motivated motions of natural beings, most notably growth, attest that which we have been looking for since the beginning of this book: the "*logos* of being," an intrinsic relation between potentiality and actuality, a genuine claim coming from the very being at hand about its own being, a true standard of being, that is, an inherent standard.

Out of the four basic meanings of *logos*, namely "standard," "ratio," "reason," and "speech," we have now come to understand the first one and accounted for its inherence: *logos* as standard.

2. The Organic

Nature then does not exclude *logos* at all, at least in the sense of inherent standard, essence, or form: natural beings are characterized by being stretched between mere being and their *logos* as what it is *for them* to be. If it is true that *logos* is inherent and that it is the expression of what it is for natural beings to be, then the meaning of *logos* would not be restricted to reason, speech, or ratio as strictly "subjective." Would this natural *logos* be derivative of the *logos* in reason, language, and logic? Would the show of natural beings be a ventriloquism, an imposition of our structures of thinking and of living onto nature? In short, how is this first, natural meaning of *logos* related to the others which seem to be "subjective"?

But, as we suggested, Aristotle's "logic," and even the most formal part of it, his syllogistic, may be seen to be inspired by and derived from the forms according to *logos* in nature. After exploring the valid syllogisms in his logic, Aristotle makes the general observation that all valid inferences require one affirmative premise and one universal premise (*APr.* I, 24, 41b7–8). And a universal premise requires a universal term (*On Int.* 7). These requirements may be considered as following from the *theôria* of the positive regularities in nature: not instantaneous miracles one after the other, but the ongoing spectacle of the revolution of stars, the periodical changes of seasons and weather, the cycles of migration, wind, rain, and snow, the growth and reproduction of plants and animals, and the show of the oak that spouts from the buried bed and thus returns to its origin.

And yet there is another sense of *logos* that does not apply to the whole range of nature as "standard." Some natural beings put up a show in a different way and they are stretched in a different way than natural beings as a whole. For instance, fire is certainly a natural being, it is inherently motivated upward or in centrifugal motion and has its "place" in the first from last sphere of the universe.[40] And yet, although it has its own *logos* as holding onto *the* hot and *the* dry without letting one yield to or overtake the other, fire is exemplary of beings that are deprived of *logos* in another, second sense that we must illuminate in this section:

> But to some the nature of fire seems simply to be the cause of nutrition and growth, for it alone of all bodies and elements appears to be nourished and grow; hence one may suppose that this is that which works in plants and animals; yet it is somehow a concomitant cause, but the cause is not simply [fire] . . . for the growth of fire is limitless [*apeiron*] as long as there is something to be burned, whereas of all things composed by nature there is a limit [*peras*] and *logos* of magnitude and growth. (*DA* II, 4, 416a10–18)[41]

Fire served us previously as a good example for showing how the Aristotelian concept of locomotion and place differs from early modern notions. But something else is going on here. As *logos* is said in many ways, fire has *logos* in one sense, as inherent standard, but not in another. True, it is "stretched" away from the center of the universe, its *topos*, unlike the early modern concept of matter, and it is "stretched" between *the* hot and *the* dry. But it simply keeps on "stretching out" however big or small it is. Although, unlike stuff, fire is *not* indifferent to its place in the universe, it *is* indifferent to its magnitude.

The Soul as Form

Nature in general or fire in particular then do not necessarily illustrate *logos* in the sense of a limit of magnitude and growth. What is it that has a "*logos* of magnitude and growth"? Right after the passage quoted above, Aristotle's answer is the ensouled, living being: "But these [limit and *logos*] belong to the soul, and not to fire; [they belong] to *logos* more than to matter" (*DA* II, 4, 416a19).[42] What then does Aristotle mean by soul such that it exhibits a new sense of *logos*? Aristotle elaborates his own definition of the soul in several steps in the first chapter of *DA* II. Let us offer a running commentary to his first sketch:

> One class of those that are, we call being; but of [being], one as matter (which in its own right is not a 'this' [*tode ti*]), another as shape [*morphê*] and form [*eidos*] (directly as a result of which something is called a 'this'), and third that [which comes to be] out of them. (*DA* II, 1, 412a6–9)[43]

This is not new to us who have seen that, insofar as each is *tode ti*, that is, an individual being that lends itself to direct perception, even natural beings are "compound"; in the context of natural beings, this "composition" (*ek toutôn*), as we also have seen, should be understood not as a "com-position" or "synthesis" in the etymological sense of putting matter and form side by side, because such juxtaposition would be precisely missing the close interconnection between the two. Aristotle continues:

> Now matter is potentiality and form is actuality, and this [i.e., form or actuality] in two ways: as knowledge [*epistêmê*] or as contemplating [*theôrein*]. (*DA* II, 1, 412a9–11)

This sentence introduces a distinction within actuality itself: form or actuality is either like knowledge is or like contemplating. Conceptually Aristotle here makes room for an actuality that is unlike the full-fledged actuality of contemplation. So far, Aristotle's elaboration of the concept of the soul goes like this: if the soul is, and if one way of being is *ousia*, and if *ousia* refers to either matter or form or the composite, and if form is said in two ways, as knowledge or as contemplating, then the soul may be either matter or form (as knowledge or as contemplating), or the composite. But which one?

> Bodies seem to be beings preeminently, and among them natural ones. For these are the sources of the others. But some natural beings have life, some do not. We are calling life self-nourishing as well as growth and wasting away. So that every natural body having a share in life would be a being, but being as composite. Since [a living natural body] is such and such a body, the soul would not be body. For the body is not among the things said of an underlying thing, but rather as an underlying thing and a matter. (*DA* II, 1, 412a11–20)[44]

If beings are mostly bodies and natural bodies, and if some natural bodies share in life, and if sharing life refers to both self-nourishing and growth and wasting away, then self-nourishing and growing bodies cannot simply be bodies, but composite bodies.[45] So if the living character is *of* the body, then body would correspond to the matter of the composite, and soul to its form. "Therefore it is necessary that the soul be being as form of a natural body having life potentially" (*DA* II, 1, 412a20–22).

At first glance, this convoluted reasoning seems less to give us information about the soul than to impose a meaning on the word: the soul is the life principle, and this life principle is *of* a body and not the other way around. Bodies having life potentially look a certain way, perform a certain work, put up a certain show. And the soul or living is that show: "self-nourishing as well as growth and wasting away." To say the least, this "most comprehensive" (*DA* II, 1, 412a6) definition of the soul is so worldly and bodily that it immediately disappoints any reader assuming the soul to be something aloof, disincarnated, and otherworldly. Eating here seems to be a sufficient condition for having a soul and a sufficient enactment of it.[46] If we are at first disappointed by this, it is perhaps because we overestimate the value of the soul and/or we underestimate the significance of nutrition.

Importantly, even as an unwarranted assumption, the claim that the soul is said of a body and not the other way around implies the impossibility of transmigration of the soul. If souls could transmigrate, then there would be absolutely no sense in observing the bodies of living beings in order to *understand* their life, since their soul would have no inherent relation to their body, and we could not do biology and any inquiry *on the soul* unless as some form of "psychics."

This "definition" of the soul, however, does not help us distinguish the natural beings that have a share in life from those that do not. Soul is defined as form, but so was nature.[47] Self-nutrition, the work minimally required for having life, may well be interpreted as a change with respect to quantity originating from the being itself. Since we saw that, for Aristotle, fire grows as much as trees and animals do, how are the latter ensouled bodies distinct from the soulless former? Despite the fact that elements can turn into one another, as stated in *GC* II, 1, 329b1, why cannot we say that, when rain falls, water is growing in puddles, just as we say that a watered plant does? Don't we *feed* fire as we *feed* our pets? How are the shows of nature as a whole and those of *living* nature any different? Doesn't each exhibit its inherent logic? Why did Aristotle suggest that the growth of fire has no limit and *logos*?

The Soul as Actuality

Aristotle does not call the account of the soul we read above a "definition" (*horos*, *horismos,* or *logos*). Despite the presence of the "therefore" (*ara*), it does not finish anything. It is rather the first step of his dialectical reasoning in this first chapter of *DA* II. In this first step, what we learned is that soul and life and self-nourishing are coextensive. Aristotle continues:

> Therefore it is necessary that the soul be being as form of a natural body having life potentially. But being is actuality; therefore [the soul is] the actuality of such a body. But actuality is said in two ways: first as knowledge, and then as contemplating. Thus it is clear that [the actuality characterizing the soul] is as knowledge. (*DA* II, 1, 412a20–24)

Let us elaborate the crucial distinction between actuality "as knowledge" and actuality "as contemplation." To say that one *knows* Latin does not require that one constantly speak, write, read, study, and think about Latin. In fact, on the contrary, a sign that one *knows* Latin is that one is able to *stop* putting to use one's acquisition, to have internalized or "digested" it. But note that in fact Latin is an odd example for soul and life, precisely because Latin is a *dead* language. But characterizing Latin as a *dead* language is itself telling. That a language is dead does not mean that no one in the world ever actually writes, reads, speaks, understands, and studies it; what it means is that nobody is able to *stop* putting their knowledge of Latin to use without immediately starting to lose it. Learning dead languages is often comparable to Sisyphus's endless struggle against the natural motion of the rock that each time rolls down the hill: however much one puts it to use, it does not quite stick. People quite often have to learn dead languages over and over again, to resuscitate them, so to speak. Generating a sentence in a dead language is like building a castle out of dry sand, and its maintenance is like the constant anxiety of keeping a house of cards straight. On the other hand, learning a *living* language leaves one enough room, energy, and time for playing with it, distorting it, being creative with it, or even forgetting about it. Knowing a living language is thus similar to life: if it slumbers, if it is inactive, this does not mean that it is dead, it rather means it is alive. Hence, in explaining the kind of actuality that characterizes the soul, Aristotle interestingly explains his example of knowledge and contemplation with yet another example he takes precisely from the realm of the soul: sleep and waking.[48] Waking is to sleep what contemplating is to "dormant" knowledge.

So, in determining the soul, Aristotle is not simply using his classical distinction between potentiality and actuality, he is refining it. It is not true that the possession of a language and sleep are states of mere potentiality and privation, because the requirements for sleep or the possession of some knowledge are results of prior preparation, the end-products of previous work. Only knowing beings contemplate, only sleeping beings wake up, only immature beings can ripen. Or else we are meaning something different by these words: if fire or a rock contemplates at all, it contemplates without ever having known; its awakenness does not emerge out of, and ever fall back into, sleep; it is ever complete without having matured at all. Speaking metaphorically and thus inexactly (*Top.* VI, 2, 139b34), fire is a narcoleptic fixated in contemplation, it is a grown-up who has not lived through childhood.[49]

This is why Aristotle suggested that the growth and magnitude of fire has no limit or *logos*. Being a natural body, the locomotion of fire has a definite inherent directionality, away from the center of the universe. But if fire has a regularly recognizable "form" or "look" (*eidos*), its pointy shape is determined not by its growth into a *telos*, but by its inherent locomotion. For the shape of fire is rather a byproduct of its natural upward impulse. Hence, once it reaches its natural place, it no longer has the same shape.[50] The ensouled being, on the other hand, presents a growth and completion we do not find in nonliving nature, an instantiation of *logos* beyond the stretch between factual being and inherent standard. Not that the soul is *more* complete than fire. In fact, fire is *too* complete to be ensouled, or *too* alive to be living.

This completion that distinguishes the soul from nature in general is the achievement of a state *for* an activity. There is an important sense in which ensouled beings are complete and, in a sense, "incomplete." Beyond the fire's stretch out toward the completion of what it is for it to be, the soul is stretched between the completion of its *past* development and its *future* exercise of vital functions. The show of the soul is the show both of a "look" toward the past (its preparedness) and a "look" toward the future (performance). In a word, the soul is characterized by being *ready*.

This is perhaps why, while nature in general was akin to *logos* as "form according to *logos*" (*Ph.* II, 1, 193a31, 193b3), the soul is also "a being according to *logos*" (*DA* II, 1, 412b11). The actuality that characterizes the soul then requires a state of growth between potentiality and actuality as such. The soul is either a second potentiality, or, as Aristotle puts it immediately after his example of knowledge and contemplation, "the first actuality of a physical body having life potentially" (*DA* II, 1, 412a28–29).

Organicity

By being the "first actuality of a natural body having life potentially," the soul is a detour between mere potentiality and actuality; what distinguishes the show of the soul from that of natural beings is that ensouled bodies precisely display this very detour. Ensouled bodies exhibit their soul by the way they have life potentially: while the immediacy between the potentiality and actuality of fire is reflected in the indifferent identity of its parts, the intermediate state of the soul is reflected in the interrelated differences of bodily parts. The *logos* as soul is such that its parts are neither fused with one another nor indifferent to one another, but exhibit at once an achievement taken one by one, and a project of cooperation. They are not fully actual, not fully at work, but as yet *for* a work. While fire *does* its work, the soul *has* work. Hence soul needs tools whereas fire needs none.

This is why, on the one hand, watching the spectacle of fire is somewhat similar to watching a chess game: one can start watching it from the middle. The show of living beings, however, is comparable to a thriller: missing the first scene where the murder is committed or the last scene where the murderer is revealed, or misunderstanding the development that leads to the revelation—this is *not* to have really seen the movie. The parts of the life of the ensouled being are spectacularly complete and "incomplete."[51]

As the soul is thus determined by a work (*ergon*) as much as by actually being at work (*energeia*) pure and simple, the parts of the body of the ensouled being are characterized by having a work (*ekhein ergon*), and the Ancient Greek adjective for having a work is *organikon*: "The soul is the first actuality of a physical body having life potentially—but such will be any body that is organic" (*DA* II, 1, 412a29–412b1).[52] The wholeness of fire does not come out of its working parts; its pointy top, its bright body, its sparkles, its flames are not qualitatively and mutually differentiated for a work, they are equally and indifferently determined by the upward motion of fire as such. It is no coincidence that the word "pyramid" comes from the Ancient Greek *pyr*, "fire," for a pyramid is precisely a shape determined by its gradually weakening upward orientation. The natural determination of fire does not offer a stage of relative indetermination such that it may then determine itself.

Let us emphasize this remarkable and surprising claim: for Aristotle, the soul of animals does not show itself beyond the body. The soul does not show itself simply in every part of the animal body taken in isolation. It rather shows itself in the body as a whole: "The parts of the plants are organs too, though altogether simple ones; for instance, the leaf is the covering for the peel, and the peel for the fruit, while the roots are similar to the mouth, for both take in food" (*DA* II, I, 412b1–4). To find the soul of living beings, Aristotle looks at their parts. The stretch that characterizes the soul in its "look" toward the past (preparedness) and the future (performance) is seen in the way the parts of a living body are at once developed and purposeful. Thus, to see the soul is, once again, to "understand how that which is disrupted has the same *logos* as itself: a back-stretching harmony as in the bow and the lyre."

That Aristotle considers the parts of an organic body as developed wholes can be seen from the fact that he takes the parts to be exemplary of the things that exist by nature as much as whole animals (*Ph.* II, 1, 192b9). That he deems the parts of animals as prepared together in order to put up a show or to exhibit a *logos* may be why precisely his work *Parts of Animals* contains so many fundamental insights into his understanding of nature and life. For instance, the following:

> One should not recoil childishly from the examination of the humbler animals. For in every realm of natural beings there is something wonderful. And as Heraclitus, when strangers who

> wanted to meet him saw him warming himself at the furnace and stopped, is said to have demanded them not to be afraid to come in as even there the divine was present, so should one go on to study each animal without distaste as in every being there is something natural and beautiful. (*PA* I, 5, 645a14–22)

Then, as distinct from merely natural beings, *living* beings will exhibit a meaning of *logos* other than "inherent standard." They will do so by the way in which their parts have work, that is, are organized.

Nutrition

What is this work of the soul? If the soul is indeed "preparation," what is it "preparation" *for*? What is that in view of which organs are arranged? What is *logos* here *logos* of—since it is not "*logos* of being" pure and simple? Just as the magnitude and growth of fire lack limit and *logos*, the "logic" of the soul will first show itself in an inherently motivated motion and rest with respect to quantity—that is, in growth. "The soul has a *logos* that increases itself."[53]

Since the organic being is determined not by a percentage of raw elements, but by its irreducibility to any lumping together of elements, its self-nourishing and growth are not reducible to the reception and accumulation of one or several elements:

> Empedocles has not spoken in a beautiful way in adding to this that growth happens to plants when they take root downward because earth moves that way by nature, and when [they spread] upward because fire moves that way . . . *what is it that holds the fire and earth together as they move in opposite directions?* For, if there is nothing to prevent this, they will be torn apart; and if there is [something to prevent this], it is the soul and it is the cause of growth and feeding. (*DA* II, 4, 415b28–416a9; emphasis is ours)[54]

This is Aristotle's crucial reservation for understanding *logos* as "ratio" in the context of living beings. The growth of organic bodies cannot be reduced to an accumulation of elements according to *any* percentage, since a percentage, although an account of the respective amounts of the ingredients, cannot account for the very fact of their togetherness, that is, for the very stretch that characterizes a vigorous body: "for [plants] do not grow up and not down, but equally in both directions, and in every direction" (*DA* II, 1, 413a28–29).[55] Within a living body, this inclusiveness of contrary directions (up *and* down) comes from the inclusiveness of different elements (fire *and* earth).

Plants fall not as plants but precisely as earthy; plants sprout not as fire, but as plants. Nutrition then is a processing and informing as much as an undergoing or receiving. If eating involves the disintegration of a being's form into its elements, it also requires the subsequent reintegration of the elements in the self-nourishing being's form. It is not sufficient to say that nutrition is a reception of a being's matter without its form. Nutrition is digestion as much as reception. It is less a process of indifferent accumulation than the reformative process of bringing and holding together the formerly contrary elements within the new form.[56]

It may be necessary to illustrate Aristotle's conception of nutrition by stating what would *not* count as nutrition, since us humans, having other powers of the soul, necessarily modify nutrition according to those other powers (hunting, tasting, gastronomy, fasting, feasting, diets . . .) and are thus susceptible of concealing it. What then would *not* count as nutrition? For instance, in English "emptiness" and "fullness" are precisely inadequate concepts for expressing nutrition, because the absence of matter in the body is by itself insufficient for explaining hunger and thirst, just as its mere introduction is for nutrition. The growth of no plant ever requires water *as such*, precisely because a plant is *not* water *as such*. Watering a plant rather takes a certain *form* precisely because a plant *is* a certain form. Similarly, taking a medicine involves a specific mode of delivery of chemicals, an exact amount, a certain diet, a certain timing, a rhythm of sleep, and ultimately a certain *form* of life. Adding water to water, flesh to flesh, blood to blood, hair to hair, is precisely failure to nourish. Similarly, merely mixing water to earth, blood to flesh, or olive oil to hair is the same failure to nourish as long as solely the quantities in the mixture are considered. Nutrition is neither a transition from emptiness to fullness, nor a delivery of matter, but a specific answer to a specific question. Put in terms of Aristotelian ethics, proper diet is not solely a matter of deduction from pre-given rules, but always a matter of employing prudence or practical wisdom (*phronêsis*). Digestion is not becoming full, but preparing matter, integrating it: "cooking" or "concocting" (*pepsis*).[57]

A new logic, a new *logos*, and a new kind of "stretch" thus emerges with nutrition: whereas natural beings are inherently motivated to hold on to what they are *and* what it is for them to be (*logos* as "standard"), here a living being does so by holding on to contrary elements according to what it is to be for itself, without simply letting one element take over or remain isolated and idle (*logos* as "ratio"). It is precisely because living beings hold together the elements according to their own form that contrary elements coexist within living bodies instead of one knocking down the other. This is the basic insight behind the second sense of *logos*: proportion, ratio, percentage.[58]

But this is not enough for capturing this second sense of *logos*. For Aristotle himself objects to Empedocles's theory that the soul is a *logos* or harmony in *On the Soul* I:[59]

> They say that harmony is a blend [*krasis*] or composition [*synthesis*] of contraries and that the body is composed of contraries. However, harmony is some *logos* of those that have been mixed [*tôn mikhthentôn*] or a composition [*synthesis*], and the soul cannot be of these. (*DA* I, 4, 407b30–34)[60]

When Aristotle articulates this criticism, his object is clear: for him the soul cannot be a harmony understood as blend or composition—a "*logos* of those that have been mixed," or a "*logos* of those that are mixed" (*DA* I, 4, 408a9). And in the following paragraph he insists that the soul cannot be the "*logos* of the mixture" (*logos tês mixeôs*) (*DA* I, 4, 408a14–28). If the soul were a harmony or *logos* of mixture, in short, a percentage, then there would be many souls each time there is a new percentage of elements in the body, for "the mixture of elements for flesh and for bone do not have the same *logos*" (*DA* I, 4, 408a15–16)[61] Just as a percentage cannot account for what holds its ingredients together, offering various percentages avoids the same question of what holds these percentages together. If soul has to do with *logos*, this will not be merely a matter of number or percentage because, however precise and many, the percentage of ingredients will not account for their unity, for the "stretch" between them, for what makes them parts of one show.[62]

The *logos* of growth then is not the percentage of ingredients: "The *logoi* of mixtures are in the relation [*prosthesei*] of numbers, and not in numbers, for instance three in relation to two and not three times two" (*Metaph.* XIV, 6, 1092b32–33).[63] This explains how Aristotle can explicitly agree with Empedocles elsewhere: "Even Empedocles says that the bone is by virtue of *logos*—which is 'what it is to be' and the being of the thing" (*Metaph.* I, 10, 993a17–19). If life and nutrition stretch out to exhibit a *logos*, this show is understandable *neither* by means of its elements *nor* by their percentages. So, if *logos* here means "ratio" or "proportion," we must keep in mind the fact that it is so not as a number, but as a relation between numbers, that is, as holding on to its different constituents and their magnitude without letting one take over the other or lie indifferent to them. "For a tragedy and a comedy come into being out of the same letters" (*GC* I, 2, 315b14–15).[64]

Reproduction

In reproduction as well as in nutrition, an ensouled being strives for the perpetuation of itself and/or of its form by integrating contraries. What reproduction teaches us is that, just as an adequate understanding of nutrition requires that we consider the parts of animals not as starting points, but as products,[65] we can be spectators of the show of living beings only when we take account not of one arbitrarily chosen segment of their life, but of their life as a whole. For instance, a squirrel exhibits its "inherent standard," its *logos* of being, its own logic, that is, what it is for a squirrel to be, not in its tail or claws taken as ends in themselves, but as *incomplete* completions, as organs. In the same way, a squirrel shows off what it is to be for a squirrel along a lapse of time and through events that stretch beyond its maturity, even before its birth and after its death. The form of a squirrel comes to appearance neither in the parts of its body, nor in the slices of its life span taken by themselves, nor in the percentage of its chemical makeup. Just as its front claws relate back to its spine, its climbing a tree refers back to its birth and nutrition, and forward to its project of reproduction. The life form called "squirrel" is nothing but an ongoing and everlasting success story. Thus we must dishabituate ourselves from viewing nature and life forms in snapshots. If they are fundamentally spectacular, they are not photogenic, and their movement is not still motion. Life forms are not photographical, but "biographical."

Natural beings exhibit their show and logic not in the way objects around us seem to be constantly available to our gaze, but in the way a war or an artwork comes into existence: the date of the birth and death of a squirrel, and even everything in between, can be recorded and documented by a camera; yet its soul as livingness extends even beyond its life and death—not as immortal, but, on the contrary, *as mortal*. Reproduction in nature indeed acquires its full significance in the context of mortal beings, of their life and death, and of their only afterlife in offspring. A livingness that extends beyond our momentary mental images demands thus a "theoretical" spectator equipped, not with "theory," but with a wonder, patience, and scientific passivity that lets the spectacle unfold through improbable influences and fortuitous circumstances.

But *On the Soul*, which does not expound on nutrition, seems to leave the topic of reproduction to *Generation of Animals*—except in this most crucial passage for the corpus as a whole:

> We must talk about food and reproduction; for the nutritive soul belongs to the others as well, and is the first and most common potentiality of the soul by virtue of which living belongs to them all. The works [of the soul] are reproduction and the use of food, for the most natural work for living beings, if it is full-grown and not defective or does not have spontaneous generation, is to make another like itself: an animal making an animal, a plant a plant, so that they may partake in the eternal and divine in the way they can.

> For all things desire [*oregetai*] that, and do everything they do by nature for the sake of it. (*DA* II, 4, 415a23–415b2)[66]

Thus, reproduction as the integration of the living being's form into the material of another body, and nutrition as the integration of the material of another body into one's own form, are two facets of the same most natural work: *oregesthai* for partaking in the eternal and the divine. Aristotle is quite explicit that the most natural appearance of life takes the form of *oregesthai*—whose first meaning is "to reach out for grasping" and "to stretch out for." Until now we used "stretch" as a metaphor. Here *oregesthai* literally means "to stretch," and only metaphorically "to yearn for" or "to desire."[67]

In an informative passage of the *Nicomachean Ethics*, Aristotle likens the love of the benefactor toward the beneficiary, and of the artist toward his work, to the love of animals toward their young:

> Every artist loves his own work more than he would be loved by the work if it were ensouled. Perhaps this happens especially in the case of poets [*poiêtas*], for they love their own poems [*poiêmata*] excessively, being fond of them as of their children [*tekna*] . . . The reason for this is that all things choose and love to be; and it is in actuality, in living and acting, that we *are*; and, being actually at work, the maker [*ho poiêsas*] is in a way the work; so he is fond of the work and thereby he is fond of being. (*NE* IX, 7, 1167b34–1168a8)

In line with our previous quotation from *On the Soul*, here Aristotle adds: "But this is natural."

We tried to show that the spectacular character of natural beings and the spectatorship of the natural scientist are textually grounded in Aristotle's work. Here we see that *On the Soul* supports our claim that natural beings are not simply "programmed," in the passive voice, to exhibit their logic, but that they stretch out themselves for this, in the middle voice. As to the natural scientist or the *theôros*, the explicit textual confirmation of his own natural yearning for watching the show of natural beings is found not in *On the Soul*, but in the first sentence of the *Metaphysics*: "All human beings by nature stretch themselves out toward knowing" (*Metaph.* I, 1, 980a21; Joe Sachs's translation).

3. Recapitulation and Reorientation

So far as this chapter of the book is concerned, we have seen how Aristotle's understanding of nature demands a conception of motion that may be intellectually remote from us because of the early modern rejection of the Aristotelian physics, but also that it is quite familiar to us on an experiential level. His concepts of motion and, consequently, of nature are fundamentally "spectacular," oriented toward the appearance of a form or look (*eidos*) and the articulation of a *logos*. As a counterpart to this "spectacular" character of nature, the natural scientist for Aristotle is a spectator, an explorer, a traveler, a *theôros* with a question, with an openness for the improbable show of natural beings. This pervasiveness of watching, of exhibition, and of expression of *logos* may suggest that it is because natural beings stretch out toward showing *themselves* that in Heraclitus's famous fragment 123, "nature loves to hide itself," while Aristotle insists that "it is ridiculous to try to prove that nature exists" (*Ph.* II, 1, 193a2–3).

As to our overall project, in section 1 of this chapter, we have seen that the *inherence* of the *logos* as "standard" may be warranted by the *inherently* motivated motions in nature. In section 2, we have seen that two among these motions, namely nutrition and reproduction, are made according to *logos* as "ratio." These two senses of *logos*, "standard" and "ratio," are not unrelated. They both refer to a relation that holds on to its terms without letting one take over or lay indifferent to the other. As "standard," *logos* is the relation between potentiality and actuality in natural motion; as "ratio," *logos* functions as holding onto previously exclusive elements within the body in the case of nutrition, and within another body in the case of reproduction.

Living beings are then minimally determined by two natural motions exhibiting that their "*logos* of being" is inherent to them: reproduction and nutrition. Of Aristotle's four kinds of motion, the latter are, respectively, change with respect to being and change with respect to quantity.[68] What about the other two kinds of motion: change with respect to quality and place? Although we claimed that plants, as ensouled bodies, integrate contrary elements, Aristotle seems to differ when he says that plants are of earth (*gês*) and have no mean condition (*mesotêta*).[69] In fact, the plants' accomplishment of integrating and reforming matter is also their limitation: plants have "no source of such a kind as to receive the forms of sensibles—they absorb them together with their matter" (*DA* II, 12, 424b2–3). So, in our next chapter, we must turn our attention to living beings that are capable of also changing without integrating matter, of changing with respect to quality and also to place: sensation and locomotion. These beings change and move in new ways, and meanwhile exhibit a show and a *logos* that are even more explicit than that of elements and plants. These beings are animals.

CHAPTER 4

Animal Motion

Logos *in* On the Soul

We are trying to understand *logos* as it appears in the *Categories* in the phrase "*logos* of being" as standard, and then in *On Interpretation* as an intrinsic relation between potentiality and actuality. In chapter 3, we saw how *inorganic* nature exhibits the inherence of *logos* as a "form according to *logos*," and how *organic* nature does so in nutrition and reproduction, a process of holding together formerly exclusive elements by "limit" and "*logos*." Besides "standard," a second meaning of *logos* turned out to be operative in the context of organic nature: "ratio." Yet, this second meaning also seems to refer to the fundamental meaning of *logos*: a relation holding on to its terms in such a way that it neither collapses them nor leaves them indifferent to one another. Thus, the overarching sense of *logos* can be compared to what Aristotle calls a "stretching out [*oregesthai*] toward the eternal and the divine" (*DA* II, 4, 415a23–415b2). Neither inorganic nor organic nature *simply exist*—the former is "stretched" between its potentiality and actuality, the latter is "tended" between the developed state of the parts it is constituted *from*, and the functions they are developed *for*. The stretch of fire away from the center of the universe, the reproductive urge to integrate form into the material of another body, or the nutritive impulse to integrate material into a being's own form are facets of the same desire.

But there is more. Not all natural motion involves the integration of matter. Some natural beings interact with beings without imposing their own forms onto others' bodies. These beings are receptive not only to others' material, but also to their form. Although, unlike fire, plants integrate bodies with contrary natural impulses, they are also limited to nutrition and reproduction.[1] As such, they are precisely impermeable to any form other than their own, since the complete destruction of others' forms is precisely the mark of successful nutrition and reproduction. This chapter of the book then deals with more than natural motion and the motion of living beings. It deals with specifically *animal* motion: sensation and locomotion.

> The nutritive power must by necessity be in all that grow and decay. But sensation is not necessarily in all that live. For those whose body is simple do not have touch, nor can those that are not receptive to the forms without the material. (*DA* III, 12, 434a26–30)

In section 1 of this chapter, "Sensation," we shall present the "paradox" of sensation, show that its solution depends on the distinction between affection, alteration, and completion, and conclude that, for Aristotle, sensation cannot be explained without considering it as a specific kind of *logos*, namely a "ratio" or a "proportion" between the state of the sense organ and the state of the sensible (*DA* III, 2, 426a8, 426a28ff.; *De Sensu* 7, 448a9–13). Section 2, "Locomotion," will introduce distant perception and locomotion as "syllogisms" necessarily joining the premise of the receptive part of the soul and that of the desiring part without letting one premise cancel out the other. In section 3, this discussion of the "practical" syllogism shall exemplify another use of *logos* as "ratio," while also gesturing toward the "unpractical" syllogisms that are the hallmark of our next chapter: human action.

1. Sensation

What can we learn from animals?

The elemental and the inorganic exert a certain charm on us: the height of mountains, the constancy of stars, the roar of the ocean, even the look of a campfire or a snowflake may seem to us as models to covet, and as inspirations of the sublime. Everybody now and then admires the solidity of rocks, the immensity of icebergs, the raw power of storms, or the transparency of still water. Inorganic nature aside, plants also contribute to this fantasy with the fertility or size of trees, the tickle of grass, and the blossoming of flowers: a peaceful life confined to nutrition and reproduction alone.

Nevertheless, we are more likely to indulge in this nostalgia while contemplating a view from a balcony in safe remove, or while looking at a landscape by Turner or Caspar Friedrich in a quiet museum, than while steering a ship in a storm. This nostalgia for the elemental and the vegetative seems to reflect an aspiration for opaqueness and determination, excluding hesitation and necessary care. Hence all these elemental or vegetal fantasies remain aspirations. To epitomize nutrition and reproduction for a human being is and always remains an endless task to fulfill, an abstraction, a pleasant imagination, a negative plan of *not* having to do things that is fulfilled, perhaps, only in death.[2]

Insofar as elemental and vegetal fantasies express a denial of aspects of *human* life beyond nutrition and reproduction, our investigation of animality may be expected to conceptualize how nutrition and reproduction are only "parts" of our soul as conceived by Aristotle. When Aristotle invites us not to refrain from studying the most humble animals, quoting Heraclitus who, warming up at the stove, calls his guests to "come in, be brave, for there are gods even here,"[3] perhaps this exhortation is made less against human contempt for "lowly" animals than against our unwillingness to leave elemental and vegetal fantasies for the hesitations, cares, and toils of all *animal* life. It is from animals, perhaps, that we may learn the life of sensation and motility.

The "Paradox" of Sensation

With sensation, we enter the animal world. "Although plants live, they do not have sensation, and the animal is distinguished from that which is not animal by sensation" (*De Sensu* 1, 436b11–12).[4] Yet sensation seems to immediately resist any conceptualization that starts from a distinction between subject and object.

Let us first open up what may be called, following Merleau-Ponty, the "paradox" of sensation. The experience of sensation requires both distance and penetration. *I* am the one *over here* sensing objects, and yet sensation seems to take place *over there*. For Aristotle, sensation is a kind of motion, namely a change with respect to quality, and thus seems much more remote and superficial than nutrition and reproduction. So, on the one hand, sensation seems to be even weaker than a qualitative change proper because the sentient is not really changed by its object, but rather seems to gather a faint and fleeting echo of it. Yet, on the other hand, Aristotle also defines sensation first as a kind of "alteration," a kind of becoming other[5] (*DA* II, 5, 416b35). So much so that it is with sensation that the animal soul becomes open to the world, instead of simply imposing itself upon it. In this spirit, Aristotle famously says: "In a way the soul is all beings" (*DA* III, 8, 431b21–22). Thus, while it seemed superficial and distant before, now sensation appears to be a penetration and access into the world incomparably deeper than reproduction, and a receptivity incomparably wider than digestion.

Aristotle begins his discussion of this paradox in *On the Soul* (II, 5, 416b35–417a1) with an implicit reference to a discussion of "affection" in *On Generation and Corruption*, which puts the paradox of sensation in the form of a dilemma borrowed by his predecessors: is like affected by like, or unlike by unlike? According to Aristotle, the two views form a false opposition: "the cause of their opposition is that, while one must watch [*theôrêsai*] a whole, they happened to say a part" (*GC* I, 7, 323b3–19).

What is this comprehensive view that solves the paradox of sensation, that abolishes the apparent opposition between activity and passivity, between a "subjective" perspective on sensation and an "objective" one? What is the middle way that was excluded or overlooked by Aristotle's predecessors on both sides of the discussion?

According to his typical strategy of dialectical synthesis of his predecessors' views by sorting out the multivocity of words, Aristotle states: "It is necessary that the agent and the patient be somehow the same, and somehow different and unlike one another" (*GC* I, 7, 324a3–5). On the one hand, a being cannot be affected by a being that is *altogether* similar and indistinct from it, since the same being would also be constantly affected by itself and there would be no distinction *away from which* the affection would happen to begin with. But, on the other hand, a being cannot be affected by a being *altogether* different from it, since then there would be no common ground *upon which* it could be affected by the other.

Aristotle attempts to solve the dilemma by stating that "it is necessary that the agent and the patient be similar and same in kind, but unlike and contrary in form" (*GC* I, 7, 323b32–34). So, this body can affect another *body*, and this color can affect another *color*. Thus, if sensation is an affection, it will happen between two beings similar on an overall level, and dissimilar on a relatively lower level.

But is sensation an affection to begin with? How does this idea of affection apply specifically to sensation, if at all? Concerning one horn of the dilemma, the identity of agent and patient in sensation would imply the self-affection of both on their own. This identity would destroy the active character of the agent as well as the passive character of the patient. Thus, if earth is perceived by earth, why doesn't the "earth" in my palm always sense the "earth" in my fingers, wrist, and knuckles? Assuming that my body is constituted from a finite number of elements, why doesn't one part of my body sense my other parts? Why don't I constantly feel that my blood is wet and warm, that my heart is elastic? Why don't I distinctly feel my inner organs, the curves of my brain, and my veins?[6] If I did feel my organs in the same way and to the same extent that I feel external objects, the distinction of external and internal would be abolished and my body would lose its integrity.

This loss of bodily integrity is not just a hypothetical scenario. Sometimes I *do* feel my own eyes or my own liver. But this happens precisely when I am feeling bad. A liver is sick when it is an object of sensation. Ache is self-affection. And disease is literally dis-ease: the diseased senses are unable to *not* feel themselves, they fall short of the ease, the relative potentiality, and the readiness that characterize the ensouled body as we saw in chapter 3. A healthy living body is a body whose parts are both developed *and* open. One can here see how Aristotle's conception of sensation is already both exemplifying his "definition" of the soul and sketching out an opposition to the nostalgia for the elemental we mentioned in the beginning of this chapter. For to feel well is to be altogether ready for and open to the world, to be perfectly "ec-static."[7] To feel well is not to *feel* well, but to feel *well*. More explicitly, to feel well is not to jealously hold on to an inner state of *well*-being. To feel well is to *do well* the work of feeling the world.[8]

So one horn of the dilemma, the horn of "like being affected by like," cannot be the whole story of sensation. As to the other horn of the dilemma, that "unlike is affected by unlike," Aristotle claims that sensation cannot be simply a transition from a state into its contrary under the influence of that contrary, because strictly and merely contrary things cannot get into contact to begin with. If they did, sensation would be mere transformation, the sensing animal would *become* its object, and it would be *eaten* and *digested* by its object, and there would be no sensation proper, but either nutrition or reproduction.

Negatively, then, sensation is neither a mere reversal of properties, nor a transmission of matter. Sensation must allow for a difference between the agent and the patient, but also for the possibility for the sentient to somehow hold onto the sensible. In this sense, just like the fundamental meaning of *logos*, the "paradox" of sensation is that it must hold on to the integrity both of the sentient and the sensible without letting one take over or remain indifferent to the other.

The Example of Fire

What distinguishes sensation from any kind of affection then? How is *feeling warmth* different from merely becoming warm, seeing from reflecting light, or hearing from reverberating? How are animals *touched* such that it is irreducible to the way inanimate objects or plants are? In response to this question, Aristotle makes what looks like a trivial remark: "That which *can* sense is not actually at work, but only potentially" (*DA* II, 5, 417a7–8; emphasis ours).

Follows the example of fire: "So it is like the combustible which does not burn by itself without something setting fire to it; for otherwise it would burn itself and would not need any fire in actuality" (*DA* II, 5, 417a8–10). Although Aristotle's recourse to potentiality and his example help us clarify what sensation cannot be by avoiding the dilemma's first horn, they do not help us understand what sensation is positively. What is the difference between the power of the eye for sight and the potentiality of a combustible to burn? The structure of assimilation can be applied to any change or affection, and although it helps Aristotle criticize and synthesize his predecessors' views, it does not tell us what sensation is. Thus, the fire example is helpful in understanding the specific way the agent and the patient are related in a change, but it does not shed light on the specific form this relation takes in sensation. The combustible is affected by fire, its potential is actualized by fire, it *becomes* fire, but it does not *feel* the fire.

The Example of Knowledge

And yet the concept of potentiality is central. In the rest of his analysis of sensation, Aristotle simply refines the kind of potentiality at stake. Just as the growth of plants was distinguished from the growth of fire by its developed organic character, that is, its being a *first* actuality, sensation is distinguished from change or affection in general by its being a *first* actuality, a developed power. An animal's power of sensation is a result of a prior development just as a plant's power of nutrition was. Thus, the key to understanding sensation is found back in the definition of the soul.

> But since we speak of perceiving in two ways (we say for that which hears and sees potentially that it hears and sees—even if it happens to be asleep—as well as for that which is actually so), so sensation would be said in two ways: on the one hand as in potentiality, and on the other as in actuality. (*DA* II, 5, 417a10–14)

When Aristotle offers his positive account of sensation, he no longer uses the example of the inorganic growth of fire. He rather takes up the example of knowing and distinguishes three stages divided by two transitions: (a) a human being has a *potentiality* to know, just by belonging to a genus that has the potentiality to know (*DA* II, 5, 417a23–25); (b) a human being may have a *first actuality* for knowing by having acquired some knowledge (say the knowledge of grammar) and is in position to contemplate or use this knowledge (*DA* II, 5, 417a25–28); (c) a human being may then actually contemplate or use her knowledge in a state of *second actuality* (*DA* II, 5, 417a29–30).

Having distinguished these three stages, let us turn to the two transitions between the first and second, and between the second and the third. The transition from potentiality to first actuality is a process of "changes by means of learning and frequent change from contrary conditions" (*DA* II, 5, 417a31–33). In the case of sensation, this process is that of the development of the sense organs themselves. But the transition from first to second actuality is not a change: it is a transition from this inoperative possession of sensation or grammar to being operational, being at work, being actual (*DA* II, 5, 417a33-b2). The second transition is not a change as the first one is. The first is a reversal, such as the transition from not-fire to fire, the wall's color turning from dark to bright, the turn of illiteracy into literacy, becoming other by no longer being itself. But the second transition, Aristotle says, "is rather the actual being's preserving [*sôtêria*, literally the "saving"] the potential being" (*DA* II, 5, 417b3–5).[9] A hand on a warm radiator touches it precisely in so far as it has already integrated the elements into a settled equilibrium so that it can then accomplish the second transition: it can now *refrain* from *merely* turning from cold to warm.[10] A dog hearing a bell hears it precisely in so far as it is *not merely* moved by the vibrations in his ear and does not simply reflect or transmit them as vibrations, however sophisticated this process may be.[11]

Sensation is "paradoxical" or riddlesome in at least two respects. First, sensation defies the false dilemma of either remaining the same or becoming other. A warm hand is different from a cold hand, but an actually feeling hand is not different in the same sense from a hand that is not actually feeling. Secondly, sensation defies the false dilemma between activity and passivity. Unlike inorganic bodies standing apart from one another in their natural places or moving in contrary directions toward them, and unlike plants striving to replenish their form by perfectly destroying other forms, animals are ready to *become* that which is unlike them, without ceasing to be what they are. They are not only ec-statically tended between their actual being and their inherent standard, they not only hold the contrary tendencies of the elements within their organism together under their own form, but they preserve themselves by being altered.

Another Wax Example

So is sensation between like and like, or between unlike and unlike? The solution of the "paradox" of sensation must take into account this second transition, the transition from the developed sense organ (first actuality) to its fully operational state (second actuality). "The sentient is potentially like what the sense object is in actuality. Thus, it is affected while being unlike, but, once affected, it is like its object" (*DA* II, 5, 418a3–6). An account of sensation must indeed allow for the distinction between potentiality and actuality, but, most crucially, for a concept of first actuality as distinct from both potentiality and second actuality. An account of sensation must acknowledge this level of preparedness, readiness, expectation, intermittence, sleep. An account of sensation must be able to distinguish between the mere lack of capacity and inoperativeness. Just as the growth of a plant was fundamentally different from the growth of fire, sensation cannot be reduced to a mere actuality—sensation must allow for preparation as well as for performance.[12]

> In all the respects in which the inanimate is altered, the ensouled is also altered; but all inanimate beings are not altered in all the respects in which the ensouled are, for [the inanimate] are not altered with respect to sensations, and while that which is undergone is unnoticed [*lanthanei*] by the latter, it does not go unnoticed [*ou lanthanei*] by the former. (*Ph.* VII, 2, 244b12–15)

The difference between the animal and the plant can be seen in that the former can *fail* to perceive in a way the latter cannot. Sensation is a realm of the possibility of distinction and relation between *lanthesthai* and *ou lanthanesthai*—perhaps quite akin to the etymological sense of *alêtheia.*

Again it is the sense of stretch that governs Aristotle's account of life and animality: opposites are maintained as opposites without one being collapsed to the other. For the animal, to perceive is neither to massively remain what it is, nor to surrender to what it is not. It is in this sense that sensation is a quite special kind of becoming other: a becoming other without ceasing to be itself, a becoming other that is the preservation (*sôteria*) and completion of what it is for an animal to be. As Aristotle says elsewhere, a house is not *changed* when its roof is put on top of it (*Ph.* VII, 3, 246a17–b3). The solution of the "paradox" of sensation lies in the definition of the soul, that is, in the concept of a *first* actuality, in a sense of "stretch" that defines animality.

At the end of book II of *On the Soul,* Aristotle recapitulates his previous account of various senses and media, and illustrates his conclusion by means of another familiar example:

> But concerning sensation as a whole, one must grasp that sensation is that which is receptive to the forms of sensibles without their material, just as the wax receives the sign of a ring without the iron or the gold, and takes up the golden or bronze sign but not as gold or bronze; similarly sensation of each thing is also affected by that which has a color or a flavor or a sound, although not as that which is said of each . . . (*DA* II, 12, 424a17–24)[13]

Like the fire example, this famous wax example is no less problematic than suggestive, again because the impressed wax is no more sensitive to the impression than the combustible is to fire. Aristotle's point seems to be that sensation is precisely irreducible to a transfer of matter, yet the example very misleadingly suggests that sensation is an external impression of a shape. For, as "being" is said in many ways, the eye *is* stretched out toward sight in a fundamentally different way than a piece of wax *is* receptive to any shape. The piece of wax, in Descartes as well as here in Aristotle, is precisely not stretched toward this or that sign on a ring, and for this reason it is an inadequate example for nature and life. In Aristotelian terms, as we emphasized in chapter 1, wax is rather a substance produced by bees, and whose consistency is between that of earth and water: it yields like water, yet it stays put like earth. For this reason wax is precisely *chosen* by humans for inscribing letters or impressing signets. But the wax is not completed at all by being inscribed or impressed. In fact, just like the fire example, terms like "inscription" and "impression" are among the inorganic or elemental, and thus inadequate, metaphors used for natural or animal processes.

Just as the fire example helped us solve the dilemma of affection while remaining fundamentally inadequate for illustrating the whole phenomenon of sensation, here the wax example, while helpfully suggesting that the potentiality of the sentient is not *any* potentiality but a specific one, constitutes only another step toward a well-founded conception of sensation that explains it without reducing it. And yet there is one last concept in the account of sensation in *On the Soul*, followed by one last example.

Sensation as *Logos*

This last concept is *logos*. Aristotle continues: ". . . the sensation of each thing is also affected by that which has a color, flavor or sound, although not as that which is said of each of these, but as being such and such [*hê toiondi*] and according to *logos*" (*DA* II, 12, 424a25). This complex sentence makes a surprising or most counterintuitive claim: that we do not sense color, sound, smell, and so on. The sentient is not affected by a color *as color* or by a sound *as sound*. An animal neither senses color as the genus of white, red, and green, nor does it sense redness. It rather senses red "as being such and such," that is, this red of something, a red that is subtended by pleasure and pain, in a word, *something* red. If the agent and the patient of sensation share the same genus, this means that animals sense things, and not neutral anonymous disinterested stimuli or abstracted notions. In other words, sensation is to get a reply to a prior expectancy, an answer to a prior question, namely the question of desire. Sensation is not of universals, it is of particulars.[14] Sensation is not like deduction, but like induction. It is the universal that emerges out of repeated sensations.[15]

But how is the sentient affected by the sensible *according to logos*? Aristotle continues:

> The sense organ is first of all that in which such a potentiality is; thus in one way they [the organ and the potentiality] are the same, in another way they are different; for that which senses would be a magnitude, but indeed neither the being of the sensitive nor sensation are magnitudes, but rather some *logos* and a potentiality of [that which senses]. (*DA* II, 12, 424a25–28)

A sense organ is necessarily extended, because necessarily composite as we saw while discussing organicity in chapter 3; but what makes it a sense organ is "some *logos*," which is not extended. This *logos* is the configuration of the sense organ, the relationship between extended things, and "hence it is clear why excesses in the sensibles sometimes destroy the sense organs; for if the motion of the sense organ is too strong, the *logos* (which is sensation) is destroyed" (*DA* II, 12, 424a29–32). If the sense organ exists according to *logos*, and if the power of sensation *is* precisely this *logos*, sensation requires that the sense organ hold on to a certain equilibrium between contrary qualities. It is the *logos* that preserves the sense organ: while feeling warmth, it also holds on to its prior equilibrium.[16] *Logos* once again names a limit of inclusivity—which, once violated, entails the destruction of that of which it is a *logos*.

Thus sensation must involve something like a minimal act of "remembering" or "comparing," a maintained equilibrium, since too strong a stimulus makes the animal "forget" its prior condition and simply yield to the new one. It is the holding together of both states that explains why sensation is *logos*. An eye is fundamentally incomparable to fire, to a piece of wax, and even to a final product of the animal's growth: the physiological development of the eye has indeed a *logos* of growth, but this is only a transition from potentiality to the first actuality, it is a reversal (*metabolê*): food "forgets" what it was to be for itself, food is *transformed*; but this perspective misses the "transition" from the first actuality to full (second) actuality: the sense organ is made *ready*—not for yet another transformation, but for a performance.

The last example of Aristotle's account of sensation is a lyre:

> [Excess destroys the *logos* that characterizes sensation] just as the *symphônia* and tone of a lyre is destroyed when the strings are struck hard. And [it is also clear] why plants do not sense although they have one part of the soul and are affected to a certain extent by tangibles—for they become warm and cold. The reason is that they have no mean [*mesotêta*], neither any such principle such as to be receptive to the forms of sensibles, but rather are affected with the material. (*DA* II, 12, 424a32–424b3)

This example can support our recurrent use of the idea of stretch, crucial to *logos*, as well as our quotation of Heraclitus's fragment 51 at the very beginning of this book: "They do not understand how that which is disrupted has the same *logos* as itself: a back-stretched harmony as in the bow and the lyre." But how does the lyre or the bow illustrate the first actuality, which is crucial for solving the "paradox" of sensation? The strings of lyres and bows are indeed stretched, and this stretch is determined neither by the string itself nor by its being attached to one extremity. The stretch is a function of the nature of the string *and* of the relatively fixed distance between its extremities. While objects seem to us to be massive or subtle, hard or soft, hot or cold, wet or dry, the lyre and the bow are good examples of objects irreducible to opaque materiality. And this idea of harmony being a result of opposition was indeed not alien to Aristotle's contemporaries, since the relational character of harmony was a great source of inspiration for the Pythagoreans as well as for Plato. Both Heraclitus and Aristotle seem to develop this intuition: *logos* as ratio is not an independent value on its own, but a relation between two numbers which can be instantiated indefinitely by other things. *Logos* as a note is not only *this* note played on *this* string of *this* lyre, but a result that can be attained, mutatis mutandis, on other strings of other lyres or even other instruments such that it is possible to play them together. Finally, *logos* as sensation is a relation between the sense organ and the sense object such that one may sense the same heat as long as the ratio between the heat of the organ and that of the object remains the same. Sensation is of that which is "hotter" than my hand, "stronger" than the air in my ear, "sweeter" than the state of my mouth. Sensation is not relativistic, but fundamentally relative or relational, that is, differential. *Logos* as sensation must preserve different terms, not only in their self-sameness, but also in their difference from one another.

Developed organs are already stretched between contraries: this sense of *logos* is familiar to us from our discussion of growth in chapter 3. But, here in our discussion of sensation, this stretch is no longer an end for *sense* organs: they also stretch out to the world for being completed. And this is what is new here. For animals, being in the world is reception as much as confrontation or assimilation. This certainly does not mean that sensation is added on to nutrition and reproduction. It simply means that nutrition and reproduction for animals are sensitive nutrition and sensitive reproduction.[17] From the point of view of growth, plants are indeed internally differentiated: they have organs; but from the perspective of sensation, they are indifferent, since they simply *become* hot or cold. They do not exhibit the sense of stretch embodied in sensation: they do not possess a range, a mean (*mesotêta*), in which they hold themselves and the forms of their object. That is why *every* stimulus is "excessive" for plants such that none really is, whereas "sensation is a *logos*, but excess hurts or destroys" (*DA* III, 2, 426b7–8). Sensation always implies compositeness, and this compositeness always implies the plurality of elements held together within the body of the animal. Yet what is specific to sensation is also the plurality of its objects: "Touch is like a mean of all tangibles, and its sense organ is receptive not only of all the differences of earth [*diaphorai gês*], but also of hot and cold and all other tangibles" (*DA* III, 13, 435a22–24). With sensation, we are dealing with a phenomenon that is no longer reducible to a form of integration, but one that constitutes a mutual *contact* with the world. The immense fabric of all the physical-mechanical interactions in the universe is subtended here and there by oases of sensation: "in a way the soul is all beings" (*DA* III, 8, 431b21–22). Having sensation by definition, this is what animals are: "in a way" all beings. And they are "saved" by being "in a way" all beings.

To conclude then, sensation is a *logos* in its second sense, "ratio," but in an even more subtle way than that of growth and reproduction. For sensation as *logos* no longer holds on to the formerly exclusive elements within its own form, it rather holds on to the *state* of the sense organ and the *state* of its object.[18] Whereas the awareness of difference was a sign of a failure in the assimilation process of nutrition and reproduction, every successful sensation is necessarily awareness of difference. Sensation is discrimination or *krisis*:

> To sense is some kind of being affected such that that which an object makes like itself is such already potentially. This is why we sense not what is as hot, cold, hard or soft as ourselves, but what is more so; thus, sensation is like a mean between contraries of sensation. For this reason the mean distinguishes [*krinei*] the sensibles. (*DA* II, 5, 418a14–16)[19]

Our elemental and vegetal fantasies are disrupted by this *krisis* that only animals are capable of.

So animal life is marked by sensation, and all sensation is not mere intake, but discrimination (*krisis*). However, we humans are somehow capable of denying our power of discrimination entailed by our animality. This sheds light on a very famous passage in the *Metaphysics*, IV, where Aristotle claims that a skeptic who objects to the principle of non-contradiction thereby claims to become "similar to a plant" (*Metaph.* IV, 4, 1006a15). I think Aristotle here is not sarcastic, but serious. For if the essential character of animal life is sensation, and if all sensation is distinction or discrimination (*krisis*), then the objector who rejects the principle of non-contradiction thereby refuses to *propose* anything whatsoever, to *engage himself* to one meaning at the exclusion of its opposite, and thus to *distinguish* affirmation from negation, pursuit from flight. According to Aristotle, by refusing the principle of non-contradiction, the skeptic is in fact gesturing toward vegetal and inorganic fantasies, mimicking a vegetative, anesthetic state, and claiming to disengage himself from commitment which lies, as we saw, at the heart of animal life.[20]

2. Locomotion

After nutrition, reproduction, and sensation, the last kind of natural motion is locomotion. Our analysis of it shall bring to conclusion the inquiry into the ways in which natural motion exhibits "*logos* of being" as an inherent standard. We shall see that an ox exhibits what it is for it to be, its inherent standard of being, by means of locomotion as much as by its reproduction, nutrition, and sensation. Yet Aristotle analyzes animal locomotion also as a *logos*, but in the sense of a "proportioning," a "rationing," or a "syllogism." This shall set up the stage for the specifically *human* senses of *logos* as "reason" and "speech" in chapters 5 and 6.

Distant Perception

Natural beings have an inherent source of motion and rest. Among natural beings, *organic* bodies further integrate the material of contrary bodies into their own form in reproduction and nutrition. And finally, among organic bodies, animals are receptive to the forms of bodies without their material in sensation. For Aristotle, however, some animals do more than receive the form of contiguous bodies (which happens with touch, and its subspecies taste);[21] they receive form through something else by means of smell, vision, and/or hearing (*DA* III, 12, 434b15–16).

Here we are on a higher level of complexity. The animal is not only holding together the *logos* of its sense organ and the *logos* of its object without letting one yield to the other, it is also doing so while holding the medium *as medium*. Not only is the animal holding together and yet distinguishing the material and form of a contiguous object, it is holding together and yet distinguishing the material object from the medium. For, although Aristotle's concept of the medium of sensation is quite complicated, this much is clear: as long as the medium itself is sensed, it is no longer a medium. The animal not only perceives an object, but perceives it *through something else*. Then if an animal is capable of distant perception, it should somehow *read* the object *off* of the medium. Instructive in this respect is Aristotle's account of memory, since just as distant perception is the sensation of an object *but also* of its distance, "whenever both the motion of the thing *and* that of time happen at the same time, then [the animal] is at work with respect to its memory" (*On Memory and Recollection* 2, 452b23–24).[22]

Just as the animal feels the warmth of water *without* simply becoming warm, in distant perception the animal must hear the bell *beyond* the vibrating air that carries the sound and strikes the ear. But as distinct from contiguous sensation, in distant perception the animal senses and holds its real object ("the bell") not only as distinct from itself, but also as beyond itself, apart and away from itself, at a distance, separated by the medium which *is* next to it. By using the medium as a medium, by sensing something *through* something else precisely as *something else*, the animal gains a sense of the *over there*. To follow Aristotle who explicitly compares distant perception and memory:

> All internal [objects of sensation] are smaller, and as it were analogous to the external ones. Perhaps just as another [being] takes something in itself analogically with forms [in sensation], something similar happens with distances. (*On Memory and Recollection* 2, 452b15–17)

For an animal that has only immediate touch and taste, it may seem that beings are revealed as something *else*. Only for an animal having sight, hearing, and/or smell may beings be revealed as else*where*. A similar argument can be made with respect to memory: for an animal to have a sense of *now* in distinction from *then*, it must be able to sense something *without* collapsing the time elapsed, *without* excluding the middle.

As memory requires a "sensation" of time, distant perception indeed requires a sensation of distance:[23]

> It is necessary to become acquainted with magnitude and motion by means of that by which one is also aware of time, so it is clear that the image is an affection of the common perceiving power. Thus it is clear that the acquaintance of these is by means of the primary power of perception. (*On Memory and Recollection* 1, 450a9–13)

Aristotle defends at length that there is a primary perceiving power for common attributes and even claims that there is a "sensation of time" (*DA* III, 1, 2; III, 10, 433b8). These sensations present the form of *krisis*, *mesotês*, or *logos*, but in a more complex way than would contiguous perception. For the form sensed here must be held together and distinguished by a spatial or temporal distance. Aristotle explicitly compares recollection to a "syllogism":

> Recollecting is like a kind of syllogism; for one who recollects reasons out [*syllogizetai*] that one saw or heard or had some such experience before, and this is a sort of inquiry. And by nature this belongs only to those beings that are capable of deliberation, since deliberating is also a certain sort of syllogism. (*On Memory and Recollection* 1, 453a10–14)

Deliberation, search, memory, and distant sensation all seem to exhibit the same structure: a holding together of something actual (a goal, an object sought for, a present sensation, or a past sensation) together with an awareness of the medium (the way to reach the goal, the very absence of the object sought for, spatial or temporal distance). Thus, the animal capable of memory and distant perception is no longer merely a sensitive living being, but an animal capable of explicit proportioning.

Animal Locomotion

Distant perception as access to *here* and *there* most crucially brings locomotion into play (*DA* III, 12, 434a34–434b9; 434b25–30). When we talk about sight or hearing, we are necessarily dealing with bodies that can move. This is not as straightforward as it may at first seem to be, since we mostly conceive of sensation as apart from locomotion, taking place in the eyes, the ears, or in the head. Apart from touch, sensation is for us humans an almost cerebral activity taking place at the upper extreme of the body, whereas for Aristotle the seat of sensation is in the center of the body, in the heart.[24] Further, the relation between sensation and locomotion is somewhat loose for us. Having potentialities with *logos*, as shown in chapter 2, we humans seem to think that indeed sensation and locomotion *may* go together, but it is not immediately clear why they would *implicate* one another. Here we may see why they would: distant perception requires the use of a medium, which itself requires a comparison or proportioning, an awareness of the *elsewhere* beyond the medium. But for a moving animal, the *elsewhere* is nothing but a potential *here* that would actually become *here* by pursuit or pull, and the *here* is a potential *elsewhere* that would become *elsewhere* by flight or push (*DA* III, 10, 433b26; *MA* 10, 703a19–20).

But why would an animal pursue or flee something contiguous or distant? Because "that which has sensation also has pleasure and pain, and the pleasant and painful, and that which has these has appetite; for appetite is desire for the pleasant" (*DA* II, 3, 414b4–7).[25] That sensation and locomotion are subtended by desire should not surprise us, first because, as we quoted in chapter 3, "all things desire [the eternal and the divine], and do everything they do by nature for the sake of it" (*DA* II, 4, 415b1–3). Thus just as we should primarily think of sensation not as a mental process but as fundamentally *bodily*, not as simply representational but as fundamentally *moving*, similarly we must conceive of animal locomotion as fundamentally *interested*. One can see in each step of our argumentation (embodiment, motility, desire) a factor that is abstracted in Descartes's wax example: for him, just as depth in space and time is not an integral part of sensation, the sensation of the wax is precisely a *disinterested* activity that does *not* move the subject—which ends up being nothing but the *mind*.[26]

For Aristotle, sensation and locomotion are not only subtended by desire like all faculties, in fact they are joined or articulated by it. For, abstracted from appetite, sensation does not entail locomotion in the form of imagination: "Imagination too, whenever it moves, does not move without appetite" (*DA* III, 10, 433a20–21). Nor does it move in the form of knowledge: "As a whole we see that the human being that has the healing art does not heal, so that there is something else that governs the making according to knowledge, but it is not knowledge itself" (*DA* III, 9, 433a3–6). Nor does it move as *nous*: "Now, *nous* does not appear to move without appetite" (*DA* III, 10, 433a23–24). Neither the sensation nor the imagination of a fact, nor the knowledge of a fact and its cause go any further than stating a fact or cause: "this is such and such," "this is water," "this is this big," "the moon is eclipsed because of the interference of the earth" . . . None of these have any moving force or practical implication without desire or interest, a way out of the animal returning to it. Hence, involvements with disinterested facts are abstractions within the context of the interested beings animals are.

In short, Aristotle analyzes locomotion as distant perception fused and fueled with desire. For him, the cause of locomotion is thus *both* universal desire and some form of receptivity to particulars, be it perception, thinking, or imagination (*DA* III, 10, 433a10–13).[27]

The "Practical Syllogism"[28]

We are not abusing the terms "premise," "rationing," or "proportioning" here, since Aristotle analyzes locomotion as if it were the result of a reasoning, a certain relating of two terms without prioritizing one over the other, a certain *logismos* (*DA* III, 10, 433a14–15). What kind of *logismos* are we dealing with?

Any predication like "this is such and such a thing," "this is such and such an action," or even "I am such and such" is in itself insufficient for explaining animal locomotion without desire.[29] Aristotle construes locomotion as a result of a *logismos* that takes the form of an inner "speaking" (*legein*) between appetite and sensation: "My appetite says [*legei*] 'I must drink'; 'this is drink' says sensation or imagination or intellect, and one immediately drinks" (*MA* 7, 701a32–33; *DA* III, 11, 434a17–22). More emphatically, Aristotle's conceptual reconstruction of locomotion in *On the Soul* takes the form of what is later to be known as the "practical syllogism":

(1) If such a human being must do such and such a thing, (the universal);
(2) and if this is such and such a thing and I am such a human being, (the particular);
(3) then I must do this. (*DA* III, 11, 434a18–20)

But, in *On the Soul*, Aristotle offers this *logismos* in parentheses, and does not dwell on its character as a syllogism or even as a *logismos*. Such a parallelism between the scientific and the practical syllogisms, however, is explicit in *On the Movement of Animals*. And there it is followed by a wealth of examples. Aristotle's major question is as follows:

> But how is it that *nous* sometimes acts sometimes not, sometimes moves and sometimes does not?[30] What happens seems parallel to the thinking-through [*dianoêsis*] and making a *syllogismos* about the immovable. But there the end is the thing contemplated (for when one thinks two premises, one thinks and puts together the conclusion), but here out of the two premises comes to be a conclusion which is an action. (*MA* 7, 701a7–13)

First example: Whenever one thinks that all humans must walk (the universal), and that he himself is a human being (the particular), then he immediately (*euthus*) walks (*MA* 7, 701a13–19).

Aristotle's second example is of the stopping: whenever one thinks that no human must walk (the universal), and that he himself is a human being (the particular), then he immediately (*euthus*) stops.

The third example is taken from art and therefore the minor is no longer the agent, but the object envisaged (*NE* VI, 4, 1140b3–5): [Whenever one thinks] "I ought to produce some good" (the universal), [and that] "a house is a good" (the particular), then he immediately (*euthus*) produces a house.

Aristotle's fourth example conjoins two syllogisms: [Whenever one thinks] "I need some covering" (the universal), [and that] "a coat is a covering" (the particular), then [one thinks] "I need a coat"; [Whenever one thinks] "I must make what I need" (the universal), [and that] "I need a coat" (the particular), then "I must make a coat." Aristotle thus suggests that these syllogisms can be concatenated at length so as to compose more and more complex sets of locomotion involving more and more sophisticated and extended spatiotemporal patterns. The minor premises of all the above syllogisms exemplify ways in which locomotion entails the use of the "common perceptive power" in the forms of distant perception, memory, imagination, a sensation of time, and the use of a medium as a medium. The various combinations of the minor premises provided by this "set" of powers give rise to diverse kinds of animal locomotion such as migration, hunt, escape, search, and so on, all reducible to pushing and pulling, or fleeing and pursuing.[31]

Despite Aristotle's wording and examples, what is at stake here is not an intellectual conception of animal motion, but rather a reminder that the disjunction between sensation and desire is derivative of their necessary cooperation in locomotion. For now, what is emphasized is the immediacy between universal desire and the perception of particulars. This immediacy is expressed in the recurrent adverb "*euthus*" in the conclusions of the syllogisms. In short, coupled with desire, all sensation involves pushing and pulling, and all distant perception involves flight or pursuit.

A Middle Term

The middle term of the practical syllogism in animal locomotion is precisely the relevance of the object sensed or imagined to desire: "This is it!" Since sensation does not by itself provide a universal,[32] the minor premise is bound to be particular, and that is why animal locomotion is particular as opposed to the "universal" locomotion of the elements.

It is the middle term that answers Aristotle's initial question: "How is it that *nous* sometimes acts and sometimes does not, sometimes moves and sometimes does not?" (*MA* 7, 701a6–8). For, disregarding the fact that all sensation is particular, the lack of action or motion can be inferred from the results of the *Prior Analytics*, I, 24. If, as Aristotle says there, in every syllogism at least one premise must be affirmative, and if no two affirmative premises result in a negative conclusion, then all negative conclusions must have one, and only one, negative premise. If the major premise is negative then the "syllogism" takes a form comparable to a Cesare. If the minor is negative then it takes the form of a Camestres. In both cases, the conclusion is negative, therefore there is no action or motion, because either the universal premise of desire or the particular premise of sensation is negative.

As can be seen, we are not totally against the comparison between the "practical syllogism" and the *syllogismos* in the strict sense, precisely because Aristotle is not against it. This being said, we should indeed emphasize that this comparison is heuristic, and should not be taken literally to envisage animal locomotion as a result of cognitive faculties. In fact, Aristotle too is aware of this misunderstanding and emphasizes the "immediate" character of the conclusion by repeating the adverb "*euthus*."[33] The comparison, if taken as a comparison, is instructive not only in terms of animal locomotion, but also in the context of *syllogismos* in the strict sense. A *comparison* already excludes mere difference, but also the identity of the terms compared, and thereby informs both. In the following section, we will dwell on the very difference between the "syllogism" that results in animal locomotion and the *syllogismos* in the strict sense it assumes in the *Prior Analytics*. Most specifically we shall see how the premises in *syllogismoi* involve a level of generality that all "practical syllogism" necessarily lacks, and which faculties come into play beyond memory, habit, desire, perception, and even beyond distant perception and experience. For the time being, we see that mediated sensation (distant perception or memory or imagination) *spills into* an immediate locomotion by means of the particularity introduced by the middle term in conjunction with the universal premise of desire.

We saw that, according to Aristotle, sensation is *logos* in the sense of a ratio that holds on to its constituents without letting one yield to the other. Here we see that a similar proportioning is at work, although in the more complex form of a *syllogismos*: Aristotle insistently uses *syllogismos*, *sylleges-thai*, and *logizesthai* for the "argument" abstracted from locomotion.[34] And in fact what explains animal locomotion is neither the universal premise of desire (common to all nature, as we have seen in chapter 3), nor a disinterested perception (which we have yet to see in chapters 5 and 6), but precisely a middle term, a particular provided by receptivity, that "matches" desire and receptivity, holds them together without letting one yield or remain different to the other.

Put negatively, rocks simply fall, that is, tend toward the center of the universe regardless of where they are. Fire is pulled outward regardless of whether it is in Alexandria or Athens, in daytime or at night, in winter or in summer. It is in this sense that elements move "universally," without regard for particularity. Animal locomotion, on the other hand, holds this "universal" impulse together with particulars perceived, remembered, imagined, or anticipated. Unlike the burning of fire or the falling of rocks, a bird in flight attends to the difference of heat, season, hour, wind, or humidity that its perception "tells." An animal never falls *as an animal*; as capable of discrimination, an animal lays down here, but "here" in a strong sense, in the sense of "*this* place rather than that other," and "now" in a strong sense reminiscent of the sense of *kairos*.

Hence both sensation and locomotion are instances of *logos* in the sense of "ratio." But, in the context of locomotion, Aristotle often uses verbs like *legein*, *eipein*, and *phanai* for the way the premises are supplied.[35] And he uses the word *logos* itself for the premises.[36] Perhaps the animal soul prefigures an environment of *logos* neither in the sense of "standard" nor "ratio" but in the sense of "speech." This prefiguration of *logos* as speech in animal locomotion should not be exaggerated, but neither underestimated nor ruled out: *logos* and *legein* in animal locomotion are precisely that which will link our ongoing survey of the word to the human world in chapters 5 and 6. In the animal world, universal desire is no longer neatly matched with, and fulfilled by, motion. Desire needs to engage all sorts of powers of receptivity for particulars: it must move in a certain way through a certain medium toward a certain object, and hence it must minimally "listen" to what perception or imagination have to say.

Beyond Locomotion

This necessary particularity of the sensed object negatively sheds light on the theoretical, apodictic, or scientific syllogism. The latter will involve not simply sensation nor even memory and habit, but the emergence of an *eidos* ("this kind of thing") out of particular experiences, thereby making possible *syllogismos* in the strict sense, and experience in a wider sense that we must clarify:

> While, then, other [animals] live by impressions and memories, they have a small share in experience; on the other hand, the human race also lives by art and reasonings [*logismoi*]. In humans, experience comes out of memory, for many memories of the same thing bring to completion [*apotelousin*] a potentiality for one experience . . . But art comes to be whenever out of many conceptions [*ennoêmatôn*] from experience arises one universal judgment [*katholou hypolêpsis*] about similar things. For, to have a judgment that this thing was beneficial to Callias when he was sick with this disease, and to Socrates, and one by one in this way to many people, belongs to experience. But the judgment that it was beneficial to all such and such people marked out as being of one form [*eidos*], when they were sick with this disease (such as sluggish or irritable people when they were feverish with heat), belongs to art. (*Metaph.* I, 1, 980b26–981a13)

Just as sensation involves a kind of form and a certain *logos*, and then, when coupled with universal desire, forms a certain syllogism, this famous passage also suggests that human phenomena entail a yet different kind of form and *logos*.[37] Animal locomotion differs from mere desire and sensation in that it forms a syllogism by means of a middle term that provides the relevance of sensation to desire; but animal locomotion also differs from art, *logismos*, and scientific syllogism because it lacks the emergence of a form beyond perceptions, memories, imaginations, and habituation. This is the "small share in experience" they are confined to. As can be seen from the quotation above, this "form" accessible to human agents falls between the particular and the universal such that the particular sensation is no longer simply subsumed under the universal premise of desire.

This explains exactly why, in the examples of the practical syllogism, Aristotle insistently uses the structure: "whenever *x*, then immediately *y*." As involving distant sensation and the sensation of time, animal locomotion is predicated on temporal relations: *this*, then immediately (*euthus*) *that* . . . One can understand the limits of these relations since, taken exclusively, these relations are precisely conducive to the *post hoc ergo propter hoc* fallacy. Think of the impossibility of understanding a lunar eclipse by means of merely temporal relations of succession. Sensation may well provide perfect information concerning the dark portion of the Moon and the rays of sunlight, but it cannot account for the role of the middle term, the interference of the Earth itself.

Then not all relations are spatial or temporal and not all *logismoi* take the form: "whenever *x*, then immediately *y*." According to the rest of the quotation from the *Metaphysics* above, it is the possession of *logos*, this time in its specifically human form, that gives humans access to causal relationships of "if *x*, then *y*," and this, not immediately (*euthus*), but according to a deliberation over conflicting interpretations of the relevance of the object sensed or imagined: "Is heat good *in this particular situation*?," "Is marble good for *this particular statue* to be erected *for this particular purpose*?," "Is defying an enemy good in the context of *this* particular front of a battle in *this* particular political context?," "Is it better to not give back my friend's weapon to him, *now that he has gone mad*?" Human action is irreducible to animal locomotion in that it not only *searches* by means of sensation and indeed subordinated locomotions, but also *interprets* the sensible from the get-go and *searches by interpreting*.

Human *logos* is certainly not a superpower at all, it does not guarantee *any* success in practical affairs.[38] If *logos* is a key, it locks as many doors as it opens. With human beings, the practical syllogism will result in action (*praxis*) instead of mere locomotion (*phora*). It will become "practical" in the literal sense, but it will also prove to be unimaginably impractical. This is the topic of the next chapter.

3. Recapitulation and Reorientation

In chapter 1, we started out with an investigation of the sense of *logos* as "standard" in the *Categories*, and, in chapter 2, we concluded that its inherence is to be found in *inherently* motivated motions, that is, natural motions: nutrition, reproduction, sensation, and locomotion. These four exhibit this inherence by differing, respectively, from mere increase of bulk, from mere coming to be, from mere alteration, and from mere change of place. We have tried to show how a second sense of *logos*, namely a certain kind of "ratio," explains nutrition and reproduction in chapter 3, and sensation and locomotion here in chapter 4. Thus, nutrition "rations" or "proportions" in the sense that it consists of holding on to formerly exclusive elements according to its own *logos* within the living being's body. Reproduction does the same thing this time inside the body of another. As to sensation, it "rations" or "proportions" in the sense that it requires that the state of organ and that of the object be both held together and discriminated in their relative differences. Finally, locomotion "rations" or "proportions" universal desire with the particulars of the sensible world. It uses "middle terms" that ration, proportion, match, or correlate receptivity with desire. By means of sensation and locomotion, animal life exhibits that which our elemental and vegetative fantasies may attempt to repress: care, the sense of something *making a difference*, the responsiveness of the soul to all things. For "in a way the soul is all beings" (*DA* III, 8, 431b21–22).

Thus, within our discussion of *logos* as "standard" or "essence" or "form," we have seen another sense of *logos* at work: *logos* as "ratio." Note that "standard" and "ratio" both refer to the fundamental meaning of *logos*: whether between "being" and "what it is for the being to be," or between potentiality and actuality, between contrary elements, contrary states, between particular sensibles and the universal premise of desire, these uses of *logos* refer to a preservation of difference as difference, that is, a relating of terms without one term yielding to or remaining indifferent to the other.

And what about the other two senses of *logos*: "reason" and "speech"? The last chapters of this book, chapters 5 and 6, are devoted to these two meanings respectively. As we have seen in *On Interpretation*, motion is "the actuality of a potentiality as such" (*Ph.* III, 1, 201a11–12, 200b27–28), but some potentialities differ from others as potentialities with *logos*. (*On Int.* 9, 13; *Metaph.* IX, 2, 5). We shall see that the beings that have these potentialities with *logos* are "slow deliberators" because their desire is problematic. For instance, they can wish for impossible things; they are "sophisticated communicators" because they communicate more than they experience, have experienced, or may experience firsthand. They are "great hesitators" because they are not only sensitive bodies in *krisis*, they also move according to the interpretation they had, have, or may have, regarding their sensations.

Hence these motions are more strictly called actions, *praxeis*. And indeed these beings are humans. Now it is time to investigate how humans exhibit their "*logos* of being" literally in action. Now it is time to approach the human, and to start to understand better the way in which "the human being alone among animals has *logos*" (*Pol.* I, 1, 1253a10–11). As we shall see, this is best done, not by immediately singling out *logos* as "reason" and "speech," but by understanding how human *logos* holds on to desire and thought without letting one take over the other term, how humans are a source—"either thought infused with desire or desire fused with thinking" (*NE* VI, 2, 1139a36–1139b7).

CHAPTER 5

Action

Logos *in the* Nicomachean Ethics

So far in our argumentative survey of the meanings of *logos* in Aristotle's philosophy, we inquired, in chapter 1, into the meaning of "*logos* of being" as "standard" in the *Categories*, then, in chapter 2, put forward the question of its *inherence* in the context of *On Interpretation*, and finally tried to show how Aristotle's *Physics* and *On the Soul* answer this question by exhibiting this inherence in the form of internally motivated motions in natural life (nutrition and reproduction) in chapter 3, and in animal life (sensation and locomotion) in chapter 4. We noted that these four motions brought into play a second sense of *logos*: "ratio," and we tried to show concretely how the two major senses of *logos* in these contexts, namely "standard" and "ratio," refer back to the basic meaning of *logos*: a relation between terms that until then were exclusive of, or indifferent to, one another. Now we shall move on to the human world in order to see how, after natural motion, human action exemplifies the inherence of humans' "standard of being" in the specifically human sense of "reason" here in chapter 5, and of "speech" in chapter 6.

Accordingly this chapter shall deal with ethics, *êthikê*, and will be structured around three interrelated concepts: habit (*ethos*), positive state (*hexis*), and character (*êthos*). In section 1, "Habit," we shall present Aristotle's analysis of the human soul as tripartite, and draw its implications with regard to habituation and imitation. In section 2, "Positive State," we shall show that, beyond habit, Aristotle is in need of the concept of "positive state" to account for human virtue, especially intellectual virtue which is a "positive state with *logos*." Finally, in section 3, "Character," we shall see how moral virtue, a "positive state according to *logos*,"exhibits itself in human action.

"The human being alone among animals has *logos*." What exactly does the verb for "to have" (*ekhein*) mean in this sentence? In what sense is *logos* something humans *have*? And how does *logos* interact with the rest of the human soul, especially desire? The following passage from the *Nicomachean Ethics* on human desire gives us the clue:

> The appetitive part or the desiring part in general somehow partakes [in *logos*] insofar as it listens to and can obey it in the sense in which we say "taking account [*ekhein logon*] of both one's father and one's friends." (*NE* I, 13, 1102b29–1102b32)[1]

The specifically human way in which we are able to take account of our friends as well as our father will lead us into the specifics of human discourse and communication in the following and last chapter of this book, chapter 6.

1. Habit

We already saw, above in chapter 3, that living nature, according to Aristotle, is governed by desire, the desire for reproduction:

> The most natural work for living beings . . . is to make another like itself: an animal making an animal, a plant a plant, so that they may partake in the eternal and divine in the way they can. For all things desire that, and do everything they do by nature for the sake of it. (*DA* II, 4, 415a23–415b2)[2]

In compensation for the limitations and mortality in the sublunar region, the most profound natural impulse is to reproduce and thus to *be in* another being having the same form.

The same holds true in humans, except that humans manage to *be in* another not only by giving birth to an offspring, but by continuously *acting*, *making*, and *doing* things to their offspring long time after they are born.[3] For humans, giving birth is only the beginning of giving life, and "reproduction" is coupled with a subsequent and lengthy "production" of the self-sufficient and mature human individual.

> Every artist loves his own work more than he would be loved by the work if it were ensouled . . . The reason for this is that all things desire and love to be; and it is in actuality, in living and acting, that we *are*; and, being actually at work, the maker is in a way the work; so he loves the work and thereby loves to be. (*NE* IX, 7, 1167b34–1168a9)

Hence humans' attachment to their children is an attachment not only to something they simply *are at work in*, not only to their humble chance for eternity, but also to a product *and* a project they *work at*.

As to the perspective of children, on the other hand, being "objects" of such attachment, "products" of such long effort, and "projects" involving such continuous care, they take on not only the look of their species and of their parents, but also their invisible aspects: their values, their emotions, their behavior, their accents, their fears, and even their unrealized potentials. Parents then may well succeed in *being in* their offspring and *speak from within* their children the words they were looking for all their life. This inheritance is so immediate that it can be recognized by children neither as an *inheritance*, nor as *an* inheritance among possible others.

But there is a twist, at least for Aristotle. Paradoxically, it is precisely when parents finally *are in* their offspring, precisely when they speak and act *from within* their children, that the latter start being what they were supposed to be all along: self-sufficient and independent mature beings; not only bundles of natural traits and environmental effects and internalized *habits* (*ethos*), but *characters* (*êthos*) with balanced ways (*hexis*) of *bearing themselves* in relation to different situations—not only the heirs of their parents, but friends to others in much larger contexts and projects than those of the household, and sometimes in brutal conflict with it.[4] The children's desire fulfills itself not simply by keeping on *being* what they already are, namely products of the desire of their parents, but by *no longer being with them*, by being with others, by being exposed to a realm of experiences and perspectives they never had firsthand, by listening to others and by *earning* recognition from them. The project of human parents is fulfilled when the child becomes a subject among nonparents. It is this development of human desire through her familial circle into a necessarily *open* environment that we shall explore here.

An Unpractical Syllogism

Somehow, human desire can "listen" in the sense of "taking account" (*logon ekhein*). For now let us make a textual remark concerning the way this listening and taking account takes place in our focal passage from the *Nicomachean Ethics*: *houtô dê kai tou patros kai tôn philôn phamen ekhein logon* (*NE* I, 13, 1102b31–33). We translated this ambiguous clause as "[the desiring part of the human soul listens to *logos* and can obey it] in the sense in which we say 'taking account [*ekhein logon*][5] of *both* one's father *and* one's friends.'" We did so in order to emphasize what appears to be an emphatic conjunction (*kai . . . kai . . .*).[6] Some translators, however, generally leave the conjunction unemphatic.[7] Some even translate it as a disjunction.[8] As arguing for a fundamental meaning of *logos* characterized by inclusiveness, we shall show that this ambiguous conjunction has significant implications insofar as it allows us to negotiate between an uncritically "rationalistic" definition of human beings by *logos*, and an understanding of humans as "either thought infused with desire [*orektikos nous*] or desire infused with thinking through [*orexis dianoêtikê*]" (*NE* VI, 2, 1139b5–7).[9]

Insofar as it can "listen," instead of merely saying, obeying, or dictating, human desire is infused with thinking through, or conversely, human sensation, imagination, memory, or thinking in general is infused with desire. Either way, the human soul is defined as an improbable inclusion, as an infusion, and even perhaps a certain confusion. Hence, whereas the "practical syllogism" applied to animal locomotion involved the subsumption of the particular premise of sensation under the universal premise of desire by means of a middle term, in the case of the human soul the particular sensuous premise is fundamentally complicated in that humans are capable of a certain hearing, that they are in a position both to *interpret* and to *have interpreted* the particular situations in contrary ways. Instead of being a univocal object of pleasure and pain, one and the same particular *may well* be conducive to good *as well as* to bad in the eyes of human beings, and conversely the human good is such that it *may well* lie in this particular action *or* in its contrary.

In chapter 2, we saw that Aristotle specifies these two-sided potentialities as "potentialities with *logos*" (*On Int.* 9, 13; *Metaph.*, IX, 2, 5). Regardless of whether we here translate and interpret *logos* as "reason," it is no coincidence that these potentialities instantiate the central meaning of *logos*: the human soul not only holds together the universal and the particular in order to literally spill immediately (*euthus*) into locomotion, but it also holds possible contrary interpretations of the particular sensible or imagined object, and thus exhibits not only a motion or change, but *action*. "We see that the source of that which will be is also something relying on deliberation and action" (*On Int.* 9, 19a7–8). The practical syllogism of animal locomotion takes the "unpractical" form of *praxis* in the human realm. To understand human action, we indeed must first take a look at the specificity of the human soul it originates from.[10]

A Tripartite Soul

In the *Nicomachean Ethics*, Aristotle's criterion for dividing the human soul is *logos*: "one part is *alogos*, while the other has [*ekhon*] *logos*" (*NE* I, 13, 1102a29–30). *Logos* not only distinguishes the human being from all other animals, it also differentiates the human soul within itself. For the time being, it seems as if both the world and the human soul are somehow infused with *logos*, but neither is so through and through.

Yet the analysis of the human soul necessitates a further distinction beyond the distinction between the *alogos* part and the part having *logos*. Nutrition and growth are simply *alogos* (*NE* I, 13, 1102a33–1102b1). They are activities of sleep at least as much as of waking, digestion being the cause of sleep (*On Sleep and Waking* 3, 456b17–18; 458a27–28). But there is another part of the human soul besides this *alogos* part as well as the one that has *logos*. This third part is somehow intermediary between the two:[11] "some other nature that, while being *alogos*, in a way partakes [*metekhousa*] in *logos*" (*NE* I, 13, 1102b13–14).

This intermediary part is said to sometimes "fight against and resist *logos*" in a way the purely *alogos* part does not (*NE* I, 13, 1102b17–18). If there is an intermediary part of the human soul such that it "has" *logos* but can resist and fight it, this "having" (*ekhein*) cannot take the form of *syn-ekheia*, mere continuity or adherence. But further, if this *ekhein* takes the form of *met-ekhein*, of "partaking" (*metekhousa*), as in the quotation above, Aristotle insists that this is not exact or clear enough by adding: "in a way," "somehow" (*NE* I, 13, 1102b13–14; *NE* I, 13, 1102b29–1102b32). How then does this intermediary part *have logos* such that this relation is neither a mere fusion (*syn-ekheia*) nor exactly an external and intermittent participation (*met-hexis*)?[12]

Although Aristotle explicitly leaves open the nature of the distinction between the "parts" of the soul, it is clear that the human soul, for him, can be neither monolithic nor simply heteroclite.[13] In other words, given that one part of the human soul can *resist* another part, the human soul cannot be a Cartesian *res cogitans*, since in that case there would be nothing in the human soul to resist *logos*. Indeed, it cannot be a *res extensa* either, since then there would be no *logos* to resist to begin with. Finally, the human soul cannot be some conjunction of a *res extensa* and a *res cogitans* either, since the two parts, although somehow adjacent, would have nothing to do with one another. The Cartesian mind and body are "metaphysical neighbors," so to speak, in comparison to the Aristotelian tripartite model of the human soul: they are born so far from one another that they are certainly not relatives, and they live infinitely far from one another so that they never come across one another and become friends or enemies except by means of an external occasionalism. To put it in another way while using this time a Hobbesian terminology, if human action is the result of a process involving resistance or listening in the soul, then action can be reduced neither to involuntary motion, nor to a voluntary motion which is, as it were, the "psychic servant" of the former.[14] Unlike the Cartesian model, the human being has *one* regime for Aristotle. Unlike the Hobbesian model, this regime cannot be merely a despotism according to these passages in Aristotle.

In Aristotle, if the human soul has parts, they are three in number. And two of these parts are not put side by side, but set in tension *against* one another: "while we see the erratic member [in a spasm] in bodies, we do not in the case of the soul" (*NE*, I, 13, 1102b22–23). This tripartite structure makes it such that the human soul is capable of a special kind of spasm, an erratic but "invisible" stretch, reminiscent of the kinds of stretch we noted in the previous parts of this book. Yet here the stretch can take the form not only of tension, but of explicit resistance, obstinacy, and fight, or explicit adherence and consonance. And even these latter terms are inadequate because they are supposed to explain human phenomena by means of physical phenomena, suggesting that the intermediary part sticks to (Latin *adhaerare*) or echoes *logos* (Latin *consonantia*). Aristotle insists that the intermediary part can "obey" (*peitharkhein*) *logos*.[15] This "obedience" may take the form of simply executing a command, but the capacity for resistance here suggests rather the etymological sense of "hearing out": the intermediary part is not simply determined by *logos*, but rather gives ear to it, listens to *logos* "in the sense in which we say 'taking account of *both* one's father *and* one's friends,'" precisely because it is able to resist it. This is not fricrion, but resistance (*antiteinein*). It is fight (*makhein*), and not clash. My sweet tooth disobeys *logos* in a fundamentally different way from the consistency of my bones and sinews. Conversely, my eating habits are obedient to *logos* in a way fundamentally distinct from the way the furniture in my apartment yield to my arrangement. This "tension" results from the intermediary part's "attention" to *logos*.

If then the intermediary part somehow can "obey" *logos*, it is not because it immediately yields to it, but because it has "given ear" to it, it has taken it into account (*logon ekhein*). The relation between obedience and audience is not only etymologically found in Latin, but emphasized in many Aristotelian texts as well as our focus text:

> At least the [intermediary part] of the self-restrained person obeys [*peitharkhei*] *logos*, and then that of the temperate and brave is best-hearing [*euêkoôteron*], for all harmonize [*homophônei*] with *logos*. It appears that the *alogos* [part in the human soul] is twofold. For the vegetative part does not share in *logos* at all, whereas the appetitive part or the desiring part in general somehow partakes [in *logos*] insofar as it listens to [*katêkoon*] and can obey it [*peitharkhikon*] in the sense in which we say "taking account [*ekhein logon*] of both one's father and one's friends." (*NE* I, 13, 1102b27–33)[16]

Our translation tries to render the strong emphasis on the argumentative, almost forensic and political, environment of the human soul, because we are trying to highlight the fact that, for Aristotle, the human soul is distinguished *neither* by being simply rational, *nor* by having a rational and an irrational part that lay side by side or are mixed indifferently, but by its inclusion of an explicit relation between its parts, of a realm where they confront one another, where they may well explicitly resist and fight one another, make compromises or come to a consensus. As distinct from dualistic or monistic conceptions of the human soul, Aristotle's tripartite human soul resembles an *agora*.

Whereas animal sensation is subtended by intermediary *degrees* of pleasure and pain, the human soul then has an intermediary *part*. Human receptivity of particulars entails an act of questioning, a task of interpretation, and thus an environment of negotiation. A knife, a retreat in battle, a glass of wine, a payment, lumber, hemlock: the sensation, memory, or imagination of these particulars does not necessarily spill into an immediate evaluation as to the *degree* of pain and pleasure they may entail and a consequent motion; they also trigger what Aristotle compared to the attention one lends both to one's father or friends. Hindering the smooth and immediate functioning of the "practical syllogism" of animal locomotion, it is this possibility of attention of the intermediary part that will assume a central function in the emergence of human action.

A Kind of Learning

What then is "in" the intermediary part? Potentialities? No. In chapter 3, we saw how the soul is an *already developed state* of a body having life potentially, and how it is indeed by nature that the human soul has these potentialities ready to work:

> Whatever grows by nature in us is bestowed on us first as potentialities, we display their actuality later. This is clear with the senses: we did not acquire the senses by repeatedly seeing or hearing, but the other way around: having them, we used them; we did not get them by using them. (*NE* II, 1, 1103a27–31)

Besides the vegetative part, human action and life are characterized by the two other parts, and as Aristotle continues we see that their development involves an almost opposite process:

> [These] perfections, we acquire by first putting them to work, just as we do other arts. For the things that one who has learned them needs to do, we learn by doing, just as house-builders become

> so by building houses or harpists by playing the harp. (*NE* II, 1, 1103a31–1103b1)

Whereas one becomes capable of sight through an embryonic development of *not seeing at all*, one becomes a harpist *by playing the harp*.

What then does the intermediary part of the human soul *have*, if not potentialities? Habits. How do habits come to be? Instead of the word "habituation," Aristotle typically uses the verb *manthanesthai*, or the noun *mathêsis*, "learning," as in the following famous passage:

> By nature, then, all animals have sensation; from this, some acquire memory, some do not. Accordingly the former are more intelligent and more capable of learning [*mathêtikôtera*] than those that cannot remember. The [animals] that cannot hear sounds [*tôn psophôn akouein*] are intelligent but cannot learn [*aneu tou manthanein*], such as a bee or any other kind of animal that might be such. Whatever animal has this sense besides memory learns [*manthanei*]. (*Metaph.* I, 1, 980a28–980b26)

The capacity to learn, unlike intelligence, requires what Aristotle calls the "hearing of sounds" besides memory.[17] Which animals are capable of "hearing sounds" and thus of being taught and of learning, and thereby of being formed by habits? One answer is found in the *Parts of Animals*: "all [birds] use their tongues also as a means of interpretation [*pros hermêneian*] with one another, and some to a larger degree than other, so that there even seems to be learning among some" (*PA* II, 17, 660a35–660b2). A more specific answer is found in the *History of Animals*:

> Among small birds, while singing some utter a different voice than their parents if they have been reared away from the nest and have heard [*akousôsin*] other birds sing. A hen nightingale has before now been seen to teach [*prodidaxousa*] her chick to sing, suggesting that song does not come by nature as *dialektos*[18] and voice does, but is capable of being shaped [*plattesthai*]. (*HA* IV, 9, 536b14–18)[19]

Aristotle emphasizes that learning here, as a process of acquiring habit, stems from the animal's environment, and not necessarily from its natural parents. The intermediary part of the human soul then includes habits, and these latter are generated not as natural potentialities are, but they are literally shaped by the environment. And "hearing sounds" is precisely hearing them for the sake of not only remembering them, but repeating them.

A Kind of Imitation

One can see the extent of learning in the sense of acquiring habits: it is imitation.[20]

> Generally there seems to be two causes of the poetics, both natural: for imitation is innate to human beings from childhood (and they are distinguished from other animals in that they are the most imitative and do their first learning through imitation), so also is it natural that they all take pleasure in imitations. A sign of this is what happens in the way we act: for we take pleasure in contemplating the most precise images of things which we would look at with pain, such as the forms of most ignoble beasts and corpses. The reason for this is that learning [*manthanein*] is most pleasant not only for the philosopher, but also for everyone else—although not much is common between them. Thus humans take pleasure in seeing images because while watching they happen to learn [*manthanein*] and to infer [*syllogizesthai*] what each thing is, such as "this is that." (*Po.* 4, 1448b4–17)

So humans have two natural inclinations toward imitation, both of which involve some "learning." In the second kind of inclination, humans take pleasure in perceiving imitations—a more or less disinterested perception of a representation which, as disinterested, requires the awareness that it is indeed a representation, in order to provide the middle term of the above-mentioned syllogism: it is the *commonness* of shapes of the noses, and not its identity, that implies that the image is *not literally* (univocally or synonymously) Socrates himself, but an image of Socrates. The "learning" involved in the second case is clearly not immediate, it is "inferential" or "syllogistic." Seeing a picture of Socrates, we seem to "infer": this two-dimensional image has a snub nose and such and such a forehead and beard, but Socrates has the same features, so this is an *image of* Socrates, homonymously speaking this *is* Socrates.[21]

In the first kind of inclination, however, humans *themselves* imitate and do their first learnings in this way. This kind of imitation is not described as requiring an "inference" or "figuring out" (*syllogizesthai*). Here imitation seems to be mere immersion, and to always start out so for Aristotle. The bird that imitates a song does not do so *as* an imitation. She mirrors rather than she represents; she repeats rather than she forms an analogy or syllogism; she echoes rather than she infers. This *natural* inclination to imitate brings it about that humans, but also small birds, are *naturally* inclined to acquire and reproduce behavior that are *not* innate to them. Here is prefigured a natural tendency to precisely transform the "innate." So, where then do habits come from, unlike the innate potentialities of the vegetative part? From the environment.

The Limitation of *Ethos*

Thus, the acquisition of habits takes the form of a learning through mere imitation. While the vegetative part of the soul at birth is ready to do its own work, the intermediary part is naturally ready to do what others do. While nature takes care of the reproduction of the life form and the corresponding development of the vegetative faculties, after that, nature leaves the care of the "reproduction" of the rest to the living being's environment. "And in all the other skills people do not generally know their tools and their most accurate reasonings by taking them from primary things; they take them from what is secondhand or thirdhand or at a distant remove, and get their reasonings from experience."[22] Indeed, "a human being generates a human being" by nature, but it is by learning that a certain song survives across generations.

In a way the tendency to imitate is the reverse of sensation: instead of *receiving* the form of external objects as in sensation, the imitating animal is *impregnated* by them, she "reproduces" them in her body, and she "becomes" them, so to speak. Imitation is almost a regression from sensation back into nutrition and reproduction. In fact, children's surprising capacity for remembering is often likened to the capacity for absorption of a sponge, or to a fertile soil. Perhaps this is why, for Aristotle, "whether one is habituated from childhood this way or that way makes no small difference, but rather a great difference, or rather all the difference" (*NE* II, 1, 1103b23–25). Between nature and *logos*, then, the intermediary part acquires habits by means of learning, which takes the form of imitation or immediate repetition.

Yet how does this fit our guiding passage? Does habit match the kind of "taking account" (*ekhein logon*) of *both* one's father *and* one's friends? As we saw, the bird can learn the songs she hears from other birds no less than from her natural parents. Yet if humans took account of others merely in the sense of imitating them, Aristotle would not insist that the desiring part "gives ear" to *logos*. And if humans took account of anybody, regardless of whether they are our fathers *or* friends, then he would not mention the latter two, but say "others" as in the end of *On the Soul* (*DA* III, 13, 435b24–26). Is it exact to say that, to return to Aristotle's examples, house building and harp playing are *habits*?

The kind of "having" (*ekhein*) which characterizes our having *logos* as humans and our taking account of our fathers and friends then does not seem to be fully captured by "habit," *ethos*. Habit takes us beyond the fulfillment of innate potentialities into the realm of the intermediary part of the human soul, and yet it does not appear to be the form of having that lends insight into the way humans have *logos*. Precisely because "taking account," *logon ekhein*, does not mean here reproduction or imitation, but "esteem," "consideration," "value," "regard."[23] The intermediary part of the human soul has the ability to resist *logos* and therefore has the ability to obey *logos* because it "respects" *logos*—again, not as blindly following it, but in the meaningful etymological sense of "respect" as "looking back" at it. In animal life, we saw sight as a kind of distant perception; here we see another kind of looking, a looking back, reminiscent of the "back-turning stretch," oriented toward "both one's father and one's friends."

Habit is indeed a crucial part of the human life and education, and yet it cannot account for the relationship between the intermediary part of the human soul and *logos*.

2. Positive State

A New Kind of Listening

If not habit, what does the intermediary part of the human soul "have" such that it can listen to *logos*? Besides the above-quoted passage from the *Metaphysics* that enables us to distinguish human beings and *some* animals from, say, bees, by the criterion of "hearing sounds," and consequently of habituation, learning, and imitation, we now need to make a further step in order to gain insight into specifically and essentially human growth. We shall do so by introducing here a helpful passage from the *Politics*, VII, which is unfortunately much less quoted than the famous *logos* passage from book I:

> There are three things by which human beings are made good and serious, these three are nature, habit and *logos*. For first one must be born a human and not any other animal, thus must have a certain body and soul. But there are some qualities that are of no use to be born with, for our habits make us revert them; in fact by nature some are liable to become for the worse or for the better by habits. So other animals mostly live by nature, some do so to a small

> extent by habits too; but the human being lives by *logos* as well, for only the human being has *logos*. So that these [three] must be harmonized [*symphônein*]. For human beings often act contrary to habituation and nature because of *logos*, if they are persuaded [*peisthôsin*] that some other way of acting is better. Now, we have already delimited the natural property of those who are to be amenable to the hand of the legislator. The work left to do is education [*paideia*], for humans learn some things by being habituated, others by listening [*akouontes*]. (*Pol.* VII, 12, 1332a38–1332b11)[24]

What is this latter and specifically human kind of listening or hearing distinct not only from hearing as mere sensation (*akoê*), but also from the "hearing of sounds" (*tôn psophôn akouein*) required for a "learning" in the sense of mere habituation and imitation? Is this the kind of listening that the intermediary part is capable of with respect to *logos* "in the sense in which we say 'taking account of both one's father and one's friends'"?

Let us start out by negative results that may narrow down the field. Aristotle's tripartite analysis of the human soul here defies many classical dichotomies such as rational and irrational, nature and nurture, activity and passivity. For the intermediary part here is neither a reservoir of natural potentialities nor a receptacle of habits. The human soul is no more divided between desire and thought, between active parts and passive parts, between innate motions and environmental stimuli. It is no more split between nature and nurture than between the rational and the irrational.[25] Just as the latter dichotomy lacks the intermediary part, the former seems to eliminate and reduce *logos* altogether. The latter dichotomy omits "childhood" while the former omits "maturity." Thus, these classical dichotomies disable us from understanding the human soul according to Aristotle.

It is exactly here that we shall see the function of *logos*: "For human beings often act contrary to habituation and nature because of *logos*, if they are persuaded that some other way of acting is better" (*Pol.* VII, 12, 1332b6–8). If there is to be *both* a childhood *and* a maturity, *both* the development of the intermediary part *and* that of the part having *logos*, the human soul must not be analyzed into acquired habits and/or natural impulses all the way down. Here *logos*, presumably in the sense of "reason," precisely is a third factor or an "included middle" that defies seemingly exclusive dichotomies. Accordingly, habits cannot remain quantifiable atomic stimuli and thus be simply contrasted to innate "faculties." Habits cannot be simply accumulated in the way fire can grow without limit or *logos*. There must be something *formed* out of habits.

What then does human action involve that is irreducible both to natural motion and to passively undergoing and repeating? On the one hand, natural potentialities of the soul are reserved to the vegetative part. And, as we have seen in chapter 3, these are developed organs ready for work. On the other hand, habits as passive exposure (*paskhein*) to, and immediate repetition of, environmental influences (*pathê*) cannot resist or obey *logos*, they repeat without listening or taking account (*logon ekhein*). What then does emerge in the intermediary part? What does human education involve that is neither a potentiality actualized at birth, nor internalized firsthand experience?[26] If it is neither *syn-ekheia*, nor *met-hexis*, then what is the substantive form of *ekhein* in relation to *logos* that makes sense of being compared to one's taking account of "both one's father and one's friends"?

Positive State

The answer is *hexis*, which we shall translate as "positive state" for lack of a better rendering.[27]

> In a word, from similar actualities [*energeiôn*] positive states [*hexeis*] come to be. Hence it is necessary to make out actualities to be of certain sorts, for the positive states follow from the differences among these. (*NE*, II, 1, 1103b22–24)

Positive states are the basic constituents of the intermediary part of the human soul. Beyond mere habit (*ethos*), positive states build up human character (*êthos*). Neither nature, nor environment, but positive states make up human *êthos*, the real *daimôn* of human life according to Heraclitus's fragment 119.

> There are three things that come to be in the soul: feelings [*pathê*], potentialities and positive states . . . By feelings, I mean desire, anger, fear, confidence, envy, joy, affection, hatred, yearning, jealousy, pity, and generally those things which are accompanied by pleasure or pain. By potentialities, [I mean] those things in accordance with which we are said to be apt to undergo [*pathêtikoi*] these, such as those by which we can feel anger or be annoyed or feel pity. By positive states, [I mean] those things in accordance with which we bear ourselves well or badly toward feelings; for instance, in relation to being angry, if we are that way violently or slackly, we bear ourselves badly, but if in a measured way, we bear ourselves well, and similarly in relation to other feelings. (*NE* II, 5, 1105b20–28)

This crucial passage gives us a clue as to why Aristotle defines humans as animals that neither *are* of a certain kind, nor *do* certain things, but *have* (*ekhei*) something, because this passage introduces a sense of *ekhein* and *hexis* that is deemphasized in other analyses of these terms in the Aristotelian corpus.[28] Aristotle here explains *hexeis* as "those things in accordance with which we bear ourselves well or badly toward feelings" (*kath' has pros ta pathê exomen eu ê kakôs*). Human beings do not simply undergo (*paskhein*) fear or confidence, they are not only influenced under (*hypo*) their impact, they maintain a relation to (*pros*) them. Human beings neither simply act (*prattein*) in fear or confidence, nor even *are* they (*einai*) simply afraid or confident, they bear themselves (*ekhein*) well or badly in relation to these feelings. If humans are defined neither by something they *are* nor by something they *do*, but by something they *have*, this may well be because *hexis* designates a kind of having that is irreducible to something humans simply *are* or *do*.

Human beings feel anger in a way fundamentally different from the way a combustible is set on fire. Humans never literally *burst* in anger, fear never literally *consumes* their hearts, the human soul is never literally *set on fire* by love.[29] Certainly, humans *undergo* pleasure or pain. In fact, all sensation entails pleasure or pain.[30] But the human soul also has an aspect *out of which* it *bears itself* (*ekhein*) toward these feelings. This is why positive states can neither be substituted by or to habits, feelings, and natural potentialities; they "grow" *out of* them. Human growth is such that it involves this *other* growth. For Aristotle, *hexis* is the proper subject matter of ethics. This is why the *Nicomachean Ethics* is far more deeply related to the *Politics* than to *On the Soul*.

Freedom

Let us flesh out this concept of "positive state" by distinguishing it from "habit" in our previous examples. Is there a strong sense in which harp playing (a positive state) is distinct from the singing of a bird (a habit)? Both are indeed examples of those apparently paradoxical activities that we become capable of by precisely exercising. They both illustrate the way habits *stick* by means of repetition in distinction from natural potentialities: "Being carried down by nature, a stone cannot be habituated to be carried upwards even if one were to habituate it by throwing it upwards ten thousand times; nor can fire be habituated to be carried downwards" (*NE* II, 1, 1103a21–23). How then does harp playing differ not only from the falling of a stone or the burning of fire, but also from the singing of a bird?

How does one become not only someone who plays the harp, but a *harpist*? Perhaps we should ask: *when* does one become a harpist? When she happens to pick up a harp and pluck its strings? Or when she is capable of perfectly repeating what the teacher plays? Or is it rather when the student *no longer needs* to imitate the teacher, when the student *no longer needs* to immediately remember all the particular instructions and all the past experiences? Just as we noted in chapter 3 that one learns a language when one "forgets" the rules, similarly one becomes a harpist when one *no longer needs* to follow one's master or to be pushed by him, but "walks her own walk." This is when one is a harpist even while not playing a harp. Similarly a house builder is someone who *does not have to* imitate his master, but who in fact *must* be able to go beyond his master in order to improvise on the particular means, materials, workers, budget, and geography, and so on in order to build each time the particular, therefore unique, house.

The settling of a positive state then is an emergence of freedom. Not a freedom *from* playing certain notes, but the freedom *to* play others instead. It is the freedom of differing without falling into contradiction, that is, without ceasing to have the exact same *logos*. A positive state is a *result* of the actualities that we become capable of by exercise. And this result at least partially transcends the preparation such that, as Aristotle says, the good shoemaker or the good general makes the best even out of bad circumstances (*NE* I, 10, 1101a1–5). Indeed, no harpist is *only* a harpist. But being a harpist does involve the human soul as a whole. For, when one is a harpist, this colors one's eating and sleeping habits, one's respiration and concentration, one's daily schedule, one's furniture and one's house, one's relation to one's body and to other people, one's career decisions, one's way of raising children, one's political views, and ultimately, depending on how serious the person is, one's life *as a whole*. Thus it is not true that some people are more harpist than others.

Medicine, Architecture, and Music

Most instructive, in this context, is a famous but lengthy passage from the *Metaphysics* that subtly defends a claim that at first may seem counterintuitive: while positive states such as art or science[31] emerge out of experience and habit, the latter two remain more general than positive states:

> While, then, other [animals] live by impressions and memories, they have a small share in experience; on the other hand, the human race also lives by art and *logismos*. In humans, experience comes out of memory, for many memories of the same thing bring to completion a potentiality for one experience . . . But art comes to be whenever out of many conceptions from experience arises

> one universal judgment [*hypolêpsis*] about similar things. For to have a judgment that this thing was beneficial to Callias when he was sick with this disease, and to Socrates, and one by one in this way to many people, belongs to experience. But the judgment that it was beneficial to all such and such people marked out as being of one form [*tois toiosde kat' eidos hen aphoristheisi*], when they were sick with this disease (such as sluggish or irritable people when they were feverish with heat), belongs to art. (*Metaph.* I, 1, 980b26–981a13)

The crucial factor is the nature of the "judgment," whether it is a judgment of mere fact or of the cause. Indeed animals often take care of themselves quite well, and human beings may manage quite well to live just by following their feeling and the familiar judgments of traditional medicine that they have been exposed to: "Such and such a potion is good for this disease," "Such and such a plant is poisonous," and so on. Similarly, one may well have memorized perfectly the traditional "judgments" concerning the "appropriate" music to play at weddings, sacrifices, funerals, and so on. An experienced manual laborer may well mechanically build up such and such walls for temples and other kinds for residences, and yet

> the experienced person knows the what, and not the why, whereas the artisan is familiar with the why and the cause. This is why we think master craftsmen in each kind of work are more honored and know more than manual laborers, and are also wiser because they know the causes of the things they do (just some inanimate things, the others do what they do without knowing, as fire burns; the inanimate things doing each of these things by nature, but the manual laborers by habit). (*Metaph.* I, 1, 981a27–981b5)

Earlier in this chapter, habit was opposed to the motion of fire. In comparison to positive states, they seem quite similar.

So positive states differ equally from habit and from mere nature by their openness to the particularity of the situation: this is good for Socrates neither because it is good in general, nor simply because it worked in the past, nor even because it worked on Socrates in the past, but *because* now Socrates is such and such in this particular situation. In fact, in this particular, unique and unprecedented situation, Socrates may well be right in thinking that drinking poison is the right thing to do for him. This wall is to be built this way, not because that is the way walls have always been built, not because I am told to build it that way, but *because* of the material, the geography, the purpose of the building, and the political significance of the building. This song is to be played this way, not because that is *the* way it is played by the masters, but *because* of the particular acoustics of the environment, the time of the day, the season of the year, but also because of the way of life it serves, the way it forms or affects the listeners of a certain kind and on a certain, unique, occasion.

In short, positive states make it possible and even necessary to go beyond the dichotomy of natural potentialities and acquired habits. Thus, human life exhibits the inherent character of its own *logos*, "standard of being," by means of these positive states. It is here, at the level of positive states, that the third sense of *logos* shows itself: reason.

Hexis Meta Logou

It is not anachronistic to associate artistic perfection and virtue in the word "virtuoso." And it certainly is not out of place to dwell on the example of music. Music is always a fundamental factor of education, and especially of the emotional education of children, in Aristotle as well as in Plato.[32] Just as the building of a house or the making of a movie involves many people having different shares in the overall purpose, similarly singing to a playback or to a karaoke, conducting an orchestra, DJing in a club, involuntarily repeating an annoying tune one has heard on the radio, whistling in the street, and playing in a military band or a jazz quartet offer a variety of distributions of "knowledge" of the causes. This wide spectrum is spread between, on the one hand, a level of mechanical repetition (imitation, mere habituation, or association), and on the other hand, a level of knowledge (art or science), of the awareness of the particular, that is of the awareness that universal "recipes" do not have univocal effects on all particulars. Here we thus find a level of holding together two possible contrary ways to go in a particular situation, and a state of deliberating well about them—a positive state with *logos* (*hexis meta logou*).[33]

The settling of a positive state is then an emergence of freedom in the sense of overcoming the exclusiveness of what presents itself initially as contrary options. As a form of human freedom from top-down applications of universal rules as well as from the sheer particularity of perceptions, our analysis of positive states with *logos* such as medicine, architecture and music here foreshadows what will turn out to be the essence of human *logos* in our next chapter: human involvement not only with one's past firsthand experiences, or with one's mechanical training, but with non-firsthand experience.

The intermediary part of the human soul, then, is not an aggregate of habits. Habits, feelings, experiences, memories *become* positive states, settled and free ways of the human soul's bearing itself toward the latter. For the time being, this seems to be the clue toward interpreting meaningfully and adequately our focal passage from the *Nicomachean Ethics* where the intermediary part of the human soul listens to *logos* the way "we say 'taking account [*ekhein logon*] of one's father and one's friends'" (*NE* I, 13, 1102b30–1102b32). It is this bearing oneself, *ekhein*, that is "crystallized" in the concept of positive state (*hexis*). Positive states are formed not by natural growth or habituation, but by education, the *other* growth required by human growth: one's listening not only to one's immediate surrounding, that is, to one's "father," whether natural or not, *but also* to those beyond, to one's "friends"—the human soul's having both of these tendencies at once. "Taking account" here means not only remembering and being habituated by means of firsthand experiences in the "household," but also attending to that which one precisely *has not* or *cannot* have experienced and even *may never* experience firsthand. For the time being, it seems as if the human being *has logos* in the sense a guitarist *owns* a guitar: not the possession of an object, indeed, neither a mastery over a memorized repertoire and over general instructions, but rather an ability to bear oneself without them and beyond them.

3. Character

Clearly this is not enough. The concept of positive state takes us further than nature and habit in accurately describing the human soul by introducing a kind of freedom. Yet while technical and theoretical positive states may color all human experience, they certainly do not exhaust it. The intermediary part of the human soul attends both to one's father and to one's friends in a nontechnical and nontheoretical way as well. We saw that harp playing and house building are instances of assuming a master's or teacher's general guidance, and then of overcoming it for the sake of freely and maturely engaging in new particular situations. And yet, while art is a positive state with *logos* (*meta logou*, *NE* VI, 3, 1140a11), the positive states of the intermediary part are *not* with *logos*, but rather according to *logos* (*kata ton logon*, *NE* VI, 1, 1138b25–29), or against it (*para ton logon*, *NE* I, 13, 1102b24). One's relation to one's master or teacher is much less intricate and profound than one's relation to one's father, and much less freely chosen and sustained than one's relation to one's friends.

Hexis Kata Ton Logon

We said that some people *are* harpists, while some are not. Yet we cannot say, in the same way, that some people are courageous while others are not.

When non-harpist adults happen to pick up a harp, they play it the way a child would, whereas cowards feel fear in a fundamentally different way than children do (*NE* III, 5, 1114a3ff.): in the latter case something is lacking, but in the former case something is *destroyed* or *out of place*. People do not take up their feelings and needs the way one may pick up a harp; people do not relate to one another the way they choose a harp teacher or are handed over to a master craftsman. When human beings produce, humans do things to objects. When they act, they also do things to themselves. Art and science are indeed positive states, and they were helpful in securing an aspect of the human soul distinct from both natural potentialities and acquired habits. Yet the basic constituent of human character is positive states that relate to feelings and desires that are as old as we are, and probably older than our very sense of who we are.

Hence perfection in art or production is not a perfection of the intermediary part of the soul, of human desire (*NE* III, 10, 1117b23–25). Art and science require that the human bear oneself in relation to objects, memories, trainings, and habits. They both do have a part in the human soul. But they are precisely too akin to *logos* and too detached from desire, they are "with *logos*" (*meta logou*). In art, "taking account" means not only remembering and being habituated by means of firsthand experiences in the "household," but also attending to that which one precisely has *not* experienced; but the other person involved remains distant, detachable, somebody who is more or less chosen, and therefore exchangeable. The father and friends we take account of in our relation to desires and fears, on the other hand, are not simply expendable or exchangeable. There is a much stronger sense in which they are unique, noninstrumental, nonexpendable. We are so deeply implicated in them that we cannot discharge them, but rather *resist them*. We do not simply deliberately follow their instructions, we take account of them in a stronger or more precise sense.

Shame

There is a phenomenon that exhibits the way a *hexis kata ton logon* takes account of others, the kind of listening and access beyond one's firsthand experiences: shame. "Shame is an impression concerning dishonor, and that for its own sake and not for its results" (*Rh.* II, 6, 1384a22–26). It is exactly here that the expression "*logon ekhein*" reappears: "[people] necessarily feel shame before those whom they take account of [*hôn logon ekhei*]" (*Rh.* II, 6, 1384a28–30). This sheds light on the kind of positive state of character that is more profound than one's relation to a harp teacher or a master architect: a fault in playing the harp in itself is a fault and nothing more; but if one feels ashamed of making that mistake before one's teacher or an audience, it is necessarily because one takes account of them beyond and regardless of their status, one listens not to their particular instructions, but to their evaluation of oneself. The kind of listening to one's father and friends involved in *logon ekhein* is then the necessary attendance to both as speakers and evaluators. Indeed this presence of others is not more audible than visible: "[People] feel more ashamed before those who will be always with them [*paresomenous*] and who keep watch on them [*prosekhontas*], because in both cases they are under the eyes of others" (*Rh.* II, 6, 1384a35–38). The phenomenon of shame seems to suggest that "respect," the sense of *logos* that prefigures rationality and speech, is a looking back, a gaze turned at the gaze of another.

After habit, and positive states as such, this is finally the correct sense of *ekhein* for understanding *logon ekhein* both in the way the desiring part "takes account of" both one's father and friends, and in the way the human being alone "has *logos*": it is not *hexis* alone, it is not *hexis meta logou*, not a *met-hexis*, but a *hexis kata ton logon*. Human character and its positive states, whether virtues or vices, will involve the gaze of others, their "presence," but also the sense that these others "will always be with" oneself. This is why human character is fundamentally interpersonal and necessarily involves a project of living together. Ultimately this is why human beings are "political animals." To *have logos* means to take account of the evaluation of others with which one has a life project, to somehow look at oneself and the world from the eyes of others, that is, from a non-firsthand point of view.

But what is this presence of others really like such that they remain *with us*? Because, although we do not feel to have failed a master's teaching while making a mistake as such on our own, we do feel shame even when others are *not* there attending our behavior. There must be a sense in which we *see* others *look* at us without them looking at us, in which they speak to us from within without giving any orders, in which they "move us" without constantly pushing or pulling us. Just as shame does not need the physical presence of others looking at us and giving us instructions, a *hexis kata ton logon* is not a state constantly generated by others, but presents a self-sustaining structure. In a way we must specify, we carry on these others in us—and not in the sense of imitating them, but in the sense of "taking account" of their evaluation of us and thereby respecting or disrespecting them.

Bodily *Hexis*

Aristotle argues that a positive state is not an alteration. In alteration the mover is continuous with the moved, whereas in positive states it is not:

> Among positive states, some are virtues, some are vices. Yet neither virtue nor vice is an alteration [*alloiôsis*], but virtue is a certain completion [*teleiôsis tis*] (for when something attains its virtue, then it is said to be complete, for then it most conforms to its nature, as a circle is complete when a circle comes to be and in the best way), and vice is its corruption and displacement [*extasis*]. (*Ph.* VII, 3, 246a11–17)

As we saw in our previous section, *hexis* as such is a self-sustaining structure, it is freed from being moved each time. Just as a harpist does not become one each time she picks up a harp, our character is not an agglomeration of atomic spontaneous choices or responses to atomic stimuli. "Neither the positive states of the body, nor those of the soul are alterations" (*Ph.* VII, 3, 246a10–11).

Bodily *hexis* may help us shed light on the peculiar way in which our father and friends *are with us*, as attested by the phenomenon of shame. "For instance, we place health and vigor in the *krasis* and *symmetria* of the hot and the cold, either in relation to themselves or in relation to their surroundings; and similarly with beauty and strength and the other virtues and vices" (*Ph.* VII, 3, 246b5–8). Now, in chapters 3 and 4, where we dealt with nutrition and sensation, we already thematized this "blending" (*krasis*) and "proportionality" (*symmetria*); but on this occasion, we can briefly touch upon some aspects of the specificity of human corporeality. Even at the level of merely bodily functions, virtues and vices are self-sustaining positive states. For Aristotle, "beauty," "ugliness," "health," and "sickness" are not simply "properties" such that they may be simply manipulated externally, that is, altered; nor are they simply natural in the sense of innate, in which case they would be constantly "moved" or "generated" by nature as such.

Note the remarkable characterization of the body here: although a body has matter and matter can be changed, a body *cannot* be made beautiful or ugly by merely external manipulations. The Aristotelian body has at once a special kind of "thickness" and a "historicality." Its beauty and ugliness has a special depth of its own, a "logic" unto itself, beyond simply the way it looks.

Thus virtues and vices are not simply a matter of sensitivity or insensitivity even at the level of merely bodily functions: "virtue makes one be insensitive [*apathes*] or sensitive [*pathêtikon*] in a certain way, while vice makes one contrarily sensitive or insensitive" (*Ph.* VII, 3, 246b18–20). In chapter 3 we saw how bodily health is not simply a matter of preestablished substances. The cause of health is a *regime*. Health depends on a diet which configures certain substances with corresponding amounts and timing, but also, precisely, on all sorts of habits, on work conditions, on familial traits, on laws, and so on. Aristotle's understanding of bodily excellence is at once substantive enough to avoid relativity, and particular enough to defy empty universal prescriptions. Experiential testimony for this can be found in the fundamental difficulty of generalizing medical issues, and often the need for family physicians, that is, physicians who not only deduce diagnoses and treatments from a first consultation, but who have a long-lasting acquaintance with us and our life, and even with our grandparents, that is, with us as a new emergent life within a long tradition. Physicians do not always calculate, they do not always deduce diagnoses from overarching principles, for the simple reason that they are unable to do so successfully or to do so as such.[34] Physicians do not manipulate or "alter" our body, because they cannot always do so successfully, or because they cannot do so at all. Hence, the Hippocratic phrase, *primum non nocere*.

Pellegrin nicely contrasts the relative stability of Aristotelian virtue with Christian virtue:

> Aristotelian virtue has nothing to do with, say, Christian virtue. The Christian saint is in no way at safety against the return of evil, and is always open to temptation. The Aristotelian wise person—just like the Platonic, Stoic and Epicurean—finds his happiness in virtue, even if happiness secondarily depends on external conditions. A person who represses his bad desires with more or less pain, the "restrained" person in Aristotle's terms, may well look virtuous externally, yet he is not so. Hence two Aristotelian claims, among others, which set his ethics apart from Christian or Kantian morality: first, the sense of modesty (*aidôs*) is not a virtue, for the accompanying shame is foreign to the virtuous. And secondly, pleasure is the genuine criterion of a virtuous act and enables us to distinguish it from forgeries.[35]

Thus, being neither a temporary affection, nor an ingrained habit, a positive state exhibits a relative stability that makes it meaningful to talk about virtue and character in ethics.

Moral Virtue

Aristotle extends his analysis of virtue and vice from the context of the body to that of the intermediary part of the soul, the seat of pleasures and pains. There we see the same irreducibility of positive states to habits and alterations in an even richer form:

> Similarly with the positive states of the [intermediary part of the] soul, since all of them consist in holding oneself in relation to something in a certain way [*pros ti pôs ekhein*], and while virtues are completions [*teleiôseis*], vices are displacements [*extaseis*]. (*Ph.* VII, 3, 246b21–247a2)

Positive states are neither feelings such as pleasure or pain, nor sensations which are always accompanied by the latter:

> All moral virtue concerns bodily pleasures and pains . . . while pleasures and pains are alterations of the perceptive part, it is clear that something must be altered both for these to be cast off and for them to be taken on. Therefore, the generation of them [of virtues and vices] is with alteration, but they are not alterations. (*Ph.* VII, 3, 247a7–19)

Just as excesses destroy the sense organs, and ultimately health as such,

> the same thing holds true for the temperance and courage and other virtues; for the man who runs away from everything in fear and never endures anything becomes a coward; the man who fears nothing whatsoever but encounters everything becomes rash . . . Temperance and courage are destroyed by excess and deficiency, and are preserved by the mean. (*NE* II, 2, 1104a18–27)

What *is* universal about courage is that it will involve confrontation and avoidance thereof. Because, in each case, courage will involve one's fear. But the object of the fear confronted and the specific way in which confrontation might happen is not universal at all; on the contrary, it is always particular, and therefore always requires a creative act, that is, an act originating from the subject in the uniqueness of his being, situation, and history.

This parallelism between bodily virtues and moral virtues may remind the reader of our discussion of sensation in chapter 4: if it is true that excess in sensation destroys the organ, sensation is a *logos* and requires a mean; similarly, excess in feelings destroy something in the human soul. We must clarify what is meant by "mean" or "excess" in this context, just as the same problem showed up in our discussion of sensation. The destruction of a sense organ is the destruction of its *logos*, of its ability to hold together contrary sensuous qualities (hot and cold, wet and dry); in other words, while the excess of heat in iron simply moves it further and further away from the cold toward more and more heat, excess of heat in a hand makes it insensitive to both cold *and* heat. The meaning of *logos* as "ratio," in the context of sensation as well as in that of the moral virtues, is not simply a matter of percentage, of quantity, of fine-tuning, but a matter of holding contraries together. But while growth holds on to actual contrary elements, and sensation holds on to actual contrary states, the human agent holds contrary possibilities. Virtue stems from the fact that the human agent is open to possible contrary interpretations of particular sensations. This seems to be the key point that so crucially distinguishes virtue from apathy or insensitivity:

> Humans become corrupted through pleasures and pains, either by pursuing or avoiding them at the wrong time or in the wrong manner or in as many ways as such things are delimited by *logos*. *This is also why some define the virtues as certain kinds of apathy or calmness*, but they do not define them well because they say this simply but do not add "as one ought" and "as one ought not" and "when" and the rest. (*NE* II, 3, 1104b21–28; emphasis ours)

Both the virtuous *and* the vicious person *act in relation to pleasures and pains, both* feel them.[36] Both the courageous and the coward feel fear, and what distinguishes the soul of the former is that it is *not only* occupied by fear, that it takes account of the particularity of the situation, and *not only* of its own emotional state or habits, of its history or present situation. The virtuous person then "listens to *logos*" by holding its emotional state together with contrary interpretations of the situation. In a sense, the virtuous person is defined not by less, but by more sensitivity—not perhaps to the pleasure and pain, but to the various and more comprehensive ways of interpreting them.

This holding together of contrary interpretations can be seen indirectly by its result: *proairesis*, "choice," literally "a taking out [*hairesis*] of one of the interpretations in favor [*pro*]." In fact, this holding together typical to all the senses of *logos* we have seen so far here goes back to the oldest sense of *logos* and *legein*: collecting, laying down one beside another.[37] And *proairesis* as a "taking out" or "picking" is precisely the result of this laying down. It is because *logos* holds together differences in their difference that *proairesis* as picking is not simply taking what it given, but taking *out*, taking *from out of* what is given, a choosing one option for the exact same reason (*logos*) one refuses the other option(s). Choice happens only *out of* a simultaneous openness to a manifold of options, and thus only *for a reason* for choosing *this* rather than *that*, that is, only *because of* an interpretative deliberation between *this* and *that*. Hence these options are not different amounts of desire or fear, but different interpretations of the same particular object.[38]

Thus we come to finally make sense of the meaning of *logos* in the expression "rational potentiality" (*dynamis meta logou*) we encountered in *On Interpretation* in our chapter 2: humans are exposed to contrary options because they hold on to contrary interpretations of situations or objects or projects. If Socrates can both walk *and not walk* out of jail, this is because Socrates has devoted his life to cultivate the ability to interpret the situation of walking away from prison in contrary ways, unlike Crito urging him to run out of jail.[39] This "motion" is what is called action (*praxis*) in the strict sense. "*Logos* goes both ways [*amphoin esti*], but not in the same manner; it is in the soul which has a source of motion, and will therefore, by the same source, set both in motion linking them [*synapsasa*] to the same *logos*" (*Metaph.* IX, 2, 1046b21–23).

Deliberation

As we said, this holding together of contrary interpretations can be seen indirectly by its result: *proairesis*, "choice," but also more directly by the very process of interpretation. Aristotle does not use the usual term for "interpretation" in Ancient Greek, namely, *hermeneia*, but that of "deliberation," *bouleusis*.

Because of its openness to the particularity of human situations, Aristotle's ethics is fundamentally irreducible to universal prescriptions and to quantitative measurements. Just as virtue is irreducible to apathy because of the latter's indifference to the particularity of the situation, defining virtue as an arithmetical mean (such as 6 being the mean of 10 and 2) is a fundamentally distorted way of looking at the human soul:

> But the mean in relation to us is not something one needs to take in this way, for it is not the case, if ten pounds is a lot for someone to eat and two pounds a little, that the gymnastic trainer will prescribe six pounds, for perhaps even this is a lot for the one who is going to take it, or a little. (*NE* II, 6, 1106a36–1106b5)

The mean, or the *logos*, is not measured, but deliberated according to the particular person and her situation. What is measured, according to Aristotle, is vice, precisely because vice is an excess *away* from virtue, which is a standard in itself. Bringing together "choice," "mean in relation to us," and indeed *logos*, moral virtue is finally defined as follows: "a positive state that makes one apt at choosing, consisting in a mean condition in relation to us, which is determined by *logos* and by the means by which a person with practical judgment [*phronimos*] would determine it" (*NE* II, 6, 1106b36–1107a2). Both desire and intellect are in fact without *logos*.[40] And neither as such characterize human beings. It is their togetherness, their interpenetration that characterizes *logos* and defines human beings. It must be recognized that even if Aristotelian ethics epitomizes divine *theôria* or the contemplative life, nevertheless his account of moral, that is, strictly human, virtue gives utmost importance to the particularities of human life. For Aristotle, this is intrinsic to ethics:

> But let this be granted in advance—that all *logos* concerning actions is obliged to speak in outline and not precisely, just as we said at the beginning that one ought to demand that *logoi* be in accord with their material, whereas matters that are involved in actions and are advantageous have nothing static about them, any more than do matters of health. And the general *logos* being like this, still more does the *logos* concerning particulars lack precision; for it falls under no art nor under any skill that has been handed down, but it is necessary for those who are acting to always look at the circumstances surrounding the occasion, just as is the case with the medical art or the art of steering a ship. (*NE* II, 2, 1103b36–1104a11)

Both "gut feelings" and general prescriptions fail to circumscribe the origin of moral virtue, the former being stuck with an unaccountable particular emotional or bodily state, the latter with an empty rule to apply. The former leave no room for listening and thus resemble habit, whereas the latter are unable to listen to the particularity of the situation human life is always confronted with. The former repeats, and the latter dictates, whereas moral virtue for Aristotle must take the form of taking account of others. If the human soul holds together contrary interpretations of one situation, it is because the human being is able to see another as herself (for "a friend is another self," *NE* IX, 4, 1166a32), but also because the human being can see herself as another, and thus can be a friend to herself (*NE* IX, 8, 1169a12). As the individual human being is a "political animal" according to Aristotle, friendship turns out to be a virtue in a special sense. (*NE* IX, 4, 1166a1ff.) In the next chapter, we shall see better how human *logos* is precisely this perceptiveness in regard to others' experiences.

Logos in the context of positive states and human character then blurs the apparent exclusivity of contrary actions, the externality of others, and a monolithic view of the integrity of the human individual. As the prudent person interprets apparently similar situations in contrary ways and apparently different ones as the same, the intermediary part of the virtuous person takes account of both one's father and one's friends not only in the sense of seeing them see oneself, but in the sense of being able to intimately assume their point of view and "listen to them" while making decisions and deliberating in situations of which one has no firsthand experience.

Circles Vicious and Virtuous

The necessarily imprecise character of ethics thus makes it impossible to draw inferences from particular actions to the "completions" and "displacements" that constitute virtue and vice. For instance, someone writing a Ph.D. dissertation knows the variety of the forms distraction can assume. Despite appearances, writing a dissertation well is fortunately not about being a good ascetic, about being a person who sharply compartmentalizes sectors of her life. The inability to concentrate does not simply mean to be unable to refrain from doing many things, from undergoing many sensations, from being constantly stimulated and excited about multifarious things. Distraction rather means to do and undergo *many* things *as many*, and not *as one*. It means to do and undergo many things *while resetting the process* with each action or passion. Vice as "displacement" refers to this necessity of resetting the process, and thus has very little to do with "evil." Vice as "displacement" is "replacement."

On the other hand, the term "concentration" also refers to the "circle" analogy, but this time not because it suggests routine, but because it incorporates *all* different points equidistant from the center. To be virtuous is to be able to go on a trip, to incorporate difference while remaining the same, whereas vice is to remain at the same place while constantly moving around. Paradoxically, a "vicious" trip is to move around, a "virtuous" trip is change and understanding. Hence being concentrated on a dissertation in philosophy in no way entails lack of interest and excitement in front of the multiplicity of actions and passions precisely because it is not an application of a rule or a report on various experiments, but, at least at first, a risk, a trip, the answering of a riddle, *a question*—an engagement into something that one knows that one does not know. Being concentrated here is rather being constantly interested and necessarily open *without having to reset one's interest*, being excited *without having to refuel one's curiosity*, doing and undergoing *without having to end and restart*. Distraction and concentration are examples of human phenomena that are environmental, that is, irreducible to motion and lack of motion, activity and passivity.[41] For one who is distracted may well be standing still, but in fact he is constantly stopping and restarting.

This is why it is not enough to stand still in order to step out of the "environment" of distraction. In order to get out of this process of constant change, one cannot simply make a change. In order to unify this multiplicity, one cannot simply add something. A child that is constantly distracted while sitting in a classroom may well become extremely concentrated while playing soccer: playing soccer creates an environment that absorbs and intensifies the soul more and more so that in the end the players are disturbed by distractions. This is why a soccer field is not a certain space *in* which things happen, it is the environment *of* those things, imbued with interpretation.

Similarly, fear is not simply an atomic feeling. For fear can "color" actions and objects, it can create environments, especially in the case of human beings which, as we shall see better in chapter 6, having *logos*, are able to understand and relay non-firsthand experiences as much as firsthand experiences. Fear is a perfect case for seeing the implications of the human capacity for understanding and relaying non-firsthand experiences. For, in an environment of fear in which I fear someone who fears me, I will be ready to express my fear in such a way as to set the other to do the same. But since I know that my violence will provoke his, I will be ready to do violence harsh enough to intimidate him definitively. Yet he knows this too and must feel pretty much the same way as I do. So he will be prepared to preempt my plans of definitively harshening my violence by even greater violence, and so on. It is precisely because the reign of fear is more than the sum of the individual motions or atomic feelings it contains, that it blurs the distinction between action and passion, between my feelings and those of my enemy. Consequently, sometimes, if not often, it unfortunately becomes very difficult to pinpoint any beginning of a long-lasting enmity, and also to foresee any short-term resolution.

The Dilemma of Character Painting

Just as the photographic approach to the spectacle of natural beings turned out to be fundamentally flawed above in chapter 3, here we may see why all representations of human character become fundamentally problematic. In his discussion of the aesthetic education of children, Aristotle argues that visual representations reflect character only to a small extent:

> These [visual representations] are not the likenesses of characters, the forms and colors produced are rather signs of characters and these are in the bodily modifications. But so far as there is a difference concerning the contemplation of these, the young should not contemplate the works of Pauson but of Polygnotus and of any other moral [*êthikos*] painter or sculptor. (*Pol.* VIII, 5, 1340a32–38)

It is exactly these two artists that Aristotle compares in the discussion of character representation in the *Poetics*: "[Those who imitate] do so either as better or as worse than us or as similar to us just like painters do: Polygnotus paints those better than us, Pauson those worse than us, while Dionysus those similar to us" (*Po.* 2, 1448a4–7). So, if character (*êthos*) defies momentary appearances, particular acts and general prescriptions, how can a painter produce a "likeness," and not a "sign," of a just person? How does one represent visually not an act or a feeling, but a positive state such as a virtue or vice? How does one illustrate not only a human body, but her *êthos*—her true *daimôn* according to Heraclitus?

Unlike a composer of music who, according to Aristotle, more directly speaks to our feelings and shapes our soul, painters of *êthos*, the "peintres de mœurs," as it is said in French, are in a dilemma: if a painter, naively speaking, has to convey on the canvas the depth of a three-dimensional body in space, a portrait painter has to somehow project on the canvas the depth of the soul in time and history. If one's goal is to represent a person as a character, one can limit oneself neither to a naturalistic representation of the model's nose, eyes, mouth, and hair as an "exact" photograph would, nor to a parable or an allegory in which the figure would be subsumed under a universal virtue or sin as can be seen in, say, Brueghel's paintings of the seven deadly sins. The representation of character should be neither merely representative nor, in this particular sense, "moralizing."[42]

Hence it may be easier to produce a conventional representation of Justice and to graphically reproduce the outer appearance of a just human being's body, than to represent a just person as such. Again this is because imprecision is inherent to ethics, because human character is irreducible to universal formulas and particular acts, because there is an impossibility to represent human deliberation and interpretation, because there is an "invisibility" of the father and friends of whom the virtuous human being takes account, and in front of whom she feels ashamed, because there is a "lack of content" in their words.

Rembrandt teaches one much about how developmental and even hereditary characteristics can be paradoxically represented in a moment and two-dimensionally. One example may be his 1653 painting of *Aristotle Contemplating the Bust of Homer*. According to our interpretation of character, there is no wonder that there is still controversy as to what the painting means, but also whether or not Aristotle is looking at the bust at all, and even whether the figure *is* Aristotle to begin with.[43] Although he has recourse to "signs," allegoric objects (in this case the bust, the golden chain with the medallion of Alexander the Great), biblical scenes and references, exotic clothes, and real-life situations and actions, Rembrandt's real tool in conveying positive states is light and darkness. His contrasts attempt to find a middle way between simply asserting the particular person in her particular time and place—say, Solon in sixth-century Athens—and making her a conventional sign of universal virtue—say, a blindfolded woman holding a balance in one hand and a sword in the other. His contrasts rather seem to be oriented towards conveying the effect that the brightness is not fully detached from the *possibility* of sinking back into darkness and that obscurity is *pregnant*. This contrast does not simply create a dramatic impression or the appearance of the depth of the soul, it allows the appearance of a status between presence and disappearance, in Aristotelian terms, between actuality and potentiality. And this is why it is able to convey the sense of a person having not only a face and an identity but also a history and a character.

So Rembrandt's contrasts convey two contradictory impressions. On the one hand, one feels that, apart from the presence of the figure that is *re*presented, the figure *could* have been somewhere else, in different clothes, in a different situation and committing a different act, and yet that it *would* be the same thing, that she *would* adapt herself and still hold the same relation to the world and to her emotions. This means that she is not confined by this particularity. On the other hand, the portrait of a magnanimous person by Rembrandt, insofar as it represents this character trait of the person, gives the impression that if somebody else were in the same situation, doing the same thing or standing in the exact same posture, it *would not* be the same thing. This means that she is not merely a universal idea, but a person.

Thus, at least as much as people are sources of actions, characters are constitutive of people for Aristotle. Just as an environment is more than the sum of the objects *in* that environment, a virtue is the environment of a soul irreducible to particular acts or general rules. The transcendence of virtue over the particular situations and general rules is at once stable and vulnerable as the transcendence of the environment over its components. The courageous person neither spontaneously *repeats* courage in his soul, nor does he *apply* a preexistent formula to his particular situation. *Hexis* names the very fact that there are neither virtuous acts per se, nor recipes for virtue other than that it involves an unforeseeable free relation to contrary extremes. The contrasts in Rembrandt's portraits reflect the necessarily deliberative character of human *logos*, its very *êthos*, its holding contrary interpretations without letting one yield to or take over the other.

4. Recapitulation and Reorientation

In chapter 1, we saw that the first sense of *logos* is "standard of being." In chapter 2, we saw that this standard must be inherent to the being in question. In chapters 3 and 4, we saw that natural beings exhibit the inherence of their "standard of being" in natural motion: nutrition, reproduction, sensation and locomotion—all of which instantiate a second sense of *logos*: "ratio." Here in chapter 5, we began seeing that human beings exhibit the inherence of their "standard of being" in human action—thus introducing the third sense of *logos*: "reason."

Our elaboration of the source of action required an analysis of the tripartite structure of the human soul, and especially of its intermediary part. Beyond dualistic as well as monistic accounts of the human soul, Aristotle holds that this intermediary part, the "desiring part," "somehow partakes [in *logos*] insofar as it listens to and can obey it in the sense in which we say 'taking account [*ekhein logon*] of both one's father and one's friends'" (*NE* I, 13, 1102b31–1103a3). As capable of listening to *logos*, of obeying or resisting it, this intermediary part has been shown to include not only habits (*ethos*) (section 1), but, more crucially, positive states (*hexis*) (section 2), and especially ones according to *logos* (section 3). Thus we tried to show that Aristotle construes virtue, especially moral virtue, neither merely as a natural potentiality nor as an acquired habit, but as a settled and free positive state of deliberating according to *logos*, that is, of interpreting particular situations beyond the mutually exclusive options of mere adherence and indifference. Our discussion of freedom, shame, deliberation, and character painting demonstrated the inadequacy of the exclusive options of past and present, of passivity and activity, of nature and nurture, and of self and other. Once again we came across the fundamental meaning of *logos*: a relation holding on to its terms without letting one yield, or remain indifferent, to the other.

Desire has *logos* in the sense in which we say "taking account" of both one's father and one's friends. Having *logos*, the human being takes account of others as herself and of herself as others—especially as "those who will always be with them" (*Rh.* II, 6, 1384a35–38). But who are they? One does not choose one's family, and especially one's parents, one's "father." But one can become a person who chooses one's friends in the polis precisely beyond the family circle. In so far as the question of ethics depends not only on one's father but also on one's friends, we must move beyond the framework of the household and make our way into the horizon of the polis.

CHAPTER 6

Speech

Logos *in the* Politics

So far we have seen three major senses of *logos* in Aristotle: "standard" in chapters 1 and 2, "ratio" in chapters 3 and 4, and "reason" in chapter 5. In each of these senses, I have argued, *logos* refers to a relation holding its terms together in their difference instead of collapsing one to the other or keeping them in indifference. In this last chapter, I turn to the fourth and last major meaning of *logos*, namely "speech." It is in this sense that Aristotle famously says: "the human being alone among animals has *logos*"[1] (*Pol.* I, 1, 1253a10–11). Yet, in the Aristotelian corpus, we do not find a unitary account of speech, any more than a unitary account of *logos*; instead we find scattered remarks that remain to be gathered and unified. It is this Aristotelian account of speech that I shall try to bring together here.

To do this, in section 1, I shall turn to animal communication, especially the modes of animal hearing directed at three different objects: noise, voice, and buzz. This will allow me, in section 2, to propose three fundamental features of speech as specifically human communication: mediation, articulation, ambiguity. By means of these three features, I shall analyze the first articulation of human speech,[2] that is, very roughly speaking, the articulation of "letters" into "words." Then, in section 3, I shall analyze the second articulation of human speech, that is, again very roughly speaking, the articulation of "words" into "sentences." This analysis will show that, while the moods of animal communication are comparable to the imperative and subjunctive, there are two moods of specifically human communication: the indicative and the optative. Here I will draw the conclusion that *logos* as speech is *the specifically human capacity for both understanding and relaying non-firsthand experience as well as firsthand experience.* In section 4, I shall test this interpretation of *logos*, and draw its implications, by confronting it with three major Aristotelian texts: *Categories*, 1, *Metaphysics*, I, 1, and indeed the famous opening of the *Politics*.

Such an interpretation of *logos* is indispensable for accounting for human predication, human experience, human community, and major aspects of the specifically human condition such as mythology, history, science, utopian fiction, philosophy, and sophistry. Even further, this final sense of *logos* as "speech" also refers to the fundamental meaning of *logos* we encountered throughout this book: specifically human communication involves apparently contradictory terms (experiences that are made firsthand, and ones that are not, will not, or even cannot be made firsthand) without reducing one to the other, or letting them remain indifferent to one another. Only then will we see that the very question of the "*logos* of being" that initiated this book (e.g., "What is it *for an ox* to be?") can actually only be asked by a being equipped with *logos* as the capacity of understanding and relaying *non-firsthand experience* as well as firsthand experience. The question of the "*logos* of being" presents itself only to a being having *logos*.

1. Animal Communication

Are bees capable of hearing according to Aristotle? This is a seemingly innocent question concerning quite a local phenomenon in "second philosophy." But, in fact, it already calls for witness the famous opening of Aristotle's "first philosophy," the *Metaphysics*, according to which the answer seems no:

> The [animals] that cannot hear *psophoi* are intelligent but cannot learn, such as a bee or any other kind of animal that might be such. (*Metaph.* I, 1, 980b23)

Yet at least two passages in the *History of Animals*, IX, suggest otherwise. The first one implies that bees do hear:

> When a swarm is about to take flight, a monotonous and peculiar voice happens [*phônê monôtis kai idios*][3] for some days, and two or three days beforehand some fly around the hive; whether the king is among these has not yet been observed because it is not easy. (*HA* IX, 40, 625b9–10; Balme's translation slightly modified)

A couple of pages later, another passage is more straightforwardly affirmative:

> At daybreak [bees] are silent until one bee arouses them by buzzing [*bombêsasa*] two or three times. Then they all fly out together to work, and on returning they are noisy [*thorybousi*] at first but

> gradually become less so until a single bee flies around buzzing [*bombêsêi*] as though making a sign [*hôsper sêmainousa*] for sleep; then suddenly they are silent. (*HA* IX, 40, 627a24–28; Balme's translation)[4]

Here we seem to face an inconsistency between Aristotle's negative position on the subject of bee hearing in the *Metaphysics* and his affirmative stance in the *History of Animals*, IX. As the so-called principle of the "excluded middle,"[5] famously first formulated by Aristotle besides the "principle of non-contradiction,"[6] forbids bees from being neither deaf nor not deaf, Balme attempted to settle the problem by assigning the two conflicting texts to different periods of Aristotle's career, claiming that he changed his mind between them.[7] This philological solution as such brings about three problems: first, generally, anyone's conflicting views can be reconciled once we assign them to different times; secondly, this solution does not answer why the author changed his mind and in what direction; and finally, in this context, such an isolation of the two conflicting claims does not help anyway, since skepticism about bees' ability to hear shows up in the following passage from the very *HA*, IX, 40, which seemed to defend it:

> Bees seem to like the rattle,[8] and so people say they collect them into the hive by rattling pots and counters.[9] It is not clear, however, if they hear it at all,[10] and whether they act thus through pleasure or through fear.[11] (*HA* IX, 40, 627a15–19; Balme's translation slightly modified)

So, assigning the *Metaphysics* and the *History of Animals* passages to two different periods does not help us know whether or not Aristotle believed bees to be capable of hearing. Then, without venturing to philologically date conflicting claims to different periods of Aristotle's career, let us attempt to philosophically interpret his seemingly ambiguous remarks in a way that makes them compatible, even mutually supportive and philosophically interesting.

Noise

For perhaps the ambiguity does not lie in Aristotle's position to begin with. Besides being the first to formulate the two "principles" mentioned above, he also famously and typically appeals to a disambiguation of our apparently univocal everyday words.[12] So in this case, the ambiguity may lie in the Ancient Greek verb *akouein*, "to hear," itself. Grammatically, this verb is often followed either by a genitive or by an accusative, mostly meaning "to listen to, to learn from"[13] or "to hear something, not *listen to*" respectively.[14] More interesting, perhaps, is the variation of the verb's meaning according to what the object is heard *as*. These distinctions may help us solve the apparent contradiction about Aristotle's position on bee hearing, not by appealing to chronological or philological emendations, but by recognizing the ambiguity of the verb as such and disentangling it.

Let us start with the *Metaphysics* passage. Here the verb takes the genitive and its object is *psophoi*, and almost all English and French translations of the *Metaphysics* translate *psophos* as "sound":[15] "The [animals] that cannot hear sounds [*hosa mê dynatai tôn psophôn akouein*] are intelligent but cannot learn, such as a bee or any other kind of animal that might be such" (*Metaph.* I, 1, 980b23). According to the distinctions above, Aristotle is claiming not that bees are simply deaf, but that they cannot listen to, or learn from, *psophoi*. What does *psophos* mean? What is the process of its production and reception? What does it mean to say that bees are unable to listen to or learn from it, as opposed to other unnamed species? And how does this align with the two passages from the *History of Animals*?

In Aristotle as well as in Ancient Greek, *psophos* is defined generically as the acoustic effect of one thing striking another. "Sound [*psophos*] comes to be in actuality always from something against something and in something, for it is the striking that produces it. Therefore if there is one [thing only], sound is impossible" (*DA* II, 8, 419b9–12). Sound results from the shock of a body against another unable to yield immediately, "for the motion of the thing striking must outrun the yielding of the air" (*DA* II, 8, 419b22–24).[16] Solid, smooth, and hollow things sound best, "because they produce many blows after the first one by bouncing back and forth, while what is moved is unable to get out" and sound expands as long as the medium is continuous and one (*DA* II, 8, 419b16–18, 34–35).[17]

One way of reacting to sound would be to reverberate or reflect it. If reverberation and reflection are not emissions of sound, they certainly are transmissions. However, as we know from chapter 4, to *perceive* a sound is a phenomenon fundamentally different from transmitting it. This is trivially clear from the fact that the lyre or the bell, when struck, does not hear, any more than a loudspeaker or a recorder, whereas the ear of an animal does hear. As we saw, "sensation is *logos*" (*DA* III, 2, 426b7; II, 12), but in a different way than the strings of lyre stand in a certain ratio or proportion in the eyes of the lyrist. Sensation requires the simultaneous grasp of the state of the sense organ *and* of the state of the object *without* letting one yield to the other. To let the organ yield to the medium would not be sensation, but reverberation; and, as we saw, to have the organ overpower the medium would amount not to sensation either, but to sound production.

In hearing, "when the [air] outside is moved, the [air] inside is moved too" (*DA* II, 8, 420a5–6; *PA* II, 10, 656b16). But the actually hearing ear does not simply yield to or overpower the motion of the incoming air: "the [air] in the ear has been walled in so as to be unmoved in order that there might be an accurate sensation of all differences of motion" (*DA* II, 8, 420a9–12).[18] To say that sensation is *logos* means nothing other than that all sensation is sensation of difference and thus requires a way of holding together the terms that are being differentiated. All sensation is sensation of a *between*, a stretch *between*: "Hearing is of the differences of sound."[19] For Aristotle, sensation is not only an undergoing or doing, but a kind of "discrimination," *krisis*.[20]

By simultaneously holding together and discriminating the motions of air inside and outside the sense organ,[21] hearing reveals to the animal the vast realm of relatively smooth, solid, hollow, and relatively quick-moving objects. But since we saw that hearing as a kind of distant perception implies locomotion for Aristotle in chapter 4, we may also infer that the animal that is the *subject* of hearing also becomes its probable *object* precisely because of its ability to move. Theoretically, all that can hear can also be heard, but indeed not the other way around. As more unimpeded and less oriented than the eyes in most animals, hearing is less restricted by the distinction between the back and the front, the left and the right, the up and down. Hearing in this sense is less focused than circumspective, opens less a *point* of view or a perspective than a surrounding, an environment, a horizon of hearing and being heard. To return to bees, if the *Metaphysics* is claiming that bees are incapable of hearing *psophos* in this generic sense of "sound," any acoustic phenomenon, then they should be simply deaf, and in that case the text conflicts with the passages from the *History of Animals*.

But, in fact, Liddell, Scott, and Jones's *Ancient Greek Lexicon* renders *psophos* not generically with "sound," but specifically with "noise."[22] It even opposes this specific sense to other acoustic phenomena exemplified in Aristotle's biology.[23] That Aristotle doubts that bees hear noise is corroborated by his skepticism about their hearing the rattling pots and counters in a passage quoted above. If *psophos* means not "sound" in its generic sense, but specifically "noise," then the *Metaphysics* passage might be claiming that bees are somehow deaf to noise only, and this passage might be brought in line with the passages in *HA*, IX, 40, that assume that bees are capable of hearing.

Yet what, if anything, would it mean to say that bees are deaf to noise, but not to all sound? What are the animal species capable of hearing noise that remained unnamed in the *Metaphysics*?[24] And further, why does the passage associate the hearing of noises with the capacity for learning (*manthanein*)? We may gather an answer from Aristotle's description of animal species that *are* capable of hearing *psophoi*:

> Among the small birds, some when singing send forth a different voice [*phônên aphiasin*] from their parents, if they have been reared away from the nest and have listened to other birds singing [*allôn akousôsin ornithôn aidontôn*]. A hen nightingale has before now been observed teaching [*prodidaskousa*] her chick to sing, which suggests that the "song" does not come naturally in the same way as *dialektos*[25] and voice [*phônês*], but is capable of being shaped [*plattesthai*]. (*HA* IV, 9, 536b14–18; Peck's translation modified)

So some small bird species, for example, nightingales, do hear "noise," that is acoustic phenomena regardless of its origin and meaning. The kind of learning they are capable of, unlike bees, results from *akouein* followed by the genitive, that is, from the listening to and learning from an external acoustic stimulus, with the consequence that the animal reproduces it mimetically.[26] "Song" does not "come naturally," but rather can be "shaped." Then, according to the *Metaphysics* passage, bees are not deaf of sound as such, but to noise, unlike some small bird species; more specifically, they are incapable of receiving the acoustic effect or a shock as such, and of relaying it without understanding it.

Voice

But deaf as they are to noise according to the *Metaphysics*, what *are* bees capable of hearing in the passages of the *History of Animals*? We saw that "when a swarm is about to take flight, a monotonous and peculiar voice [*phônê monôtis kai idios*] happens for some days" (*HA* IX, 40, 625b9–10). This suggests that bees are capable of hearing voice: *phônê*.[27] If so, our apparent contradiction may be solved by stating that bees are sensitive to voice only, and not to noise, as some imitating bird species are.

Yet this is impossible. Aristotle insistently and clearly denies that insects can utter "voice" in the strict sense of the word. "Now the only part of the body with which an animal can utter a voice [*phônei*] is the pharynx" (*HA* IV, 9, 535a29–31; *DA* II, 8, 420b10). In general voice is a sound produced by an animal, "but not by any random part" (*DA* II, 8, 420b14); technically speaking, it is "the striking of inhaled air against the part called the 'windpipe' by the action of the soul in these parts" (*DA* II, 8, 420b27–29, 14–17). So the production of voice requires that the animal neither inhale nor exhale, but withhold air, "for the one who withholds [air] moves it" (*DA* II, 8, 421a2–4).[28] Unlike the continuous alteration of inhaling and exhaling in respiration, voice has a discontinuous character. And unlike the immediate mimetic relay of sound by some bird species, voice presents a certain reflexivity or middle state in the animal body. Furthermore, in voice production, the respiratory functions of the lungs, the windpipe, the tongue, and of the air within and without are all reorganized.[29] Thus, voice production entails reorganization in the organic body as well as in the animal's relation to its environment. This reorganization is made in such a way that voice is reducible neither to the effect of a motion against another motion where the striking object is external to the object struck, nor simply to a sound coming from within the animal body.[30]

Buzz

Bees match none of these physiological requirements for uttering voice. Since the "monotonous and peculiar voice" mentioned above is nevertheless uttered by a bee, could bees be capable of producing a counterpart (*analogon*) of voice?[31]

This counterpart to voice is *bombos*, the "buzz." The parallelism between voice and buzz can be found in their respective physiology. The "striking of inhaled air against the 'windpipe'" in breathing animals is clearly paralleled in the "friction of the internal *pneuma*" in some insects, such that the buzzing bee presents a reflexivity and reorganization analogous to the ones with which we previously characterized the uttering of voice:[32]

> Thus insects produce neither voice nor speech [*oute phônei oute dialegetai*], though they produce a sound [*psophei*] by their internal *pneuma* (not externally emitted *pneuma*, for none of them breathes), but some of them buzz [*bombei*], for instance the bee and other winged insects, and some 'sing' as the saying is, e.g., the cicada. All these insects produce a sound [*psophei*] by means of the membrane which is under the *hypozoma* [the division between thorax and abdomen] (this of course refers to those whose bodies are divided at this point), e.g., a certain kind of cicada, which makes the sound by friction of the *pneuma* [against the membrane]; and so do flies and bees and all the others, as by their flying they produce the lifting and contracting movement: the noise [*psophos*] is actually the friction of the internal *pneuma*. (*HA* IV, 9, 535b3–12; Peck's translation)

So Aristotle has an account of buzzing, although unfortunately he has pretty much nothing to tell us about the physiology of bees' hearing.[33] There are two texts that support the parallelism between breathing animals and insects such as bees: *On Sleep and Waking* 2, 456a11ff., and *On Respiration* 9, 474b31ff. In these, the external *pneuma* inhaled by breathing animals is correlated with the internal *pneuma* of insects; the second text correlates the lung motion of breathing animals, the movement of fishes' gills, and the friction against the membrane in insects.

However, the parallel drawn here is not between voice and buzz, but between the motion of respiration in breathing animals and the motion of buzzing in some insects. In other words, if there is a kind of buzzing among bees that is a counterpart to voice production, it must be not a constant sound (*psophos*) comparable to the heartbeat,[34] but a different buzz that is discontinuous and occasional. This character of the buzzing becomes manifest when we mark the temporal qualifications in our second passage from the *HA* IX, 40:

> At *daybreak* they are silent *until* one bee arouses them by buzzing [*bombêsasa*] *two or three times*. Then they all fly out together to work, and *on returning* they are noisy [*thorybousi*] *at first* but *gradually* become less so *until* a single bee flies around buzzing [*bombêsêi*] as though making a sign [*hôsper sêmainousa*] for sleep; *then suddenly* they are silent. (*HA* IX, 40, 627a24–28; Balme's translation, our emphases)

It is clear that Aristotle distinguishes the "making noise" (in this case, *thorybein*) and the "buzzing" (*bombein*). Hence, this passage brings us to the most crucial aspect of the parallelism between voice and the buzz, and to what distinguishes both from noise. Whereas it was unclear above whether bees acted "through pleasure or through fear" upon hearing the rattle, here the buzz is explicitly said to be heard *as though meaningful* (*hôsper sêmainousa*). In voice, unlike noise, "the striking object must be ensouled and have some imagination [with it], for in fact voice is a signifying sound, but not [signifying] the inhaled air as a cough" (*DA* II, 8, 420b31–421a1). While sound as such is simply *of something against something*, "voice is a sound of an ensouled being" (*DA* II, 8, 420b6).[35] Even further, "voice is a sound of an animal" (*DA* II, 8, 420b13–14). Voice production is always coupled with the animal's capacity for sensation and, probably, for locomotion. Thus, a voice is a quite explicit demand for "attention" coming from, and addressed to, an animal. Whereas sound means friction or excess of *touch*, voice is of an animal making *contact*.

The primary phenomenon of voice, and of the discontinuous buzz in bees, is thus a demand for attention, a call, even a kind of claim.

For, most importantly, "voice is a sign [*sêmeion*] of the painful and pleasant" (*Pol.* I, 1, 1253a11–14). Regardless of whether it is reflex or deliberately encoded, an "effect" or a "message" of pleasure and pain, voice seems thus infused with desire just as locomotion.[36] Like voice, locomotion is an embodiment of pleasure and pain in the forms of flight from, and pursuit of, particular objects. And yet, the structure of voice cannot be reduced to the "practical syllogism" of locomotion, because voice is precisely *not* flight or pursuit, but rather a "sign." In light of this, the animal making such a "sign" may be doing so precisely because the object of interest is *not* attainable by the motion of the individual animal. One obvious example of this is reproduction which mostly necessitates a cooperation between male and female (*Pol.* I, 1, 1252a).[37] This also ties in with the animals' use of voice for calling their lost babies.[38] Voice conveys a "particular premise" ("this is pleasant" or "this is painful") to *another* animal in order that they move *together*. Subjoining a "particular premise" to desire for a possible cooperation, voice is inherently "tactical," assuming the mood of a subjunctive or *hypotaktikê* in later Greek grammar.

If so, whereas the mechanical reproduction of a sound or noise never becomes a premise, being meaningless and disinterested in itself, the "practical syllogism" of voice and buzzing operates in an environment of *common* interest and desire, in a minimal possible community through which individuals are not only formed out of organs, but themselves become part of a possible "organization" or *taxis* for fleeing danger and pursuing common pleasure. An animal that emits a voice in order to mark its territory, to mate, to threat, to find its babies, or to warn another animal is in each case an animal that perceives the means of its desire beyond its own immediate motion or rest and thus convokes another for cooperation. Uttering voice or buzzing implies the significance of others animals and, to some degree, of their perspective, their interests, their evaluation. Voice and the buzz thus are not marked by the immediacy of the individual animal's flight or pursuit that resulted in the "practical syllogism," since they demand immediate cooperation *from another*. They constitute a motion withheld in the individual animal's body in order to be translated into the language of common interest, an outer organ used to reorder the world *with* and also *for* others. For Aristotle, it is precisely this common work that characterizes political animals such as human beings, wasps, ants, and bees (*HA* I, 1, 488a7–10).

So, we are back to bees. Now that we have seen that voice, or its counterpart "buzz," is essentially infused with a meaningful and interested project of cooperation, we can accept Aristotle's position in the *Metaphysics* while also making more sense of our two passages from the *History of Animals*: in the first passage in the *History of Animals*, the bees' hearing the "monotonous and peculiar voice" was immediately followed by their preparation to take flight; in the second passage, they clearly go to sleep and wake up upon hearing the buzz. In both cases, the bees seem to immediately move cooperatively in reaction to the buzz of another bee, and probably not to the sound of the rattle. While, as the *Metaphysics* suggests, some bird species are able to perceive and relay *noise* regardless of its meaning, of its source, or of the interests involved by the sender, the passages in the *History of Animals* show that bees immediately receive *voice*, or more specifically, *buzz*, as a meaningful and interested call to cooperation or synergy.[39]

This brings us to the third meaning of the verb *akouein*, again typically followed by the genitive: "to obey."[40] The Homeric examples denote obedience to a king (*Iliad*, XIX, 256) or a people's hearkening to a king as to a god (*Odyssey*, VII, 11). This converges with the idea that bees have a "king"[41] whose voice they "listen" to, not in order to imitate and thus relay the sound heard, but in order to execute his orders. In fact Aristotle says that "it is commonly agreed that [bees] follow [*epakolouthein*] the kings because their birth depends on these bees (for if there were no such dependence, the facts concerning their hegemony [*ta symbainonta peri tên hêgemonian autôn*] would have no reason)" (*GA* III, 10, 760b15–18).[42] This detail may explain why, in an earlier passage, we saw Aristotle expecting the "king" to be among the bees that alert the others for the approaching flight, saying "whether the king is among these has not yet been observed because it is not easy" (*HA* IX, 40, 625b9–10). Unlike noise hearing, immediately relayed by imitation regardless of its content or source without any particular mood, the cooperation implied in voice is injunctive and imperial ("hegemonic") in character, and its mood is the imperative (*prostaktikê*). In hearing noise, some bird species relay without understanding; in hearing voice, bees do not relay, but understand and obey.[43]

So are bees capable of hearing according to Aristotle after all? We saw that the answer is yes. But more importantly, we saw that this question was flawed, for it assumes a false dilemma that may lead one to "solve" it by dating the "contradictory" texts to different periods of Aristotle's career. A better formulation of the question is the following: what exactly, if anything, are bees capable of hearing according to Aristotle? The exact answer is the following: not *psophos* in the generic sense of "sound," nor *psophos* in the specific sense of "noise," nor voice as such, but a counterpart of voice, namely the buzz, or to be as exact as possible, not the continuous buzz, but the discontinuous and occasional buzz. This disambiguation solves the apparent contradiction between the texts:[44] the *Metaphysics* passage emphasizes that bees are incapable of hearing noises in the sense of meaningless acoustic objects to be relayed, and hence of learning in the sense of imitating, reproducing, and relaying them; whereas the two *HA* passages point out that they *are* capable of hearing, if not voice per se, at least its counterpart, the discontinuous and occasional buzz, acoustic objects as meaningful and interested calls for cooperation.[45] Some bird species are capable of relaying without understanding, while bees understand but do not relay.[46]

2. Human Speech: From "Letters" to "Words"

As we just saw, some bird species are capable of relaying non-firsthand experiences without understanding their content. Honeybees, on the other hand, show themselves able to understand the content of non-firsthand experiences, but they do not relay them to yet another honeybee. In this section and in the following one, I shall propose and develop the following claim: the ability to both understand and relay non-firsthand experience as well as firsthand experience is precisely what Aristotle means by *logos* in the exclusively human sense of "speech." As in the other three major senses of *logos*, namely "standard," "ratio," and "reason," the meaning of *logos* as "speech" is thus again a kind of relation, of gathering, of inclusiveness between terms that previously may have seemed mutually exclusive or indifferent: contents of firsthand experience, *and* contents that are not, may not be, or even cannot be, experienced firsthand.

Previously, we distinguished three senses of the Ancient Greek verb *akouein*: sound hearing, voice hearing, and listening in the sense of obeying. Yet there is a fourth sense of *akouein*: "understand, [to] take *in a certain sense*."[47] This definition suggests that what is heard here may be taken *in another sense*. Then what is heard is somehow not straightforward, but fundamentally opaque, unlike voice which, as we saw, "comes naturally" and cannot be "shaped" (*HA* IV, 9, 536b14–18). The message here is not just taken in naturally and entirely, but remains open to interpretation and indeed misinterpretation, leaving a gap between sound and meaning. In this kind of *akouein*, we then move from the fact of having sense to the task of making sense. In short, according to the definition, the object of this kind of hearing is characterized by three features: mediation, articulation, and ambiguity.

Mediation

So indeed is *logos* in the sense of "speech," as I shall now try to demonstrate by bringing together Aristotle's scattered remarks on the matter.

Mediation is clearly found in Aristotelian remarks concerning human speech. As speech, *logos* is never immediate, just as it never is in any sense in Aristotle. More specifically, even the material of speech is not immediate as voice is. There are passages in Aristotle which suggest that the material of speech is voice.[48] And yet other passages stress that the voices to be used as material of speech are modified: "Now speech is signifying not with voice, but with its modifications [*pathê*], and not because [the one who utters speech] takes pleasure or suffers" (*Prob.* 10, 895a4–14).[49] The rest of this passage names the unit through which *logos* is articulated out of voices: "Letters [*grammata*] are modifications of voice." Then the specific material of *logos* is "letters":[50] "Speech is composed of letters through voice" (*PA* II, 16, 660a3–4). The mediation that makes *logos* possible and distinguishes it from other acoustic phenomena involves the production of letters, and this production differs from voice production both physiologically and semantically.

First, the physiology of the production of letters differs from that of voice production. We saw that the production of voice involves the pharynx and lungs, and also a special use of the windpipe.[51] Speech, however, is produced by means of the mouth, the teeth, the larynx, the pitch of the voice, tongue, and the lips.[52] "The voice and the larynx send forth the vowels, and the tongue and the lips the consonants, of which language [*dialektos*] is constituted" (*HA* IV, 9, 535a29–b1). Thus letters are not only a selection of voices, they are distinguished among themselves into two interrelated groups. While vowels have an audible voice, some letters have a voice only in conjunction with vowels: "A consonant is that which has no voice by itself with *prosbolê*, but becomes audible with one that has voice" (*Po.* 20, 1456b28–29). The production of consonants involves a new physiological aspect, *prosbolê* and *symbolê*: "Speech is composed of letters through voice; but if the tongue was not this way, or if the lips were not wet, most of the letters could not be uttered; for some are impacts [*prosbolê*] of the tongue, some are closings [*symbolê*] of the lips" (*PA* II, 16, 660a4–7). Thus, just as the production of vowels brought into play the larynx, now consonants engage the lips and the tongue:

> Voice and sound are different, and language [*dialektos*] is a third. No part ever emits voice apart from the pharynx; thus, those that have no lungs, never utter; but language is the articulation [*diarthrôsis*] of voice by means of the tongue: the voice and the larynx send forth the vowels, the tongue and the lips [send forth] the consonants, of which language is constituted. Therefore those that have no tongue or no loose tongue do not use language [*dialegetai*]. But sounding belongs to other parts as well. Thus, insects neither emit voice, nor

> use language, but emit sound to the interior of their lungs, not outside. (*HA* IV, 9, 535a27-b5; 536a32–536b4)

Thus Aristotle distinguishes a letter from sounds, from voices, from vowels if the letter is a consonant, or from consonants if it is a vowel, and finally from other vowels if it is a vowel, and from other consonants if it is a consonant. For instance, the "letter" /u/ heard or produced as a letter is determined in a fourfold way: it is not a wuthering (not only a sound); it is not a howl (not only a voice); it is neither /b/ nor /t/ nor /s/, and so on (not a consonant); it is neither /a/ nor /e/ nor /i/, and so on (not any vowel).

Hence, learning a new language requires not only that one widens the range of one's phonatory equipment quantitatively, but also that one modifies it qualitatively. For uttering new letters requires a new cooperation between the larynx, the lungs, or the lips and tongue. Even at the apparently rudimentary level of sound production, the acquisition of a new language demands an extensive rehabituation of the body. Thus the mediated character of speech can be seen in the physiological aspect of its production through letters.

Just as the basic material of speech involves a meticulous process of production, the reception of a letter *as a letter* also involves a quite sharp perception or intricate discrimination of acoustic differences. This is reminiscent of Aristotle's wonder in front of the distinct perception (*diaisthanesthai*) that some bird species are capable of (*HA* IX, 1, 608a17–21). One may claim that, for Aristotle, languages differ from one another not only in their syntax, grammar, and vocabulary, but all the way down to their letters.[53] Thus, the ear tended toward letters is tended toward something that is not simply a sound, because letters are not reducible to physical shocks and strokes; not simply voice, because letters are not *any* voice, but a selection of voices; not simply a voice from within a selection, because letters are also modified physiologically and acoustically by the distinction between consonants and vowels; and not simply a preselected acoustic unit that has a voice either independently or dependently, because consonants are finally differentiated from the other consonants, and vowels from the other vowels.[54]

Yet the crucial aspect of the mediated character of speech is not physiological, but semantic. Because letters are meaningless.[55] While voice is itself meaningful and composed out of meaningful parts, *logos* is meaningful, but composed out of *meaningless* parts. Beyond a merely physiological modification of voice, letters involves a fundamental semantic modification of voice, of one's relation to desire, to meaning, and to others. To learn to speak is not to add cries and shouts in various combinations, it is to recharge voice at its natural roots. Even to supply the material which speech will further articulate, one must not only learn to reorchestrate one's respiration, larynx, tongue, and lips, but, most importantly, one must be able to "redefine," as it were, one's most elemental pleasures and pains. Just as animal voice was possible only by refraining from both inhalation and exhalation, from both flight and pursuit, here the basic material of speech requires that one *not* emit a voice, that one go beyond the dilemma of invoking or threatening others. To learn letters is to fundamentally modify one's behavior in order to learn to commit the voice and silence of one's body to others.

There is textual evidence in Aristotle for the psychological significance and ethical exemplariness of learning letters. The *Nicomachean Ethics* uses *grammatikê*, "literacy,"as a paradigmatic kind of knowledge, and as an example of a positive state: it is by performing literacy that one becomes literate (*NE* II, 3, 1105a20). Yet literacy is not merely a matter of imitation:

> One may in fact write letters by chance or with the support of another. One will then become literate only when, while writing letters, one does in a literate way, that is, according to the literacy in oneself. (*NE* II, 3, 1105a22–24)

Hence literacy is defined not only by knowing how to write, but also by knowing how to read (*Topics* VI, 5, 142b31). It is this crucial aspect of literacy, its being "in oneself," that distinguishes it from all kinds of imitation, however perfect, as the ones we saw some bird species to be capable of. Hence language for Aristotle is psychological, ethical, and political all the way down to its material. No wonder listening to speech, or reading, contributes most to learning and prudence:

> Hearing conveys the differences of sounds, but in some animals it also conveys the differences of voice. Incidentally hearing makes the largest contribution to prudence, for speech is the cause of learning by being audible, but it is audible not in itself but incidentally, for speech is composed of nouns and each noun is a symbol. (*De Sensu* 1, 437a10–15)

As we saw, voice is meaningful through and through. It is a natural outer "organ" intended to "organize" others by means of orders (the imperative mood) and threats or promises (the subjunctive mood). Letters, however, precisely evacuate meaning from voice, revert the natural reorganization of voice, and *stop* invoking others for the sake of its desire. It is on the foundation of such negation that speech can be mediated in a strong sense by means of "letters," that speech can be "taken *in a certain sense*," and that a letter can have a function without having a meaning.

Articulation

My use of the word "articulation" here may remind the reader of a concept introduced in twentieth-century linguistics: "double articulation" (Martinet) or "duality of patterning" (Hockett)—the articulation of meaningless units ("phonemes") into meaningful units ("morphemes"), and the articulation of these meaningful units into syntactic wholes. This is not a coincidence. For, when talking about the formation of words, Aristotle explicitly and insistently uses a word that means the process of organic differentiation in the embryo, *diarthrôsis*, "articulation":[56]

> Voice and sound are different, and language [*dialektos*] is a third. No part ever emits voice apart from the pharynx; thus, those that have no lungs, never utter; but language is the *diarthrôsis* of voice by means of the tongue. (*HA* IV, 9, 535a27–b1; 536a32–b4)

So is there a parallel between the articulation of speech and the formation of the embryo?[57]

On a lower level, voice is comparable to elements constitutive of organic bodies: both voice and elements lack *logos*. We saw in chapter 3 that fire was ever too complete to be proportioned into the growth of an organism ("fire grows without any limit or *logos*");[58] similarly, the voice of a crying baby is already too meaningful to be *integrated into* a meaningful whole. On the higher level too, *logos* is comparable to the organic body: just as the organic body is not reducible to an agglomerate of elements, but rather needs an intermediate level of articulation into nonuniform parts, similarly *logos* is irreducible to a series of natural "uniform voices" and requires the intermediate level of articulation into highly determined, "modified," and meaningless units, namely letters.[59] So, just as elements cannot account for *diarthrôsis* in the sense of organic formation, voice cannot account for *diarthrôsis* in the sense of the articulation of speech. In both cases, *diarthrôsis* names a process which goes beyond mere uniform units.

The word Aristotle uses for "uniform unit" in these contexts is *stoikheion*, meaning alternatively "natural element" or "uniform voice." Aristotle's uses of this word support the parallelism above. *Stoikheia* account for voice, as it is "like water is part of water":[60] "The elements of a voice are that out of which voice is composed, and that into which it is ultimately divided, and these are not divided into other voices different from them with respect to their form"

(*Metaph.* V, 3, 1014a27–32).[61] Yet, unlike voice, speech, even a syllable, is not an agglomerate of elemental sounds, but rather an articulation of letters:

> The syllable is not its elements [*stoikheia*], nor is BA the same as B and A, nor is flesh fire and earth; because after dissolution they no longer exist, neither flesh nor the syllable, whereas the elements and both fire and earth do exist. Thus the syllable is something, yet not only its elements, vowels and consonants, but something else; and the flesh is not only fire and earth, or hot and cold, but something else. (*Metaph.* VII, 17, 1041b11–19)

Thus, the parallelism between organ formation and the formation of *logos* can be established: neither body parts nor speech parts are agglomerations of raw elements or *stoikheia*, since both require the articulation of a preformed material that has no meaning or life on its own, but only a function.

What is this function? What are letters articulated into? "*Logos* is a signifying voice, one of whose parts is signifying separately, not as an affirmation [*kataphasis*], but as an expression [*phasis*]" (*On Int.* 4, 16b26–28). Then letters, meaningless as such, are articulated into an expression that is separately meaningful.[62] Whatever the vague word *phasis* exactly means,[63] Aristotle says: "Let noun and verb be the only expressions" (*On Int.* 5, 17a17–18). So letters are ultimately articulated into nouns and verbs, the result of the first level of the articulation of *logos*.[64]

Nouns, the products of the first articulation of speech, introduce three aspects that define speech: its conventional (*kata synthêkên*),[65] composite (*synthetê*),[66] and symbolic character (*symbolê*).[67] So firstly, with regard to the *conventional* character of nouns, we saw that speech is irreducible to a series of natural voices.[68] Since letters were already conventional, it is not surprising to see that a noun, and a fortiori full-fledged speech, signify "according to a convention" and not as an "organ" (*On Int.* 2, 16a20–21; 4, 16b33–17a2). Aristotle explains: "According to a convention, because no noun is by nature, but when a symbol comes to be; letterless [*agrammatoi*] sounds, for instance those of wild beasts, *do* make something manifest, but none of them is a noun" (*On Int.* 2, 16a26–29). In Ancient Greek, *synthêkê* means "a compound," but also "convention," especially in Aristotle and Plato, and it is usually contrasted to the "natural." A voice as such is never a noun any more than it is a letter, because voice does not signify by means of a convention. One never hears a voice *as voice* in a noun, nor a noun *as noun* in a voice.

Secondly, as to the *composite* character of nouns, this should not be surprising to us either. For we already saw that a noun uses a certain kind of voice as material. The sound /u/ may well happen to correspond to the English second-person pronoun ("you"), or the name of the letter *u*, or a voice (an expression of surprise), or even a sound (the wuthering of the wind). Yet such an ambiguity does not disprove the existence of differences, but proves it: /u/ may be one of all four *because* there *is* a fourfold distinction to begin with. To take the wuthering of the wind for a dog howling, or a dog howling for the pronoun "you," is precisely a case of confusion between distinct registers. Because languages are conventionally determined all the way down to their basic constituents, we can hear nouns or verbs as mere voices or sounds only by *forcefully* abstracting their meaning, particular situation, or context.[69]

The third characteristic of nouns, their *symbolic* character, is new to us. For, while letters are no more symbolic than voice, nouns come to be "when a *symbolon* comes to be" (*On Int.* 2, 16a28). In fact, *On Interpretation* opens with this idea: "Those in the voice are symbols of the affections in the soul" (*On Int.* 1, 16a3–4). Then, the composite and conventional character of a noun goes together with its being a *symbolon*. But what does *symbolon* mean? Closely related to *symbolê* which appeared above as the "closing of lips" in our discussion of the physiology of voice production (*PA* II, 16, 660a7), Aristotle uses the word *symbolon* in meanings that are pretty much unrelated to the English word "symbol": it means a "complementary factor" in the context of Empedocles's understanding of the relation between male and female (*GA* I, 18, 722b12); it appears in the context of air's being composed out of the wet and the hot "as from *symbola*" (*Mete.* II, 4, 360a26); and it is used in the context of the generation of a constitutional government "taking a *symbolon*" from both oligarchy and democracy (*Pol.* IV, 7, 1294a35).

Most concretely *symbolon* means a "*tally*, i.e., *each of two halves* or *corresponding pieces* of an astragalos or other object, which two *xenoi*, or any two contracting parties, broke between them, each party keeping one piece, in order to have proof of the identity of the presenter of the other."[70] This last and most concrete sense of *symbolon* best designates the conventionally and compositely significant character of nouns or verbs. For, whereas the hot and the wet, male and female, democracy and oligarchy have a certain existence apart from the other, a tally by itself means nothing at all. If it means at all, it does so only potentially.[71] For, before broken into two tallies or *symbola*, the *astragalos* is a bone, thus a natural organ. But once broken in two, it can no longer fulfill its natural function. When two strangers break an *astragalos* among them and deprive it from its first function, they instill the two pieces with a fundamentally new interdependent meaning: each tally designates its unique counterpart in distinction from all other tallies. Thereby the two holders of the tallies mutually identify themselves on the basis of the very moment of the unique breakage of the *astragalos*.

This sense of *symbolon* also sheds light on the kind of people the tally holders may be, and prefigures the fundamental role of speech in the founding of the polis. An *astragalos* taken as a bone may roughly match another bone: two relatives may have similar bone structures, and they may identify one another just by looking at such similarities. As a bone with a certain form (*eidos*), the *astragalos* may bring together relatives. Yet, once broken into two tallies, an *astragalos* may bring together *any* two people. This is why even strangers or guests can break *astragaloi*. Hence Aristotle uses *symbolon* in this sense of a "tally" being a "friend" to its counterpart and "stretching out" toward it to form a whole:

> But in a way the friendship of the opposite is also friendship of the good, for [opposites] stretch out [*oregetai*] toward one another through the middle. For they stretch out to one another as tallies do, because that way one middle thing results from both. (*EE* VII, 5, 1239b30–33)

This "one middle thing" resulting from both seems to be exactly the *symbolon*, an essential feature of nouns and hence of speech. Identification and *mis*identification do not become an issue in a context involving no strangers or guests, in the context of a household, a village, or an isolated city. This is certainly not neglected by the fifth- and fourth-century ancient Greek culture developing into cities with a background of their alliance against the Persians. Thus, Oedipus *misidentifies* himself and his parents only because *both* he is cast out of his fatherland Thebes *and* returns there afterwards. His mother fails to recognize his face and natural bone structure only because she is led astray by his conventional identity as the son of the king of Corinth or as the witty stranger that saved Thebes from the Sphinx. As we shall see better in our conclusion, the tragedy of *King Oedipus* pivots around human immersion in the conventional and symbolic character of *logos* and the open environment provided by the polis. For all characters, except Teiresias, are fixated on the ambiguity of the oracles and overinterpret them. Oedipus solves the Sphinx's riddle thanks to his dexterity in the face of this ambiguity. The tragedy is made possible because, as citizens, everybody in the play is thinking merely in terms of the conventional symbolism and compositeness of *logos*. On the contrary, again as we shall see in our conclusion, village life as such is fixated, not on ambiguity or homonymy, but on synonymy or literality. It is too closed to such conventional *mis*identification, because it is closed to conventional and symbolic identification.

So how does a noun work as a tally? What are the two tallies in our context? Arguably, one is the "sounds" uttered, and the other is the "affections of the soul." A tally is able to fulfill its function whether the bone is broken this way or that way *as long as both parties have one piece*; similarly, the affections of the soul may well be expressed by these sounds or those ones. It is precisely this contingency that we do not find in voice or natural organs. Considered as mere voice, a noun is as useless as a broken bone. It is precisely an inconsistent, unintelligible sequence of vocalized demands. But once one envisages a noun as a noun, as a meaningful unit that is conventionally combined out of meaningless units, then one embarks on a process of finding a matching tally—the meaning.[72]

This explains why for Aristotle a noun is quite a strong threshold for meaning. For he insists that the parts of a noun are meaningless. According to him, even a noun such as *Kallippos*, which is obviously a compound of *kalos* ("beautiful") and *hippos* ("horse"), is *not* composed out of meaningful parts (*On Int.* 2, 16a21–22; *Po.* 20, 1457a12–14). *Hippos* is indeed a noun on its own, but not as part of *Kallippos*. Just as the wind does not utter the voice /u/, and just as /a/ in "apple" is *not* a noun, /kalli/ is *not* meaningful in *Kallippos*. The meaning of a noun is not to be found in the meaning of its parts. Further, just as *hippos* in *Kallippos* does not count as a noun, neither does "not-human" (which is an "indefinite noun") nor "Philon's" (which is a declension), "because it is not true or false with 'is,' 'was' or 'will be'" (*On Int.* 2, 16a29–16b3). So if for Aristotle a noun is a strong threshold of meaning, it is because a noun depends on whether it will contribute to a truth or falsity when it is coupled with the verb "to be." This is the first clue of the meaning of "meaning": the possibility of truth or falsity when coupled with the verb "to be." Presumably this is why the noun, and not the verb, constitutes the first articulation of speech.

As to verbs, Aristotle has similar strong restrictions: compound verbs are *not* composed out of nouns and verbs that by themselves have meaning (*Po.* 20, 1457a15); a form like "isn't recovering" does not count as a verb, it is only an "indefinite verb"; forms such as "will recover" and "recovered" do not count as verbs either, they are declensions of verbs: "they differ from the verb in that the verb designates [*prossêmainei*] the present time, whereas the others denote that which is around [the present time]" (*On Int.* 3, 16b17–18). A verb "is always a sign of that to which it belongs, for instance, of the underlying things" (*On Int.* 3, 16b9–10), so much so that a *logos* need not contain a verb: the definition of "human being" is a *logos* that does not contain a verb

(*Po.* 20, 1457a24–27). "[*Logos*] is composed of nouns each of which is a symbol" (*De Sensu* 1, 437a13–15). Meaning is the *possibility* of truth and falsity when coupled with the verb "to be." "Cleon" means something because "Cleon is" is either true or false. And further, "Cleon walks" signifies something, and it is a *logos*, it contains a part that by itself signifies something: "Cleon" (*Po.* 20, 1457a27–28). But "walks" or even "is" does not mean anything on their own, that is, they are meaningful as something said of an implicit "Cleon" (*On Int.* 3, 16b22–23).[73]

Aristotle's positing of the noun as the first level of articulation of *logos* is implicitly an argument against infinite regress in meaning: as conventional, composite, and symbolic, a noun, the basic meaningful unit of *logos*, is and should be able to *refrain from referring back to more elementary meaningful parts*, and to precisely mark the beginning of a realm of meaning to which no voice can access. Voice, on the contrary, is composed out of meaningful parts all the way down—a long cry may indeed be composed out of short cries that do not mean the same thing, but *do* mean something, a slight emphasis in the pain or pleasure, a minor nuance of threat or invitation.

What is entailed in hearing a noun? To my knowledge, there is only one passage, an obscure one, where Aristotle seems to address the issue of *understanding* a noun instead of hearing mere voice:

> Verbs said by themselves are nouns, and they signify something—for the speaker puts the thought, and the hearer remained at rest [*êremêsen*]—but in no way does it signify whether it is or not. For "to be" or "not to be" are not signs of a thing, not even if you said "the being" [*to on*] on its own. For it itself is nothing, but designates some *synthesis* which cannot be thought without the components.[74]

Aristotle here spells out both the productive and receptive side of the expression of nouns: "the speaker puts the thought, and the hearer remained at rest." To hear and understand a noun involves rest. What kind of rest?

The nature of this "rest" in hearing a noun may become clearer if we recall the essentially moving or motivating characteristic of voice. As we saw, voices "move," they "invite" or "threaten." They are imperatives or conditionals: they imply order, threat, or promise. If the hearer of a voice as voice is neither impelled nor repelled away, it is simply because it is insensitive to the threat or invitation. Rest as a response to voice is thus contempt or indifference. Listening and understanding a noun as a noun, however, is precisely to "remain at rest" at least for a "moment" of understanding, that is, of receiving the meaning by remaining open to its possibility of truth *and* falsity. "Rest" here is not at the expense of a relation to one's interlocutor. The "rest" of understanding is not due to insensitivity, but due to the consideration of possibilities at least momentarily considered as options. The first articulation of speech is then received by a being capable of holding the possibility of truth and that of falsity without letting one yield to the other.[75]

This structure of "momentary rest" in front of two contraries matches the structure of the "potentialities with *logos*" we saw in chapter 2: understanding a noun as a meaningful unit necessitates that the listener stay open to *both* of contrary possibilities, just as the "potentiality with *logos*" implies a "moment" where Socrates must "stand still" and weigh the option of fleeing *together with* the possibility of not-fleeing.[76] "There must be some other dominant factor [*to kurion*], I mean desire or choice" (*Metaph.* IX, 5, 1048a10–11). Desire or choice—but which one holds both possibilities open? The faculty that holds them open may be imagination. But Aristotle argues that the imagination combining perceptions, and therefore pleasures and pains, must be distinguished from an imagination involving the work of *logos*—a deliberative, "logistic" imagination:

> So a sensory imagination, as was said, belongs to other animals as well, whereas the deliberative one belongs to those that are *logistikê*: for, whether one shall do this or that is already a work for *logismos*, has to be measured by one [criterion], since one is looking for the better. Thus one is able to make one thing out of many images. This is the reason why [other animals] do not seem to have opinion, because they do not have opinion that comes from a *syllogismos*, while others do have it. Desire does not have the power of deliberating, but at one time this desire wins out and knocks away that one, and at another time that one wins out and knocks away this one, like a ball, when there is lack of self-restraint. But by nature the higher is more governing [*arkhikôtera*] and moves. (*DA* III, 11, 434a6–16)

Here we see that deliberative imagination is the realm of *logismos*, that realm belonging only to the *logistikos*, where motion is not produced by the stronger desire's knocking away the others, but by a "momentary rest" of the immediate provocation of desires in consideration: "desires come to be contrary to one another, which happens whenever *logos* and appetite are contrary to one another, and comes about in beings that have perception of time" (*DA* III, 10, 433b5–8). In other words, the ability to foresee the future as possibilities, to grasp and make a decision about one's life as a whole, and not as an agglomeration of atomic moments, decisions, and motions, requires having *logos* as "reason" and acting according to it. Since the motion dominated by *logismos* does not conquer desire, it cannot be insensitive or repressive toward it. *This* motion is action.

To return to *logos* as speech, to hear a noun as a noun is to be open to a kind of meaning that is irreducible to the massive meaningfulness of voice, to be open to a certain field of *possible* truth and falsity beyond the field of immediate pleasure and pain. Sensation of proper sensibles, and the pleasure and pain accompanying them, are so revealing that their truth is not an issue.[77] Speech, however, is such that it always entails truth *as an issue*. The "rest" that constitutes the completion of the first articulation of speech for Aristotle then is a paradoxical rest in hesitation—not the hesitation between two almost equal pleasures or pains, but that between the possible truth and falsity that the noun may instantiate, a minimal patience for interpretation, one might say "hermeneutical patience."

> In general a sign of the one who knows and the one who does not know is being able to teach, and for this reason we regard art, more than experience, to be knowledge, since the one can, but the others cannot teach. (*Metaph.* I, 1, 981b7–10)

Just as a sign of knowing is here the ability to reformulate the content of knowledge to others in other particular circumstances *instead of merely repeating it*, a sign of the one who has understood a noun is his ability to reformulate the same thing with other words, to paraphrase it, to make variations on it while preserving the exact same "truth values." A sign that one has understood the word "Socrates" is one's ability to paraphrase it with "a philosopher," "a meddlesome busybody," or "a Brazilian soccer player," without changing the "truth values" it may have when coupled with "is" or "is not."

A symptom of the understanding of a noun then is the listener's readiness to proceed from the first level of articulation of *logos* to the level of its full, second, articulation. To understand the word "Socrates" is tantamount to fall in a preliminary aporia, to assume "hermeneutical patience," and to be provoked to ask: "So what *about* Socrates?"

Ambiguity

Ambiguity is the third central feature of human speech, after mediation and articulation. It follows from the symbolic character of nouns. For, precisely because nouns necessarily open up a distance between the sounds uttered and the meaning, the same things are said in many ways not only in different languages, but even within one language, and the same nouns can refer to fundamentally different things. In a word, the first level of articulation of speech is what opens the possibility of ambiguity, equivocation, *homonymia*. It is because there is homonymy that even the hearing of the most common noun may require a search for the exact meaning. Even the most elementary words, such as "man," "stone," "bird," or "hit" necessarily partake in ambiguity, as we saw in the riddle at the very beginning of chapter 1.

Yet now we can see why the "flaw" of ambiguity or homonymy, inherent to nouns, precisely goes hand in hand with their convenience. Ambiguity is a necessary consequence of the infinite economy of language: "Nouns and the quantity of *logoi* are finite, whereas things are infinite in number; thus it is necessary that the same *logos* and noun signify a number of things" (*SE* 1, 165a11–14). This enables Sophocles to skillfully show how erroneous Oedipus is in promising his citizens to *either* kill whoever killed Laius *or* die himself—without ever imagining that this is not an either-or situation, since the two options are synonymous (*King Oedipus*, ll. 132–46). Speech articulates a *potentially* unlimited number of nouns out of a limited number of basic conventional units, and stands for an infinite number of particular affections of the soul, but this economy is at the price of possible tragic ambiguities.

The necessarily ambiguous character of what is "heard" in the last sense of *akouein* (after hearing sound, hearing voice, and obeying) also shows up especially in the opening lines of the Aristotelian corpus which distinguish homonyms and synonyms (*Cat.* 1, 1a1–12). The human condition, that is, the condition of an animal having *logos*, situates us in an unavoidable gap between names and beings. For synonymy entails the commonality of both names and "*logos* of being," while, as seen in chapter 1, we can always address beings homonymously, that is, with respect to their name only, since language is conventional. The mediation of speech through meaningless parts frees or detaches meanings from voices, and makes synonymy not a given, but a continual task. No wonder languages change. This is because of homonymy, the unavoidable ambiguity of language. It is very telling that Socrates, Plato, and Aristotle are all extremely aware of ambiguity and view disambiguation as a major philosophical task, while none of them seem to have ever hoped to eradicate ambiguity from natural language. Quite in opposition to much later aspirations and attempts for a perfect, unambiguous language in Descartes, Leibniz, Enlightenment philosophers, and most notably John Wilkins,[78] it seems as if Aristotle, a pioneer in axiomatic science and formal logic, believes that language is *necessarily* ambiguous because he seems to think, like Wilhelm von Humboldt, that language is "the infinite use of finite media."[79] Only a dead language can be a perfect one.

Since specifically human hearing is understanding, that is, "taking *in a certain sense*," and since the bond between meaning and sound is detached in human speech, it is possible to interpret the same letters (say, *l*, *o*, *g*, *o* and *s*) in different meanings, as "standard," "ratio," "reason," "speech," or as my spell-check does in interpreting *logos* as the plural of "logo." For the same reason, it is possible to rephrase one same meaning in different letters, one same idea in other words. As we saw earlier in this chapter of the book, to hear a voice was to be moved by its meaning, even if in the form of indifference. The semantics of human speech, however, is fundamentally exposed to paraphrase, interpretation, and translation by a mediator, a translator, an interpreter, a Hermes, or a *hermêneus*.

3. Human Speech: From "Words to Sentences"

Finally, after our survey of animal communication, and our analysis of the first articulation of speech, from "letters" to "words," through mediation, articulation, and ambiguity, we now come to the full articulation of speech. In this section, we shall see that, unlike voice which was bound by imperative or subjunctive moods, speech can be construed in two other moods as well: the indicative and the optative. We already saw how, by means of imitation, some bird species relay non-firsthand experiences without understanding them, while, in their obedience and cooperation, bees understand them, but do not relay them. The elaboration of the indicative and optative moods will put us in a position to argue that *logos* in the sense of "speech" names the specifically human capacity for both understanding and relaying non-firsthand experiences along with firsthand experiences.

The Indicative

Just as speech first articulates voiced and unvoiced units (vowels and consonants) for the sake of meaning, the meaningful unit itself is determined in terms of a second articulation: namely, the articulation of that which has meaning on its own (a noun) and that which has meaning only when coupled with a noun (a verb) for the sake of possible truth or falsity. The *possibility* of truth and falsity appears as the central factor of speech. Thus, the "final cause" of the first articulation of speech points to the second level of articulation. "Letters," however functional, were not meaningful in themselves; nouns, in turn, however meaningful, are not ends in themselves.

Thus we come to the most common meaning of *logos* as speech: *logos apophantikos* or "declarative sentence." We saw Aristotle's definition: "*Logos* is a signifying voice, one of whose parts is signifying separately, not as an affirmation, but as an expression."[80] *Logos* has a meaningful part, but this second level of articulation also relates that independently meaningful part to that which applies and does not apply to it (*hyparkhein*) with temporal specification.[81] In the first case, indeed, the declarative sentence is affirmation (*kataphasis*), in the second, it is negation (*apophasis*): "Affirmation is a declaration of something concerning something [*kata tinos*], whereas negation is a declaration of something against something [*apo tinos*]."[82]

The duality of affirmation and negation is explained by the duality of truth and falsity, and this latter by the truth of the principle of non-contradiction: concerning the very same subject matter, a declarative sentence is necessarily open to *both* truth and falsity. Therefore any such sentence can be negated. Here we see that truth or falsity, the radical breakthrough out of voice into speech, puts at work that which was potential in expression: "Socrates is executed" is not simply an expression of something ("Socrates"), but an expression of *something* about it. But what? The declarative sentence enjoys a "freedom" that is almost as unlimited, a "freedom" that extends far beyond the unique "correct" match, and is entangled in the myriads of ways of being "incorrect."

This is why such correctness is not a fact, but an issue. For structural and necessary reasons, speech is certainly not a perfect means to truth as correspondence.[83] For humans, truth as correspondence is almost a nostalgia for the strictly animal condition, for the full experience of sensation:[84] for presence, for pure experience, for apperception, for sheer firsthand experience, for the apodictic certainty, for seeing everything from one's own eyes, or at least for the self-evidence of *imagining* that one sees everything from one's own eyes. For humans, firsthand experience and direct perception are, more often than not, a task, if not an impossible one.

There is an Ancient Greek word that perfectly corresponds to this ideal of apperception: *autopsia*, "seeing from one's own eyes," "firsthand experience," "witnessing." Aristotle uses *autoptês*, "eye witness," exactly in the sense of firsthand knowledge as opposed to mere *legein*: "As we said, the largest rivers flow indeed from the highest mountains. To those who look at maps of the earth this is clear, for they have been drawn by means of *in situ* investigation or, if not seen firsthand [*autoptas*], then by means of those who speak" (*Mete.* I, 13, 350a14–18).[85]

So having *logos* is particularly ill-suited to the ideal of *autopsia*. There may well be an ancient Greek epistemic ideal of *autopsia*.[86] But if *autopsia* can become a *concern* at all for the ancient Greeks, but also for Descartes or for human beings in general, this is because the human condition is not confined to it. The human condition, but also perhaps ancient Greek philosophy, are understandable less by asserting the preeminence of sight or hearing or language as such, or by noticing the quantitative complexity of human life and communication, than by emphasizing the irreversible human detachment from, and occasional yearning for, *autopsia*. It is the forms of "not seeing with one's own eyes," but indeed also of "not hearing with one's own ears," that characterize the human condition.[87]

Unlike imperatives and the subjunctive conditions implied by them in animal communication, declarative speech corresponds to the indicative mood. Not that it *indicates* the truth. On the contrary, because what it can indicate drives the human condition away from *autopsia* toward a vast and confusing realm where unjustified, unjustifiable, and unfalsifiable sentences proliferate.

The Optative

We have already seen how animal communication was mostly governed by the imperative (*prostaktikê*) and the subjunctive (*hypotaktikê*) moods. Besides these two moods, we just saw the second articulation of human speech in the sense of "declarative sentence" in a third mood: the indicative (*horistikê*). And yet there is another mood specific to *logos*: this is the optative mood (*euktikê*).[88] Aristotle is sharply aware of this mood. For, according to him, all declarative sentences are indeed *logoi*, but not the other way around. Despite what his critics claim,[89] Aristotle does *not* reduce speech to declarative sentences: "Not all *logos* is declarative, but the *logoi* to which truth or falsity belong. For instance, a *eukhê* ["prayer" or "wish"] is a *logos*, but it is neither true nor false."[90]

In order to develop this marginalized or totally neglected aspect of human speech, let us first trace out the Aristotelian concept of *eukhê* as a kind of *logos* in its own right, then analyze the state of the soul that is expressed by it, and finally differentiate the optative mood from the other three moods.

In Ancient Greek, *eukhê* means "prayer," "vow," "wish," "aspiration," "curse."[91] Despite being a *logos*, "prayer" is *not* susceptible of truth or falsity. Although the human being is distinguished by *logos*, not all *logos* is declarative. Beside the declarative, propositional, or indicative mood of *logos*, grounded by the principle of non-contradiction and constitutive of logic and science, *eukhê* is this other kind of *logos*, somehow detached from truth and falsity, a *logos* that is not *predicative*, but rather *precative*. Yet, as Aristotle adds, the analysis of this kind of *logos* must be relegated, for its proper place is not in *On Interpretation*, which is reserved to declarative *logos*, but in the rhetoric and the poetics. Thus one would expect a satisfying account of *eukhê* in the *Rhetoric* and in the *Poetics*.

In the *Rhetoric*, unfortunately *eukhê* appears only twice in the same sentence, and this in its verbal form of *eukhesthai* in the discussion of the "depreciative metaphor."[92] According to this passage, although praying (*eukhesthai*) is honorable and begging is dishonorable, both belong to the same genus: demand (*aitêsis*). This point confirms that *eukhê* is not a declarative *logos*, but it remains too generic since we have seen that animal voice (*phônê*) was also precisely a kind of demand. How does *eukhê*, as a demand, differ from the kind of demand we found in animal voice?

The promised analysis of *eukhê* is to be found no more in the *Poetics* than in the *Rhetoric*. In the *Poetics*, *eukhê* is briefly mentioned as a form of expression (*skhêma tês lexeôs*) among others: "What is a command [*entolê*]? What is a prayer [*eukhê*]? and a narration [*diêgêsis*], a threat [*apeilê*], a question [*erôtêsis*], an answer [*apokrisis*], etc.?"[93] Then *eukhê* is to be distinguished from "narration" and "answer." But also, while probably belonging to the genus "demand," *eukhê* is distinguished from "question." Although both are neither true nor false, the act of questioning may still seem like a "quest," thus a readiness to move and investigate, while *eukhê* lacks these characteristics. Finally, this passage suggests that *eukhê* differs from the kind of demand we saw in our analysis of animal voice: whereas the demand expressed in animal voice took the form of a threat or a promise made to another animal in a "subjunctive" (*hypotaktikê*) mood, this passage clearly distinguishes *eukhê* from "threat." Whereas animal voice was "imperative" (*prostaktikê*), Aristotle's list of forms of expression implies that *eukhê* is semantically, if not grammatically, also distinct from "command."

The same distinction between command and *eukhê* is found in the next lines of the *Poetics*. Here Aristotle objects to Protagoras's criticism of Homer, and while doing so underlines the semantic, if not grammatical, distinction between the imperative and the optative:

> Why would one agree with Protagoras in criticizing [Homer] because, while supposedly praying [*eukhesthai*] [the Goddess], he commands [*epitattei*] her by saying: "Sing goddess the wrath . . ."?[94]

Apparently Protagoras criticized Homer for addressing the Goddess in the imperative mood instead of the precative/optative mood. Aristotle finds this criticism irrelevant: poetic license tolerates the use of the imperative for expressing what is clearly a *prayer* to the goddess. Either way, the texts referred to in Aristotle's remark concerning *eukhê* in *On Interpretation* were the *Rhetoric* and the *Poetics*; we have seen that, although these two texts do not supply the promised analysis of *eukhê*, the *Rhetoric* determines the genus of *eukhê* as "demand" (*aitêsis*), and the *Poetics* distinguishes *eukhê* from other kinds of demands such as "threats" and "questions."

To recapitulate, then, *eukhê* is a *logos* that is not declarative or "indicative" of a present, past, or future state of affairs, as a narration or an answer may be. As a form of expression, it belongs to the genus "demand" (*aitêsis*). It is distinguished from other species of demand: it differs from "question" in that it is not a demand for a verbal response; more importantly, it is different from the subjunctive mood of threats and from the imperative mood of command which both characterized animal voice. *Eukhê* does not suggest potential harm or profit as threats and promises do; it does not expect a verbal response as a question does. In this sense, *eukhê* is an unaccountable *logos*, a *logos* exempt from truth and falsity, confirmation and falsification: since it does not *indicate* or *propose* an actual or even potential state of affairs, it cannot be held accountable for a commitment it does not make; but since it is not a question, it is also unanswerable; finally, since it is not a promise, a threat, or a command, it offers nothing to be broken, nothing to be obeyed or disobeyed.

The optative mood of prayer is then to be strictly distinguished from the imperative and subjunctive moods. Yet these grammatical terms may be misleading, for, as we saw in Aristotle's dismissal of Protagoras's criticism of Homer, a verb that is grammatically in the imperative mood may well have an optative meaning as when one says "Help me, God!" or even "Good morning!" The semantically optative sentence "Good morning!" does not express the *desire* one feels for the other's having a good morning in the sense that one has thus committed oneself to making the other's morning a good one.

But what is the state of the soul that is expressed by the optative? A desire, to be sure. But how is *eukhê* as an expression of desire any different from animal voice, equally an expression of desire? What are the kinds of desire and what kind does the optative express? We may find a hint not in *On Interpretation*, in the *Rhetoric*, or in the *Poetics*, but in the *Nicomachean Ethics*, III, 2 and the parallel text in *Eudemian Ethics*, II, 10. In this passage, Aristotle distinguishes "choice" (*proairesis*) from "desire" (*orexis*) by showing that choice corresponds to neither of the three kinds of desire: neither to "appetite" (*epithymia*), nor to "spiritedness" (*thymos*), nor to "wishing" (*boulêsis*):

> But [choice] is surely not wishing either, even though that appears a close approximation to it, since there can be no choice of impossible things, and if anyone were to claim to choose something impossible, that person would seem to be foolish; but there is wishing even for impossible things, such as deathlessness. And there is also wishing for things that can in no way be done by oneself, such as for a certain actor to win an award, or for an athlete to win a contest, but no

> one chooses such things, but only those things one believes could come about by one's own act. Also, wishing is rather for an end, while choice is of things that are related to the end; for example, we wish to be healthy, but we choose those things by means of which we will become healthy, and we wish to be happy and say so, while it would not fit the meaning to say we choose to be happy, since, universally, choice seems to be concerned with things that are up to us.[95]

Eukhê seems to express just this state of the human soul: wish, *boulêsis*.[96] From the verbal expression, we have thus moved to the psychic state, and from there we are led to the object of that state. What kind of desire is wish? Wish is a kind of desire distinguished by its objects: (1) impossible objects (such as immortality) beyond plans for any possible ones; (2) objects that are not realizable or attainable by ourselves (like the victory of a team in a match); (3) the ultimate objects of our decisions and choices (such as health or happiness). Just as *eukhê* was reserved to human beings as an instance of speech, here the wish expressed by it may well be an exclusively human desire. In fact, Aristotle clearly says in *On the Soul* that "*boulêsis* comes to be in the *logistikê* part [of the soul]."[97] Similarly, in the *Nicomachean Ethics*, Aristotle says that beings deprived of *logos* (*alogoi*) have "appetite" and "passion," but do not partake in "choice,"[98] which is a "close approximation" to wish. Just as *eukhê* was an atypical *logos* for not being susceptible of truth and falsity, wish belongs to the *logistikê* part of the human soul in a problematic way: wish is a peculiar kind of desire that does *not* move the being that expresses it. But neither does it move the being that is addressed, as does animal voice. For the object of wish is envisaged precisely as simply unattainable by the individual animal as well by an alliance with others.

In order to sketch out the "wishful attitude," let us then bring together the main features of *eukhê* with wish, this atypical, nonmoving, kind of desire:

First, the difference between *eukhê* and declarative *logos*. The optative is not the indicative. Unlike declarative sentences, *eukhê* is a *logos* that somehow has access beyond past, present, and futures states of affairs; it opens up the realm of impossibility that is not susceptible of truth and falsity. The desire behind *eukhê* is susceptible of "extending" or "stretching" into mere unreality, infinitely beyond the actual and even all potentials. Hence wish and prayer are immune to the control of verification and falsification, of corroboration and elenchus, regardless of whether they *happen* to come to pass. For it is not exact to say that a wish *becomes true* in the sense that a bet *turns out to be true*, since that which becomes true is not the wish, but a future state of affairs extracted from the *content* of wish (namely, a bet); yet, as we saw, wish is not reducible to its content since it belongs to a specific mood, the optative. For instance, when one wishes the execution of Socrates and he is executed, what *becomes true* is not the *wish* (the desire) itself, but the declarative or indicative proposition: "Socrates will be executed."[99] Further, reaching beyond the realm of truth as correspondence to reality, the fundamental dimension of unreality in the optative mood penetrates the past as profoundly as the future. For, having *logos*, being thus capable of wishing without regard to any limit, reality, and likelihood, human beings are precisely capable of desiring a counterfactual, saying, for instance, "If only we had not executed Socrates!" Indeed, in English, the semantically optative "if only" here is to be distinguished from the subjunctive or imperative phrase "only if" of commands and demands. While offering humans access to truth and to correspondence with reality by means of logic and science, *logos* also exposes humans to the realm of unreality. Unlike other desires that are geared toward the future, the wishful attitude is particularly important in understanding the relationship to the past in human experience. Having *logos*, human beings are exposed to regret, guilt, and bad conscience.

Secondly, *eukhê* is distinct from conditionals. In other words, the optative is not the subjunctive. The object of wish is not limited by the realm of reality, of possibility, and of conditions. The wish for Socrates to be executed is modally different from a conditional sentence expressing that he will be executed if he does not stop doing philosophy. In the same way, curses differ from threats, as blessings do from promises. Phrases such as "God willing," "Deo volente," or "Inshallah" cannot be literally meant as conditional clauses if they are to take part in *eukhê*, in the optative mood. Literally, the sentence "God willing, we shall succeed" is not an *eukhê*, unless what is meant by the sentence is: "May God will that we succeed." Again, wishes cannot be literally expressed with expressions like "please" or "if you will." For *eukhê* must be beyond the imperative of "pleasing" and the eventuality of one's willing to please. For, oxymoronically, *eukhê* is a disengaged promise. It is not "tactic," "prostactic," or contractual. My wishing somebody a happy birthday in no way binds me at the level of action; in no way am I thereby obligated to make plans and predictions and to take responsibility. We have seen that animal voice necessarily implies a threat or a promise made to the other animal; we have come to see why wish is neither. Being unconditional, wish is not subject to conditions, eventualities, justifications, refutations, confirmations, or denials. As we just saw in our lengthy quotation from the *Nicomachean Ethics*, one then *may* wish an impossibility, beyond actual or even possible experience. One *may* wish that one had not undergone a trauma, that the Trojan War had not happened, that Socrates had not been executed. All kinds and senses of *eukhê* (with the important exception of "vow") are expressions of an *intention* without any regard for its realization and for a trial of its correspondence with reality. So among the forms of *eukhê* and expressions of wish are salutations, best wishes, congratulations, prayers, blessings, swears, and curses.

Thirdly, *eukhê* differs from commands which may appear equally unconditional or categorical—the optative is not the imperative. In the *Poetics*, we saw Protagoras criticizing Homer for using an imperative for addressing the Goddess; yet, for Aristotle, this criticism was not valid since it wrongly assumes that semantics is determined by grammatical tense. For a prayer may well be expressed by an imperative without signifying a command. A wish is precisely not a frustrated desire "translated" to another as a call for cooperation by means of animal voice. Wish differs from other kinds of desire in that it does not "immediately" (*euthus*) spill into any action or even into any *call* for action. "Save Socrates!" is a linguistic expression of a desire that is intended to move its listener, a desire that would put the subject himself in motion *had he possessed or perceived the means for satisfying it*. The *wish* to save Socrates, however, although a desire, is a "universal premise" fundamentally detached from any "particular premise" susceptible of triggering motion. Other desires move the animal, wish does not. Voice is a call for cooperation and project for action, *eukhê* is not.

This optative mood subtends not only wishful thinking and prayer, but also regret, guilt, even certain kinds of dreams and reveries. Indeed, wishing does not imply wishing *well*, and not all prayers are for the *good* of someone. Curses are *eukhai* as well. Thus, the wishful attitude is found not only in the form of gratitude and hope, but also in the form of resentment. The human soul, having *logos*, thus capable of wishing, exposes itself to passions that would seem utterly absurd and irrelevant to other animals, since *eukhê* is a desire that moves nothing. Wish gives access, or supposes access, to a vast domain of detachment and abstraction from facts, possible alliances, and conceivable individual or common projects. Thus, by definition, wish is exempt from invoking others; it remains isolated and absolutely "verbal." Although situated outside the domain of logic, *eukhê* is in a sense *logos* par excellence, for it remains strictly *logikôs*.[100]

One cannot fail to notice that the four exemplary objects of wish in the above passage from the *Nicomachean Ethics* are of the utmost importance in human life according to Aristotle: Immortality, success, health, and happiness. There even the central concept of "choice" in Aristotelian ethics is said to be subsumed under such objects of wish. For Aristotle, then, wish seems to be our psychological relationship to our highest aspirations which exceed our knowledge and planning, and they find their expression in *eukhê*: faring well (*eu prattein*), long life, prosperity, rejoicing (*khaire!*), success, good luck. In short, *eukhê* is a *logos* that acknowledges the vulnerability of *logos* itself at the face of contingency, when things are *not* "up to us." In this respect, the wishful attitude may be seen as a corrective of hubristic claims of rationality for self-sufficiency. In this sense, the wishful attitude maintains a constant reserve for gratitude and for the recognition of our limitations, as well as our constant possibility for hope. So in this respect, for the wishful attitude, the world is fundamentally open, undetermined by history, rational planning, or human understanding.

Hence, there is a political implication of this wishful attitude. Being the only animal capable of *logos* and thus of *eukhê*, the human political animal is capable of transcending all realpolitik and of finding refuge in a strictly *logikos* discourse: utopianism. It is not surprising that the word *eukhê* occurs regularly in Plato's *Republic*. There it designates the "ideal" city, which, although impossible, is eminently worthy of wish—a city that has no place in reality, but can always be envisaged precisely through *logos*, a city constituted in *logos* alone.[101] Similarly, the major Aristotelian text in which *eukhê* most occurs is neither the logical nor the psychological works, but the *Politics*, where it appears in the phrase *kat' eukhên* qualifying a constitution that is most wishable.[102]

Let us then conclude our elaboration of the optative mood. The wishful attitude is not only possible, it is a perpetual possibility for animals having *logos*, since it is ultimately irrefutable by demonstration. As having *logos*, human beings are uniquely capable of interpreting the world as mere happenstance, of denying their own agency and responsibilities, and of relating to unreality and to contradictions at the risk of claiming to become "similar to a plant."[103] Being the "precative" animals we are, human beings are capable of desiring that which is refused even to gods themselves, according to Aristotle's quotation of Agathon: namely "to make undone whatever has been done."[104] The human soul, by having *logos*, and by being able to simply wish things, is exposed to hopes and fears that would indeed have seemed odd, fantastic, or simply irrelevant in the animal realm, because the *logos* of wish is the expression of some interest that does not move the subject. Most importantly, being irreducible to voice which simply *indicates* the desire of the animal's soul, wish as *logos* is the expression of something one has not experienced, may never experience, and may know well that one will never experience. If wish is a *logos*, and if wish implies that one transcend all actuality and even all possibility, then *logos* must offer an access specifically beyond any firsthand experience.

Logos as Access beyond Firsthand Experience

We have now come to the end of our elaboration of specifically human *logos* as speech in this chapter of the book. Let us recapitulate the major steps we made in our previous three sections.

In section 1, we explored animal communication. We noted that animal voice was fundamentally geared to move another animal in a way comparable to the subjunctive mood (threats, promises) and imperative mood (orders). We saw that bees were capable of *understanding* a non-firsthand experience expressed to them by another bee (since they seemed to obey the order given), but also that bees *did not relay* the non-firsthand experience to others; conversely, we saw that, in imitating the sounds they hear, some bird species were capable of *relaying* what they heard, *but without understanding it.*

In section 2, we proposed the hypothesis that *logos* as human speech for Aristotle is this ability to both understand and relay non-firsthand experiences as well as firsthand experiences. To substantiate this hypothesis, we analyzed human speech in its three major features: its mediated, articulated, and necessarily ambiguous character. Being mediated, articulated, and ambiguous, *logos* enables and destines humans to understand and communicate experiences neither the sender nor the receivers have had or may ever have. This is why *logos* is properly received neither by a memorization and repetition of its form, as we saw some bird species to be capable of in hearing sound, nor by obedience to its content, as we saw in bee communication.

In section 3, we moved from the level of "words" to "sentences," and showed that, besides the subjunctive and imperative moods governing animal communication, human speech has two other moods: the indicative mood, and the often neglected optative mood. As an expression of pain and pleasure, voice always signifies a firsthand experience (*autopsia*), and it is fundamentally oriented toward moving its hearer, even if the hearer ends up remaining unmoved; the indicative mood of human speech, however, is capable of refraining from trying to move its hearer, and of indicating, of making her "believe," "agree," or "understand." This means not that *logos* is necessarily indicative of the truth or of the true essence of things, but that it exposes humans to *claims* to truth, to the *issue* of truth. As it is mediated through meaningless units, as it is conventional and thus necessarily ambiguous, *logos* removes us from any felicitous match between voices and meanings, homonymy and synonymy, belief and truth. As Aristotle quotes from Euripides, "if there are persuasive false designations among mortals, you should also admit the contrary, that disbelieving the true befalls mortals."[105] The optative mood, specific to human speech, governs expressions of desire for things beyond the realms of *actual* firsthand experience and even of *possible* firsthand experience.[106]

This is then the wonder of *logos*: that we can even *claim* to understand things we have never experienced or or may never experienced firsthand—say, about bee communication or about the "essence" of an ox, about "what it is to be for an ox"; and further, "even worse," that we can relay our claims to still others. Because *logos* is mediated by convention, that is, it is detached from the immediate meaningfulness of pleasure and pain, and because *logos* is articulated through letters, that is, it is detached from the natural vocal expression of pleasure and pain, we can understand non-firsthand experiences, when we hear a *logos*, without having to experience them firsthand, and we can relay meaning without even having to reproduce the same words. In comparison to sound and voice, *logos* as human speech is the ability to understand non-firsthand experiences (just as voice hearing, but unlike sound hearing) *as well as* to relay them along with firsthand experiences (just as sound hearing, but unlike voice hearing). This ability to understand and relay both firsthand experiences and contents never experienced firsthand sheds light on the specifically human character of historiography, of oracles, of mythology, of the necessary accumulation of information in science, of sophistry and philosophy.[107]

4. *Logoi*: Definition, Account, and Law

In order to offer textual support for this claim concerning human *logos*, and to draw its implications, let us turn to three major Aristotelian texts in which this sense of *logos* is used. We shall see that Aristotle's accounts of the role of *logos* in human claims to definition, to causal accounts, and to law presuppose exactly such an ability to understand and relay non-firsthand experience as well as firsthand experience.

Human Predication (*Categories*, 1)

Human beings are capable of *claiming* to define beings other than themselves. This claim to make essential predications, to formulate "essences," to access "forms" or "inherent standards" of beings other than themselves, clearly presupposes human *logos* as the ability to understand and relay non-firsthand experiences. This is how humans can even claim to understand and to formulate not only the pleasant or painful aspects of, say, an ox, but *what it is to be* an ox—an idea that, by definition, no human can gather from firsthand experience. It is in this sense that the "*logos* of being" only shows itself to a "being having *logos*."

This seems confirmed in the opening of the *Categories* where synonyms are distinguished from homonyms as sharing not only a conventional name but also the *logos* of their being. Aristotle is clear that "*logos* of being" here refers not to what, say, an ox may be *for us*, but "what it is *for it* to be an animal":

> Those whose names only are common, but whose *logos* of being according to this name is different, are called homonyms, such as "animal" for both the human being and the representation; for if one supplies what is it for each of them to be animal, one will supply a particular *logos* for each. Those whose names are common and whose *logos* of being according to this name are also common are called synonyms, such as "animal" for both the human being and the ox; for each of these are addressed with the common name "animal" and their *logos* of being is the same. For if one supplies the *logos* of what it is for each to be animal, one will supply the same *logos*. (*Cat.* 1, 1a1–13)[108]

Having *logos*, we are such that we are able to claim to address other beings not only from our own perspective as determined perceptually or practically ("this is black [to me]," "this is powerful [for me]," "it is time to sleep [for me]," "this is dangerous [to me]," etc.), but from *their* own perspective: "this is a living being." In other words, if we had no *logos* and thus no claim to access the "essence" of beings from a third-person perspective, we could not but admit that all our predications are subjective accidental, momentary aspects and that all our addresses are homonymous, and there would be neither any sense of *ousia* nor any appeal to the principle of non-contradiction.

> In general those who say this [those who deny the principle of non-contradiction] do away with being and what it is for something to be. For it is necessary for them to say that all things are incidental [*symbebêkenai*] and that there is no such thing as the very thing it is to be human or animal. (*Metaph.* IV, 4, 1007a20–23)[109]

Even assuming that relativism was somehow the truth, which is paradoxical in itself, we would need to explain the illusion of nonrelativistic claims, and these would require an ability to somehow suppose an access to a "measure" that is not ourselves. In other words, if we did not have *logos*, if we had no access beyond firsthand experience at all, we all could not but be followers of Protagoras (and thus actually his refuters).

Human Experience (*Metaphysics*, I, 1)

This brings us back to the famous passage from the *Metaphysics* we quoted at the beginning of this chapter. This passage also warrants our use of the word "experience" in claiming that *logos* names our ability to claim to access non-firsthand *experience*. For here Aristotle claims that, unlike sound and voice, human experience mediated through *logos* includes the ability to understand and relay causal accounts beyond "impressions and memories." Once we read the rest of the passage with occasional paraphrases using what we have learned so far, we see that human experience proper is distinguished by *logos*:

> Animals are by nature born having sensation [and "that which has sensation also has pleasure and pain"][110] . . . The [animals] that cannot hear noise are intelligent but cannot learn, such as a bee or any other kind of animal that might be such. Those that have this sensation [i.e., the capacity to hear noise] besides memory learn [e.g., some bird species]. Thus the others live by impressions and memories, and have but a small share of experience [*empeirias de metekhei mikron*]. But the human kind [lives] also by art and reasoning [*logismos*] . . . Indeed, we see people of experience succeeding more than those having a *logos* without experience; the reason is that experience is familiarity [*gnôsis*] with the particulars, but art, of universals. . . . Nevertheless we consider that knowing and acquaintance [*to ge eidenai kai to epaiein*] belong to art rather than to experience and take the artisans to be wiser than people of experience in that wisdom rather follows knowing in all cases. For the former know the cause while the latter do not. (*Metaph.* I, 1, 980a27–981a28)

Aristotle recognizes the wonders of *logos* as well as its limits: while it transcends the experience of particulars and looks more like wisdom to people, *logos* is not necessarily more successful in practice. First, people may well be, and often are, more successful even if they do *not* have a *logos* and do *not* know causes or the universals; secondly, by giving us access beyond our firsthand experience, human *logos* exposes us to the possibility of being *mistaken* about causes in a way other animals do not seem susceptible. Similarly, *logos* makes it possible that, of two people who lack experience and are unsuccessful with particulars, one be wise and the other simply unwise. Finally, the rest of the passage claims that, unlike mere experience of fact, *logos* includes *both* the understanding of a causal account, which was not confined to firsthand experience, *and* the ability to relay it—that is, to teach it:

> Thus [master craftsmen] are wiser not because they are practical, but because they have a *logos* and know the causes. As a whole, a sign of knowing and not knowing is the ability to teach [*didaskein*], and hence we think that art rather than experience is scientific knowledge; for [artists] can teach while the others cannot. Further, we do not consider any of the senses to be wisdom. They are indeed our chief sources of acquaintance with particulars, but they do not tell the reason [*to dia ti*] for anything, as for instance why fire is hot, but only that it is hot. (*Metaph.* I, 1, 981b5–13)

As opposed to the way some small bird species "learned" whatever sounds they heard, in the sense of becoming capable of relaying them without understanding them, here we see that *logos* enables us to both understand and relay our accounts of non-firsthand experience. Without *logos*, we may well know, remember, and even predict that fire is hot, yet *logos* enables us to *claim* to understand why it is so, and to teach this to others. Being disconnected from sensation, thus from pleasure and pain, and from the particular practical necessities of life, *logos* connects humans with disinterested wonder and innovation, and with the leisurely satisfaction of their natural desire for knowledge, that is, with *philosophia*.

Then, just like the *Categories* passage, this opening chapter of the *Metaphysics* seems to confirm that, for better or for worse, *logos* enables us to understand and relay even that which is beyond the possibility of firsthand experience. This ability to claim to disengage from firsthand experiences also sheds light on Aristotle's typical methodological procedure from what is clear and known to us toward what is clear and known "simply or by nature."

Human Community (*Politics*, I, 1)

Finally, let us turn to the most famous Aristotelian passage on human *logos*:

> It is clear why the human being is a political animal in a greater degree [*mallon*] than any bee or any gregarious animal. For nature, as we say, does nothing in vain, and among animals the human being alone has *logos*. Voice is indeed a sign [*sêmeion*] of the painful and of the pleasurable, and so is possessed by other animals as well (for their nature has developed so far as to have sensation of the painful and pleasant, and to signify [*sêmainein*] these to others), yet *logos* is for showing [*dêloun*] the advantageous and the harmful, and thus the just and the unjust; for it is peculiar to

> humans in distinction from the other animals to have the perception of the just, the unjust and other qualities, and it is community [*koinônia*] in these that makes a household and a city. (*Pol.* I, 1, 1253a10–18)[111]

Indicating the advantageous or the harmful by means of *logos* is then crucially different from signifying pain and pleasure by means of voice—*logos* is the ability to understand and relay advantages and harms never experienced firsthand, to even indicate justice and injustice. Thus even in practical matters, *logos* does not simply demand obedient cooperation by means of a "prostactic" (imperative) order, or by a hypothetical or "hypotactic" (subjunctive) threat. In the "horistic" (indicative) mood, *logos* is able to delimit and define an ethical-political realm. In the "euctic" or "precative" (optative) mood, *logos* is able to project justice against all odds.

Human presence is shot through with *logos*: being able to detach themselves from that which is standing right in front of them, human beings stand in front of, and interact with, things in a specific way. Since humans are able to somehow "witness" that which they have not witnessed firsthand, the following question is more telling in this context than its answer: "—Yourself, were you with Socrates yourself the day he drank the poison in prison or did you hear it from someone else?—Myself, I was there myself Echecrates" (Plato, *Phaedo*, 57a). This is a paradigmatic situation that characterizes human dialogues: the speaker may well be relaying his firsthand experiences, his *autopsia*, but not necessarily so:

> Since it is impossible to discuss by bringing in the things themselves, but we make use of symbols in the place of things, we think that what happens with names also happens in the case of things, just as people who count pebbles [*psêphôn tois logizomenois*]. (*SE* 1, 165a6–10)

Once we are dealing with human *logos*, we are no longer simply dealing with "things themselves"; the awareness of "things themselves" becomes a task to fulfill, a goal to attain, or, as it so often happens, a target to irrevocably miss. It is this hermeneutical task that is implicit to Aristotle's *logikê* in general, but also to the ambiguous Platonic strategy of *writing dialogues*. As the human speaker is capable of relating both her experience and that which she has not experienced, the human listener is able to consider that which she hears as either of the two. Echecrates *can* believe that Phaedo is relating his firsthand experience, but he does not have to; it is human *logos* that necessarily brings along trust and distrust as open options. We *can* believe what Phaedo or the *Phaedo* says, but the point is that we can do so only as irredeemably exposed to do otherwise.

Aristotle employs above the expression "counting pebbles" in its literal sense of counting on an abacus—and precisely *not* with abstract symbols and numbers. But indeed the ancient Greeks' usage of pebbles goes far beyond counting pebbles *as pebbles*. They are also used for *representing something*. Most notably pebbles are used as votes, that is, as representing people's opinions.[112] And it is true that for Aristotle there is something fundamentally inadequate to the human condition in simply *counting votes* for and against a proposal in decision-making: simply voting for and against is in fact a regression into expressions of pleasure and pain. Hence the exclusive options of protesting and applauding, of calling *aye* and *no*, are often expressed by the word "voice" in English, for instance, in expressions like "to collect the voices" or "voice vote." On the contrary, for Aristotle, what gives life to laws, contracts, or decisions, what establishes the very options to be subsequently voted for, is the excellence of *deliberation*: "law has a compulsory force because it is a *logos* emanating from some prudence and intelligence" (*NE* X, 9, 1180a22–23). But again, this is the foundation of sophistry and demagogy as much as that of genuine political participation. Sophists and demagogues are able to manipulate their audience in ways a tyrant may not be able to, because, exercising *logos*, the sophist accesses the experiences of others, and because, having *logos*, the demagogue is able to view the world not only in terms of his own agenda, but also from the standpoint of the people.

In short, as an access beyond firsthand experience, *logos* enables us to assume not only a third-person perspective on nature and on ourselves, but also to take on the point of view of other people. Hence, when Aristotle distinguishes four kinds of *logoi* or "arguments" in discussion ("didactic arguments, dialectical arguments, examination arguments and contentious arguments"),[113] all four are explained in a short sentence which each time implies *the assumption of somebody else's point of view*: "Didactic arguments are those which reason from the principles appropriate to each branch of learning and not from the opinions of the answerer, for he who is learning must take things on trust."[114] With respect to the first kind of argument, didactic argument, this is exactly what we meant by saying that science requires an accumulation of knowledge that is obviously impossible without the capacity for understanding and relaying that which one has not experienced firsthand. Secondly, Aristotle continues: "Dialectical arguments are those which, starting from widespread opinions, reason concerning a contradiction."[115] We dealt with the importance of dialectical method in our introduction, so here let us only note how it requires human *logos* as being specifically oriented *to* that which is not clear to us, but is clear by nature. The starting point of dialectic already requires that the questioner assume what is for him a non-firsthand stance: the stance of the answerer. But further, the dialectic refutation also necessitates that both parties come to recognize something that exceeds both of their firsthand experiences: a contradiction. Thirdly, in examination arguments, the questioner must again tune into the mindset of the answerer.[116] Finally, contentious arguments "are those which reason or seem to reason from opinions which appear to be, but are not generally accepted."[117] This last sense, like the previous ones, is inconceivable so long as we interpret *logos* merely as "reason," "statement," "sentence," "inference," or "argument": *logos* means "argument" not in the sense of a private reasoning, but in the sense of a reasoning from or towards somebody else.

The community that *logos* makes possible is not only any political community. It is the polis. Although there are many nonhuman "political" animals, there is no nonhuman polis according to Aristotle. We have seen that political animals such as human beings, wasps, ants, and bees are characterized by common work.[118] The implication seems to be that, properly speaking, a city is fundamentally irreducible to a "household," a "family," a "beehive," a "workshop," a "corporation," an "alliance," or a "body politic":

> Yet it is clear that if one goes further in unifying the city, it will not be a city at all. For in its nature, the city is a multiplicity [*plêthos*]; if further unified it will become a household, and further it will become a single human being . . . And a city consists not only of many people, but also of people differing in kind [*eidei*]. Because a city does not come to be from similar people; for a city and an alliance [*symmakhia*] are different things. An alliance is of value by its quantity (since the alliance is naturally for the sake of military strength [*boêtheias*]), just as a weight would be worth more if it weighed more, whereas the parts which are to make up a unity must differ in kind. (*Pol.* II, 1, 1261a18–25)

This implies that the city, founded on *logos*, is fundamentally unexplainable by the imperative or subjunctive moods of, say, bee cooperation, let alone by bird imitation. Then *logos* must be irreducible to strategic contracts for mutual aid (*boêtheia*), and might even be an expression of a content that cannot or may never be experienced firsthand. The specific form of *logos* in this function may well be, not a particular command, but law or a general rule, designed precisely to apply to an infinite number of instances: "Paternal authority does not have the force of necessity, neither does an individual in general, unless he is a king or the like; law has compulsory force because it is a *logos* emanating from some prudence and intelligence" (*NE* X, 9, 1180a19–29). Not being confined to firsthand experience, *logos* is capable of defining (*horistikê*) a level of generality and universality irreducible to any tactical cooperation (*hypotaktikê* or *prostaktikê*). Detached from firsthand experiences, in its indicative (*horistikê*) mood, *logos* is thus able to lie at the basis of all sorts of myths, narratives of creation, of afterlife, of apocalypse; and in its optative (*euktikê*) mood, *logos* makes possible the human experiences of wishful thinking, of utopian fiction, of greeting and blessing, as well as of cursing and remorse.

Recapitulation

This chapter of the book was focused on the full phenomenon of human *logos* as "speech."

In section 1 we turned to animal communication and distinguished two kinds of hearing in animal life in the context of a discussion of bee communication in Aristotle: "noise" appeared as an acoustic object stripped from the interests and meanings invested by the transmitter, as some bird species hear and reproduce with astonishing accuracy the sounds they hear regardless of its origin. On the other hand, "voice" and its counterpart in bees, the discontinuous and occasional "buzz," manifested themselves as coming from an animal in the form of an essentially meaningful and interested claim for attention and call for cooperation, as we observe bees hearing commands to wake up, to go to sleep, and to prepare for flight. We drew two conclusions from this discussion. First, bee communication suggested two moods in animal communication: the imperative of commands, and the subjunctive of threats and promises. Secondly, we noted that bees *understand* the non-firsthand contents they "hear," since they obey the orders given, but do not *relay* it further to other bees, while some bird species, in imitating the sounds they hear, *do relay* them, but without *understanding* their possible content.

In section 2, we formulated the hypothesis that *logos* as specifically human speech names precisely the capacity for both understanding non-firsthand experiences (like the bees, but unlike the imitating birds), and relaying them (like the birds, but unlike bees). To unpack this hypothesis, we turned toward the kind of hearing specifically oriented toward speech, and not to sounds, voices, or commands. We saw that this kind of hearing meant "understanding or taking *in a certain sense.*" We unpacked this definition by noting that it implies speech to be mediated, articulated, and necessarily ambiguous. These implications enabled us to mark out the true material of speech ("letters"), and to describe the first level of its articulation ("words").

Then, in section 3, we moved from the level of "words" to the level of "sentences," that is, from the first articulation of speech to the second. We noted that *logos* as "sentence" introduces two moods besides the imperative and subjunctive moods of human communication: first, the indicative mood whereby affirmations and negations necessarily transcend expressions of firsthand experiences, and expose humans to understanding and conveying non-firsthand experiences; secondly, the optative mood by which humans understand and convey sentences that are not susceptible of truth and falsity, that express desires beyond any actuality and even any possibility.

Finally, in section 4, we tested our hypothesis about human speech on three major Aristotelian passages on human *logos*. We saw that the hypothesis sheds light on the human ability to *claim* to access anything like the essence of other beings in the *Categories*, causes in the *Metaphysics*, and laws in the *Politics*, while also suggesting the necessary function of *logos* in historiography, in news media, in utopian fictions, in remorse, in mythology, in science and philosophy.

All Aristotle's texts are indeed *logoi*. And if we are correct in explaining human *logos* as the ability to understand and relay firsthand and non-firsthand experiences, we must be able to illustrate this in the case of Aristotle's works themselves. In fact, on the one hand, Aristotle's works contain the amazing wealth of observation found in his philosophy of nature or "second philosophy," for example, the observation of the honeybees' waggle,[119] or his report on the phenomenon of what would come to be named "Halley's comet."[120] But, on the other hand, they also incorporate extremely general claims that are not and cannot be based on firsthand experience, for example, the "principle of non-contradiction" or the universal claim that "all humans by nature desire to know" at the opening of his "first philosophy," such that we can hear, through the relay of innumerable hands of disciples and detractors, copyists, translators, editors, companions, and commentators, the "monotonous and peculiar voice" of Aristotle today.[121]

So, after the three senses of *logos* we elaborated in the previous chapters of this book, namely, "standard," "ratio," and "reason," this is the fourth and last major meaning of *logos* in Aristotle: the specifically human ability to understand and relay firsthand experience as well as non-firsthand experiences. Although further extended into "sentence," "discourse," "oration," "book," and so on, this last meaning still refers back to the basic meaning of *logos*: just as "standard," "ratio," and "reason," *logos* as speech is, once again, a relation that holds on to its terms without collapsing or isolating them. Specifically, human speech holds on to one's *own* experience not at the expense of that which extends beyond it into the "wonders" that Sophocles says humans *may be*, and even into that which a human being *will never be*, such as the standard of being of an ox, "what it is *for it* to be," its "*logos* of being."

The question of the "*logos* of being" shows itself only to a "being with *logos*."

CONCLUSION

1. Overview

The Project

Thus, we come full circle. In this book, we started out from the question of the "*logos* of being" of, say, an ox—its "inherent standard" of being (chapters 1 and 2). After exploring how this inherent character shows itself as a kind of "rationing" or "proportioning" in natural and animal motion (chapters 3 and 4) and as "reason" in human action (chapter 5), we have come to see in chapter 6 what kind of being *we* must be to even ask the question of the "*logos* of being": a being that has *logos* as "speech" in the sense of the specifically human ability to understand and relay even that which is by definition beyond her firsthand experience, in this case, what it is *for an ox* to be. It is because all along we ourselves, animals having *logos*, were able to understand and relay that which we never experienced firsthand that we have been able to raise the question of the "*logos* of being" of an ox in the first place.

It is in this sense that the question of the *logos* of being presents itself only to a being having *logos*. Yet, by the same token, we have completed our survey of the four major meanings of *logos* in Aristotle's philosophy: standard, ratio, reason, and speech. These four meanings of *logos* all refer to the fundamental meaning of "gathering," quite in conformity with the etymology of the word. More specifically, the fundamental meaning of *logos* falls within the category of "relation" (*pros ti*) as a relation that holds on to its terms in their difference instead of collapsing one to the other or holding them in indifference. In this basic sense, *logos* typically names a synthesis of terms otherwise thought as mutually exclusive, without violating the "principle of non-contradiction." It introduces a third option, a *via media*, or a middle way that was unnoticed or ruled out, and it does so not at the expense of the "principle of the excluded middle."

The Argument

So, in chapter 1, we started out by noting that the word *logos* appears at the very beginning of the Aristotelian corpus in the phrase "*logos* of being" which distinguishes synonymy from homonymy. We claimed that there "*logos* of being" must mean the standard of being of a being. This was the first major meaning of *logos* in Aristotle: standard, form, essence, or "essential formula." In this meaning, *logos* functioned as answering the question: "What is it for this thing to be?" *That a being has such a standard means that it holds on to its aspects as well as to a certain "claim" concerning what it is for itself to be, without letting one yield, or remain indifferent, to the other.*

In chapter 2, we asked what warrants for the fact that this standard is not arbitrarily imposed from without, but *inherent* to the being at hand. For a being to have an inherent standard implies that it is neither indifferent nor identical to it, and that its meeting the standard is neither merely necessary nor an eventuality on a par with an infinite number of others. *To have a "logos of being" for a being, then, means for it to hold its actual state together and an inherent potentiality together without letting one yield, or remain external, to the other.* Since the actuality of a potential as such is precisely Aristotle's definition of "motion," and since nature is an inherent source of motion and the "form according to *logos*," we concluded that the inherence of the standard of being thus must be illustrated, if anywhere, in natural motion (chapters 3 and 4), and in human action (chapter 5).

Accordingly, chapter 3 dealt with natural motion. We noted how, as simply natural beings, elements are not simply located at certain coordinates in space. Rather, *while being at their actual location, they potentially have their place that they are to rest at, that tend toward and back to*. Further, we saw how *living* beings instantiate the inherence of their standard of being by reproduction and nutrition. *Living beings not only hold on to their place, as elements do, but also, in nutrition, hold together contrary elements within the "logos of growth" in their own body without letting one take over or lay indifferent to the other; in reproduction they do the same in another body*. Thus, as governed by a *logos* of growth, these motions introduced the second major meaning of *logos*: ratio.

Chapter 4 further explored specifically animal motion: sensation and locomotion. "Sensation is a *logos*" by *holding together the state of the organ and that of the object in their very difference instead of being indifferent to or overtaking one another*. Perception is an affection coming from without that completes the body of the animal from within. As to locomotion, it is analyzed as the result of the "practical" syllogism in which, unlike the case of elemental motion, *universal desire in nature is held together with diverse forms of receptivity to particulars*—thus giving rise to various forms of motions: flight, pursuit, hunting, and migration.

Chapter 5 introduced the third major sense of *logos*: reason. It is in action that humans exhibit the inherence of their "standard of being." The defining trait of action is choice, and choice is defined by holding one "option" above others, thereby requiring a prior state of the human soul (*hexis*) in which *it holds on to contrary interpretations of the particular sensible.* This precisely complicates the immediacy of the "practical" syllogism beyond all forms of natural motion and animal locomotion: the particular premise is no longer provided by immediate sensation, but rather reelaborated by positive states (*hexeis*). While intellectual virtues such as art, science, and prudence presuppose "potentialities with *logos*," that is, two-sided potentialities, virtues of character hold contrary interpretations of particular sensibles in so far as the latter are objects of desire, pleasure, or pain. As Aristotle says, "the desiring part in general somehow partakes [in *logos*] insofar as it listens to and can obey it in the sense in which we say 'taking account [*ekhein logon*] of both one's father and one's friends'" (*NE* I, 13, 1102b31–1103a3). The *Politics* takes this metaphor of "taking account of father and friends" literally by claiming that *logos* establishes both the household and the city.

So in chapter 6, we developed an Aristotelian account of "speech"—the fourth major meaning of *logos*. We argued that speech is the human ability to understand and relay firsthand experience *as well as* experience which is not and even cannot be made firsthand. *Logos as speech dissolves, or at least dilutes, the boundary between what one has experienced and what one has not. Human beings are able to have firsthand experience not at the expense of understanding and relaying those they never had or may never have.* In its indicative and optative moods beyond the imperatives and subjunctives of animal motion, this ultimate meaning of *logos* founds both the household and the city, provides a necessary condition for legislation, historiography, myth, politics, science, sophistry, and philosophy. Hence this capacity is what enables us humans, along with Aristotle, to even inquire into what it is for another being to be, by asking: "What is it *for an ox* to be?"

The Results

Here are the results of the argumentative survey we have conducted.

First, *logos* in Aristotle never refers to anything simple, pure, or immediate. It always refers to a relation, a mediation, or a synthesis, in all of its meanings without exception. In this sense, *logos* must be contrasted with *nous* as we shall briefly do at the very end of this book. Secondly, in its specifically human sense, *logos* is strictly and rigorously secular, mundane, full of "wonders," but never mystical. It is never associated with any other animal nor with anything divine. This may be fruitfully contrasted with the Stoic, Gnostic and Christian uses of the word.[1] Thirdly and finally, it is possibly because it refers to something so humble, prosaic, or at least lacking purity and divinity, that this ambiguous but common word has remained unthematized, riddlesome, hidden in plain sight, both in Aristotle and in his posterity.

Once *logos* is restored and brought into play in its fundamental meaning, one can see compelling reasons for thinking Aristotle as a thinker of inclusion.[2]

As to the implications of our claim that *logos* as speech for Aristotle means the specifically human capacity for understanding and relaying firsthand as well as non-firsthand experiences, there are two things to note in order to grasp its significance. First, once the communicating parties possess this ability, the rate of information relay should increase exponentially. Since there is no relay among bees, the scout bee who has found a resource must inform other bees directly one by one, hence the propagation of information follows *a linear growth*. Both bees and the imitating bird species are thus sealed off from the wild proliferation of non-firsthand experiences: bees do not relay them, while the birds do not understand their content when they imitate them. Among humans, however, the "middle man" both understands and relays. So, the capacity for understanding *and* relaying non-firsthand experiences unavoidably boosts the speed with which the information is propagated. Since the receiver can also relay the message without having to undergo the experience firsthand, the propagation of information increases *exponentially*.

Secondly, once the communicating parties possess this specifically human ability, there is no preestablished control over the truthfulness of the messages. Having this capacity, a human being views her human interlocutors as possibly conveying something they have not experienced either. Hence, as Aristotle quotes from Euripides, "if there are persuasive false designations among mortals, you should also admit the contrary, that disbelieving the true befalls mortals."[3] I am exercising my ability to understand and relay non-firsthand experiences not only when I say "Socrates was executed in 399," but also when I say "Socrates was *not* executed in 399." Similarly, one is necessarily drawing on one's capacity to understand and relay non-firsthand experiences when one says that Socrates's execution was the right thing to do, that it was *not* the right thing to do, that the world was created in six days, that it will come to an end, that there are igneous rocks on the surface of the moon, or that all lines contain an infinite number of points. In a way, we are all "middle men."

Thus, this ability is key to understanding the human condition insofar as it is constituted by history, science, education, news media, myth, propaganda, utopian fiction, sophistry, and philosophy. For, if human beings were not receptive to experiences they have not made firsthand, information could not be accumulated, articulated, and propagated in the complex forms of diverse sciences *in order then to be repeated and made public*. Each scientist would start over all experiences and experiments, and would have to be the *first* scientist deprived of all traditions and institutions.[4] Further, without such a human capacity, there could also be no limitless propagation, accumulation, and reception of misinformation. There could be no discourse about the creation of the universe, about the origin of species in general, about "our" species, or about any community in its mythical form, since there would be no ethnic or familial genealogy claiming to "purity" or "nobility." Each human being would have to be the first being on earth, the first human being, the first ancestor of his descendants, the founder of his city, a child of no one. There would indeed be no true fiction, no true experimentation, no true improvisation, no historiography, no prophecy, since by definition all these require access to that which one has not experienced. There would be no awareness of one's life span as a whole, which is requisite for happiness according to Aristotle, and thereby no sense of one's own death other than something that did, does, and will happen to others. There would be no propaganda, no rumors, no deliberately impossible and yet deliberate desires, that is, no utopian fiction and no nostalgia, no true remorse or bad consciousness. There would be no *debatable* principles of living, since all principles would be immediately subjugated to the preservation of the individual and/or of the species. Thus, there would be no genuine compromise, no promises held or betrayed, no true sacrifice because there would be no sense of "good" and "bad" beyond the "painful" and "pleasant." There would be no possibility for pleasure and pain to assume not an *immediate*, but an *accompanying* role. Conversely, there would be no otherworldliness, no eschatology deferring one's pains and pleasures to an afterlife. There would be no true accountability, and thus no true, unaccountable forgiveness. There would be no way to detach oneself, for better or for worse, from one's own first-person perspective, no way to be with others beyond the spectrum of allies and enemies, of cooperators and opponents, of masters and servants. In short, there would be no intermediary room for a *xenos* to remain a *xenos*—a welcomed guest or a potential rival. Finally, if humans did not have *logos*, they would not only be less wonderful or terrifying, they would also lack the sense of wonder and terror. They could not love that which they know they cannot have. There would be no philosophy in the Socratic sense. Philosophy is in another's language. *Philosophia* is, in a sense, *xenophilia*.

Doesn't it make sense to say that one learns another's language, reads another's book, listens to another's ideas, enters another's land, and is initiated in another's way of living *precisely because* one already has the feeling that it is *there*, in *their* syntax or *their* words, in *their* customs and rituals, that wisdom lies?[5] Don't the monuments of unknown cities, the sinuosities of their streets, the traces of the sedimentation of their laws and customs, the fleeting intonations of their sentences, and the divergent categories of their thought appear as promises, rather than as obstacles or indifferent alternatives? Isn't wonder irreducible to both exoticism and fantasies of assimilation? Would the world then seem like our only and ultimate school? What would the world look like if it were our only and ultimate school? It would look exactly as it is.

2. The Human Condition: The Cycloptic and the Oedipal

For better or for worse, these are the implications of *logos* in the specifically human condition. To give these implications a concrete form, let us see two limiting cases, one of which lacks *logos*, while the other is immersed in it in a specifically human way. "Since those who imitate imitate acting people which are necessarily either serious [*spoudaious*] or lowly [*phaulous*] . . . they imitate them either as better than us or as worse, or as similar to us, just like painters" (*Po.* 2, 1448a1–6). The character that is "worse than us" is the figure of the Cyclops.

The Cycloptic

Although they appear in many important passages of the Aristotelian corpus,[6] the Cyclopes appear in the *Poetics* as figures well-suited to comedy, being "worse [*kheirous*] . . . than the people today" (*Po.* 2, 1448a17). In the debate between conservatism and reform in the *Politics*, they appear as "earth-born" and *not* to be followed since "they were just like ordinary and foolish people" (*Pol.* II, 5, 1269a7–8). The Cyclopes are representatives of ancient customs that should be reformed with caution, even if they are written down. Most importantly, the following discussion concerning the priority of law as *logos* over paternal rule suggests that what is at stake is less a group than a way of life qualified as "cycloptic" (*kyklôptikôs*):

> Paternal authority does not have the force of necessity, neither does an individual in general, unless he is a king or the like; law however has compulsory power, being a *logos* originating from some prudence and thought. Now among humans, those who oppose people's impulses are hated, even when they do so rightly, but the law is not hated when it orders what is decent. But in the city of the Lacedemonians alone, or among few others, does the lawgiver seem to have taken care for upbringing and exercises, while in most cities they have been most careless about such things, and each person lives the way he wants, laying down the law "for his

> children and wife" in the manner of a Cyclops [*kyklôptikôs*]. (*NE* X, 9, 1180a19–29)

What makes the Cycloptic way of ruling and living "worse" is then simply that it is at least *second best*, compared to what *is* best according to Aristotle: that upbringing be a common concern.[7] In the terms of the *Nicomachean Ethics*, human life is impoverished by no longer "taking account of *both* one's father *and* one's friends."[8]

This ties in well with Aubenque's emphasis on the role of deliberation and necessarily of compromise as much as consensus in ethical and political affairs according to Aristotle. Aubenque claims that in fact the middle ground in discussion has nothing to do with mediocrity for Aristotle, just like the middle term in logic and the mean in ethics has nothing mediocre about them. The search for including such a middle path is not a way of "playing it safe," but in fact the search for "excellence between two extremes." In Aubenque's words:

> In the political order, this excellence is friendship which is the basis of a genuine city in opposition to associations motivated by private interests. The human being accomplishes herself in community, in the coexistence and the conviviality [*synousia*] whose intellectual condition of possibility is common deliberation. It is in this sense that the "government of the middle," which we call "constitutional government" ["*politie*" in the French text] or "democracy," is the most "excellent" of constitutions.[9]

Genuine compromise is impossible without *logos*, without an immersive access into another's perspective, without at least an opening toward that in which one does *not* take pleasure, without sacrifice, that is, without a *proairesis*, a preference, an interpretation as good, of that which one does not and may never benefit from. Genuine compromise is impossible without an eye for the mindset of another. Other than their paternal rule and lack of care for upbringing, what does the Cycloptic life look like?

Law

The Cyclopes lack nothing but lack itself.[10] Living on an island of the blessed, similar to the golden race in Hesiod,[11] the Cyclopes "lack" concern and work, as is made unmistakable in the Homeric text by the wealth of privative adjectives and the recurrent contrasts with the human condition: they have no plow, no sowing, no hunting, *hence* no carpenters and no ships . . . (Homer,

Odyssey IX, 125). No wonder that Odysseus, assuming the point of view of an entrepreneur or of a colonizer, fantasizes about the city they would have been able to build if they had had some ships, and about the abundant agriculture they would have had thanks to the fertile soil (*Odyssey* IX, 126–41). The idyllic environment of the Cyclopes is reflected by their regimen. Coming upon one of them, Odysseus immediately contrasts his diet to human nutrition: "[He was] not like a man that lives by bread [or grain, *sitos*], but rather like a wooded [*hylêenti*] peak of high mountains, which stands out to view alone, apart from the rest" (*Odyssey* IX, 190–92). This inhuman diet and vegetal ("hylic") or elemental stature seems connected with their sporadic way of life remarked by Aristotle in the *Politics*.[12]

Hence, they "lack" the need for deliberation and cooperation. As Aristotle quotes, "each gives law to his children and spouses" in his own cave[13] (*Odyssey* IX, 107–15). Indeed, they are "arrogant and lawless" (*Odyssey* IX, 106), and yet this is not because they are wicked, but rather because they are blessed in some way. The Cyclopes may remind one of Aristotle's characterization of the kind of human being that is by nature deprived of the polis. According to another Homeric quotation in Aristotle, this "apolitical" person by nature is "'clanless, lawless, hearthless,' and also a lover of war. He resembles an isolated piece at draughts."[14] To vary Aristotle's striking metaphor, the Cycloptic routine is that of a king on an empty chessboard, checkered in black and white.

The Cyclopes lack neither a common location,[15] nor houses, caves, or streets, nor common goals and *therefore* common strategies.[16] Yet a community is not simply made out of allies, and a city is not made out of neighbors.[17] What the Cyclopes "lack" is an agora. They do not lack the mental capacity for deliberating, but rather a sense of the human condition and situatedness which make it *necessary* to deliberate:

> For it is impossible to lay down a law about things people deliberate over. Therefore they do not deny at least *this*: that the human must judge about these, although not one human being, but many. For each ruler judges beautifully when he has been educated by the law, and it would seem out of place if one person saw better when judging with two eyes and two organs of hearing, and acting with two feet and hands, than many people with many, since even today the monarchs make many eyes and ears and hands and feet their own, for they adopt persons that are friendly to their rule and to themselves as their fellow-rulers. (*Pol.* III, 11, 1287b23–32)[18]

So if the Cyclopes seem to "lack" one eye by birth, their character is no less formed by their environment. Hence Odysseus never seems to suggest that they have an evil or wicked nature, but rather insists on their self-sufficient environment (*Odyssey* IX, 190–91). Of course, all this inference is made in contrast to the human condition which has less to do with birth, say the number of eyes one has, than with their interaction with their environment.[19] And human environments are not always as blissful as the island of the Cyclopes. Homeric, Platonic, Euripidic, and Aristotelian texts all depict the Cyclops as having one eye because of a more fundamental political and interpersonal shortcoming, *and not the other way around.* Hence the number of "eyes" or "hands" always remains often misleadingly metaphorical. To vary examples around this insight as we shall see Aristotle doing, what makes a conversation is not two speakers, what makes a good one is not even *more* speakers, and a friendly gathering is not enriched simply by more and more food or more and more hosts and guests, but by their variety, that is, their difference. The reason why a crowded jury may be better than a restricted one is not the number of the jury members, but their diversity that does not necessarily follow from such a number:

> It is possible that the many, although not each one is serious [*spoudaios*], yet when they come together, may be better [*beltious*] than those who are so, just as public dinners to which many contribute are better than those supplied at one's cost; for where there are many, each one may have some portion of virtue and prudence, and when they have come together, just as the multitude becomes one human being with many feet and hands and senses, so also it becomes one with regard to moral and intellectual faculties. This is why the many judge musical and poetic works, for each can judge a different part and all of them all of the work. (*Pol.* III, 6, 1281a42–1281b10)

The Cyclopes are not stupid or logically defective. They lack a portion of "virtue and prudence." Their condition is *apaideusia,*[20] a lack of education, perhaps the condition that, according to Aristotle, makes one demand a demonstration even for the principle of non contradiction, or for the very existence of nature.[21] Thus this "shortcoming" is *not* simply foreign to humans, or at least to their "past."

Now we are in a position to read Aristotle's famous quotation of the Homeric story of the Cyclops:

> Formerly the cities were under kingly rule as some peoples still are, because they came [to form a city] out of kingly rule, for every household is under the kingly rule of its oldest member so that the colonies were so too, given the kinship of their members. And this is what Homer says: "and each gives law to his children and spouses," for they were scattered, and that is how people used to live. (*Pol.* I, 1, 1252b19–26)[22]

Not having any notion of law beyond his sporadic life, being the lonesome powerful king on the empty chessboard, no wonder the Cyclops is unfamiliar with any kind of "law of hospitality" (*Odyssey* IX, 259–71), but instead seems to embody different impoverished forms of the "law of the middle excluded": I am either this or that, this is either my place or not, this is either mine or not, this is either a friend or a foe . . . He considers another viewpoint as contrary, contradictory, or confrontational. *Being* the son of the sea god Poseidon and a sea nymph, Polyphemus the Cyclops in fact *has* no Cyclops parents, and even no gods properly speaking (*Odyssey* IX, 275–80),[23] therefore no law reaching out of the cave, no openness, because no need for openness, to a perspective beyond his pleasure and pain.

Of course, Odysseus is depicted as a diametrically opposite character. The Cyclopes were characterized by privative adjectives: "*a-phrêtôr*" ("clanless"), "*a-themistos*" ("lawless"), and "*a-nestios*" ("hearthless").[24] On the contrary, Odysseus's famous epithets insist on his openness to a plurality: he is the "*poly-tropos*" ("much-wandering"), the "*poly-mêtis*" ("man of many counsels"), the "*poly-mêkhanos*" ("resourceful"), the "*poly-tlêmôn*" ("much-enduring"), the man of many twists and turns, of much contriving and endurance. As opposed to the literally autochthonic Cyclopes, Odysseus is the voyager, the perennial *xenos*, the one displaced and also stretching back to his origin. For instance, when he lands on the island of the Cyclopes, he takes the best wine he has, and once arrived at Polyphemus's cave, despite his famous cunning, he refuses his fellow men's proposal to run away with the goods they found in there—not because he believes in the natural goodness of humans and Cyclopes, but rather because he expects generosity in return (*Odyssey* IX, 228–30). To use the metaphor of chess once again, Odysseus is not a pawn at all, he is comparable to a queen surrounded by bishops, knights, and rooks.

So Cycloptic life "lacks" *logos*. The Cyclopes are not *alogos* as such, but *alogos* precisely in the way a human may be, may have been, or may come to be. The "lack" of the Cyclopes is only seemingly anatomical, and the Cycloptic life is "worse" not because they are literally monocular, but because they "lack" the need of deliberation, of immersing themselves into the perspective of others. "Lacking" *logos*, the Cyclopes are blissfully "confined" to their first-hand experience, to their *autopsia*.

Language

This shows in the language of Polyphemus the Cyclops. He does attempt to make Odysseus tell him where his ship was.[25] Indeed, Odysseus immediately deciphers Polyphemus's malice and tells him that their ship dashed into pieces (*Odyssey* IX, 279–85). In a dramatic reversal, the very weakness of Polyphemus's attempt to manipulate inspires Odysseus to manipulate him in turn, and this time successfully. It is at this moment that, calming his immediate anger (*Odyssey* IX, 299–305) without altogether suppressing it (*Odyssey* IX, 504),[26] Odysseus pays heed to *logos* and appeals to his openness to a life altogether foreign to him by taking a look at the world from Polyphemus's round eye.

Besides his resources of art and indeed the cooperation of his fellow men in the fabrication of the spear (*Odyssey* IX, 319–35), Odysseus makes and works out his plan by means of language. The night before he blinds him, Odysseus has a little chat with Polyphemus while offering his good wine as if asking for mercy (*Odyssey* IX, 347–52); and when in drunkenness Polyphemus asks his name (*Odyssey* IX, 355–59), he springs his trap by famously telling him that his name is "Nobody" (*Odyssey* IX, 366).

The rest of the story is well known. When Polyphemus tells the other Cyclopes that "Nobody is killing me" (*Odyssey* IX, 408) in the hope of organizing them, both Polyphemus and the other Cyclopes are responsible for the miscommunication. For Polyphemus takes "Nobody" for a proper name, while the other Cyclopes take it as a pronoun, unable as they are to notice Polyphemus's shortcoming, and immersed as they are in the literal and correct sense of this word. They fail to become "many eyes and ears and hands,"[27] regardless of how many and how well-armed they may be (*Odyssey* IX, 410–12). Polyphemus then fails to attune himself not only to Odysseus's plans, but also to the mindset of the other Cyclopes. Otherwise he would explain to them that the word "Nobody" is homonymous, to use Aristotelian terms, and does not only mean "nobody," but in this context is the name of the evil Greek guest. But nor do the Cyclopes put themselves in Polyphemus's shoes and notice that *clearly* "Nobody is killing me" is an awkward answer to their question in that context. Both sides take the word "Nobody" univocally, but unfortunately in different senses, precisely as Odysseus planned in using this ambiguous name. Cyclopes act as if words simply match beings, as if there is only one word for one being or one kind of being.[28]

This is the story Aristotle has in mind when he calls the life of the Cyclopes as second best, that is, as falling short of the potential of human law and language. We saw at the beginning of this book how Aristotle characterizes this univocal, nonarbitrary, and essential relationship between nouns and beings: the Cyclopes "lack" *logos* not because they lack language, but because their language is immersed in synonymy.[29] In a word, Cyclopes seem to lack the sense of riddles.[30]

In the Homeric text, the life of Polyphemus seems to have been perfect until the cunning and colonizing Odysseus arrived. The latter laughs at the shortcomings of Polyphemus, and so might the reader think he is expected to do. In fact, it is this passage that Aristotle quotes in the *Rhetoric* as testimony that the more one is angry at somebody, the more he will want his enemy to *know* who retaliated.[31]

Love

And yet, there is more to Polyphemus's story.[32] For there is an unsaid in the Homeric text, a backstory that remained untold until the later tradition. This prequel reveals to us a Polyphemus that is not merely an exemplar of the limited capacities in matter of law and language among Cyclopes, but a particular person with a particular past, and with a personal story about that past—a past which was not as idyllic as a reader of Homer might have thought. This story puts Polyphemus in a new and even more problematically human contrast with Odysseus who was famously awaited at home by Penelope and Telemachus.

Because this story is a love story. It is told in the eleventh idyll, "The Cyclops' Serenade," by Theocritus, a Sicilian poet from the third century BC.[33] This text is extremely suggestive as to what it means to lack *logos* not only in social organization and communication, but also in individual emotional life, a life unable to access resources and assume mindsets beyond its own firsthand experiences. It shows why, however "worse" Cyclopes may be, their situation must at least be *plausible* in the eyes of the spectators for the play to be a comedy.[34] It shows how the world is not split into mythical grotesque beings lacking *logos*, and cunning humans possessing it. It blurs such a distinction in line with Aristotle who situates an *alogia* at the very center of the human soul, that is as characteristically human as *logos*.[35] It relates a story of Polyphemus that teaches us something about the human condition.

For Polyphemus, it turns out, was a heartbroken lover. Theocritus's idyll opens thus in Verity's translation (Theocritus, 2002: 33, ll. 1–18):

"Nicias, there is no remedy for love, no liniment,
As I believe, nor any balm, except the Muses.
Theirs is a gentle, painless drug, and in men's power
To use; but it is hard to find. You know this well,
I think; you are a doctor, and one whom the nine
Muses love above all. This at any rate was the way
My countryman the Cyclops eased his pain,
Polyphemus long ago, when he loved Galatea,
When the down was fresh about his mouth and temples.
He loved, not with apples, roses, or curls of hair,
But in an outright frenzy. For him, nothing else existed.
Often his flocks would come of their own accord
Back from green pastures to the fold, while he, alone
On the weed-strewn shore, would sing of Galatea from
Break of day, wasting away with love. Deep inside he bore
A cruel wound, which mighty Cypris' dart had driven
Into his heart. But he found out the cure: he would sit
On some high rock, and gazing out to sea would sing."

Polyphemus was not only madly in love with the sea nymph Galatea. He also wrote poetry—the only remedy for a broken heart, according to the narrator: sitting on a rock, gazing at the sea, and singing.

There follows Polyphemus's love song. Here is the opening (ll. 19–29):

"O my white Galatea, why do you spurn your lover?
Whiter to look at than cream cheese, softer than a lamb,
More playful than a calf, sleeker than the unripe grape.
Why do you only come just as sweet sleep claims me,
Why do you leave me just as sweet sleep lets me go,
Flying like a ewe at the sight of a grey wolf?
I fell in love with you, my sweet, when first you came
With my mother to gather flowers of hyacinth
On the mountain, and I was your guide. From the day
I set eyes on you up to this moment, I've loved you
Without a break; but you care nothing, nothing at all."

There are two important aspects of this opening. First, by means of this *logos*, we get to understand something we have not experienced firsthand: how Polyphemus himself saw Galatea. More exactly, we get to understand how

Polyphemus thought he would praise Galatea to herself in such a way that would convince her to join him on his island. The first adjective he uses, "white," is pretty redundant, since the name Galatea already strongly brings to mind "milk," *gala* in Ancient Greek.[36] Similarly, the metaphors he uses to praise her seem to be chosen to reflect his limitation to his own firsthand experience, his inability to go beyond synonymity, literality, or univocality: for Galatea's whiteness brings to his mind "cream cheese," her softness a "lamb," her playfulness a "calf," her sleekness an "unripe grape," her fleetingness "a ewe."

The second important related aspect of the opening is Polyphemus's general tone of complaint and his avowal of not understanding her. But then he tries to understand her by looking at himself from a non-firsthand point of view (ll. 30–33):

> "I know, my beautiful girl, why you run from me:
> A shaggy brow spreads right across my face
> From ear to ear in one unbroken line. Below is a
> Single eye, and above my lip is set a broad flat nose."

All along, we seem to be called by Theocritus to ridicule Polyphemus: his linguistic capacities, his incapacity for assuming somebody else's point of view, his looks, and so on. This seemingly ridiculing tone continues as Polyphemus tries to convince Galatea. Polyphemus interprets the situation in a clearly self-centered way, foreshadowing his later inability to communicate with the other Cyclopes in the Homeric episode. So he makes propositions, offerings, and promises to Galatea that are very much irrelevant to a sea nymph (ll. 34–49):[37]

> "Such may be my looks, but I pasture a thousand beasts,
> And I drink the best of the milk I get from them.
> Cheese too I have in abundance, in summer and autumn,
> And even at winter's end; my racks are always laden.
> And I can pipe better than any Cyclops here,
> When I sing, my sweet pippin, deep in the night
> Of you and me. For you I'm rearing eleven fawns,
> All marked on their necks, and four bear cubs too.
> O please, come. You will see that life is just as good
> If you leave the grey-green sea behind to crash on the shore,
> And at night you will find more joy in this cave with me.

Here there are bays, and here slender cypresses,
Here is sombre ivy, and here the vine's sweet fruit;
Here there is ice-cold water which dense-wooded Etna
Sends from its white snows—a drink fit for the gods.
Who could prefer waves and the sea to all this?"

There follows an explicit foreshadowing of the *Odyssey* (ll. 50–53):

"But if you think I'm a touch too hairy for you,
I have oak logs here, and under the ash unflagging fire.
Burn away my life with fire—I could bear even that,
And my single eye, my one dearest possession of all."

Then, instead of a "plan of action," we read Polyphemus blaming his mother and then nature in general (ll. 54–59):

"I wish my mother had given me gills when I was born,
Then I could have dived down and kissed your hand,
If you denied me your mouth, and brought you white
Snowdrops or delicate poppies with their scarlet petals.
One grows in summer and the other grows in winter,
So you see I could not bring you both at once."

Can't he build a ship? Can't he at least learn to swim? Ironically, indeed, he wishes for "some mariner" to visit him, in another reference to the *Odyssey*. Once again, the blame is on anybody else but him (ll. 60–66):

"It's not too late, my sweet, for me to learn to swim;
If only some mariner would sail here in his ship,
Then I could fathom why you nymphs love life in the deep.
Come out, Galatea, come out and forget your home,
Just as I sit here and forget to return to mine.
Follow the shepherd's life with me—milking,
And setting cheese with the rennet's pungent drops."

Finally, the blame turns definitely toward the mother. Instead of engaging in action to meet Galatea *on her own terms*, Polyphemus yields to his resentment for his mother and to wishful thinking *in his own terms*. Polyphemus dreams of punishing his mother by exhibiting his own suffering (ll. 67–71):

> "It's my mother who does me wrong; it's her alone I blame.
> She's not once spoken a gentle word to you about me,
> Although she sees me wasting away, day by day.
> I'll see she knows how my head and feet throb with pain,
> So that her torment will be equal to what I suffer."

Despite his self-centered but passionate desire, Polyphemus's so-called plan of "action" involves optatives, or contrafactual conditional sentences, or conditions depending on Galatea, on his mother, on nature, on a possible stranger—in short, on pretty much everybody *but him*.

The end of Polyphemus's love song is bitter. Quite unlike Odysseus trying to go back to Penelope and Telemachus, Polyphemus convinces himself to come to his senses, to stay where he is, and to distract himself from his love for Galatea. Beyond being born in a legally and linguistically limited environment, Polyphemus here chooses to take account of a voice in himself as one takes account of both one's father and one's friends (ll. 72–79):

> "O Cyclops, Cyclops, where have your wits flown away?
> Show some sense, go and weave some baskets, collect
> Green shoots for your lambs. Milk the ewe
> At hand; why chase the one who runs away? Maybe
> You'll find another Galatea, and a prettier one too.
> I'm invited out for night-time play by lots of girls,
> And they giggle together as soon as they see I've heard.
> On land I too am clearly a man of some consequence."

However grotesque it may appear at first, Polyphemus's situation is by no means one unfamiliar to human beings.[38] Hence we entered this detour beyond the Aristotelian and Homeric texts simply to make the point that Polyphemus in fact partakes in a special modality of *logos* we encountered in chapter 6: the optative mood, the mood of wishing and praying. His self-centered interpretation of the situation and his complete lack of commitment for changing it precisely fit the structure of wish, a desire that is cut off from all action. And however comedic, it is in fact this aspect of Polyphemus that is humane, and Theocritus clearly ends up sympathizing with him (ll. 80–81):

> "So by singing the Cyclops shepherded his love,
> And more relief it brought him than paying a large fee."

For, while we can easily think how Polyphemus could have indeed joined Galatea, we can also imagine a situation where this is simply impossible, where Polyphemus's "cure" or plan of "action," namely "poetizing," may well have been the *only* resource. Galatea could have simply refused Polyphemus. She could have been prevented from seeing Polyphemus by her family. She could have been dead. In such a case, Polyphemus may have wishfully imagined to join her in an afterlife, in a world to come, in another Ithaca. And this is as specifically human as Odysseus's inventiveness in remedying his *nostalgia* and returning to the arms of Penelope.

What this supposedly comedic Polyphemus teaches us about *logos* is then the following: since human *logos* is an exposure, beyond *autopsia*, to that which one has not experienced firsthand, human beings are able to remain stuck in their own perspective and experience, be it idyllic or traumatic, in a specific way, that is, in a humane way. It is precisely because they *can* overcome their own perspective that human inability to do so takes a specific form, the form of Job's long-repressed protest against God, the form of wish in all its frustrated versions: remorse, resentment, obsession, utopian fiction, nostalgia, or melancholy. Human *alogia* is as wonderful or terrifying than human *logos*.

The Oedipal

So much then for the character who is "worse than us" according to Aristotle's *Poetics*. Who is the character that is "better than us" again such that it may well shed light on the human condition from the reverse angle? Aristotle suggests that characters that are "better than us" are to be found in tragedy, not in comedy.[39] More specifically, the Aristotelian paradigm of tragedy is Sophocles's *King Oedipus*.[40] The paradigmatic tragic hero is Oedipus whose action he precisely qualifies as *deinon*.[41] Here human blindness is more tragic than Polyphemus's, since it results not from human confrontation with impossibility, but comes forth through human possibilities, deliberate decisions, words, and actions. As Cycloptic blindness illustrates something about human confinement in *autopsia*, Oedipal blindness may have something to teach us concerning a life altogether detached from *autopsia*.

There are a great number of ways in which Oedipus can be contrasted to Polyphemus. Unlike Polyphemus who *has* no god because he is the son of one, Oedipus is the son of a human, and he is a zealous follower of god's oracles. Instead of having limited linguistic skills like the solitary heartbroken shepherd Polyphemus, Oedipus is the very one who cunningly solves the riddle of the Sphinx and becomes at once the savior of a city, the father of a family, and a bold king. With all his messengers, soldiers, oracles, family members, and advisors at the opening of the tragedy, Oedipus appears as a panoptic character. At the very opening of the tragedy, he is all eyes, hands, and feet at the throne of his city in the middle of the stage facing a new riddle in the form of a wicked epidemic, something unthinkable in the blessed island of the Cyclopes. This multiplication of the "organs" of the King of Thebes is a perfect example of human *logos* as our ability to understand and relay that which we have not experienced firsthand: the messages carried by messengers, the oracles related by soothsayers and then relayed by others, the numerous stories handed on from generation to generation, the various genealogies, orders, threats, inferences, curses, vows, and promises . . . In *King Oedipus*, the whole action is speech, and speech is hyperactive. Unlike Polyphemus who either becomes a "lover of war" or fails to identify himself with the desires of his loved one, Oedipus the *xenos* is welcomed by the Thebans and saves them, marries their widowed queen, and becomes king. And in contrast to the frustration, rage, and resentment of Polyphemus, Oedipus is majestic, righteous, and magnanimous.[42] Compared to the Cyclopes' xenophobic island, finally, Thebes is a cosmopolitan and liberal environment, the xenophile city par excellence.

The contrast shows itself best in the context of language. Called out for help by Polyphemus, the Cyclopes fail to understand that "nobody" does not have a univocal sense in that context, that is, that "nobody" and "Nobody" are homonyms. Oedipus and other characters in the tragedy do the exact opposite: they all fail to notice that "the killer of Laius," "the one who slept with his mother," "Laius and Jocasta's son," and "Oedipus" are all synonyms. Whereas the Cyclopes were limited to the literal senses of words ("Nobody" as a proper name), the Thebans are so immersed in the multivocity of *logos* that they precisely *fail* to take things literally. The oracles are always over-interpreted, they are understood not literally, but are constantly distorted by the assumptions of the listener.

Jocasta, for one, does not recognize the face of her own son.[43] She fails to recognize his natural identity, because she is led astray by his conventional identity as the "son of the king of Corinth" or as the "witty stranger that saved Thebes from the Sphinx." So she takes him to be a *xenos*. Oedipus, in turn, *misidentifies* himself and his parents only because he is cast *out* of Thebes and returns there afterwards. Rural life as such is closed to such conventional *mis*identification, because it is closed to conventional identification. The tragedy is made possible because, as citizens, everybody in the play is thinking merely in terms of conventional symbolism.

The symbolic character of nouns entails a structurally determined confusion: precisely because nouns necessarily open up a distance between the sounds uttered and the meaning, the same things are said in many ways not only in different languages, but even within one language, and because the same nouns can mean fundamentally different things. In a word, the first level of articulation of *logos* opens the possibility of ambiguity, equivocation, homonymy. It is because of homonymy that even nouns are subject to interpretation. In chapter 6, we saw how this inherent "flaw" of nouns follows precisely from their convenience, and why homonymy is a necessary consequence of the enormous economy of language: "Nouns and the quantity of *logoi* are finite, whereas things are infinite in number. Thus it is necessary that the same *logos* and noun signify a number of things" (*SE* 1, 165a11–14). This enables Sophocles to beautifully show Oedipus tragically determined to *either* kill whoever "himself" killed Laius *or* die "himself"—supposing these synonymous designations to be *homonymous*.[44]

To sum up our comparison between the character who is "worse than us" and the one who is "better": the Cyclops lives a self-centered, closed, rural life of synonymy where things that share names also share their "*logos* of being" naturally as animal voices are signs of pleasure and pain, as bones fit into their joints; Oedipus, on the other hand, lives a political life of homonymy, a life open and devoted to others, a life of conventions, contracts, symbols, and interpretations. As the Cyclops was blind to others and was exposed to being blinded by another's cunning or beauty, Oedipus is oblivious to himself and, sure enough, ends up blinding himself.[45]

When Aristotle insists that there be nothing in the plot of the tragedy itself that is *alogos*, but only in past events, his example is *King Oedipus*.[46] It is his disregeard for his shady natural roots that ruins Oedipus's plans for starting over and freely redefining himself. After Jocasta recognizes who Oedipus is and condemns herself to silence, Oedipus, seeing her terror, bravely cries:

> Let whatever disaster come! However lowly it may be, I want to see my origin [*sperm' idein*]. In her womanly arrogance, she is ashamed of my ignoble roots. But I consider myself to be the child of Fortune [*paida tês Tychês*] the generous, and I am not ashamed of it. It is Fortune who was my mother, and the years of my life that made me lowly and great. This is my origin, nothing can change it: why would I refuse to learn who I was born from? (1076–85)

Oedipus's true hubris, his true misunderstanding of human limitation, exhibits itself in this claim to be a purely rational agent, a self-transparent individual, freely defining himself, consciously engaging with others through contracts, the child of no real parents, but "the child of Fortune." This is what makes him "bigger than nature," "better than us," detached from the *alogia* of his past, and so terrifying. And this makes his downfall not simply realistic, but paradigmatic. This detachment from his natural roots could make Oedipus simply neglect the question of his origins. And yet, on the contrary, it pushes him forward in the gradual unfolding of his self-recognition.[47]

We have thus come to the end of our elaboration of Polyphemus and Oedipus as two figures that shed light on the human condition as having *logos*, that is, as having access to that which one does not and may never experience firsthand. Repeatedly used by Aristotle as paradigms, they both instantiate specifically human forms of *alogia*. The one is immersed in his cave, in his self-centered life, in his rural familial circle, in his natural environment and in a language innocent of the ambiguity that is typical to *logos* and always requires interpretation. The other one lives his cosmopolitan and public life as a self-determining rational individual agent detached from his natural origins, so wrapped up in his free interpretations and assumptions that he is blind to his familial origins, to his irrational attachments, and to his childhood.

So the Cycloptic and the Oedipal are two limiting-cases of human *logos*, or, alternatively, two forms of specifically human *alogia*: a deficiency in *logos* and an exclusive immersion in it that is wonderfully and terrifyingly possible only for a being that has *logos*.

3. *Nous*

Yet not all *alogia* is human. Aristotle's works present a sense of *alogos* that is not a *privation* of *logos*, but is altogether foreign to *logos*. In contrast to Cycloptic or Oedipal *alogia*, this one is *positive*, a positive state, a *hexis*.[48] Thereby this *alogia* testifies that, despite its extremely varied functions, *logos* is not a key opening all doors and the single overall logic of all being. For Aristotle there *is* a form of carelessness that is not vice, a kind of a lack of prudence that is not foolish, a way of being that does not hold onto different terms in their difference. For Aristotle there *is* a state that has no extremes and thus no middle to exclude or include. It is different from science, but it is not ignorance. Beyond compositeness and manifoldness, the world, even the sublunar realm, has oases of positive simplicity, of pure acts.[49]

This is *nous*.[50] And *nous* is to be distinguished from *logos* on all levels.[51] Unlike composite beings that have a "*logos* of being" in the sense of "standard" (see our chapter 1), *nous* is everlasting transparency and purity: "There is a sense in which *nous* makes all things; this is a positive state like light: for in a way light makes colors in potentiality into colors in actuality. This *nous* is separable, impassive, unmixed, since it is at work in its being" (*DA* III, 5, 430a14–17). Unlike beings that are *both* potentially *and* actually so that what it is for them to be is at issue (see chapters 2 and 3), *nous* leaves no room for change, for decisions and choices, for deliberation, for consensus or compromise, for intermittence, for *not* being at work, and for somehow not being what it is for *nous* to be: "*Nous* does not think intermittently. Separated, it is only what it truly is, and this alone is immortal and eternal . . . and nothing thinks without this" (*DA* III, 5, 430a18–25).[52] Unlike sensation as a *logos*, holding on to the form of sensibles without yielding to them or affecting them (see our chapter 4), "*nous* is the form of forms" (*DA*, III, 8, 432a3). Unlike locomotion which takes the form of a practical syllogism, *nous* is not moved, but rather moves without itself being moved.[53] Unlike prudence (see chapter 5), "*nous* apprehends the terms of which there is no *logos*" (*NE* VI, 8, 1142a25–26).[54] Unlike *logos* as predication, affirmation, or negation, "*nous* is not something in relation to something else [*ti kata tinos*]" (*DA* III, 6, 430b26–29). *Nous* is thus naturally associated not with the strictly human, but with the divine in the human.[55]

> Since, among the intellectual positive states by which we are in truth, some are always true (knowledge and *nous*), and some admit of falsity like opinion and calculation, and since no other kind of knowledge is more accurate than *nous*, and since the sources are more knowable than demonstrations and all knowledge is with *logos*, thus there would be no knowledge of the sources; and since no knowledge admits of being more true than *nous*, then *nous* would apprehend the sources; from this one sees also that the source of demonstration is not demonstration, just as the source of knowledge is not knowledge. So if we have no kind of truth other than knowledge, then the source of knowledge would be *nous*; it would be the source of the source, just as all knowledge stands to all things. (*APo.* II, 19, 110b5–17)

On a similar line of demarcation, Aristotle writes in the *Politics* that "*logos* for us, and *nous*, is the *telos* of nature" (*Pol.* VII, 13, 1334b15). Reason, rationality, or intelligence may appear to us today as a superpower defining and distinguishing human beings. We hope to have shown that for Aristotle *logos* distinguishes humans from other animals in two of its senses ("reason" and "speech"), but that these two together with the other two senses of *logos* ("standard" and "ratio") all refer back to one basic meaning shared by all living nature and most of nature as such. Yet Aristotle does not hypostatize or epitomize *logos* in the context of beings as such (since God and the ultimate constituents of the cosmos seem to lack it), nor in the context of ultimate human capacities and happiness, since *nous* is without *logos*. And if *logos* has been surprisingly neglected both by Aristotle and by his posterity, it may be because *logos* has been eclipsed by the priority and divinity of *nous*, thereby abandoning its worldly, observant, deliberating, concrete, hesitant, and humane character in order to become the Word.

NOTES

Preface

1. This claim that the specificity of human communication lies in the double ability to understand and relay non-firsthand experiences also seems quite in line with twentieth-century discoveries and discussions around bee communication. See Frisch, 1993: esp. 43, 55–56; Benveniste, 1971: 53; Deleuze and Guattari, 1987: 77. For a detailed discussion, see chapter 6.

Introduction

1. Chantraine explains the etymologically fundamental meaning of *logos* as follows: "Le sens originel est 'rassembler, cueillir, choisir' . . . , d'où 'compter, dénombrer' . . . *legô* signifie parfois 'énumérer,' etc. . . . 'débiter des injures,' au moyen 'bavarder, discourir' . . . Ainsi est né l'emploi au sens de 'raconter, dire,' etc." (1984: 625). Heidegger's interpretation is in line with Chantraine: "[*Legein*] means what our similarly sounding *legen* means: to lay down and lay before. In *legen* a 'bringing together' prevails, the Latin *legere* understood as *lesen*, in the sense of collecting and bringing together. *Legein* properly means the laying-down and laying-before which gathers itself and others" (Heidegger, 1984: 60; see also Heidegger, 1959: 123–79). See also Hoffmann, 2003: 27–53, whose claim that focal reference of the various senses of *logos* is "composition/gathering" is quite cogent to ours here, although made in a wider, mostly sophistical and rhetorical context that is very neglectful of Aristotle's usage. In Book V, definition 3 of the *Elements*, Euclid defines *logos* as a "*poia skhesis*," a certain state, condition, or relation, not *between* but *of* two homogenous magnitudes of the same kind with respect to their size (Euclid, 2007: 291).

2. Unless noted otherwise, all translations from Ancient Greek and Latin are my own. In transcribing the Greek texts, I shall use *ê* for êta, *ô* for ômega, *kh* for khi, *u* or sometimes *y* for upsilon, and *i* for the iota subscript. In this fragment by Heraclitus, I adopt the reading of *homologeein* ("agreeing," "having the same *logos*") for *xympheretai* ("brings together") as in the text of Hippolytus who is "the fullest source" (KRS, 192). For *homologeein*, see Heidegger, 1984.

3. While belonging to the post-Aristotelian tradition, the division of the Aristotelian corpus into three parts (logic, physics, and ethics) is a procedure which itself is not altogether foreign to Aristotle. See *Top.* I, 14, 105b19ff.

4. Plato, *Republic*, V, 479B11–C5; *Euthydemus*, 300D. The whole text of the riddle is quoted in the scholiast. (Hermann, 1853: 34)

5. *Po.* 22, 1458a26-27: "The idea of riddle is that one conjoins impossible things while telling existing things."

6. S.v. "*logos*" in LSJ, 1057–59. For the increase of frequency of its use from Homer until the fourth century, see Hoffmann (2003: 30).

7. Here are the major headings in the LSJ:

   I. computation, reckoning;
   II. relation, correspondence, proportion;

III. explanation;
IV. inward *debate* of the soul;
V. continuous statement, narrative, oration;
VI. *verbal expression* or *utterance*;
VII. *a particular utterance, saying*;
VIII. *thing spoken of, subject-matter*;
IX. *expression, utterance, speech* regarded formally;
X. the *Word* or *Wisdom* of God.

This extensive list covers all major meanings given in Chantraine (1984: 625), and most of those in Guthrie except perhaps Guthrie's emphasis on "definition, essential formula" and "worth, esteem, fame, regard" (Guthrie, 1979: 38, 419–25).

The *Anecdota Graeca* compiles sixteen senses of *logos*, out of which we may mention the following: temper of mind, constitution (the text's example is of human being as having *logos*), *dynamis* or essential native power, a complete, independent meaning (*sêmainomenon . . . autoteles*?), book (*biblios*, roll or case for holding a papyrus case), role of an actor, voice (*phônê*), and standard (*kanôn*) (1887: 327–28).

Cassin et al. (2014: 586) give the list of the senses of *logos* in a marginal scholium of a manuscript of the *Tekhnê grammatikê* by Dionysius Thrax (Dionysius Thrax, *Scholia in Dionysii Thracis artem grammaticam*, in *Grammatici Graeci*, vol. 1, fasc. 3). Of these twenty-two meanings, the following may be of interest: concern (*phrontis*) and consideration (*logariasmos*)—which are akin to "worth" in Guthrie above—justification (*apologia*), *logos* of expenses, conclusion, natural potentiality (*dynamis*), and again, par excellence, God (*kat' eksokhên ho theos*).

Heidegger usually reduces these senses to four: "speech," "reason [*Vernunft*]," "foundation [*hypokeimenon*]," and "proportion" (Heidegger, 2008: 50; 1984:60). His earlier interpretations of *logos* determine its basic underlying meaning as "making manifest" (Heidegger, 1996: 28–30 (§7b); 1997: 139–41 (§28c); 1985: 84–85 (§9aβ)). Inspired by Heidegger and Sallis, Hoffmann gives a similar fourfold distinction: "account," "composition," "speech," and "reason" (Hoffmann, 2003: 33; see also Robinson, 2010: 24–26; Robberechts, 1993: 336).

8. For purposes of comparison between Aristotle's strictly secular uses of *logos* and its later evolutions, it may be helpful to mention some significant senses listed in Lampe's *Patristic Greek Lexicon* (1961: 807–11): "*ground* [of cosmic order]," "second Person of Trinity," "unity of Godhead," "Christ incarnate," "source of man's rationality and of his communion with God," the eternal and immanent (*endiathêtos*) Logos about which Lampe says: "the distinction between *logos endiathêtos* (*immanent reason*) and *logos prophorikos* (*uttered word*) used to illustrate the unity of Father and Logos and the distinction between them (from the standpoint of the finite observer) through the act of Creation and redemption in which Logos is the expression of the infinite Father" (Lampe, 1961: 809). The Gnostics employed the word *logos* for the "rational cosmic principle controlling the fate of men" in the poems of Aratus, and associated the word with the "*ogdoad*," the eight deities of Hieropolis. See also Mortley, who claims that the distinction between immanent (*endiathêtos*) *logos* and uttered (*prophorikos*) *logos* can be traced back to Aristotle's use of *eksô logos* in *APo.* I, 10, 76b25 (Mortley, 1986: 26). More generally, see Sorabji, 1993.

9. *Logos* occurs in the very opening of Aristotle's corpus (*Cat.* I, 1a1–13). Further in his logical works, one reads that some potencies are with *logos*, some without (*On Int.* 13,

22b38–23a1; *Metaph.* IX, 2, 5.), that a premise and a syllogism are somehow both *logoi* (*APr.* I, 1, 24a15, 24b19), or else that knowledge implies the possession of the *logos* of the "why?"(*APo.* I, 6, 74b27–28; II, 19, 100a1–3).

In his philosophy of nature, one reads that nature lies less in the material than in the form according to *logos* (*Ph.* II, 1, 193a31ff.), that living beings nourish themselves and reproduce not according to a mixture or separation, but according to a *logos* (*GC* II, 6, 333b916; *DA* II, 4, 416a16–18), that sensation is not only according to *logos* (*DA* II, 12, 424a25), but that "sensation is a *logos*" (*DA* III, 2, 426a8, 426a28ff.), and that locomotion originates from one universal and one particular *logos* (*DA* III, 11, 434a17–22; *MA* 7).

As to his ethical and political works, finally, Aristotle uses *logos* for distinguishing the parts of the human soul (*NE* I, 13, 1102a29–1102b34). Most famously, indeed, humans are defined as the only kind of animal that has *logos* (*Pol.* I, 1, 1253a10–11; VII, 12, 1332b5–6) and *logos* remains at the basis of their education (*Pol.* VII, 12, 1332a38–1332b11; 13, 1334b7–28) as of the household and city (*Pol.* I, 1, 1253a18).

10. Bonitz, 1955: 433–37. Most lists of the meanings of *logos* mention not "standard," but "essence," "law," "notion," "essential formula," or "form." As an exception, see "*kanôn*" in the *Anecdota Graeca* (1887: 327–28); for the closely related later meaning of "formative and regulative *law* of being, *essential disposition*," see Lampe, 1961: 808. Similarly, apart from the senses of "capacity for reasoning" and "capacity for discourse," Mortley mentions the sense of "appropriate system of functioning," most significantly in *DA* II, 12, 424a31, and *PA* I, 1, 639b15 (Mortley, 1986: 26).

Leaving the discussion of *logos* as "standard" to the first chapters of this book, for now let me say that this sense of *logos* is not primarily linguistic, nominal, mental, or subjective. (Compare Winslow, 2007.) For Aristotle's essentialism, see Barnes's introduction to his translation of the *Posterior Analytics* (Oxford: Clarendon, 2002, xiii).

A fifth sense of *logos* in Aristotle may be "esteem, worth, value, consideration." Compare, for instance, *NE* I, 13, 1102b31–32, but also the "*Logos*" article I.4, in LSJ, 1057. See also Guthrie, 1979: 419–25, mentioned above; Herodotus, 2.85, 7.5; Theon of Smyrna, 1878: 72–74; Lampe, 1961: 808.

11. In the corpus, there is one definition of *logos* in the sense of "sentence": "*Logos* is a signifying voice, one of whose parts is signifying separately, not as an affirmation, but as an expression" (*On Int.* 4, 16b26–28; *Po.* 20, 1457a23–24). Yet, far from mentioning the other meanings of *logos*, this definition does not even cover the sense of *logos* as "sentence." For our elaboration of this topic, see below section 3 of chapter 6.

For Aristotle's discussion of the ambiguity of words, see, for instance, *Cat.* I, 1a1ff. For his insistence on disambiguating terms, see *Top.* II, 2, 110a22ff.; *SE* IV–VI; *Rh.* II, 24, 1401a10ff. For his own analysis of the ambiguity of fundamental philosophical terms, see, for instance, indeed, *Metaph.* V.

12. Let us mention the exceptions. Besides the *Anecdota Graeca* mentioned above, Theon of Smyrna gives an important list of the "Peripatetic" meanings of *logos*. To the lists of the meanings of *logos* mentioned above, Theon adds the technical sense of syllogism and *epagôgê* as well as the definitely non-Aristotelian, Stoic phrase *logos spermatikos* (Theon of Smyrna, 1878: 72–74). Porphyry mentions the multivocity of *logos* in his commentary on the *Categories* (64, 28), but he does not attempt to account for this multivocity and even leaves out the sense of "ratio" (Porphyry, 1992: 44–45). His remarks in the *Commentary on the Harmonics of Ptolemy* (12, 6–28), although very interesting, are not concerned with *Aristotle's* uses of *logos*. Let us also note that, according to Diogenes Laertius, Sphaerus the

Stoic, a pupil of Zeno of Citium and Cleanthes, wrote a lost book entitled *Peri logou* (*Lives and Opinions of Eminent Philosophers*, VII, 178).

13. Let me give a brief literature review and some bibliography here. To my knowledge, the only work that deals with *logos* in Aristotle's corpus as a whole and recognizes its neglect is Barbara Cassin's *Aristote et le logos* (Cassin, 1997: 9, 25, 153; see also Cassin, 1996). Siding with the Sophists, Cassin characterizes Aristotle as a thinker of exclusion, of common sense, of *doxa*, of banalities, as the paradigm of the "phenomenologically correct" (1997: 4), and attempts to show the conveniently neglected incompatibilities of his various uses of *logos* (1997: 151). In diametrical opposition to Cassin, I shall approach Aristotle with the principle of charity and justify this by my preliminary openness to the *doxa* in our discussion of method, and end up demonstrating that the various senses of *logos* do fit together as, each time, a relation that holds on to its terms in their difference without collapsing them or simply isolating them.

I must also mention Cassin's *Dictionary of Untranslatables* in which *logos* occupies its rightful place. Although this source has come to my attention only after the final draft of this manuscript, I am pleased to see both the many points where my work is confirmed and those on which my work will provide a new or fuller account.

According to the account by Cassin et al. 2014, the untranslatability of *logos* stems from its polysemy. This polysemy may appear to be a mere homonymy. According to this view, *logos* would have several homophonic roots, especially one denoting "saying" (as in *dialogos*, *mythologos*) and the other denoting "gathering" (as in *syllogos*, *lithologos*). Yet, this semantic bipartition does not map onto the morphological distinction between -*lógos* as making "action nouns" (*dialogos*, *syllogos*) and -*lógos* as making "agent nouns" (*mythologos*, *lithologos*). In fact, the distinction between the two main senses of *logos*, as "saying" and "gathering," becomes blurred especially in scientific terms: an *astrologos*, a *botanêlogos*, a *genealogos*, and an *etymologos* can be viewed both as collectors of items as well as specialized speakers on those items.

There are even uses of *legô* in Greek and *lego* in Latin that suggest that *logos* has one single root and one fundamental meaning—that of "gathering." Expressions such as *legere oculis*, *lire*, *collecte*, as well as Homeric uses (*Iliad* 23.239, 21.27, 2.222; *Odyssey* 11.374; see also *katalegein* and derivatives in *Iliad* 24.380, 656; *Odyssey* 1.169, etc.) suggest the way in which the fundamental sense of "gathering" may have been extended into the sense of "saying," "counting," "speaking" and even "reading [aloud?]." Hence, Cassin et al. quite rightly stress that *logos* in the register of "speech" never means a "word"; in the register of "counting," it never means an isolated "number"—in either register, it always refers to something having a "syntax": "the constitution or consideration of a series, of a notionally complex set" (Cassin et al., 2014: 583). My work has come to the exact same conclusion; see pp. 21–22 and 191–94 in this volume.

After a review of Ancient Greek dictionaries, Cassin et al. ask the following question: "Was the mathematical sense primary, with relationality and proportionality serving as a paradigm, even a matrix, of a syntagmatic structure in general, in a line that ran from Pythagoras to Plato and then Neoplatonism? Or rather, from a structural perspective that is no doubt more Aristotelian (Bailly, Bonitz), is mathematical technique simply one application of the human *logos*?" (Cassin et al., 2014: 583). I touch upon this issue in chapters 3 and 4.

Cassin et al. rightly remark the striking absence of a thematization of *logos* in *Metaphysics* V and elsewhere. They remark that *logos* can be used in different senses in one and the same work and give the example of its uses in *On the Soul*. In *On the Soul*, one network links *logos* with *eidos*, *to ti ên einai*, *entelekheia*, and *horos*. A second network connects it to "voice," "discursiveness," and "rationality" proper to humans, a network gathering anatomy and physiology with politics and ethics. A third network allows Aristotle to define sensation as a *logos*—in the sense of "relation," "proportion," a *ratio*. Finally, a fourth network of meanings gathers *logos* in the sense of "statement." But in distinction from the second network, here the subject of *legein* is sensation itself—be it of humans or of another animal. Cassin et al. conclude their remarks on the multivocity of *logos* in Aristotle in the following way: "This survey of the meanings of *logos* makes their disjunction, as well as their systematization, apparent: so a gap remains between the mathematical *logos*, which calculates sensation, and the *logos* proper to man, who makes statements, constructs arguments, and unites and persuades citizens. It is as if the Greek language contributed to confusing, and thus to foreclosing, a certain number of questions that Aristotle, 'compelled by truth,' nevertheless persisted in asking" (Cassin et al., 2014: 585; here they seem to draw on Cassin, 1996).

Cassin et al. quite rightly distinguish the Stoic use of the polysemy of *logos* from Aristotle's in that, for the Stoics, "throughout, *logikos* indissociably means both rational and discursive" (586). Their account is also good for tracing the senses of *logos* beyond Aristotle, in Latin texts in the double form of *ratio* and *oratio*, through Lucretius, Cicero, Seneca, and then John's Gospel and the Hebrew underpinnings of *logos* such as *hokmah* and *dâvâr*.

Besides Cassin's sustained work on *logos* in Aristotle, there is one essay that is central to this discussion as a whole. In his essay "Man and Language," Gadamer argues that *logos*, as it appears in Aristotle's famous characterization of human being, should not be translated as *ratio*, "reason," or "thought," but as "language." (Compare Heath, 2005: 6.) He argues that language is neither a mere tool one can pick up and put down at will, nor a conscious, individual, and subjective act or capacity (Gadamer, 1976: 59–68). I agree with Gadamer's criticisms, but I disagree with the "linguistic turn" he endorses. I equally disagree that "the distinguishing feature of man . . . is his superiority over what is actually present, his sense of the future . . . [that] he can make what is not present manifest through his speaking, so that another person sees it before him." I cannot help but think that animal signaling, for instance in front of danger, does make manifest something that is not present. Most importantly, the phrase "non-present" is ambiguous. The "present" may well be contrasted to the "future," or to "common concepts," as Gadamer does; but it may well be contrasted to the "past," the "possible," even the "impossible." Gadamer's account does not elaborate on this. In any case, I will claim in chapter 6 that the distinguishing feature of human speech is not its relation to what is present or non-present, but its understanding and relaying non-firsthand experience as well as firsthand experience.

Mortley offers a survey of the various meanings of *logos* in Aristotle without getting into details and without addressing the question of the relationship between these meanings. This is understandable given Mortley's task of offering a very large-scale picture of the history of the uses of *logos* in general. This wide perspective is helpful at points, but it also causes the author to project onto Aristotle's philosophy some post-Aristotelian notions such as the hypostatization of *logos*, and the distinction between internal (*endiathêtos*) *logos* and outward (*prophorikos*) *logos* (Mortley, 1986: 25–30). Winslow's *Aristotle and Rational Discovery* is not intended as a comprehensive and systematic study of the different uses of *logos* in Aristotle (Winslow, 2007; see also Winslow, 2006). And yet, although the book lacks much in terms of clarity in organization, in argumentation, in reference, and even in transliteration, I enjoyed it for some of its bold insights, and for the partial corroborations it provided me. (Winslow, 2007; see also Winslow, 2006)

Among the recent works on *logos* in more or less larger parts of Aristotle's corpus are Baracchi, 2007; Long, 2011; Rese, 2005; Weigelt, 2002. I have not been able to find and read Irina Deretić's "Logos, Platon, Aristotel" and "Aristotelov metafizički pojam logosa." For accounts of *logos* not restricted to Aristotle's philosophy, see Heidegger, 1996: 28–30 (§7b), and his various preparatory lectures, 1997: 139–41 (§28c); 1985: 84–85 (§9aβ); Brague, 2005: 69–82; Brague, 1988; Brague, 1978 which enumerates many of the meanings of *logos* we shall analyze, and interprets them often exactly like we shall end up doing (Brague, 1978: 171). See also Brun, 1961: 22–27. Apart from these, we should point out two notes that concentrate on our problem here: Hicks, 1915: 1–2; Stocks, 1914: 9–12. Also, in the introduction to his translation of the *Parts of Animals* (Cambridge, Mass.: Harvard University Press, 1937, 26ff.), Peck notes the variety of the meanings of *logos* within one and the same work (640a32, 646b2, 678a35, 695b19, 639b15 . . .), and considers them to be "correlated" without showing what this correlation is. The same is true of Lear who notes that "*logos* is a protean word," but does not go beyond saying that "there is no equivocation" between *logos* as definition and *logos* as form (Lear, 1988: 28–29).

For broader accounts of the development of the philosophical senses of *logos*, see Guthrie, 1979: 38, 419–25 (mostly specific to Heraclitus's fragments); Kerferd, 1981: 78–84 (in which one paragraph, on pp. 83–84, distinguishes the meanings of *logos* and specifies its "focal reference" quite exactly as we shall do, although in the context of sophistic and rhetoric); Chieza, 1992: 15–30; Heath, 2005: 8ff.; Robinson, 2010: 24–26; Fattal, 1988; Fattal, 2001: esp. 27–48; Robberechts, 1993: 336; Lallot, 1988, 15; and Hoffmann, 2003: 27–53, which, although quite akin to our approach and conclusion, devotes no more than a short paragraph to Aristotle's use of *logos* and, disregarding the fact that Aristotle emphasizes that all *logos* is *not* declarative (*apophantikos*) (*On Int.* 4, 16b33–17a4, see our chapter 6, section 3), marks him as the beginning of the "logical prejudice" whereby the sense of *logos* loses its focal reference to "composition/gathering."

14. Since I shall only briefly touch upon it in what follows, let me refer the reader to the wide range of scholarly views on the subject illustrated in Sim, 1999, especially the introduction. See also Ward, 2008: 43–56.

15. *APo.* II, 19, 100b2–4; I, 2, 72a1–5; *Top.* VI, 4, 141b5–14. For the use of both widespread opinions (*endoxa*) *and* perception (*aisthêsis*) see *GA* III, 10; *APr.* I, 30, 46a17–22; *Cael.* III, 7, 306a3ff.; *DA* I, 1, 402b21ff. See also Owen, 1975; Nussbaum, 1982; Aubenque, 2002, 83–93; 2009: 44. See also Bolton, 1990: 190–95; 1991: 11. It is true that Aristotle often stresses that, when possible, one should always uphold perception over *endoxa* (*Cael.* III, 4, 303a20–23; III, 7, 306a3–17; *GA* III, 10, 760b27–33; *APr.* I, 30, 46a17ff.). Yet, for the most part, if not always, widespread *endoxa* seem to overlap with perception.

16. For instance, see my article "Aristotle at Work—Method in *GA*, III, 10," *Epoché* (forthcoming in 2017). See also Hamlyn, 1990: 475–76.

17. *Top.* I, 12, 105a13–17; *APo* II, 19, 100a15–100b4. In a certain sense, book III, the "book of aporias," is well placed right after the "doxography" of book I of the *Metaphysics* (Nussbaum, 1982: 276).

18. See also *Metaph.* I, 1, 982b17; III, 1, 955a35; *NE* VII, 1, 1145b2–6; *MM* II, 6, 1200b20–24.

19. For an influential discussion of this point, especially but not exclusively in regard to the *Physics*, see Owen, 1975; Nussbaum, 1982; Evans, 1977: 77–80.

20. This clause seems to be an echo of, if not a clear reference to, Plato's *Parmenides*, 136A and the following, and thus betrays Aristotle's indebtedness to Zenonian dialectic (Berti, 1978: 354–55; see also Dumont, 1992: 178–79). For Aristotle's relationship to Plato's *Parmenides*, especially in the *Physics*, see Owen, 1975.

21. See also *APo.* I, 11, 77a26–30. Compare Evans, 1977: 31–32.

22. For the distinction between dialectic and special sciences, see Evans, 1977: 5: "But what marks off the sciences from dialectic is that they embody a correct view of reality . . . Dialectic, by contrast, should not embody any view of reality—neither a correct one . . . nor an incorrect one." See also Dumont, 1992: 178–79; Granger, 1976: 72: "Sans doute la dialectique ne saurait-elle avoir elle-même de principes propres (à un type d'être) pour la guider, et son action est-elle ce tâtonnement plus ou moins systématique qu'évoque le mot PEIRASTIKÈ."

23. Berti, 1978: 347–70. See his reservations on pp. 351–52. See also Seaton's criticism of Berti (Seaton, 1980: 283–89), and Berti's reply (Berti, 1980: 290–92).

24. Nussbaum insists that Aristotle's concept of the "unhypothetical" is radically different from Plato's. Since I do not agree with her claim that Plato's unhypothetical principle is known "entirely independently of all conceptualization and thought," I do not agree with the sharp contrast she draws between Plato and Aristotle here. (Nussbaum, 1982: 288) I am sympathetic to Roochnik's criticism of Nussbaum in Roochnik, 1990: 203. See also Evans, 1977: 21–25.

25. See Matthews, 1999: 125–36. MacIntyre claims that, for Aristotle, "dialectic is no longer the road to truth, but for the most part only a semi-formal procedure ancillary to enquiry." On this issue, he contrasts Aristotle first with the tragic poets, and then with Socrates and Plato: "Where Socrates argued dialectically with particular individuals and Plato wrote dialogues, Aristotle therefore produces expository lectures and treatises" (MacIntyre, 2013: 184). Yet if dialectic is not the road to truth for Aristotle, how is one to explain Aristotle's *explicit* remarks on dialectic in *Top.* I, 2, 101a35–101b4? Further, how are we to characterize Aristotle's *implicit*, but typical, procedure starting from the *phenomena*, the *endoxa*, or simply the *legomena* in most of his major works? How is the text of the *Metaphysics* or, say, the first book of the *Physics*, *On the Soul*, or the *Nicomachean Ethics* an "expository" lecture or treatise that does not take off from a critical engagement with his predecessors views or with widespread everyday assumptions? Indeed these are not dialogues, but it is difficult to see how they do not employ a dialogical procedure between openly conflicting views.

26. For textual evidence see *APo.* I 1, 71a1–11; *Top.* I, 2, 101a35–b4; *Ph.* I, 1, 184a16–22; *DA* II, 2, 413a11–13; *Metaph.* I, 1; II, 1; VII, 3, 1029b3–12; *HA* I, 6, 491a7–14. Perhaps the most famous expression of this procedure is the one at the beginning of the *Nicomachean Ethics* where Aristotle pays tribute to Plato: "We should not overlook the distinction between the *logoi* that start out from principles and those that lead to principles. For it was well that Plato too raised this question, and inquired whether the way is from principles or toward principles, just as in a race one may run from the judges to the boundary or the other way" (*NE* I, 4, 1095a31 1095b2. See Plato, *Republic* VI, 509D–511E. See also Sparshott, 1994: 27–29). In front of this dilemma, Aristotle seems to open up an obvious safe ground: "One must begin from what is known; but this has two meanings: things known to us and things known simply. Perhaps then we, at any rate, ought to begin from the things that are known to us" (*NE* I, 4, 1095b2–4; VII, 1, 1145b2–7. Indeed, the major text for this idea is *APo.* I, 2, 71b23–72a5. See *EE* II, 1, 1220a15–22. See also Ross, 1949: 38; Evans, 1977: 52).

27. See *Metaph.* IV, 2, 1004b25–26; *SE* 34, 183a39ff; *Top.* VIII, 5, 159a33. See Aubenque, 2009: 55; Bolton, 1990.

28. *Top.* I, 2, 101a35-b4. For the association between *peirastikê* and *exetastikê* in the context of dialectic, see also *Rh.* I, 1, 1354a5; *Top.* VIII, 5, 159a25, 33. Compare Plato, *Apology* 22E–23C; *Protagoras* 348A.

29. *SE* XI, 172a18.

30. Bolton, 1990: 200–203. *Metaph.* IV, 2, 1004b26; *Top.* I, 1, 100b23ff.; VIII, 14, 163b12–16; *SE* 11. Compare *Metaph.* III, 1, 995b2–4.

31. In this respect, I am in much agreement with Enrico Berti who, in an article I will often refer to in this part of the book, follows Aubenque (1962) in defending that a dialectical procedure is employed in Aristotle's *Metaphysics* (most notably in the discussion of the principle of non-contradiction in book IV) and in his classification of animals by species and genera (Berti, 1978). I am also in agreement with Baracchi's approach to Aristotle's dialectical method and to *logos* (Baracchi, 2007: 1–15).

32. Evans, 1977: 5–6.

33. For the role of homonymy in Aristotle, see Ward, 2008. Biographical sources strongly suggest that Aristotle made a collection of proverbs early on in his career (Natali, 2013: 25). Natali also notes that this research "is also a facet of the attention given by Aristotle to common opinion and to the *phainomena*, those impressions and beliefs that seem evidently true to various people." For a list of passages where Aristotle uses popular sayings and proverbs, see the article "*paroimai*" in Bonitz, 1955: 569–70.

34. Aristotle explicitly deals with his own assumption not in the *Categories*, but in *SE* I, 165a6ff.

35. If we are to follow the *Organon*, we find him later taking up and scrutinizing gradually wider phenomena. In the *Categories* and *On Interpretation*, he shifts his focus from words to assertions (subjects, predicates, statements, modalities, etc.), in the *Prior Analytics* to syllogisms (premises, conclusions, moods and figures of syllogisms, etc.), then in the *Posterior Analytics* to demonstrations and science (knowledge, proof, definition, principles, etc.), and finally to less rigorous or simply invalid arguments in the *Topics* and in the *On Sophistical Refutations*. The Arabic tradition included the *Rhetoric* and the *Poetics* in the *Organon*, and these two can be seen as studies of large units of *logos*.

36. Brentano, 1975: 128.

37. See Eco, 1994: 28; Pinker, 1999: 10.

38. For a discussion of this point, see Benveniste, 1966: 64–70. But compare Vuillemin, 1967: 76–77; Granger, 1976: 60. For a discussion around Aristotle's genuineness in the face of impasses, see Aubenque, 2009: 39–52. For a fuller account of the deep link between Aristotle's methodology and things said (*ta legomena*), see Long, 2011: 49–70. One indication that Aristotle is not simply imposing Ancient Greek "categories" onto beings as such may be found in his pointing to "anonymous" phenomena. (See, most typically, *NE* II, 7, 1107b31; III, 10, 1115b26; IV, 10, 1125b17, 26; for a list of "anonymous" virtues and vices, see the article "*anônymos*" in Bonitz, 1955: 69.)

39. Later in this chapter, I shall address the claim that Aristotle "surrenders" to his native language and uncritically transposes its structures onto his logic and ontology. For the time being, let me note that his seminal distinction between homonymy and synonymy is precisely intended to challenge the prima facie univocality between a single noun and one kind of thing. The later distinctions between subject and predicate, between premise and conclusion, between different kinds of syllogism and arguments are all made for the sake

of challenging and then nuancing or often refuting an apparent sameness in language or exposing illegitimate conflations and superfluous differences.

40. Plato, *Theaetetus*, 148E–151D.

41. For an influential discussion, see Owen, 1975; Nussbaum, 1982; Irwin, 1982: 250. Compare Bolton, 1991, who argues that the method of natural science recommended in *Physics* I, 1, is not dialectic, but "empirical." According to this view, the starting point is not the views of the many or the wise, but "experience" or perception. It is not exactly clear to me why one should choose either one or the other; on the contrary, taking both the widespread opinions and our experiences together as a starting point at least explains why Aristotle so typically starts out his inquiries by relating and critically discussing the views of his predecessors, by laying out material from his "library," his collection of Greek constitutions, or the secondhand accounts about different species of animals, and so on. Bolton seems to hedge his view on dialectic by saying that dialectic "must somehow be in aid of the general inductive procedures which constitute the proper scientific method for reaching the first principles, since that is the way the scientist reaches them" (Bolton, 1991: 22).

42. See Balme's introduction to his translation of *HA* VII–X (Cambridge, Mass.: Harvard University Press, 1991). We shall discuss the "theoretical" character of Aristotelian natural science in chapter 3. For now, let us simply point to a passage from *On Generation and Corruption*: "The reason of the inability to see admitted facts as a whole [*ta homologoumena synoran*] is lack of experience. Hence those who have lived more closely with natural phenomena are better able to lay down such principles as can be connected together and cover a wide field; on the other hand, those who do not watch [*atheôrêtoi*] the present things because of lengthy discussions prove to have a narrower view. One can also see from this the difference between those who inquire by nature [*physikôs*] and those by discussions [*logikôs*]" (*GC* I, 2, 316a5–12).

Let us also note that Charles Darwin salutes Aristotle, in an 1879 letter, "as one of the greatest, if not the greatest observers, that ever lived." In his 1882 letter, he famously wrote: "Linnaeus and Cuvier have been my two gods, though in very different ways, but they were mere school-boys to old Aristotle." Gotthelf argues that these expressions of admiration are not mere gestures of politeness, but genuinely enthusiastic responses, and that the increase in Darwin's admiration for Aristotle was prompted by his reading of the introduction and parts of translation of the *Parts of Animals* by Ogle (Gotthelf, 1999: 16).

43. See especially Lang, 1998; Roochnik, 1990: 29–31; and Peck's introduction to Aristotle, *History of Animals* (Aristotle 1965: x, xi).

44. See Aubenque, 2002, 83–93. For the influence of the Platonic dialogical form on Aristotle, see Jaeger, 1950: 24ff.; Irwin, 1988: 7ff. "When Aristotle sits on the shore of Lesbos taking notes on shellfish, he will be doing something that is not, if we look at it from his point of view, so far removed from his activity when he records what we say about *akrasia*. He will be describing the world *as it appears to*, as it is experienced by, observers who are members of our kind" (Nussbaum, 1982: 274).

45. For an exemplary dialectical approach, see *Metaph.* I, 3–10. See also Berti, 1990: 261; Irwin, 1988: 22. The discussion of *akrasia* in *Nicomachean Ethics* VII, a passage often quoted in the discussion over the methodological role of *phainomena* and *legomena* in Aristotle (see, for instance, Nussbaum, 1982), also proceeds in three steps: first the gathering of appearances (*phainomena*) and of claims (*legomena*) about the subject matter, then the drawing of *aporiai* from them, and finally the working out of these puzzles (Cooper and

Aubry, 2009: 9, 239). *On Generation and Corruption* I, also proceeds dialectically (Burnyeat, 2004: 7, 10, 16, 22; Wildberg, 2004: 230). For Aristotle's collectorship in general, see Natali, 2013: 96–113.

46. If in claiming this Aristotle could have hardly avoided looking into his own soul and his own relations, one may ask who Aristotle's own fathers and friends were. And who were Aristotle's own fathers and friends? His own work gives us a good idea: among them were indeed the Platonists, and even Plato himself, but also his predecessors such as Empedocles, Democritus, Parmenides, Eudoxus, and Heraclitus. For an elaboration of Aristotle's relation to the "things said" (*ta legomena*), see Long, 2011: 49–70.

47. Rorty, 1980: 2; Evans, 1977: 89–94.

48. Evans, 1977: 5.

49. *Rh.* I, 2, 1356a25–26. "And, as in Protagoras, also in Aristotle, dialectic and rhetoric find their most natural terrain of application in political life, where democracy accepts the free confrontation of opinions: rhetoric in fact, says Aristotle, is like an offshoot of dialectic and of the treatment concerning peoples' customs which is rightly called politics" (Berti, 1978: 364).

50. See, for instance, Ross, 1949: 59. For an overview of the recent discussions of dialectic in Aristotle, see Bolton, 1990: 185–236.

51. In the introduction to his translation, Barnes views the *Posterior Analytics* as concerned not with "methodology of research," but with "the organization and presentation of the results of research" (Oxford: Clarendon, 2002, xiii). This changes the relationship one expects between the *Analytics* and Aristotle's scientific work: "Since *A Pst* does not describe a scientific methodology, it would be misconceived to complain that the methods which Aristotle follows and occasionally describes in the scientific work do not fit the prescriptions of *A Pst*. Again, in so far as the biological writings do not purport to present a *finished* science, we should not expect them to exhibit the organization and structure which *A Pst* describes" (xix).

52. Many recent scholars agree with this point of view. See Berti, 1990: 261. See also Bolton who cites Owen, Barnes and Burnyeat (Bolton, 1990: 186). It is worthwhile to note that Aristotle's approach often tends toward exposition precisely when his field of inquiry is a new one, that is, one that precisely *lacks* widespread opinions to proceed from. See also *SE* 2, 165b1–3: "Didactic arguments are those which reason from the principles appropriate to each branch of learning and not from the opinions of the answerer, for he who is learning must take things on trust."

53. *Cael.* II, 12, 292a15–17. See also Burnyeat, 2004: 15.

54. Berti, 1978: 366; Aubenque, 1963.

55. Owen, 1975: 88; Nussbaum, 1982; Irwin, 1982: 250.

56. Berti, 1990; Irwin, 1982: 250.

57. See Ross's introduction in Aristotle, 1924: lxxvii. See also Ross, 1949: 48; Berti, 1991: 59; Babür, 2002: 7–20; Ward, 2008: 43ff. On the relationship between apodictic and dialectic, see especially Aubenque, 2009: 55–60: "La science, n'étant démonstrative que dans sa phase finale, doit être préparée par un examen critique des opinions en présence, qui doit permettre de démasquer les points de vues erronnés parce que contradictoires, soit intrinsèquement soit par rapport à des propositions déjà reconnues comme vraies (par exemple, des propositions d'expérience), et de parvenir ainsi par élimination aux prémisses 'vraies et premières,' sur lesquelles s'appuiera la déduction proprement scientifique" (Aubenque, 2009: 90).

58. For the distinction between the sublunar and the supralunar realms in Aristotle, see *Mete.* I, 2, 339a19–20; 3, 339b5.

59. Aristotle often stresses that the kind and amount of certainty to be expected in a discipline depends on the subject matter of the discipline itself (*NE* I, 3; *Protrepticus* in Aristotle, 2015: 16). According to the tradition, Thales not only made exact and profitable deductions concerning heavenly motions, but also advised the Ionians to build up a central chamber for deliberating issues that involve a modality that is fundamentally inadequate for such exactness and predictability (KRS: 78–79)

60. *APo.* I, 30, 87b20; II, 12, 96a8; *APr.* I, 13, 32b4–13. See also *On Int.* 9, 19a18–22; *Metaph.* V, 30, 1025a14–21; VI, 2, 1026b31–33; *Cael.* I, 12, 283a32–b1; III, 2, 301a7; *GC* II, 6, 333b5; 9, 336a27; *Ph.* II, 5, 196b10, 20; II, 5, 197a32; II, 8, 198b35; II, 8, 199b24; *PA*, III, 2, 663b28–29; *GA*, IV, 8, 777a17–21; *EE* VIII, 2, 1247a31–33; *Rh.* I, 10, 1369a32–b2. See also Natali, 1989: 143–45; Evans, 1977: 89–94. For a bibliography of the more standard and traditional view that Aristotle's method is narrowly demonstrative, and of the recent recovery of the function of dialectic in Aristotle, see Berti, 1978: 366, n. 82.

61. We are roughly following Denver, 1991: 73–83. See also Ross, 1949: 31.

62. Compare the case of the hermaphrodite goats in *GA* IV, 4, 770b35–36. See also Judson, 1991: 82–89.

63. Our example is partially inspired by Carlo Natali's seminar entitled "Le Premier Traité d'éthique—La structure et les desseins de l'*Ethique à Nicomaque*" that took place at the University of Paris I in February-March 2006. See also Sparshott, 1994: esp. 28.

64. Sparshott, 1994: 25.

65. "Especially in the *Ethics*, Aristotle tends to use terms *critically*, not simply as standing for established notions" (Sparshott, 1994: 12).

66. See also *EE* 13, 1215a4–5. In this definition of happiness, only the concept of "actuality" is Aristotelian.

67. That Aristotle takes his definition of human happiness as a "principle" can be seen from *NE* I, 7, 1098b2–12. It is exactly here that Aristotle emphasizes the modality of dialectic, "for the most part," by discussing the extent to which external goods, fortune, and even the fate of one's descendants may impact human happiness.

68. Sparshott, 1994: 23–25. For a similar defense of Aristotle's dialectical approach to practical philosophy, see Berti, 1990: 259, 262.

69. *Metaph.* V, 30, 1025a14, 1025a30; VI, 2, 1026b27, 1027a8; *Ph.* II, 8, 198b34–199a3.

70. See also Aubenque, 1963: 37–41; Rorty, 1980: 2–3.

71. In fact, Aristotle may be linked further back into the emergence of dialectic in Zeno and/or in Protagoras (Berti, 1978: 354–55; see also Dumont, 1992: 178–79). For the "Platonic Influence on Aristotelian Homonymy," see Ward, 2008: 40–42.

72. Plato, *Theaetetus* 189E.

73. See also Plato, *Sophist* 263E, and *Philebus* 38C–E. According to Aubenque, these may be the passages Aristotle alludes to in *Top.* VIII, 14,163a36–163b3: "If we have nobody else, we must [argue for and against] with ourselves" (Aubenque, 2002: 256, n. 3). See also *Cael.* II, 13, 294b8.

74. Unlike Socrates in the *Phaedrus* 230D.

75. Cicero, *Tusculan Disputations* V, 10.

76. If it is true, as Berti says, that Socrates was the first to know "how to bring the two requirements of dialectic," namely the value of opinion in Protagorean dialectic, and the principle of non-contradiction implicit in Zenonian dialectic, Aristotle puts dialectic to

work in the investigation of nature (Berti, 1978: 355). For explicit Aristotelian criticisms of Socrates's turn away from nature, see *Metaph.* I, 9, 992a24–28, b8–9.

77. "Dialectic also arrives at its most complete development which is at the same time a recapitulation of the most important of the preceding stages" (Berti, 1978: 363). On this dialectical and elenchic character of Aristotelian method, see Ross's introduction to Aristotle, 1924: xxxv; Morel, 2003: 82; Berti, 1991: 59; Natali, 2013: 67. For the extent and depth of Socrates's influence on Aristotle, see also Jaeger, 1950: 21–22, 47ff. For Aristotle's more radical conception of dialectic in comparison to even Plato, see Aubenque, 2009: 64. In light of the recognition that Aristotle's method is for the most part dialectic, I am more tempted to see him in continuity with Plato, than to oppose his "demonstrative" method to the Platonic privilege of dialectic.

78. See also *Metaph.* I, 3, 983b3–7.

79. From here one may also quantify the frequency of the word *logos* in Aristotle's "books" and compare it with similar statistics extrapolated from Plato, Heraclitus, or the Gospel according to St. John. This procedure would be convincing, clear, and easily knowable by just looking. But, as Aristotle remarks, deduction is more efficacious against objections. Hence the inductive "results" can never be bulletproof or even conclusive, since any number of statistics can by definition be refuted by a higher number of samples to the contrary. To take up Aristotle's example of the skilled person above, one can discuss at length whether a skilled killer, liar, or thief is also the best—a classical problem in ethics in ancient Greek philosophy.

80. See Berti, 1978: 364.

81. See for instance, Brunschwig, 1991: 11–40.

82. Frede, 1996: 157–73; Sorabji, 1996: 331.

83. Thus, Sallis's warning for *logos* in Plato may be repeated in Aristotle's case: "When we regard it as self-evidently correct to allow *logos* to be taken as ratio, hence, as reason, we reaffirm, without even really considering the matter, one of the most overwhelmingly decisive transitions in that movement away from the Greeks that constituted the course of Western thought. To assume, in advance, a specific, well-defined determination of *logos* in this direction—to take for granted in an interpretation of Platonic writings subsequent notions of 'rationality' and 'demonstrative argument'—is to be misled by the tradition, made possible by Plato's work, into ignoring the original struggle with the problems of determining *logos* which takes place in Plato's writings" (Sallis, 1996: 14–15).

84. For, sure enough, there the same problem emerges because the task of understanding was deferred: what does *ratio* mean in Thomas Aquinas or *aql* in Ibn Rushd? (For *logos* as *nutk,* see Averroès, 2000: 141, 179; for *logos* as *aql,* see Averroès, 2000: 109.) Further, why didn't Aristotle use *nous* in the sentence from the *Politics,* given that *nous* is equally translated and interpreted as "intelligence" by many "authorities"? If, in the context of the *Politics, logos* is to be understood as "reason" in the sense of "intelligence," so is *nous* in other contexts. If *logos* is translated as "reason" in the sense of "cause," so is *aition*. If *logos* is translated as "definition," so is *horos* and *horismos*. If *logos* is translated as "relation" in one context, so is *pros ti* in many others. What warrants Aristotle's use of *logos* in one context and of another word in another?

85. Jaeger, 1950; Ross, 1949: 18.

86. Jaulin, 1999: 8–11; Guthrie, 1981: 14–15: "Jaeger took these facts, that Aristotle started his career as a Platonist and finished it as something different, and was inclined

to conclude on no other grounds that the development of his philosophy took the form of a steady and continuous movement away from Platonism; and to use this conclusion as a premise for all subsequent deductions. Thus, when a new portion of the Aristotelian corpus came up for discussion, he asked the question: 'how far removed from Plato is its philosophical position?,' and according to the answer assigned it its place, early or late, in the chronological series of Aristotle's writings." Similar remarks concerning Jaeger's genetic interpretation of the diverse uses of *phronêsis* in Aristotle can be found in Aubenque, 1963: 15–31.

87. But did Aristotle leave Athens *after* Plato's death to begin with? Compare Diogenes Laertius, V, 2. For a general discussion, see Natali, 2013: 31–32.

88. Cited by Aristocles in Eusebius, *Praeparatio evangelica* XV. See Jaeger, 1950: 106–7. For a similar criticism of Jaeger's thesis in the context of Aristotle's concept of "prudence," see Aubenque, 1963: 20. For a judicious account of the sources concerning Aristotle's biography in general, see Natali, 2013: 17–31.

89. "While appreciating the seriousness of all these analyses, one cannot but remark that they all stem from Jaeger's assumption that Platonism is simply identical with the doctrine of Ideas, and their abandonment means turning one's back on it" (Berti, 1981: 8).

90. For "*logos tou einai*" see also Plato, *Sophist*, 78D1ff. Perhaps it is no coincidence that one of the earliest uses of the adjective *dialektikôs* is found in Plato's *Meno* (75D), so famous for its discussion of the paradox of inquiry.

91. Grene meaningfully compares this procedure with Heraclitean flux: "from one page to the next one is never reading the same Aristotle, and finally there is no Aristotle left to be read at all" (Grene, 1963: 27–28, cited in Lang, 1998: 14).

92. Our two-sided criticism of "inductive" and "deductive" methods agrees almost point by point with Lang's criticisms of both "genetic" and "acontextual" methods; both start out as looking contrary, but end up equally vacuous, arbitrary and insufficient (Lang, 1998: 13–18).

93. The reader will notice that the use of *logos* in the *Metaphysics* (especially books VII and VIII) is scattered throughout the book.

94. Both animals and elements are capable of locomotion. What distinguishes the two is precisely *logos*: if displaced elements have an impulse for locomotion, animals *hold that impulse together with particular sensations* as a result of which they move. So, elements are not self-movers in the latter sense (*Ph.* VIII, 4, 255a5–10).

95. See also *Rh.* II, 6, 1384a23–25; *EE* II, 1, 1219b27–1220a11. Again, *NE* VI, 2 states: "Thus choice is either thought infused with desire or desire infused with thinking through, and such a source is the human being."

96. See also *Pol.* VII, 12, 1332b5–6; *NE* IX, 9, 1169b20–21; *EE* II, 8, 1224b30. But see also *NE* VIII, 12, 1162a15–25.

97. Hesiod's uses of *logos* emphasize that a *logos* can be second or third hand, or that it might be simply deceitful. See Hoffmann, 2003: 32, n. 12.

98. *NE* IX, 4, especially 1166a32 b2: "a friend is another self . . . It would seem that there could be such a love [friendship toward oneself] insofar as each person is two or more, and because the *hyperbolê* of friendship resembles friendship toward oneself."

99. It is true that Aristotle himself often exaggerates the distance between him and Heraclitus. See also Cherniss, 1935: 380–81.

100. See Lampe, 1961: 807–11. Compare the divine use of language in Heath, 2005: 209–12.

Chapter 1

1. The traditional arrangement of Aristotle's corpus indeed goes back not to Aristotle, but to Andronicus of Rhodes who is said to have had access to original manuscripts in Rome and arranged the Aristotelian corpus in the second half of the first century B.C.E. See Ross, 1949: 7n.

2. *On Int.* 2, 16a19–20, 16a26–29; 4, 16b33–17a2; *Po.* 20, 1456b35, 1457a2, 11, 14, 23.

3. At the rudimentary level of word count, however, *logos* is not a frequent word in the *Categories*. It occurs there forty-six times. Even when *logos* does occur in the text, Aristotle mostly employs it in its nontechnical meaning of "something said" (e.g., nine occurrences of *logos* in *Cat.* 5, 4a23–4b11) or of "assertion." (e.g., *Cat.* 10, 12b7–10). At first, then, *logos* does not seem to be a theme or explicit focus in the *Categories*. In fact, the *Categories* is traditionally considered as a text not on *logos*, but on its constituents. See, for instance, *Cat.* 4, 1b25: "Each one of those that are said without combination [*tôn kata mêdemian symplokên legomenôn* . . .] means either *ousia* or how-much . . ."

4. This point is developed only in other texts such as *SE* 1, 165a6–14 and *On Int.* 9, 18b38–19a1. See especially *Metaph.* IX, 10, 1051b7ff.

5. In Ancient Greek, *onoma* can mean "noun" as opposed to "verb" (*rhêma*) as well as "name" and "reputation." See the "*onoma*" article in LSJ, 1996: 1232.

6. *Gegrammenon*. Although there is indeed no word for "representation" in Ancient Greek, especially no word that has the same strong philosophical connotations, the meaning of "representation" can be compared to *gegrammenon* which can mean "that which has been drawn," but also "that which has been written down" or even "the one whose name has been written."

7. Dexippus explains the clause "according to this name" in the follow way: if this clause was omitted "it would have been possible to show that the same things were homonyms and synonyms, as for instance the Ajaxes, for if the definition had not been specified as 'corresponding to the name,' one and the same definition could have applied to them as men" (Dexippus, 1990: 45).

8. For "*logos tês ousias*" in Aristotle's biology, see *PA* IV, 13, 695b19.

9. See also *PA* I, 1, 640b34–641a7; or *DA* II, 1, 412b20–22: "the eye is the material of vision, and if vision is left out there is no eye, except homonymously, as for instance the stone or painted [*gegrammenos*] eye." For the distinction between representation and the represented, see *On Memory and Recollection* 1, 450b15–451a14.

10. See *Ph.* VII, 4, 248b7–249a8. For a discussion, see Ward, 2008: 17ff. The case of homonymy between a species and its genus is especially puzzling, since calling a species (say, "ox") by its genus ("animal") is precisely Aristotle's example of synonymy. Thus, if homonymy operates between a species and a genus, it seems like it is reserved to instances where a genus is addressed as one of its species and *not vice versa*.

11. See also *NE* I, 6, 1096b25–30. Compare Heraclitus's play on the ambiguity of *bios* in Fragment 48.

12. *On Int.* 2, 16a19–20, 16a26–29. For an explanation of *synthêkê*, often translated as "convention," see also *On Int.* 4, 16b33–17a2; *Po.* 20, 1456b35, 1457a2, 11, 14, 23. We shall elucidate this word in chapter 6, section 2. For a cogent discussion of the question as to whether homonymy holds between two things or two names, see Ward, 2008: 13.

13. See also *Top.* VI, 10, 148a23–25.

14. Sorabji, 1993: 62ff.

15. This version constitutes the first step away from Protagorean dialectic toward Aristotelian dialectic. See Berti, 1978: 355: "if Protagoras discovered the value of opinions for dialectic and hence for freedom of speech, a thing neglected by Zeno, then Protagoras in his turn neglected the value for dialectic of the principle of non-contradiction and hence of refutation."

16. See also *Metaph.* XI, 5, 1062a31–35; IV, 4, 1006a4–5, 1006b34–1007a1; *On Int.* 5, 20a16–17. For another ambiguously critical reference to Heraclitus in this context, see *Metaph.* IV, 8, 1012a33.

17. See also *SE* 4, 165b39–166a7.

18. Our analysis in this part of the book seems roughly in line with Kosman, 1967.

19. *Ph.* I, 2, 185a5.

20. Aristotle's more central objection to the hypothesis of Parmenides and Melissus stems from his investigation of the precise way in which "being" and "one" are meant. *Ph.* I, 2, 185a22ff.

21. *Ph.* I, 3, 186a34–35; 3, 186b17–18; 4, 187a13; 4, 187a19.

22. This structure of contraries and the thing underlying them is in fact a leitmotif in the Aristotelian corpus. See *Metaph.* IV, XII, or *Ph.* I, 6, 189b12–22: "this opinion seems to be the ancient one, that the one and excess and deficiency are the sources of beings . . . If among four, there were two oppositions, there would need to be present some nature in between, apart from each pair [of contraries]." Aristotle's conclusion concerning the number of sources in this first book of the *Physics* is the following: "It is impossible for contraries to be acted upon by one another. But this is solved because the underlying thing is something different. For it is not a contrary. So in a certain way the sources are not more than the contraries, but two in number in this way of speaking; but neither are they altogether two on account of there being the [underlying thing] different from them—but three" (*Ph.* I, 7, 190b33–191a2).

23. Aristotle is arguably the one who introduced the term *hypokeimenon* as a philosophical term, perhaps taking it from its momentary but highly suggestive occurrences in Plato's dialogues. See especially Plato, *Protagoras* 349B. See also Plato, *Republic* IX, 581C, and *Cratylus* 422D.

24. The same definition is given in *Top.* VI, 10, 148a23–25.

25. The only change that beings do not undergo in the proper sense is coming-to-be and passing-away. (See *Ph.* V.) We will indeed return to this crucial exception in chapter 3. See *On Int.* 13, 23a21–25; *Metaph.* IX, 8, 1050b6–35; XII, 1, 1069a30–1069b2.

26. See especially its legal senses, such as "a cause, judicial process, lawsuit, the hearing before the decision, . . . a business undertaken . . . a concrete question, case for discussion." Charlton T. Lewis, *An Elementary Latin Dictionary* (Oxford: Oxford University Press, 1918), 116.

27. Just as *res* and *causa* in Latin often mean much less a "mere object" than an "issue," a "matter of concern," and so on, *pragma* in Greek often refers to a matter of public concern. For instance, in the *Rhetoric* Aristotle employs *pragmata* as "the main issue to be discussed" and "the proper subject-matter of rhetoric" (*Rh.* I). In chapter 2, we shall return to this issue in the context of the connection between *pragma*, *pragmateuesthai,* and *praxis*.

28. For a discussion of this point in connection with *Metaph.* IV, see Jaulin, 1999: 35.

29. For a good analysis and elaboration of this point, see also Aubenque, 2002: 83–93.

30. For one of the many discussions of the denial of this qualification in the Aristotelian corpus, see *SE* 22, 178a17–19.

31. Why does Aristotle omit the clause "in relation to the same" (*pros to auto*) that we find in Socrates's version? It indicates the fact that *x* cannot be, say, both bigger and not bigger than *y*, although it may well be bigger than *y* and not bigger than *z*. Indeed, this is a crucial theme in many dialogues such as the *Parmenides* and the *Republic*. Since Aristotle has an extensive account of relation (*pros ti*) both in *Categories* 7, and in *Metaphysics* V, 15, he cannot have been unaware of this qualification. The only possibility seems to be that he did not deem this qualification to be crucial in that it is superfluous to indicate that something can have properties that stand in opposite relations to different objects. Thus, a statement such as "this finger is longer" or "this boy is the nephew" would be, in the eyes of Aristotle, an inherently incomplete statement.

32. Fragment 84.

33. For an analysis of this articulation of motion and rest in living bodies, see *MA* 1, 698a7–698b8.

34. In my discussion of the principle of non-contradiction and of the top example, I have benefited much from Recco, 2007.

35. *DA* III, 10, 433b27.

36. Many famous examples in the history of philosophy have exploited the fact that wax is almost pure matter without form. Plato, *Theaetetus*, 191C–D; Aristotle, *On Memory and Recollection* 450a32–b11; *GA* I, 21, 729b17; *Ph.* VII, 3, 245b11; *Cael.* III, 7, 305b30; *DA* II, 1, 412b7, III, 12, 435a2. See also Klein, 1998: 187; Themistius, 1999: 58. In chapter 4, we shall discuss another famous use of the wax example in Aristotle from *DA* II.

37. *Cat.* 2, 1a20–1b8; 5, 2b3–5.

38. See also *HA*, V, 21; V, 22, 553b31–554a1. According to the *Meteorology*, wax is composed out of both water and earth, can be impressed, squeezed and melted, and is soft, malleable, and more inflammable when mixed with other things than by themselves (*Mete.* IV, 9).

39. See also Aristotle's refutation of the Megaric view of potentiality in *Metaph.* IX, 3.

40. We shall touch upon problems concerning the pictorial representation of human character in chapter 5, section 3.

41. Nietzsche, 1962: 107. There is indeed truth to Nietzsche's claim. See especially *Ph.* I, 2, 185b20; *Metaph.* XI, 5, 1062a32 and XI, 6, 1063b24. And yet *Metaph.* IV, 3, 1005b25 and IV, 5, 1010a13 clearly distinguish Heraclitus from what is said about him and from his followers. *Top.* VIII, 5, 159b31 and *Metaph.* IV, 7, 1012a24 do not provide sufficient support for simply confronting Aristotle and Heraclitus as Nietzsche does. Furthermore, there is an explicit sentence in the Aristotelian corpus where a contradiction is said to be "quite reasonable [*mal' eulogon*]" (*EE* VII, 12, 1246a13).

Chapter 2

1. In fact, modern physics and metaphysics took this option quite seriously *against the Aristotelianism of their time*. But it is not the case that nobody thought of such a possibility in ancient Greece; in fact, Aristotle himself defends the multivocity of being explicitly and insistently against the tenets of a view according to which there is no such thing as potentiality, namely the Megaric school (*Metaph.* IX, 3). He may also have the Atomists in mind. For a clear exposition of Aristotle's position with regard to the multivocity of being, and his modern critics, see Berti, 2001: 185–207.

2. *Metaph.* IX, 3, 1047a14–15.

3. *On Int.* 13, 23a21–22. Again, for the distinction between the sublunar and the supralunar realms in Aristotle, see *Mete.* I, 2, 339a19–20; 3, 339b5.

4. For the fragile sense of divinity *in* or *around* nature, see, most famously, *PA* I, 5, 645a15–23, and *Metaph.* XII, 8, 1074b1–14.

5. See the pseudo-Aristotelian *Oeconomica* I, 1, 1343a5–7: "Some of the arts are divided into two, producing [*poiêsai*] and using the product [*khrêsasthai tôi poiêthenti*] do not belong to the same, just as the lyre and the flute . . ."

6. *Cat.* 1, 1a3, 1a8–12; 5, 2a16–18ff.

7. Annick Jaulin and Hakan Yücefer objected to my interpretation of the phrase "*logos* of being" as an *inherent* standard of being. For, they said, even an artifact can have a "*logos* of being," and, thus, "*logos* of being" need not be inherent to the being under question, but can equally be imposed from without as in artifacts. This objection poses a serious threat not only to my point here, but also to my overall argument in this book. For if artifacts have a "*logos* of being" as much as natural beings, then the "*logos* of being" of something may well be imposed from outside, without the being itself having a "say" on what it is, contrary to my claim here. Then there may be no necessary connection between the question of the "*logos* of being" and natural beings, living beings, and humans as I shall claim in the following chapters of this book.

This objection seems to be supported by at least three major Aristotelian texts: the *logos* of the house in *DA* I, 1, 403b4–8, the soul or form of the axe in *DA* II, 1, 412b12–16, and the true nature of the bed in *Physics* II, 1, 193a11–b19. Yet the objection seems to lose its power once the contexts are taken into account. For all three texts try to establish the difference between matter and form *in non-artifacts*. Aristotle uses artifacts as examples in discussions about form in non-artifacts not because artifacts have form in the same way non-artifacts do, as the objectors claim, but simply because form is much easier to differentiate from matter in artifacts. So the distinction between form and matter is clearer in a "house" than in an affection of the soul such as "anger" in *DA* I, 1, 403b4–8; the distinction between soul and body would be quite clear if we imagined an axe to have a soul ("chopping") in *DA* II, 1, 412b12–16; and, as to *Physics* II, 1, 193a11–b19, it is easier to see how form (or *rhythmos* or *logos*) is destroyed in a bed than in a natural being, for artifacts ultimately dissolve into natural beings, while natural beings dissolve again into natural beings: "Bodies seem to be beings [*ousiai*] to a highest extent, especially natural ones; for, the latter are the sources [*arkhai*] of the former" (*DA* II, 1, 412a11–13; also see *Metaph.* VII and VIII generally, especially VIII, 3, 1043b21–22; *Ph.* II, 1, 192b33, where the example of house occurs precisely in distinction from beings who all "are beings [*ousiai*]").

Artifacts are convenient examples in the study of non-artifacts (ensouled beings, animals, or natural beings) not because they are beings or have form or a "*logos* of being" in exactly the same way non-artifacts do, but rather because, on the contrary, their form is precisely imposed from without, that is, because their "standard of being" or "*logos* of being" is *not* inherent to the being at hand. Hence, when the distinction between form and matter is no longer a central issue, Aristotle clearly reverts to non-artifacts, as can be seen by the frequency of the term "*logos* of being" applied to living beings in the biological texts as in the opening of the *Categories* and indeed later in *Cat.* 5. Not only are artifacts derivative of natural beings, but art in general imitates nature for Aristotle (*Ph.* II, 2, 194a22; II, 8, 199a15–21, where again the example of "house" is used). So if artifacts are derived ultimately from natural beings or imitate them, then the "*logos* of being" should apply primarily to natural beings. I think this discussion and Aristotle's examples here support my point that, unlike the derivative or heuristic use of "*logos* of being" for artifacts, the "*logos* of being" referred to at the opening of the *Categories* means an *inherent* standard of being. (Compare the Idea of the Bed in Plato's *Republic* X, 596A–597D.)

8. See also Klein, 1965: 148.

9. The ambiguity of Socrates's *active* and *deliberate* not-moving is indeed at the heart of his protest against Anaxagorean accounts of nature in the preceding crucial discussion in the *Phaedo* 98E–99A.

10. Note that even here we have not departed from our implicit dialogue with Descartes. In the *Meditations*, one of the things that are explicitly bracketed is the concept of life. Similarly, the concept of soul (*anima*) as a principle of life is bracketed as unclear, and yields to the concept of mind (*mens*) which is "distinct and clear" to itself: clear in its immediate self-grasping, and distinct from the body.

11. For the multivocity of being for Aristotle and its implications, once again see Berti, 2001.

12. See, most famously, *Metaph.* XII, 3, 1070a10ff.

13. See *Ph.* III, 4, 203b6ff. "Un monisme serait *alogos*, en ce qu'il ne peut pas expliquer la différence entre le principe et ce qui n'est pas lui . . . La cellule minimale est la dichotomie qui permet d'accéder au *logos*" (Brague, 1978: 178).

14. Of course, this central concept of Aristotelian philosophy is used and thematized in many parts of the corpus. See, most famously, *Metaph.* V, 12; *Metaph.* IX; *Ph.* III, 1–3.

15. See Aristotle's mention of the Megarics' use of potentiality in *Metaph.* IX, 3.

16. Aristotle's exception is affirmations or negations that are predicated of universals but *not universally*. Aristotle addresses this at the end of chapter 8 of *On Interpretation*.

17. In some manuscripts the word "*melan*" (black) here appears as "*mega*" (big, large).

18. A similar necessitarian point of view, defended sub specie aeternitatis, and its pessimistic (and, according to us, vacuous) implications, can be traced in the discourse of a character, probably "Heraclides," in Aristotle's *Protrepticus*: "for to those who behold anything eternal it is silly to take seriously those things [things that seem to us great, secure, beautiful, and honorable]. What is great or what is long-lasting in human affairs? No, it is owing to our weakness, I think, and the shortness of our life, that even this appears anything great" (*Protrepticus* in Aristotle, 2015: 20–21).

19. The "kinds" (*genê*) here are indeed the kinds of change (*Ph.* III, 1, 200b33–34).

20. According to the famous manuscript E (Parisinus gr. 1853): "For nature too comes to be in the same; for it is in the same genus as potentiality."

21. The broad and politically oriented scope of *praxai* may gesture back to our emphasis in chapter 2 on the word *pragma* as not simply meaning "object" or mere "thing," but also act, deed, work, matter, affair, duty, business, a thing of consequence or importance. The first chapters of the *Rhetoric* may provide good examples for the usage of *pragmata* not as "object," but as "issue."

22. See Ross's "Introduction" in Aristotle, 1924: cxxvii.

Chapter 3

1. *DA* II, 4, 416a10ff.

2. This point is expressed, although not developed, in Sparshott, 1994: 44.

3. According to Aristotle's *Protrepticus*, the origin of the comparison between a natural philosopher gazing at the heavens and a spectator at a festival can be traced, through Anaxagoras, to Pythagoras (*Protrepticus* in Aristotle, 2015: 22–23). In this context it is interesting to note that, in his philosophy of nature, Aristotle might be the *theôros* not

exclusively of the heavenly spheres, like Pythagoras and Anaxagoras, but also of the most humble life forms on and under the earth (*PA* I, 5, 645a22–23).

4. Aristotle clearly calls physics (*physikê*) an *epistêmê theôrêtikê* (*Metaph.* VI, 1, 1025b27). See *EE* I, 5, 1216b11ff.; and *PA* I, 5, 645a8–11, which emphasizes the "theoretical" aspects of natural science. But compare also *PA* I, 1, 640a1ff.

5. That *physis* is less determinable and yet perhaps wider than our concept of "nature" can be seen in its uses in early Greek thinkers such as Heraclitus and Empedocles. It is true that medieval and modern philosophy has thought in terms of dualities that set up nature against history, production, spirit, nurture, culture, or divinity. (See Heidegger, 1998: 183–85.) Aristotle does admit that there is, besides nature, at least one other cause or source of coming-to-be in *Ph.* II, 1, 192b8–9. He names these causes or sources in the *Metaphysics*: "[A being] is generated by art [*tekhnêi*], by nature [*physei*], by fortune [*tykhêi*] or by chance [*automatôi*]. Then art is a source in another whereas nature is a source in [the being] itself (for a human being begets a human being), and the other causes are privations of these" (*Metaph.* XII, 3, 1070a4–9).

One can see that, although art is named as a source of generation besides nature, its opposition to nature is much less emphatic than their structural parallelism (see also *PA* I, 1, 639b15–30). Aristotle's main point remains that being is generated from a synonym—whether the source of generation is outside of it (as in art) or inside it (as in nature). In the *Physics* again, he insists that art imitates nature and that, just like it is obviously absurd to think of the matter without any form, this is because it is equally absurd to think of nature as mere matter (*Ph.* II, 2, 194a19–28; see also Aristotle, *Protrepticus* in Aristotle 2015: 22).

6. "That which comes from these [*morphê* and *eidos kata ton logon*], such as a human being, is not nature, but by nature [*physei*]" (*Ph.* II, 1, 193b6–7).

7. "According to nature are both these and as many things as belong to these in virtue of themselves, as being carried up belongs to fire. For this is not a nature, nor does it have a nature, but it is by nature [*physei*] and according to nature [*kata physin*]" (*Ph.* II, 1, 192b35–193a2).

8. For Aristotle's analysis of "being-in," see *Ph.* IV, 3.

9. Themistius, Simplicius, and Philoponus suggest that "according to nature" is a narrower specification than "by nature," and give the example of monstrosities that are "by nature" but not "according to nature" (cited in Aristote, *Physique*, trans. Pierre Pellegrin [Paris: Flammarion, 2002], 117, n. 3. Pellegrin adds that it is difficult to find warrant for such a distinction in Aristotle's text).

10. Although we claim in this part that Aristotelian physics can be accessed by a dismantling of modern physics, some claim that Aristotelian physics constitutes "the physics of commonsense." See Jean Rosmorduc, *Histoire de la physique et de la chimie* (Paris: Seuil, 1985), cited in *Histoire des sciences*, ed. Philippe de la Cotardière (Paris: Tallandier, 2004), 111, n. 5.

11. The following overview should indeed be supplemented by the works of historians of science such as Leclerc, 1972, and Koyré, 1957.

12. See the "*aitia*" article in LSJ, 1996: 44.

13. See the "*hylê*" article in LSJ, 1996: 1847–48.

14. One explicit example of this usage of *hylê* is even found in *GC* I, 10, 327b12.

15. "In the context of nature, [one must consider] the composite and the whole being, and not that which never occurs apart from their being" (*PA* I, 5, 645a35–37).

16. Hobbes, 1968: 86. For a similar line of demarcation between Aristotle and Hume, see Lear, 1988: 30–32.

17. These four kinds of motion are in turn derived from the categories that do admit of being otherwise (*Metaph.* XI, 12; *Ph.* V, 2). One can see here why Aristotle spends so much time discussing whether a given category admits of contraries in the *Categories* (for instance *Cat.* 5, 4a10–4b19; 6, 5b11–6a18; 7, 6b15–26).

18. Again, the idea that matter is not generated and does not perish is found in, and fundamental to, Aristotelian metaphysics and physics. See *GC* I, 4, 320a2 and *Metaph.* VII, 7, 1032a17. For Aristotle's discussion of such theories, see *Metaph.* I, 3–4 and *Ph.* II, 2–4.

19. "A proper assessment of the rationale of Aristotle's procedure in the analysis of the most basic materials and the processes of their combinations explains at the same time, however, why he was not predestined to become the 'father of chemistry,' as he became the father of so many other disciplines. If his study of the elements and their properties did not encourage the development of chemistry in antiquity, this is because of the constraints imposed by his principles" (Frede, 2004: 313).

20. This idea of a "lump," "bulk," or "mass" of stuff deprived of unity is also a prevalently but not exclusively modern one, and is often termed *onkos* in Ancient Greek. Aristotle mostly uses *onkos* as synonymous with *sôma* and as opposed to *kenon* (void). Among its recurrent uses in philosophical contexts (in Empedocles, Parmenides, Plato, Aristotle, and later Epicure), its in-depth treatment in the seventh deduction of Plato's *Parmenides* (especially 165B and the following) is relevant to our discussion here.

21. See, for instance, *DA* III, 9–11.

22. *Ph.* IV, 4.

23. *Ph.* IV, 5, 212b16–17: "Besides the all and whole [*pan kai holon*], there is nothing outside of the all." We must point out here the informative etymology of *kosmos* which makes the word "cosmetics" intelligible: *kosmos* means order in a strong sense, both physically and almost aesthetically. This sense of *kosmos* is by no means obsolete at the time of Aristotle. See for instance *Mete.* I, 1 338a23, and other instances of *kosmos*, *kosmopoiia*, *diakosmein*, *diakosmêsis*, *kosmein*, *kosmêsis*, and so on in Bonitz, 1955.

24. Compare *Ph.* IV, 5, 212b20–24: "The earth is in the water, and the water is in the air, and the air is in the aether, and the aether is in the heaven, but the heaven is no longer in anything else."

25. One can see here the early modern breakdown of the Aristotelian distinction between natural motion and forced motion. See, for instance, *Cael.* I, 2, 269a7.

26. *Ph.* IV, 5.

27. It may be helpful to contrast Aristotle's discussion of the wholeness of the universe in *On the Heavens* or *Phyics* IV, 5, with his definition of the "infinite" in *Physics* III, 6, 207a1–2.

28. Compare the concept of *koinos topos* "in which all bodies are," in *Ph.* IV, 2. For the details of the long evolution which we necessarily simplify here, see Leclerc, 1972.

29. For the meanings of *pathos* and *pathein*, see *Metaph.* V, 21.

30. Compare the Cartesian idea that the essence of bodies is extension precisely in a space understood as *partes extra partes*. If space is defined by the mutual exclusiveness of its parts, what does it mean to say that a body is defined by its occupying various parts of space at once? What warrants for the unity of that body stretched along mutually exclusive parts? Of course, these questions are ones Descartes is prepared to face by means of his methodological skepticism.

31. See *Ph.* I, 1, 184a16–22; *NE* I, 4, 1095b1–5; *Metaph.* VII, 3, 1029b3–12.

32. Lang, 1998: 6–7.

33. It is indeed an *impoverished* version of it, because the source of motion that is a kind of cause for Aristotle is the *first* source of motion (*protê arkhê kinêseôs* or *metabolês*) and certainly not the immediate source such as a moving hand.

34. See especially *APo.* II, 2, 3.

35. "It is ridiculous to judge from the outside" (*On Breath* 9, 485b4).

36. René Descartes, *Discours de la méthode*, VI.

37. See also *Pol.* I, 1, 1253a32–38. Compare Heraclitus, Fragment 30. Compare also Lloyd, 1983: 27–35.

38. Here I am following Joe Sachs's translation in Aristotle, 1995.

39. This point converges with Aristotle's assurance that the heavens and the order in the cosmos are eternal, and not threatened by any apocalypse (*Cael.* II, 1).

40. *Ph.* IV, 4; IV, 5; *Cael.* I, 8, 277a12–277b9; *Mete.* I, 3, 340b24–341a9; I, 4, 341b13–24.

41. See also the un-Aristotelian *On Breath* 9, 485b18: "Fire exhibits differences with respect to more and less."

42. See again *On Breath*, 9 485b7–10: "The arts use [fire] as an instrument, nature [uses it] also as matter. Indeed this is not a difficulty, [the difficulty lies] rather in the fact that nature, which uses [the fire], itself thinks [*noêsai*], also providing at the same time the *rhythmos* to sensible affections [*hêtis hama tois aisthêtois pathesi kai ton rhythmon apodôsei*]."

43. "*legomen dê genos hen ti tôn ontôn tên ousian, tautês de to men hôs hylên, ho kath' hauto men ouk esti tode ti, heteron de morphên kai eidos, kath' hên êdê legetai tode ti, kai triton to ek toutôn.*"

44. "*ousiai de malist' einai dokousi ta sômata, kai toutôn ta physika. tauta gar tôn allôn arkhai. tôn de physikôn ta men ekhei zôên, ta d' ouk ekhei. zôên de legomen tên di' autou trophên te kai auxêsin kai phthisin. hôste pan sôma physikon metekhon zôês ousia an eiê, ousia d' houtôs hôs synthetê. epei d' esti soma toionde, zôên gar ekhon, ouk an eiê to soma psykhê. ou gar esti tôn kath' hypokeimenou to soma, mallon d' hôs hypokeimenon kai hylê.*"

45. Later, Aristotle implies that there is an important exception to the requirement of nutrition and generation for sharing in life: "This [potentiality to absorb food] can exist apart from the others, but the others cannot [exist apart] from this *in mortal beings*" (*DA* II, 2, 413a31–33; emphasis mine). See also the famous passage about the immortal and everlasting in *DA* III, 5, 430a23.

46. See also *PA* II, 10, 655b32–33.

47. *Ph.* II, 1, 193a31, 193b2.

48. For the same example, see *Protrepticus* in Aristotle, 2015: 26.

49. *Metaph.* IX, 8, 1050b28–30. See also Lang, 1998: 10–11.

50. For the relation between the locomotion and shape of fiery beings in the sublunar sphere, see *Mete.* I, 4.

51. *Metaph.* VII, 16, 1040b5ff. Compare the structure of fire and that of living beings with Aristotle's distinction between simple plots and complex plots in the *Poetics*, and his doctrines of the unity, length, and structure of tragedy (*Po.*, 6, 7, 8, 10; esp. 8, 1451a34–36).

52. We are well aware that we have skipped one step between elements and organs: the distinction between uniform and nonuniform parts. Yet this distinction does not contribute to our main goal of understanding the inherence of *logos* first in nature as such, and now, more specifically, in living beings. So let me refer the reader to, for instance, *PA* II, 2ff.

53. Heraclitus, Fr. 115.

54. See also *GC* II, 6, 334a9–15.

55. Even mixture in an inorganic level involves more than *any* percentage. The following passage on mixture by Dorothea Frede is extremely close to the Heraclitean idea of self-opposition (she even talks about "mutual tuning," 2004: 305) and to our claim that the fundamental meaning of *logos* is a relation between terms that preserves them together in their difference instead of collapsing one term to the other or holding them in indifference: "If one ingredient overpowers the other, there will be no mixture, but only an increase in the bulk of the predominant element. Thus a drop of wine does not mix with ten thousand pints of water but loses its *form* and merges entirely with water. Only if the ingredients are *somehow equal in power* can there be mixture. In that case there is change in both constituents, but neither will turn into the other. Instead, the mutual change will result in a dominant state (*kratoun*) that is 'in between and common' (*metaxu kai koinon*) to both. Given that mixables must be able to affect each other, there must be a basic opposition (*enantiôsis*) between them" (Frede, 2004: 295; emphasis mine). Mixture is indeed one of the most interesting and intriguing questions in *GC*, and became an intense topic of discussion through Alexander of Aphrodisias.

56. *Metaph.* VII, 16, 1040b5–16.

57. For the close affinity between concocting, digestion and growth, and even maturing, see *GA* I, 1, 715b24; II, 6, 743a31ff.; I, 12, 719a34.

58. See, for instance, later in Euclid, *Elements*, Book V, definition 3: "Ratio [*logos*] is a certain type of condition [*skhesis*] with respect to the size of two magnitudes of the same kind" (Euclid, 2007: 291).

59. See also *PA* I, 1, 621a138–144. For the genesis of the Aristotelian idea that the soul is a harmony, see Jaeger, 1950: 39ff.

60. It is not entirely clear to me whether *toutôn* refers to "*logos* and *synthesis*" or is an apposition to "*tôn mikhthentôn.*" This will not affect our argument, since we will argue that if the soul is a *logos*, it is not a *logos* as the quantitative percentage of ingredients.

61. Of course, Aristotle's major text on mixture is *GC*, especially I, 10 and II, 6, but also I, 5–6. In I, 10, Aristotle resolves problems arising from explaining change by appealing to the distinction between action and passion, and potentiality and actuality: "Neither the art of healing nor health make health by mixing bodies" (*GC* I, 10, 328a22–23).

62. I take it that this same point is made in *Metaph.* VII, 17 and VIII, 3.

63. For flesh as *logos*, see also Averroès, 1998: 91, 249.

64. In this last sentence, *On Generation and Corruption* may be gesturing toward the spectacular character of nature and life in Aristotle's philosophy. The same text also explicitly identifies the work of the natural scientist as *theôrein* in the sense of watching. For, those who argue that all change happens between like beings and those who argue that it happens between unlike beings oppose one another simply because, "while it is necessary to watch [*theôrêsai*] a whole, they happened to express a part" (*GC* I, 7, 323b18–19). (For a similar methodological point, see *Pol.* III, 9, 1280a9; *Ph.* III, 6, 206a13; IV, 9, 217b20–23; II, 2, 194b11; I, 2, 186a1.)

65. *Metaph.* VII, 16, 1040b5–10.

66. See also *Metaph.* XII, 7, 1072b3, 26, *GC* II, 10, 336b25–337a7, and *EE* I, 5, 1216a11–14: "Now they say that Anaxagoras was questioned with respect to such problems and asked why one should choose to be born rather than not; he said 'for the sake of *theôrêsai* the heaven and the order around the whole *kosmos.*'"

67. See also Long, 2011: 18; Labarrière, 2004: 179.
68. *Ph.* III, 1, 200b33–34.
69. *DA* III, 13, 435b2; II, 12, 424b1.

Chapter 4

1. *DA* II, 2, 413a26–413b1; *HA* VIII, 1, 588b24–25.
2. "You ought to remember that you are a human being—not only in living well, but also in doing philosophy" (*On the Good*, Fragment 1, in Aristotle, 1955: 113). See Aristotle's comparison of the skeptic aspiring to reject the principle of non-contradiction to a "plant" (*Metaph.* IV, 4, 1006a15). Later in this chapter, we will have the opportunity to interpret this characterization in a way more subtle and philosophical than as an expression of sheer meanness against the skeptic (see pp. 100–101 in this volume).
3. DK22A9 cited in Aristotle's *PA* I, 5, 645a22–23.
4. See also *On Youth and Old Age, On Life and Death* 1, 467b23–26; *DA* II, 2, 413a21ff.; *PA* II, 10, 655b28ff.
5. For the sake of sheer consistency, here we shall translate *alloiôsis* by "alteration" and *pathos* by "affection."
6. This point is nicely put by Heidegger: "Were our hearing primarily and always only this picking up and transmitting of sounds, conjoined by several other processes, the result would be that the reverberation would go in one ear and out the other. That happens in fact when we are not gathered to what is addressed" (Heidegger, 1984: 64–65).
7. Again Heidegger puts it nicely: "We hear when we are 'all ears'" (Heidegger, 1984: 65).
8. For *logos* as "health," see Nussbaum, 1994: 49ff. Compare Polyphemus's use of *logos* as "remedy" in section 3 of the conclusion to this book.
9. See Burnyeat, 2002: 28–90.
10. Brentano, 1977: 54–55.
11. To put it in contemporary terms: "How exactly the senses acquire the appropriate content or provide the appropriate information to the rational capacities without becoming colored is the Aristotelian analogue of a problem that troubles modern researchers, namely, how the *non-representational, non-computational* sensory system can provide information which the *computational* brain can access" (Silverman, 1989: 279).
12. For Aristotle's classical refutation of the Megaric view that reduces all potentiality to actuality, see again *Metaph.* IX, 3.
13. For another instance of wax being used as a metaphor of receptivity, see *DA* III, 12, 435a2–10; *On Memory and Recollection* I, 44931–450b1; and also Plato, *Theaetetus* 190E5–196C5.
14. *DA* II, 5, 417b23; *APo.* I, 31.
15. *APo.* I, 31, 88a3–5; II, 19; *DA* II, 5, 417a30–417b2; perhaps also *Metaph.* I, 1 981a1–7.
16. For sight, see *GA* V, 1, 780a22–25; for hearing see *DA* II, 8, 420a9–12; for touch, see *DA* III, 13, 435a21–b3.
17. See *HA* VIII, 1, 588b27–31 and Balme's note in Aristotle, 1991.
18. For the distinction between two senses of *logos* in order to account for Aristotle's understanding of sensation beyond the dilemma of a literal, purely physicalist reading (which reduces sensation to "physical change") and of a non-physicalist interpretation, see Bradshaw, 1997: 143–61.

19. See also *DA* II, 11, 424a3–7; III, 2, 426b10–23; III, 3, 427a17–21; III, 9, 432a15–17; *APo.* II, 19, 99b35; *Top.* II, 4, 111a16; *Mete.* IV, 4, 382a16–20; *MA* 6, 700b20; *Protrepticus* (in Aristotle, 2015: 26). See also Narcy, 1996: 239–56; Bradshaw, 1997: 146.

20. Barbara Cassin claims that the challenger of the principle can exempt himself from being refuted in face of his own contradiction because he is precisely laying claim to his right to contradiction. But, if I am understanding Cassin correctly, in his claim to his right, the challenger cannot appeal to the principle since he must distinguish being granted this right and being refused it. Aristotle's point seems to be that the challenger cannot *lay claim* to anything, be it the claim to contradiction. "To destroy a *logos*, one stays behind [*hypomenei*] a *logos*" (*Metaph.* IV, 4, 1006a26). The challenger cannot pragmatically *refuse* to engage in the "dialectical game" either, because refusal *is* commitment. The challenger can only *imitate* a vegetative state (Cassin, 1997: 13). See also Lear, 1980: 103–14: "But Aristotle is not arguing with a vegetable. He is arguing with someone who can present a coherent, if fallacious, argument for the falsity of the law of non-contradiction" (194).

21. *DA* III, 12, 434b18.

22. See also Aristotle's example of a shield struck by a spear in *DA* II, 11, 423b12–17.

23. The terms "distant sensation" and "sensation of time" are not stretches of the Aristotelian terminology. He in fact names this anticipatory sensation "*proaisthêsis*" (*De Sensu* 1, 436b21), and insists, as we shall see, that some animals have a "sensation of time"—all functions of the "common sensory power" (*DA* III, 10, 433b8; see also *On Memory and Recollection* 2, 452b8; see Labarrière, 2004: 179–80).

24. *PA* II, 10, 656a27–28; *De Sensu* 2, 439a2–5; *MA* 11, 703b22–23.

25. See also *DA* II, 2, 413b24–25; III, 9, 432b29–30.

26. AT, VII, 29.11–18; AT, IX, 23.

27. This latter is characterized in almost complete opposition to what we understand from imagination today; far from being a capricious, disinterested, arbitrary, or creative fancy of the mind, *phantasia* here is fundamentally interested; it is primarily fused with desire.

28. Let us note that this famous expression is not found in Aristotle. See Labarrière, 2004: 195ff; Morel, 2003: 80–89.

29. For the "universal premise of desire" see also Nussbaum, 1994: 81.

30. The reason why Aristotle puts the question of motion and action in terms of the continuity and intermittence of *nous* is presumably that he has in mind some opinions, such as that of Anaxagoras, according to which *nous* would be the *arkhê* of all.

31. *DA* III, 10, 433b26; 9, 432b29–31.

32. *DA* II, 5, 417b2022–23; III, 11, 434a16–21; *APo.* I, 31, 87b28ff; *NE* VII, 5, 1147a25–26.

33. See the eight occurrences of the word or its cognates in *MA* 8. Cf. Sorabji, 1993: 40.

34. *MA* 7, 701a9; *DA* III, 11, 434a7–10.

35. *DA* III, 11, 434a18; *NE* VII, 3, 1147a27, 35; *MA* 7, 701a32, 33.

36. *DA* III, 10, 433b6; III, 11, 434a17; *NE* VII, 3, 1147b1ff.

37. *APo.* II, 19, 100a1–6. It is this disambiguation of *logos* that seems to be lacking in Lee and Long, 2007: 348–67.

38. *Metaph.* I, 1, 981a12–23.

Chapter 5

1. See also *Rh.* II, 6, 1384a23–25; *EE* II, 1, 1219b27–1220a11.

2. See also *GA* II, 1, 731b18ff.

3. *Pol.* I, 3, 1256b10–15; VII, 12, 1332a38ff.

4. Berti, 1990: 261–62.

5. David Konstan translates this phrase as "it 'is heeding of it'" (Aspasius, 2006: 37). Richard Bodéüs nicely notes about this passage: "La même expression ambiguë (*logon echein*) sert en grec dans les deux cas: (a) pour dire qu'une partie de l'âme 'rend compte de' quelque chose (et est ainsi rationnelle en elle-même) et (b) pour dire qu'une autre partie 'tient compte' de quelque chose (et est ainsi rationnelle par participation)" (Aristotle, 2004: 98). See also Sorabji, 1993: 69–70.

6. But compare a few lines later, *NE* I, 13, 1103a2, where only the "father" appears.

7. See, for instance, H. Rackham's translation: "in the sense in fact which we speak of 'paying heed' to one's father and friends" (Aristotle, 1926: 67).

8. See, for instance, the rendering of W. D. Ross: "this is the sense in which we speak of 'taking account' of one's father or one's friends" (Aristotle, 1966). Sachs also prefers the disjunction: "In the same way too we call listening to one's father or friends 'being rational'" (Aristotle, 2002: 21). In his commentary, Sparshott seems to be clearly aware of Aristotle's reference to the relation and possible conflicts between family and the state (Sparshott, 1994: 28).

9. In this regard, we are quite in line with Baracchi's approach (Baracchi, 2007: 175–79).

10. For the complications arising from the practical syllogism in the case of humans, see also Sparshott, 1994: 7.

11. This intermediary part brings to mind many passages from the Platonic corpus such as *Republic* IV, 439E3–441C3; *Timaeus* 70A5; *Phaedrus* 253D8.

12. For Aristotle's analysis of *ekhein*, see *Metaph.* V, 23; *Cat.* 15. As we shall see, these two analyses will prove to be insufficient for understanding *ekhein* in this context.

13. *NE* I, 13, 1102a30–34; *DA* I, 5, 411a24–411b31.

14. Dodds points out how the irrational part of the soul became gradually neglected after Aristotle (Dodds, 1951: 239).

15. *NE* I, 13, 1102b26, 31, 33.

16. See also *Pol.* VII, 13, 1333a16–18.

17. See also *HA* IV, 9, 536b3–5; *Prob.* 11, 898b34–899a4.

18. This word means "language," "dialect," "accent," and even "speech" in Aristotle as well as in Hippocrates and others. (See Zirin, 1980: 339.) Here, however, it cannot but mean "idiom" in a very loose sense, which Aristotle mentions in the following sentence: "Inanimate beings never utter voice, but are said only by resemblance to do so, just like a flute, a lyre or any other inanimate being that has a musical compass, tune and *dialekton*" (*DA* II, 8, 420b6–8). Accordingly, Hett translates *dialektos* here as "modulation."

19. For a contemporary discussion of nightingales, see Anderson, 2013: 30. For plasticity, see Anderson, 2013: 19; Langues, Petri, Nespor, and Scharff, 2013: 228. For later Greek attitudes toward bird "language," see Sorabji, 1993: 80.

20. *GA* V, 2, 781a26–30; *Rh.* I, 11, 1371b8–9; III, 9, 1409b1ff.; III, 10, 1410b15ff; see also the non-Aristotelian *On Things Heard* 800a29–31.

21. For a similar connection between *eikasia* and *syllogismos*, see *On Memory and Recollection* 1, 450b20ff.

22. *Protrepticus* in Aristotle, 2015: 25. A similar remark occurs in *Metaph.* I, 1, 981a27–981b5.

23. "*Logos*" article I.4, in LSJ, 1996: 1057. See also Guthrie, 1979: 419–25; Herodotus, 2.85, 7.5; Theon of Smyrna, 1878: 72–74.

24. After a lengthy and sometimes quite detailed survey of human education that will spill into book VIII, the triad "nature," "habit," and "*logos*" is taken up again in the context of education in *Pol.* VII, 13, 1334b5. See also *NE* X, 9, 1179b21ff.

25. Berti, 1990: 261.

26. For the idea that "learning" (*mathêsis*) is only one part of education (*paideia*), see *Politics* VII, VIII, and especially *Pol.* VII, 15, 1336a24ff.

27. I am sympathetic to Joe Sachs's remarks on *hexis*. Yet his rendering of it as "active condition" unduly associates the term with activity. I am trying to emphasize that *hexis* is an "included middle" beyond the false dilemma of activity and passivity (Aristotle, 2002: xii).

28. For *ekhein*, see *Metaph.* V, 23, and *Cat.* 15. The analysis of *hexis* in *Metaph.* V, 27, is promising, but excessively cryptic and elusive. In fact, the most informative passage on *hexis* we have encountered in the corpus is *Ph.* VII, 3, 247b1–18. We shall discuss this passage shortly.

29. For an example of human love, see section 2 of the conclusion to this book.

30. *DA* II, 3, 414b4–7; also see II, 2, 413b24–25; III, 9, 432b29–30.

31. See *NE* VI, 3, 1139b32; VI, 4, 1140a11. For the connection between art, action, and truth, see Roochnik, 2004: 144–48.

32. *Politics* VII and VIII. Most specifically, see the extremely detailed discussion of music in education starting at 1339a11 and that runs all the way to the end of the *Politics*. See also, indeed, Plato, *Republic* II, VI and VII.

33. "Everybody somehow seems to divine that virtue is a certain *hexis*, a *hexis* according to *phronêsis*. But this must be slightly modified: Virtue is a *hexis* not only according to *orthos logos*, but with *logos*" (*NE* VI, 13, 1144b24–28).

34. *Metaph.* I, 1.

35. Pellegrin, 2009: 107–8; my translation.

36. For the distinction between suppression and virtue, see also Nussbaum, 1994: 82, 93.

37. Chantraine,1984: 625; Heidegger, 1984: 60; 1959: 123–79; Hoffmann, 2003: 27–53.

38. It is important not to confuse a two-way capacity (with *logos*) with two one-way capacities (without *logos*). See Makin, 2000: 147–48.

39. I grant that the function of Socrates's *daimôn* must be taken into account here.

40. For the *alogos* character of desire as such, see again *DA* III, 11, 434a12–15. For the *alogos* character of *nous* as such, see *NE* VI, 8, 1142a26–27; VI, 11, 1143a36–1143b1; for the superhuman character of *nous*, see also *NE* X, 7, 1177b30ff.; VI, 7, 1141b1–3.

41. This is why the couple potentiality/actuality cannot and certainly should not be thought as mapping on to passivity/activity. During a concert, the guitarist, the guitar, the audience, and even, or most of all the compositor, are *all at-work, in actuality*—except if one is distracted or in mere routine. For Aristotle's analysis of passive actualities, see *Metaph.* IX, 2; also see the *Protrepticus*: "when some one word means each of two things [the potential sense and the actual sense], and one of the two is so called *either by acting or being acted on*, we shall attribute the term as applying more to this one [the actual sense]" (Aristotle, *Protrepticus* in Aristotle, 2015: 26; emphasis mine).

42. MacIntyre is driven to ask and answer very similar questions about the problem of portraying virtue and vice (MacIntyre, 2013: 207, 220).

43. See, for instance, Carroll, 1984: 35–56; and Rousseau, 1962: 149–56.

Chapter 6

1. *Pol.* VII, 12, 1332b5–6; *NE* IX, 9, 1169b20–21; *EE* II, 8, 1224b30. But see also *NE* VIII, 12, 1162a15–25. For the power of speech as a human "privilege" and foundation of community, see also the "Hymn to *Logos*" in Isocrates, *Nicocles or the Cyprians* 3.5–9; also 15.253, 15.273, 4.48ff.; Xenophon, *Memorabilia* 4.3.11ff.

2. As will be seen in this part of the book, I talk about "double articulation" (or "duality of patterning") because I find the idea and even the term (*diarthrôsis*) in Aristotle. Nevertheless I am indeed aware of its immediate connotations in twentieth-century linguistics. See also Labarrière, 2004: 27ff.

3. For reasons that will become clear shortly, I adopt neither Balme's translation of "*phônê*" as "hum," nor D'Arcy Wentworth Thompson's as "sound," nor Barthélemy Saint-Hilaire's and Tricot's as "son."

4. See Pliny the Elder, *Naturalis Historia* XI, 10, (p. 432 Littré), who represents the hive like a camp of soldiers under most severe and wise orders. Virgil also talks about an arguably similar sound made in the evening, followed by the bees' murmuring around the edges and threshold of the hive (*Georgics* IV, 188; see also ll. 71–72). Earlier, in *HA* IV, 8, 534b16–17, Aristotle makes a more general, but less clear-cut point: "The Cephalopods, the Crustacea and the Insects possess all the senses; all, for indeed they possess [sight and] both smell and taste." The bracketed words are omitted by Wimmer in Aubert and Wimmer's edition, as approved by A. L. Peck.

5. *On Int.* 9; *Metaph.* III, 2, 996b26–30; 7, 1011b26–27; IV, 4.

6. *Metaph.* IV, 3, 1005b19–20ff.

7. Balme, 1962: 91.

8. Balme translates *tôi krotôi* paraphrastically as "the sound of a rattle," Thompson as "a rattling noise," Barthélemy Saint-Hilaire and Tricot as "bruit." Compare Pliny the Elder, *Naturalis Historia* XI, 22 (p. 438 Littré).

9. With a view to our later discussion of *psophos*, let us remark that here *psêphois*, "counters," appears in some manuscripts as *psophois*, "sounds" or "noises," and this reading is supported by some Latin translations. See Balme's footnote on his translation of *HA* IX, 40, 627a18.

10. *Esti mentoi adêlon holôs ei akouousin*, to which Balme adds the object "it," standing for the "sound of a rattle." The sentence is translated quite differently by Thompson ("it is uncertain, however, whether or not they can hear the noise at all . . ."), Saint-Hilaire ("Toutefois on ne sait pas du tout si elles ont la faculté de l'ouïe, ou si elles ne l'ont pas"), and Tricot ("On n'a pu encore déterminer toutefois d'une manière absolue si elles possèdent ou non le sens de l'ouïe"). Balme's footnote explains his emendation: "In the context the question seems to be, not generally whether bees are deaf, but whether they hear this sound at a distance . . ." In any case, he takes this passage to conflict with *Metaph.* I, 1, 980b23.

11. It is interesting to see that recent bee research seems to agree with Aristotle on the ambiguity of bee hearing in general, but also with his skepticism about the possibility of summoning bees by beating implements like pots: "Bees make various sounds—for example, the piping of virgin queens as they prepare to emerge from their cells, the warbling of the nurse-bees when they are producing more 'bee-milk' than can be consumed by the larval bees, and the hissing of the workers when the wall of the hive is knocked—and these are all produced by the exhalation of air from the spiracles (or lung valves) on the thorax. The wing-beat frequency of the hive, if detectable, is an excellent warning system

indicating the imminence of a swarm . . . But bees have no known auditory equipment beyond the ability to sense surface motion and the oscillation of air-borne particles, and the purpose of these utterances is so far unknown. Thus, various extremely ancient and persistent superstitions about 'tanging' the bees (calling them by beating on metal implements) are almost certainly meaningless" (Preston, 2006: 21).

12. In cases of "homonyms" in Aristotle's terms, this ambiguity is not always philosophically interesting, given that names are conventional according to him (*On Int.* 2, 16a26–29; 4, 16b33–17a2), especially if the two beings in question are mere namesakes such as a worker "bee" and a spelling "bee." Yet, there is a middle ground between trivial multivocity and downright univocity: in philosophically interesting cases of ambiguity, like that of "being," "life," and "good" according to Aristotle, the word in question refers neither to one single being or kind, nor has an arbitrary manifold of meanings. This point is nicely made in Shields, 1999. See also Ward, 2008.

13. "*Akouein* . . . meaning *to hear from, learn from,* take[s] the genitive of the actual source" (Smyth, 1920: 324). But compare *Cael.* I, 11, 281a22.

14. "*To hear a thing* is usually *akouein ti* when the thing heard is something definite and when the meaning is simply *hear*, not *listen to*" (Smyth, 1920: 324). A typical example of this accusative use of *akouein* in Aristotle may be the following: "So, what you have hear, you can utter [*hôsth' ho êkouse, tout' eipein*]" (*GA* V, 2, 781a30).

15. Jaulin and Duminil are the exception, since they translate *psophos* here as "bruit," unlike their predecessors, Cousin, Saint-Hilaire, Pierron and Zevort, and Tricot, who render it as "sons." Similarly, Ross and Barnes translate it as "sounds," William of Moerbeke as "sonus."

16. *De Sensu* 2, 438b20. See also the non-Aristotelian *On Things Heard* 800a1ff.

17. The striking object and the object struck may seem to be identical as in a bell, but it is we who detect or rather impose such an identity through our concept of an "object." The ringing bell is not one undifferentiated entity any more than two clapping hands are. A bell has a necessary internal differentiation, functionally interconnected parts, that is, "organs," an unmoving part and a moving one very much like articulations in the bodies of animals capable of locomotion (*MA* 1, 698a15ff.). The parts of the water that stir up one another and thereby emit the roaring of a tide, taken by themselves, are external to one another. Even in the snapping of fingers taken as pure sound, the palm is precisely used as something external to the fingers. In short, sound is a shock, a stroke, that is, the effect of a motion *against* another motion. A human being may put these two motions in a certain order by understanding a strictly mathematical proportion (*logoi*) between them in a Pythagorean or Platonic way. We saw in chapter 4 how Aristotle himself compares the destruction of the *logos* of a sense organ to the destruction of the harmony of a lyre (*DA* II, 12, 424a29–33; *De Sensu* VII, 448a9).

18. Compare the case of touch in *DA* III, 13, 435a21–b3, or the case of sight: "The sight of the eye which is intermediate between too much and too little liquid is the best, for it has neither too little so as to be disturbed and hinder the movement of the colors, nor too much so as to cause difficulty of movement" (*GA* V, 1, 780a22–25).

19. *De Sensu* I, 437a10.

20. *DA* III, 2, 426a8ff.; III, 3, 427a19; *APo.* II, 19, 99b35–36.

21. Compare *De Sensu* 2, 438a13–17, b5–16, where Aristotle says that vision requires that the pupil or eye-jelly be transparent.

22. See also Georgin, 1961: 871: "*psophos*: BRUIT; son."

23. *DA* II, 8, 420b29; and *HA* IV, 9, 535b31. *LSJ*, s.v. "psophos."

24. Warrington suggests that ants are among these unnamed species, and refers to *PA* II, 4, 650b26 (*Aristotle's Metaphysics,* ed. and trans. John Warrington [London: J. M. Dent and Sons, 1956], 51, n. 2). Yet the mentioned *PA* passage suggests no more than that ants and bees have a more intelligent [*synetôteran*] soul than some blooded animals. On the other hand, Asclepius gives the following examples, none of which are Aristotelian: "The dog, the parrot, the horse, the donkey, etc." (Asclepius, in Brandis, *Scholia Graeca in Aristotelis Metaphysica* [Berlin: Berolini Typis Academicis, 1837], 552).

25. As mentioned before, this word means "language," "dialect," "accent," and even "speech" in Aristotle as well as in Hippocrates and others. (See Zirin, 1980: 339.) Here, however, it cannot but mean "idiom" in a very loose sense, which Aristotle mentions in the following sentence: "Inanimate beings never utter voice, but are said only by resemblance to do so, just like a flute, a lyre, or any other inanimate being that has a musical compass, tune and *dialekton*" (*DA* II, 8, 420b6–8). Accordingly, Hett translates *dialektos* here as "modulation."

26. See also *PA* II, 17, 660a35–660b2; and *GA* V, 2, 781a26–28: "Learning [*mathêsis*] of things said happens in such a way that one can repeat what is heard [*antiphtheggesthai to akousthen*]." One of the major passages concerning the role of imitation in learning according to Aristotle is indeed *Po.* 4, 48b4–28. See chapter 5, section 1 above.

27. See also the passage just quoted, *HA* IV, 9, 536b14–18: "Among small birds, some when singing send forth a different voice [*phônên*] from their parents, if they have been reared away from the nest and have listened to other birds singing."

28. In the Pseudo-Aristotelian *Problems,* it is said that withholding breath sharpens hearing as well, "this is why in hunting they recommend one not to breathe" (*Prob.* 11, 903b34–36, 904b11–14).

29. *PA* II, 17, 660a29–660b2; *DA* III, 13, 435b25.

30. In *Cael.* II, 9, 290b12ff., one can see that Aristotle is sensitive to the difference between a sound (*psophos*) and a voice (*phônê*) when he first uses the traditional term "*symphonia*" in discussing the Pythagorean/Platonic "harmony of spheres" of stars, but then reverts to his own perhaps corrected term: "sound" (*psophos*).

31. As in the case at hand, analogous features occur between genera, like feathers of birds and scales of fish, whereas different species of the same genus exhibit features that differ by the "more-and-less," like birds having long feathers and birds with short feathers. "In distinguishing extensive kinds from one another, this term [analogous structures] usually refers to a relationship between structures which at a very abstract level perform a similar function for their possessors, but do so by different means, and are not structural variations on a common theme, i.e. are not open to more/less comparison" (Lennox, 1987: 341n). See also Balme's introduction to his translation of *History of Animals* VII–X, p. 16.

32. Although Aristotle does not himself use the word *analogon* for the buzz and its physiology, our usage of the word here is warranted by his canonical account of *analogon* in *PA* I, 5, 645b8–21, where counterparts of lung are associated with the lung in terms of their functions (*praxeis . . . koinas*).

33. Aristotle does not have more than one line to talk about antennae or "horns" (*HA* IV, 7, 532a26–27).

34. It is this sound that has been metaphorically named a "song," "hum," or "murmur," and imitated musically. "But whether 'bee dance' is a charming misnomer or not, bees really do seem to sing. The variations in pitch produced by the irregular flight of a foraging

worker bee—the 'slender sound' and 'faint utterance' which Wordsworth remembered had accompanied 'ages coming, ages gone,' the sound of summer days which William Cullen Bryant imagined as a murmuring wind, and Emerson as a 'mellow breezy bass'—is reproduced by Rimsky-Korsakov's famous 'The Flight of the Bumble Bee'" (Preston, 2006: 110–11).

35. See also *Po.* 1, 1447a20–1447b2.

36. For a discussion, see Labarrière, 2004: 23–26.

37. *Pol.* I, 1, 1252a. For information on the behavioral function of tympanal hearing in insects, without, unfortunately, any mention of honeybees, see Hoy and Robert, 1996: 439–41; Hoy, 1998: 1–17.

38. See chapter 4 of Darwin, 1998.

39. Note that all we are claiming is that bees do not hear "noise" while they are capable of hearing a counterpart of voice. We are indeed not claiming, and do not need to claim, that birds are incapable of hearing voice according to Aristotle (which is not true). Just to mention a striking example: "all [birds] use their tongues also as a means of interpretation [*pros hermêneian*] with one another, and some to a larger degree than other, so that there even seems to be learning [*mathêsin*] among some" (*PA* II, 17, 660a35–660b2). Compare *HA* IX, 40, 626b4, which states that the young bees make combs roughly "out of ignorance" (*anepistêmosynên*). See also Labarrière, 2004.

40. LSJ, s.v. *akouein*, A.II.2. Many other languages, including Turkish, English, Latin, and Arabic, associate the idea of "listening" directly to that of "obeying." One striking example of this kind of "voice" is found in Aristotle's remark that, when an elephant is subdued in fight, he "really becomes a slave [*douloutai iskhyrôs*] and is won over by the voice" (*tên tou nikêsantos phônên*) of the winner (*HA* IX, 1, 610a17).

41. That the head bee is female was not suggested until 1586 (Preston, 2006: 169). Despite its some questionnable inferences, see also Byl, 1978: 17.

42. See also Plato, *Statesman* 301E. For more information, see my article "Aristotle at Work: Method in *Generation of Animals*, III, 10," *Epoché*, especially footnote 52 (forthcoming in 2017).

43. Contrast the lazy, irascible, annoying, and careless attitude of drones in *HA* V, 22, 553b12; IX, 40, 624b16, 28; 625a15–33; 625b1–6; 626a14–15.

44. We should note that, to our knowledge, there is only one Aristotelian passage that threatens our interpretation: "Hearing is of the differences between sounds only, [it is] of the differences between voices for a few" (*De Sensu* 1, 437a10–11).

45. Similarly, a note by Daniel J. Castellano interprets the *Metaphysics* passage as indicating not that bees are deaf as such, but that they are "unable to understand the sound they hear"—which is John McMahon's translation that Castellano quotes and supports albeit not without reservations (http://www.arcaneknowledge.org/philtheo/aristotlebees.htm). Yet Castellano's argument does not provide much textual evidence and does not distinguish, for that matter, between "sound," "noise," "voice," and "buzz."

46. Before moving on to the next chapter, it may be of some interest to compare our conclusions about Aristotle's remarks concerning bee communication with twentieth-century research on bees, especially Karl von Frisch's following notes: "Sound waves borne by the air are not perceived by bees, and . . . hence they cannot hear in the customary sense. In this respect bees differ from grasshoppers, cicadas, and many other insects that, by means of drumlike structures, are able to perceive sounds . . . Kröning (1925) tried in vain to train bees to tones. Hansson (1945) conducted training experiments too, with better

technique but with no better results" (Frisch, 1993: 285). Yet, Frisch also notes a positive outcome: the "piping" and "quacking" of the queens are heard. "According to Simpson (1964) the tones—like those in the workers' tail-wagging dance—are produced by the flight musculature and conveyed to the substrate by pressing the thorax against it" (Frisch, 1993: 287). Frisch concludes: "Thus the ancient concepts of a 'language of sounds' among bees belong in the realm of fantasy. There is indeed communication by means of sounds, but it is a most primitive kind." Most importantly, in the concluding retrospective section of his book, Frisch states that the famous "bee dance" is accompanied or emphasized by buzz: "[The tail-wagging dance] is emphasized sharply by the tail-wagging movements and by a buzzing noise—the greater the distance the longer the duration of the tail wagging and the accompanying sound during each run" (Frisch, 1993: 524). In more recent research, James L. Gould and Carol Grant Gould state that the forager's buzzing at a 280Hz frequency, along its famous waggle-dance, indicates the distance to resources. They also add that, unlike the case in human language, local characteristics are genetic in honeybees. If German bee larvae are carried to hives in Italy, they will grow up to "speak German" and cause confusion in their new hives. (See chapter 5 of Gould and Gould, 1994. For more recent work, see http://www.beekeeping.com/articles/us/bee_dance_2.htm; W. H. Kirchner, "Acoustical Communication in Honeybees," *Apidologie*, no. 24 [1993]: 297–307; Eileen Crist, "Can an Insect Speak? The Case of the Honeybee Dance Language," *Social Studies of Science* 34, no. 1 [February 2004]: 7–43.) Compare Sorabji's discussion of the idea that Polish horses may not learn English (Sorabji, 1993: 82).

More relevant to our purposes, bees' inability to relay messages is suggested by Karl von Frisch (Frisch, 1993: 43, 55–56). This has been underlined by Benveniste: "There is no indication, for example, that a bee goes off to another hive with the message it has received in its own hive. This would constitute a kind of transmission or relay" (Benveniste, 1971: 53). Finally, Deleuze and Guattari have noticed the significance of this feature: "Benveniste denies that the bee has language, even though it has an organic coding process and *even uses tropes*. It has no language because it can communicate what it has seen but not transmit what has been communicated to it" (Deleuze and Guattari, 1987: 77).

47. LSJ, s.v. *akouein*, A.II.3 and A.IV.

48. *GA* V, 7, 786b22; *Prob.* 11, 898b31. See also *Cat.* 4b34–35.

49. See also *Prob.* 11, 905a30–34; and *HA* IV, 9, 535a27–b5; 536a32–536b4.

50. *On Int.* 2, 16a19–21; *Po.* 20, 1457a10–12; *Prob.* 10, 895a4–14. Most significantly, the sounds of "beasts" are characterized as *agrammatoi* in *On Int.* 2, 16a27.

51. *DA* II, 8, 420b27–29; *HA* IV, 9, 535a27–29.

52. For the role of the mouth, see *PA* III, 1, 662a17–27; for that of teeth, see *GA* V, 8, 788b3–6; *PA* III, 1, 661b1–17; for that of the larynx, see *HA* IV, 9, 535a27–b2; for the role of the pitch of voice, see *GA* V, 7, 786b19–22; finally, for the function of the tongue and lips, see *PA* II, 16, 659b27–660a8; *DA* II, 8, 420b18–23; III, 13, 435b25–26; *On Respiration* 11, 476a19–20. For a general critical discussion of "Man as Model in Aristotle's Zoology," see Lloyd, 1983: 27–35.

53. *On Int.* 1, 16a5–6. See also *Prob.* 10, 895a4–14. In this sense, even birds have different "languages" (*dialektoi*): "Both voices and languages [*hai phônai kai hai dialektoi*] differ according to locality. Thus, voice clearly differs according to its high or low pitch, but its form [*eidos*] does not differ within one kind; on the other hand, articulated [*en tois arthrois*] voice, which one might describe as a language [*dialekton*], differs in different animals, and also within one and the same kind of animal according to locality: thus, some

partridges cackle, others make a shrill noise. Among small birds, while singing some utter a different voice than their parents if they have been reared away from the nest and have heard other birds sing" (*HA* IV, 9, 536b8–17).

54. The situation becomes even more complex if one takes the semivowels into account, as Aristotle does in *Po.* 20, 1456b24–34. This lengthy argument concerning the crucial difference between *logos* and animal communication may be best contrasted with Porphyry's arguments in *On Abstinence from Animal Food* 3.3–6. See Sorabji, 1993: 82ff.

55. *On Int.* 2, 16a19–21; *Po.* 20, 1457a10–12; *Prob.* 10, 895a4–14.

56. *GA* II, 6, 744b11; *HA* VII, 3, 583b23. For "*adiarthôtos*," see also *HA* VI, 30, 579a24. Already Socrates denies articulation to animals (Xenophon, *Memorabilia* 1.4.12). I do not agree with Sorabji's rendering of *diarthrôsis* as "segmentation of utterance" and his association of this with *dialektos* (Sorabji, 1993: 81).

57. Even though not as extensively as *stoikheia*, the *grammata* are often used as basic components of more complex structures, including organic ones, for instance in the *Protrepticus*: "For whether it is fire or air or number or any other natures that are causes and first principles of other things, it would be impossible to be ignorant of these things and to recognize any of the other things; for how could anyone either be familiar with speech [*logos*] who was ignorant of syllables, or have knowledge of these who understand nothing of the letter?" (*Protrepticus* in Aristotle, 2015: 12). The parallelism between the organic body and linguistic units is a fascinating question that has tempted many, including, most prominently, Plato, Darwin, and Saussure.

58. *DA* II, 4, 416a10–18. See also *On Breath* 9, 485b18: "Fire exhibits differences with respect to more and less."

59. The material of *logos* is not as "raw" as one might think, just as the uniform parts of the animal body are not mere elements. See particularly *PA* II, 2ff.

60. Compare Plato, *Theaetetus* 202B. See Brague, 1978: 174.

61. *Metaph.* III, 2, 998a24–26; I, 9, 993a4–10.

62. For the sake of convenience, we are leaving aside the level of syllables. "The syllable is a meaningless voice, composed out of an unvoiced letter and a voiced one" (*Po.* 20, 1456b34–35). Thus, before being meaningful, letters are put into cooperation by center-periphery relations between vowels and consonants. Indeed, a syllable ("ah") may well correspond to a meaningful unit on its own as a sigh, but not *as* a syllable—any more than a letter as such would be meaningful.

63. Compare Bonitz, 1955: 813, which does not seem be of much help. See also Ross, 1949: 24 n.

64. Plato, *Sophist* 261D–262D.

65. Besides the passages from *On Interpretation* referred to below, see "*synthêkê*" in LSJ, 1996: 1717. See *APr.* I, 44, 50a19; *Rh.* I, 15, 1376a33. See also *Pol.* III, 5, 1280b11; *NE* V, 5, 1133a30, and V, 7, 1134b33, where *synthêkê* is used respectively for "law," "money," and "rules of justice."

66. Compare *Po.* 20, 1456b35, 1457a2, 11, 14, 23.

67. See *On Int.* 2, 16a28; *On Int.* 1, 16a3–4; even *PA* II, 16, 660a7; *GA* I, 18, 722b12; *Mete.* II, 4, 360a26; *Pol.* IV, 7, 1294a35.

68. Compare Antisthenes's idea, in Plato's *Theaetetus* 206E7–208E6, that complex entities could be defined only by *enumerating* their elements. "Antisthène ne fait qu'*aligner* bout à bout les mots sans pouvoir par là recouvrir l'espace à définer" (Brague, 1978: 174; see also *Metaph.* VIII, 3, 1043b23–8).

69. Of course, this foreshadows the question of writing, which is much more susceptible of being taken out of context.

70. LSJ, 1996: 1676–77. See Roochnik, 2004: 142–44.

71. See again *Metaph.* VII, 17, 1041b11–19.

72. This idea is at the foundation of Socrates's interpretation of the oracle (Plato, *Apology*, 21A1 and the following). Brague express the same idea concerning *logos* in Plato's *Meno*: "L'irrationnel devient rationnel quand il est multiplié par soi-même. La raison provient de l'élévation au carré de l'irrationnel. [La 'clôture du discours'] est d'abord, au niveau du sens, la constitution du sens par la courbure sur soi du non-sens" (Brague, 1978: 171).

73. How are we to understand the priority of the positive over the negative (such as "nonhuman" or "does not walk"), and of the present over the future and the past (such as "will walk" and "walked")? The reason may be similar to that of the priority of the noun over the verb. Just as the meaningfulness of "walks" implies a subject, the meaningfulness of "not-human" depends on "human," that of "will walk" or "walked" on "walks": Aristotle prioritizes the *tode ti*, and the actual. The negative, the future, and the past are again derivatively meaningful. This is certainly in line with his understanding of beings: in the terminology of the *Categories*, primary beings (particular *tode ti*) and secondary beings (species and genus) are prior to their predicates (*Cat.* 5); the future and the past are derivative of the present, and most fundamentally actuality is prior to potentiality (*Metaph.* IX, 8).

74. *On Int.* 3, 16b19–25.

75. For Aristotle's extremely interesting, but often very difficult, interpretations of rest (*êremia*), see his interpretation of *noêsis* and *syllogismos* as rest in *DA* I, 3, 407a33–35. For his further analyses of positive states and virtues and vices as rest, see *Ph.* VII, 3, 246a10ff.

76. *On Int.* 9, 13; *Metaph.* IX, 2, 5.

77. *DA* III, 3, 427b13.

78. Pinker, 1999: 10; Eco, 1994: 28.

79. Cited in Pinker, 1999: 10.

80. *On Int.* 4, 16b26–28.

81. *On Int.* 6, 17a23–24. Thus, it is clear that the infinitive is not a verbal form.

82. *On Int.* 6, 17a25–26.

83. *SE* 1, 165a6–14.

84. *DA* III, 3, 427b13.

85. For the other three occurences of *autoptês*, see *HA* VIII, 29, 618a18; 37, 620b23; 41, 628b8.

86. Brague, 2005: 72–74.

87. For a contemporary account of the importance of the social aspect of specifically human communication, see Burling, 2007: 181–209, especially 184, 208–9.

88. Indeed, the *enklisis euktikê* according to Alexandrian grammar. Smyth, 1920:107, 406; Dionysius Thrax, *Art of Grammar* 13, 638b8; Apollonius Dyscolus, *Syntax* 245.27. Dionysius Thrax adds also the infinitive mood (*enklisis aparemphatos*) (13, 638b7; Apollonius Dyscolus, 226.20). Compare Dionysius's fourfold distinction with Farabi, *Commentary and Short Treatise on Aristotle's "De Interpretatione."* For a comparison between Greek and Latin, which is instructive in that Latin does not have an optative, see Buck, *Comparative Grammar of Greek and Latin*, 299–301; Moore, *Comparative Greek and Latin Syntax*, 98–101.

89. This is where we depart fundamentally from Heidegger's analysis of *logos* in Aristotle which puts exclusive emphasis on *logos apophantikos*. See Heidegger, 1992: 39; 1996: 28–30 (§7b), 196–211 (§44); 1984: 64; Weigelt, 2002: 61; Sheehan, 1988: 75.

90. *On Int.* 4, 16b33–17a4.

91. Aeschylus, *Seven Against Thebes* 819–820 ; Euripides, *Phoenician Women* 70. See also Bailly, 2000: 863–64; LSJ, 739.

92. *Rhetoric* III, 2, 1405a16-18. In order to compare the Aristotelian conception of *eukhê* with its posterity, let us point out that the *Definitions* of Aquilius put prayer (*eukhê*) under the same genus (namely, *aitêsis*) and define it as a "demand of goods from the Gods" (*aitêsis agathôn para theôn*). Yet, probably dating from the Roman imperial period according to Marwan Rashed, this definition bears obviously post-Aristotelian (pseudo-Platonic and Stoic) influences. Most importantly, *eukhê* here is reserved to an address to God or to Gods, whereas it is *not* in the Aristotelian corpus (compare the mention of *eukhê* as a more honorable kind of demand than begging). Further, in contrast to the Classical Greek usages of the word as in Aeschylus and Euripides, *eukhê* in Aquilius does not contain the sense of imprecation (*ara*) which is defined by Aquilius as *another* kind of demand, namely a "demand of punishment from the Gods" (*timôrias aitêsis para theôn*). See Rashed, 2012: 149–50. See also Rashed's analyses of "vow" (*orkos*) as a "speech act" (150–153). Our analysis of *eukhê* in the following pages are in line with Rashed's remarks. I would like to thank M. Rashed for sharing his erudition and his article with me.

93. *Po.* 19, 1456b8–13.

94. *Po.* 19, 1456b15–17.

95. *NE* III, 2, 1111b20–31 (trans. Joe Sachs).

96. No wonder the word for the optative mood comes from the Latin verb *optare,* which means "to wish." Compare the verb *precare* ("to pray"), the root of the adjective "precative."

97. *DA* III, 9, 432b5–6.

98. *NE* III, 2, 1111b12–113.

99. Again, this is why the semantics of *eukhê* is a fundamentally different question than the famous problem of future contingents in *On Int.* 9.

100. See, for instance, *EE* I, 8, 1217b21.

101. See Plato, *Republic* VI, 499D, but also V, 450D; VII, 540D. All three highlight the impossibility of the city described. Plato employs the same word, *eukhê*, for a child's wish in the *Sophist* 249D. For a more extensive discussion of the relationship between *logos* and "prayer," see Nussbaum, 1994: 50.

102. *Pol.* IV, 1, 1288b23; IV, 9, 1295a29–30; II, 1, 1260b28–29; see also the verbal forms of *eukhê* in *Pol.* VII, 13, 1334b22; VII, 12, 1332a30; VII, 10, 1330a37.

103. We are referring to our discussion earlier (100–101 in this volume) concerning Aristotle's characterization of the skeptic as "similar to a plant" in *Metaph.* IV, 4, 1006a15. Let us add some further questions to be answered: What is the role of imagination in the wishful attitude? Does one imagine an impossibility wished for? Similarly, does this non-practical attitude relate to hope, to infinity, and to contemplation? Further, even though prayers and wishes cannot be refuted in the sense in which declarative sentences can be, how can one account for the fact that prayers and wishes can contradict one another?

104. *NE* VI, 2, 1139b10–11 (trans. Joe Sachs).

105. Euripides, *Thyestes* (Fr. 396, *Tragicorum Graecorum Fragmenta*), quoted in *Rh.* II, 23, 1397a.

106. While contemporary linguistic theories of "displacement" specify human language as having access beyond the "present" or the "here and now" (an idea shared by Gadamer [1976: 59–68]), we think that this might not be exact. For animal signals in case of danger, for instance, must have some content involving the future, the non-present. (See, for

instance, Burling, 2007: 36–37; Anderson, 2013: 19; Gärdenfors, 2013: 140, 145, 156–57; Gibson, 2013: 217, 218, 221; Langus et al., 2013: 230. For a good discussion of the ancient Greeks on this topic, see Sorabji, 1993, especially 79ff.) According to our account, then, human communication is specified not by *spatiotemporal* displacement, but by *modal* remoteness. While contemporary theories of "displacement" seem to miss the point, according to our account, contemporary theories concerning the "theory of mind" are welcome to our account as crucial, although not exhaustive, examples of the capacity for understanding and relaying non-firsthand experience. For my ability to think that you have a mind and are thinking of *x* requires a preliminary access that I must have to something that is not and cannot be *my* firsthand experience.

107. Compare Gibson, 2013: 209: "many species of vertebrates, including some fish, some birds, and many mammals socially transmit information and habits (Box and Gibson 1999; Fragaszy and Perry 2003)."

108. For "*logos tês ousias*" in Aristotle's biology, see *PA* IV, 13, 695b19.

109. See also Aristotle's cogent refutation of the Megaric view of potentiality in *Metaph.* IX, 3.

110. *DA* II, 3, 414b4–7; also see II, 2, 413b24–25; III, 9, 432b29–30.

111. See also *Pol.* VII, 12, 1332b5–6.

112. Pseudo-Aristotle, *Rhetoric to Alexander*, 1433a23; 1424b2; Aristotle, *The Athenian Constitution* 69.1.

113. *SE* 2, 165a38–165b1.

114. *SE* 2, 165b1–3.

115. *SE* 2, 165b3–4.

116. *SE* 2, 165b4–6.

117. *SE* 2, 165b6–9.

118. *HA* I, 1, 488a7–10.

119. *HA* IX, 40, 624b6–8. For a discussion of this passage, see my article "After Autopsy: An Introduction to *Logos* in Aristotle," forthcoming in *A Companion to Ancient Greek Philosophy*, ed. Sean Kirkland and Eric Sanday (Evanston, Ill.: Northwestern University Press, forthcoming).

120. Recent studies suggest that the first record of Halley's comet was due not to the observation by Chinese astronomers in its orbit in 240 BC, but to a report of its appearance in its 466 BC orbit by Aristotle a century later in *Mete.* I, 7, 344b31–34 (http://journalofcosmology.com/AncientAstronomy106.html).

121. *HA* IX, 40, 625b9–10.

Conclusion

1. See Lampe, 1961: 807–11; Sorabji, 1993.

2. Fattal's characterization of Aristotle's uses of *logos* as mostly critical and analytic, and not as synthetic as we claim here, may be due to the fact that he seems to be more interested in Aristotle's posterity, especially in the later interpretation of *nous* in *DA* III, 6, than with Aristotle's own use of *logos* (Fattal, 1988; Fattal, 2001: 15, 20–21, 197–212).

3. Euripides, *Thyestes* (Fr. 396, *Tragicorum Graecorum Fragmenta*), quoted in *Rh.* II, 23, 1397a.

4. *Metaph.* II, 1, 993b12–19.

5. Loose and perhaps subjective as they are, these suggestions are not altogether unfamiliar to Aristotle: "Humans are the same in relation to *xenoi* and to their own citizens

as they are in relation to style: thus [in poetry] one should make one's language foreign, for things that are remote are wondrous [*thaumastai*], and wondrous things are pleasant" (*Rh.* III, 1, 1404b8–11; along the same lines, see the use of the adjective *xenikos* against *barbarismos* in *Po.* 22).

6. *Po.* 2, 1448a15; *Pol.* I, 1, 1252b22–23. But see *NE* X, 9, 1180a29; *Rh.* II, 3, 1380b. For an implicit but clear reference, see also *Pol.* I, 1, 1253a5–7, and the intriguing parallel in *Pol.* III, 11, 1287b25ff. The figure of the Cyclops is the one we encounter in Homer's *Odyssey* IX, 114ff., and in this sense Aristotle develops a figure already present in Plato, *Laws* 680B, 682A. But the earth-born beings in *Pol.* II, 5, 1269a6–7 refer to the other figure of Cyclops we find in Herodotus, IV, 27; Hesiod, *Works and Days* 108, Pindar, *Nemean* 6.1.

7. See *Pol.* VIII, 1, 1337a22ff.

8. *NE* I, 13, 1102b31–34. Emphasis is ours for reasons exhibited in chapter 5.

9. Aubenque, 1988: 38.

10. Theocritus, 1999: 221.

11. Hesiod, *Works and Days* l. 108. See *Pol.* II, 5, 1269a7.

12. *Pol.* I, 1, 1252b24.

13. *Pol.* I, 1, 1252b19–26.

14. *Pol.* I, 1, 1253a5–8. The quotation from Homer is from the *Iliad* IX, 63. For a brilliant discussion of the apolitical man in Aristotle's *Politics*, see J.-L. Labarrière, "L'Homme apolitique: *Pessia*, *polis* et *apolis*" (forthcoming). For references to the Cyclops as *amousos*, see Theocritus, 1999: 221.

15. *Pol.* III, 1, 1274b39–1275a24ff.

16. *Pol.* III, 5, 1280b24ff.

17. There is a specific term for the prepolitical agglomeration of households in Aristotle: *kômê*. (See *Pol.* I, 1, 1252b16ff.)

18. The same idea appears in *Pol.* III, 6, 1282a16–23. For the association between *logos* and *synopsia*, see also *Pol.* VII, 1, 1323b6–7.

19. *Pol.* III, 1, 1275b22ff.

20. Euripides, *Cyclops* 493. Although I have reservations for her argument as a whole, Nussbaum makes this exact same point and refers to this exact same passage (1982: 284).

21. See 100–101 in this volume. *Metaph.* IV, 3, 1006a5; *Ph.* II, 1, 193a1. See Nussbaum, 1982: 284, 289.

22. See Aristotle, fr. 172 Rose.

23. See also Homer, *Odyssey* IX, 275–78.

24. *Pol.* I, 1, 1253a5–8. See note 14 above.

25. It is unclear to me what someone like Polyphemus exactly wants to do with the ship here. Perhaps it might have some relevance as we shall see him *needing* a ship below.

26. *Rh.* II, 3, 1380b.

27. *Pol.* III, 11, 1287b23–32.

28. *SE* 1, 165a11–14.

29. *Cat.* 1.

30. For the significance of the "linguistic defects" of the Other in Greek culture, see Heath, 2005: 174: "Linking *all* marginal groups in Greece was the lack or deprivation of authoritative speech. All except animals of course *could* speak, but they were each thought to have a language disability of some sort." Heath also nicely points out the circularity between Greek imputation of linguistic defects to the "Other" and their exclusion from public speech. "Women, for example, were politically silent because they were not allowed

to speak publicly; they were publicly silent because they had no political role" (174, 190). But see also Heath's conclusion: "I am suggesting, then—without irony—that the very nature of Greek Otherness has helped, indeed has been and will continue to be required to mitigate the evil consequences of dogmatism. The Hellenic foundation of difference was such that it is bringing about the collapse of the hierarchical structure it helped to build" (176–77). For a judicious account of the Cyclops, or Polyphemus, as fitting the Greek stereotype of a barbarian, see again Heath, 2005: 193–95.

31. *Rh.* II, 3, 1380b.

32. Already in the Homeric text, because Odysseus somewhat hubristically announces to Polyphemus who he really is, Odysseus exposes himself to the wrath of Polyphemus's father, Poseidon. The end of Odysseus's encounter with the Cyclops is thus not simply a victory of the former over the latter.

33. Not to be confused with Theocritus of Chios (Theocritus, 2002: 33–35). I must thank Eric Sanday for pointing out this text to me.

34. For the subtle relationship between plausibility and possibility in tragedy and comedy, indeed see *Po.* 24, 1460a26ff.

35. *NE* I, 13, 1102a28ff.

36. But compare Theocritus, 1999: 230.

37. Compare Ovid's Galatea telling her story (Ovid, *Metamorphoses* 13.738–897).

38. As Hunter remarks, "Desperate desire is the negation of self-sufficiency, the painful acknowledgement of 'otherness,' and so the Cyclops is a limit-case of general experience" (Theocritus, 1999: 222).

39. *Po.* 2, 1445a17–19.

40. *Po.* 11, 1452a25, 33; 13, 1453a11, 20; 14, 1453b7, 31; 24, 1460a30; 16, 1455a20; 26, 1462b2.

41. *Po.* 14, 1453b31.

42. The passage we have in mind is *Pol.* VII, 6, 1327b23–33. See also the more famous passage in *Pol.* I, 1, 1252b5–9. See also *Pol.* VII, 6, 1328a8–13: "Spiritedness [*thymos*] is something dominant and indomitable; but it is not beautiful to say that [the guardians] are cruel to strangers; for one must not be this way to anybody, and men of great-souled nature are not fierce except toward wrongdoers, and even more so against their companions if they think these are wronging them, as said before."

43. Most dramatically, when she describes Laius to Oedipus, Jocasta says: "His look was not very different from yours" (743). It is exactly upon this phrase that Oedipus realizes that he *is* Laius's killer.

44. Sophocles, *King Oedipus*, ll. 132–46.

45. "King Oedipus might have had one eye too many" (Hölderlin, 1984: 251). Aristotle also uses this metaphor and he may have Oedipus in mind in *NE* VI, 13, 1144b8–12.

46. *Po.* 15, 1454b6–8; 24, 1460a26–32.

47. It is a pity that Aristotle's insightful emphasis on "recognition" (*anagnôrisis*) seems to have been understood as a momentary outburst due to an extraordinary incident (as in a poor science-fiction movie), or due to the outstanding skill of one protagonist (as many mystery novels appeal to a keen detective for solving the mystery, or as the scenes in many comedy movies pivot around one central *factor* of funniness, the withdrawal of which renders the situation back to its "commonness"). See *Po.* 16, 1455a16–18: "The best kind of recognition is the one that comes out of the things themselves [*hê ex autôn tôn pragmatôn*], of the unfolding [*ekplêxeôs*] that happens by means of plausible events, like Sophocles'

Oedipus . . ." The all too well known Aristotelian precept that in tragedy "one should prefer a likely impossibility to an unpersuasive possibility" in fact grants events the power to be likely and persuasive without appealing to strict logic (*Po.* 24, 1460a26–27). But this is precisely granted to *events* in a tragedy. The designed unfolding of events is such that it makes even the impossible *likely*. This means that a good intrigue, the heart of tragedy for Aristotle, is capable of making the impossible *likely*, and that a bad plot fails even to make a possibility even persuasive.

48. *NE* VI, 6ff.; see also below, *DA* III, 5, 430a14–17.

49. Despite his many points converging with my argument here, I disagree with Long's claim that "God is relationality" (2011: 237). All levels of relationality involve *logos* according to my central thesis, and God or any divinity is never ascribed *logos* in the Aristotelian corpus. Therefore, God cannot be relationality. As we shall see below, this discussion boils down to the interpretation of the relationship between *logos* and *nous*. "All knowledge is with *logos*, but there is no knowledge of the principles" (*APo.* II, 19, 100b10–17; see also Aubenque, 2009: 66). Further, for Aristotle's prioritization of sensation over *logoi*, see *GA* III, 10, 760b27–33; *APr.* I, 30, 46a17ff.

50. Arendt, 1972: 65; Rorty, 1992: 9. See also Simplicius, *in de An.* 40. 20–2; 102. 11–12; Simplicius (?), *in de An. 3*, 217. 28–32; 281. 29–32; 220. 21–26, 28–34; 221. 24–28. Compare the use of *nous* in *HA* IX, 610b22. See Sorabji, 1993: 13.

51. Lee and Long try to establish a close relationship between *nous* and *logos* (Lee and Long, 2007: 348–67). This seems to require not only a disambiguation of the term *nous*, which the authors provide (e.g., from *NE* VI, 9, 1143a35–b5), but also a disambiguation of the term *logos*, which is supplied neither by Aristotle nor by the authors. It is the same problem of disambiguating *logos* which is underlined in Gonzalez's review of Long's 2011 book (*Bryn Mawr Classical Review*, August 13, 2011). I have similar reservations for using *logos* and *nous* interchangeably as "reason." See, for instance Frede, 1996: 157–73; Sorabji, 1996: 331; Sorabji, 1993: 69; Baracchi, 2007: 175.

Besides, in light of Aristotle's sharp distinction between *nous* and *logos* (see below), I am not convinced that *logos* is intrinsically related to *nous* beyond perhaps being the "condition of possibility for noetic insight" (Lee and Long, 2007: 366). Aristotle's God must be beyond any *logos*, and a fortiori beyond dialogue. Again, I agree with Gonzalez's review where he says: "In short, the unmoved mover's eternal 'thinking of thinking' appears to be the very antithesis of a dialogical conception of truth."

52. See also *GA* II, 3, 736b28.

53. *Metaph.* XII, 7, 1072a24–1072b4.

54. *NE* VI, 5, 1141a5–8; VI, 9, 1143b1.

55. *NE* X, 7,1177b30–1178a2; X, 8, 1179a23–31.

BIBLIOGRAPHY

Reference Works

Bailly, Anatole. 2000. *Dictionnaire Grec-Français*. Paris: Hachette.

Bonitz, Hermann. 1955. *Index Aristotelicus*. Graz: Akademische Druck und Verlagsanstalt.

Buck, Carl Darling. 1933. *Comparative Grammar of Greek and Latin*. Illinois: University of Chicago Press.

Chantraine, Pierre. 1984. *Dictionnaire Étymologique de la langue grecque*. 2 vol. Paris: Klincksieck.

Diels, Hermann, and Walther Kranz. 1956. *Die Fragmente der Vorsokratiker*. 3 vols. Berlin: Weidmannsche Verlagbuchhandlung.

Georgin, Charles. 1961. *Dictionnaire grec-français*. Paris: Hatier.

Guthrie, W. K. C. 1979. *A History of Greek Philosophy: The Earlier Presocratics and the Pythagoreans*. Vol. 1. Cambridge: Cambridge University Press.

———. 1981. *A History of Greek Philosophy: Aristotle, An Encounter*. Vol. 6. Cambridge: Cambridge University Press.

Lampe, G. W. H. 1961. *A Patristic Greek Lexicon*. Oxford: Clarendon.

Liddell, H. G., R. Scott, and H. S. Jones. 1996. *Greek-English Lexicon*. 9th edition. Oxford: Clarendon.

Moore, R. W. 1934. *Comparative Greek and Latin Syntax*. London: G. Bell and Sons.

Smyth, Herbert Weir. 1920. *Greek Grammar*. Cambridge, Mass.: Harvard University Press.

Primary Sources

Plato

Plato. 1914. *Euthyphro*, *Apology*, *Crito*, *Phaedo*, *Phaedrus*. Translated by Harold North Fowler. Cambridge, Mass.: Harvard University Press.

Plato. 1921. *Theaetetus*, *Sophist*. Translated by Harold North Fowler. Cambridge, Mass.: Harvard University Press.

Plato. 1925. *Statesman*, *Philebus*, *Ion*. Translated by Harold North Fowler and W. R. M. Lamb. Cambridge, Mass.: Harvard University Press.

Plato. 1926. *Laws*. Translated by R. G. Bury. Cambridge, Mass.: Harvard University Press.

Plato. 1929. *Timaeus*. Translated by R. G. Bury. Cambridge, Mass.: Harvard University Press.

Plato. 1930–35. *Republic*. Translated by Paul Shorey. Cambridge, Mass.: Harvard University Press.

Plato. 1996. *Parmenides*. Translated by Mary Louise Gill. Indianapolis, Ind.: Hackett.

Aristotle

Athenian Constitution

Aristotle. 1935. *The Athenian Constitution*. Translated by H. Rackham. Cambridge, Mass.: Harvard University Press.

Categories

Aristotle. 1938. *Categories.* Translated by Harold P. Cooke. Cambridge, Mass.: Harvard University Press.

Aristote. 2002. *Catégories.* Translated by Frédérique Ildefonse and Jean Lallot. Paris: Seuil.

Eudemian Ethics

Aristotle. 1952. *Eudemian Ethics.* Translated by Hugh Rackham. Cambridge, Mass.: Harvard University Press.

Fragments

Aristotle. 1955. *Aristotelis fragmenta selecta.* Edited by W. D. Ross. Oxford: Clarendon.

Generation of Animals

Aristotle. 1942. *Generation of Animals.* Translated by A. L. Peck. Cambridge, Mass.: Harvard University Press.

History of Animals

Aristotle. 1965. *History of Animals.* I–III. Translated by A. L. Peck. Cambridge, Mass.: Harvard University Press.

Aristotle. 1970. *History of Animals.* IV–VI. Translated by A. L. Peck. Cambridge, Mass.: Harvard University Press.

Aristote. 1987. *Histoire des animaux.* Translated by Jean Tricot. Paris: Vrin.

Aristotle. 1991. *History of Animals.* VII–X. Translated by D. M. Balme. Cambridge, Mass.: Harvard University Press.

Magna Moralia

Aristotle. 1935. *Magna Moralia.* Translated by G. Cyril Armstrong. Cambridge, Mass.: Harvard University Press.

Metaphysics

Aristotle. 1924. *Metaphysics.* 2 vols. Introduction and commentary by W. D. Ross. Oxford: Clarendon.

Aristotle. 1933. *Metaphysics,* I–IX. Translated by Hugh Tredennick. Cambridge, Mass.: Harvard University Press.

Aristotle. 1935. *Metaphysics.* X–XIV. Translated by Hugh Tredennick. Cambridge, Mass.: Harvard University Press.

Aristotle. 1956. *Metaphysics.* Edited and translated by John Warrington. London: J. M. Dent and Sons.

Aristotle. 1999. *Metaphysics.* Translated by Joe Sachs. Santa Fe, N. Mex.: Green Lion.

Aristote. 2008. *Métaphysique.* Translated by Marie-Paule Duminil and Annick Jaulin. Paris: Flammarion.

Meteorology

Aristotle. 1952. *Meteorologica.* Translated by H. D. P. Lee. Cambridge, Mass.: Harvard University Press.

Minor Works

Aristotle. 1936. *Minor Works.* Translated by W. S. Hett. Cambridge, Mass.: Harvard University Press.

Movement of Animals

Aristotle. 1937. *Movement of Animals.* Translated by A. L. Peck. Cambridge, Mass.: Harvard University Press.

Nicomachean Ethics

Aristotle. 1926. *Nicomachean Ethics.* Translated by H. Rackham. Cambridge, Mass.: Harvard University Press.

Aristotle. 1966. *Nicomachean Ethics.* Translated by W. D. Ross. Oxford: Oxford University Press.

Aristotle. 1986. *Ethica Nicomachea.* Translated by I. Bywater. Oxford: Clarendon.

Aristotle. 2002. *Nicomachean Ethics.* Translated by Joe Sachs. Massachusetts: Focus.

Aristote. 2004. *Éthique à Nicomaque.* Translated by Richard Bodéüs. Paris: Flammarion.

Oeconomica

[Aristotle]. 1935. *Oeconomica.* Translated by G. Cyril Armstrong. Cambridge, Mass.: Harvard University Press.

On Generation and Corruption

Aristotle. 1955. *On Coming-to-Be and Passing-Away.* Translated by E. S. Forster. Cambridge, Mass.: Harvard University Press.

On Interpretation

Aristotle. 1938. *On Interpretation.* Translated by Harold P. Cooke. Cambridge, Mass.: Harvard University Press.

On Sophistical Refutations

Aristotle. 1955. *Sophistical Refutations.* Translated by E. S. Foster. Cambridge, Mass.: Harvard University Press.

On the Cosmos

[Aristotle]. 1955. *On the Cosmos.* Translated by D. J. Furley. Cambridge, Mass.: Harvard University Press.

On the Soul

Aristotle. 1936. *On the Soul.* Translated by W. S. Hett. Cambridge, Mass.: Harvard University Press.

Aristotle. 2001. *On the Soul.* Translated by Joe Sachs. Santa Fe, N. Mex.: Green Lion.

On Virtues and Vices

[Aristotle]. 1935. *On Virtues and Vices.* Translated by H. Rackham. Cambridge, Mass.: Harvard University Press.

Parts of Animals

Aristotle. 1937. *Parts of Animals.* Translated by A. L. Peck. Cambridge, Mass.: Harvard University Press.

Aristote. 1995. *Parties des Animaux, Livre I.* Translated by J.-M. Le Blond. Paris: Flammarion.

Parva Naturalia

Aristotle. 1936. *Parva Naturalia, On Breath.* Translated by W. S. Hett. Cambridge, Mass.: Harvard University Press.

Aristotle. 2001. *On Memory and Recollection.* Translated by Joe Sachs. Santa Fe, N. Mex.: Green Lion.

Physics

Aristotle. 1929. *The Physics.* Translated by Philip H. Wicksteed and Francis M. Cornford. Cambridge, Mass.: Harvard University Press.

Aristote. 1969. *Physique.* Translated by Henri Carteron. Paris: Belles-Lettres.

Aristotle. 1995. *Physics*. Translated by Joe Sachs. New Brunswick, N.J.: Rutgers University Press.

Aristote. 2002. *Physique*. Translated by Pierre Pellegrin. Paris: Flammarion.

Poetics

Aristotle. 1995. *Poetics*. Translated by Stephen Halliwell. Cambridge, Mass.: Harvard University Press.

Politics

Aristotle. 1944. *Politics*. Translated by H. Rackham. Cambridge, Mass.: Harvard University Press.

Aristote. 1993. *Les Politiques*. Translated by Pierre Pellegrin. Paris: Flammarion.

Posterior Analytics

Aristotle. 1960. *Posterior Analytics*. Translated by Hugh Tredennick. Cambridge, Mass.: Harvard University Press.

Aristotle. 2002. *Posterior Analytics*. Translated by Jonathan Barnes. Oxford: Clarendon.

Prior Analytics

Aristotle. 1938. *Prior Analytics*. Translated by Hugh Tredennick. Cambridge, Mass.: Harvard University Press.

Problems

Aristotle. *Problems*, 1–21. Translated by W. S. Hett. Cambridge, Mass.: Harvard University Press.

Progression of Animals

Aristotle. 1937. *Progression of Animals*. Translated by A. L. Peck. Cambridge, Mass.: Harvard University Press.

Protrepticus

Aristotle. 2015. *Protrepticus*. Provisional reconstruction by D. S. Hutchinson and Monte Ransome Johnson. http://www.protrepticus.info/protreprecon2015i20.pdf.

Rhetoric

Aristotle. 1926. *Rhetoric*. Translated by John Henry Freese. Cambridge, Mass.: Harvard University Press.

Topics

Aristotle. 1960. *Topica*. Translated by E. S. Forster. Cambridge, Mass.: Harvard University Press.

Secondary Sources

Ackrill, J. L. 1962. *Aristotle's "Categories" and "De Interpretatione."* Oxford: Clarendon.

Anderson, Stephen R. 2013. "What Is Special about the Human Language Faculty and How Did It Get That Way?" In *The Evolutionary Emergence of Language—Evidence and Inference*, edited by Rudolf Botha and Martin Everaert, 18–41. Oxford: Clarendon.

Anecdota Graeca e codd. ms. Bibliothecarum Oxoniensium. 1887. Edited by J. A. Cramer. Oxford: Clarendon.

Arendt, Hannah. 1972. *La crise de la culture*. Paris: Nouvelle Revue Française.

Aspasius. 2006. *On Aristotle, Nicomachean Ethics*. Translated by David Konstan. London: Duckworth.

Aubenque, Pierre. 1963. *La Prudence chez Aristote*. Paris: Presses Universiatires de France.

———. 1988. "Aristote et la démocratie." In *Individu et société: L'influence d'Aristote dans le monde méditerranéen*, 31–38. Istanbul: Isis.

———. 2002. *Le Problème de l'être chez Aristote*. Paris: Presses Universitaires de France.

———. 2009. *Problèmes aristotéliciens*. Paris: VRIN.

Aubry, Gwenaëlle. 2009. "*Nicomachean Ethics* VII.14, (1154a22-b34): The Pain of the Living and Divine Pleasure." In *Aristotle: Nicomachean Ethics, Book VII, Symposium Aristotelicum*, edited by Carlo Natali. New York: Oxford University Press.

Averroès. 1998. *L'Intelligence et la pensée*. Translated by Alain de Libera. Paris: Flammarion.

———. 2000. *Commentaire Moyen sur le "De Interpretatione."* Translated by S. Diebler. Paris: VRIN.

———. 2000. *L'Islam et la raison*. Translated by Marc Geoffroy. Paris: Flammarion.

Babür, Saffet. 2002. "Aristoteles'te *episteme*." *Yeditepe'de Felsefe* 7: 7–20.

Balme, D. M. 1962. "Development of Biology in Aristotle and Theophrastus: Theory of Spontaneous Generation." *Phronesis* 7, no. 1: 91–104.

Baracchi, Claudia. 2007. *Ethics as First Philosophy*. Cambridge: Cambridge University Press.

Barnes, Jonathan. 1969. "Aristotle's Theory of Demonstration." *Phronesis* 14: 123–52.

———. ed. 1995. *The Cambridge Companion to Aristotle*. Cambridge: Cambridge University Press.

Bayraktar, Mehmet. 1988. "L'Aristotélisme dans la pensée ottomane." In *Individu et société: L'influence d'Aristote dans le monde méditerranéen*, 191–211. Istanbul: Isis.

Benveniste, Émile. 1971. *Problems in General Linguistics*. Translated by Mary Elizabeth Meek. Florida: University of Miami Press.

Ben-Ze'ev, Aaron. 1986. "Making Mental Properties More Natural." *Monist* 69: 434–46.

Berti, Enrico. 1978. "Ancient Greek Dialectic as Expression of Freedom of Thought and Speech." *Journal of the History of Ideas* 39, no. 3: 347–70.

———. 1980. "Reply to James Seaton." *Journal of the History of Ideas* 41, no. 2: 290–92.

———. 1988. "L'Idée aristotélicienne de société politique dans les traditions musulmane et juive." In *Individu et société: L'influence d'Aristote dans le monde méditerranéen*, 99–116. Istanbul: Isis.

———. 1990. "La Philosophie pratique d'Aristote et sa 'réhabilitation' récente." *Revue de Métaphysique et de Morale* 95, no. 2: 249–66.

———. 1991. "Les Méthodes d'argumentation et de démonstration dans la *Physique*." In *La "Physique" d'Aristote*, 53–72. Paris: VRIN.

———. 1991. "Les Stratégies contemporaines d'interprétation d'Aristote." *Rue Descartes*, 1–2: 33–55.

———. 1996. "Reconsidérations sur l'intellection des 'indivisibles' selon Aristote." In *Corps et âme—Sur le "De Anima" d'Aristote*, edited by Cristina Viano, 391–404. Paris: VRIN.

———. 2001. "Multiplicity and Unity of Being in Aristotle." *Proceedings of the Aristotelian Society*, New Series, vol. 101: 185–207.

Bolton, Robert. 1990. "The Epistemological Basis of Aristotelian Dialectic." In *Biologie, logique et métaphysique chez Aristote*, edited by Daniel Devereux and Pierre Pellegrin, 185–236. Paris: Editions du CNRS. Reprinted in Robert Bolton. 1999. *From Puzzles to Principles? Essays on Aristotle's Dialectic*, edited by May Sim, 56–105. Lanham, Md.: Lexington Books.

———. 1991. "Aristotle's Method in Natural Science: *Physics I*." In *Aristotle's "Physics": A Collection of Essays*, edited by Lindsay Judson, 1–29. Oxford: Clarendon.

Bradshaw, David. 1997. "Aristotle on Perception: The Dual-Logos Theory." *Apeiron* 30, no. 2: 143–61.

Brague, Rémi. 1978. *Le Restant: Supplément aux commentaries du "Ménon" de Platon*. Paris: VRIN.

———. 1980. "De la disposition." In *Concepts et catégories dans la pensée antique*, edited by Pierre Aubenque. Paris: VRIN.

———. 1982. *Du temps chez Platon et Aristote*. Paris: Presses Universitaires de France.

———. 1988. *Aristote et la question du monde*. Paris: Presses Universitaires de France.

———. 2005. *Introduction au monde grec*. Chatou: Transparence.

———. 2005. "La Leçon des anciens." *Le Point: Les Textes Fondamentaux de la Pensée Antique* 3: 7–11.

Brentano, Franz. 1975. *On the Several Senses of Being in Aristotle*. Translated by Rolf George. Berkeley: University of California Press.

———. 1977. *The Psychology of Aristotle*. Translated by Rolf George. Berkeley: University of California Press.

Brogan, Walter. 2005. *Heidegger and Aristotle: The Twofoldness of Being*. Albany: SUNY Press.

Brun, Jean. 1961. *Aristote et le lycée*. Paris: Presses Universitaires de France.

Burling, Robbins. 2007. *The Talking Ape*. Oxford: Oxford University Press.

Burnyeat, M. F. 2002. "*De Anima* II 5." *Phronesis*, 47/1: 28–90.

———. 2004. "Introduction: Aristotle on the Foundations of Sublunary Physics." In *Aristotle: "On Generation and Corruption," Book I, Symposium Aristotelicum*, edited by Frans de Haas and Jaap Mansfield, 7–24. New York: Oxford University Press.

Byl, Simon. 1978. "Aristote et le monde de la ruche." *Revue Belge de Philologie et d'Histoire* 56, no. 1: 15–28.

Carroll, Margaret Deutsch. 1984. "Rembrandt's 'Aristotle': Exemplary Beholder." *Artibus et Historiae* 5, no. 10: 35–56.

Cassin, Barbara. 1996. "Enquête sur le *logos* dans le *De Anima*." In *Corps et âme—Sur le "De Anima" d'Aristote*, edited by Cristina Viano, 257–93. Paris: VRIN.

———. 1997. *Aristote et le logos: Contes de phénoménologie ordinaire*. Paris: Presses Universitaires de France.

———. ed. 2014. *Dictionary of Untranslatables: A Philosophical Lexicon*. Translated by Steven Rendall, Christian Hubert, Jeffrey Mehlman, Nathanael Stein, and Michael Syrotinski. New Jersey: Princeton University Press.

Cherniss, Harold. 1935. *Aristotle's Criticism of Presocratic Philosophy*. Baltimore: Johns Hopkins University Press.

Chieza, Curzio. 1992. "Le Problème du langage intérieur dans la philosophie antique de Platon à Porphyre." *Histoire Épistémologie Langage* 14, no. 2: 15–30.

Cooper, John M. 2009. "*Nicomachean Ethics* VII.1–2: Introduction, Method, Puzzles." In *Aristotle: "Nicomachean Ethics," Book VII, Symposium Aristotelicum*, edited by Carlo Natali. New York: Oxford University Press.

Crist, Eileen. 2004. "Can an Insect Speak? The Case of the Honeybee Dance Language." *Social Studies of Science* 34, no. 1: 7–43.

Darwin, Charles. 1998. *The Expression of the Emotions in Man and Animals*. New York: Oxford University Press.

Davies, Malcolm, and Jeyaraney Kathirithamby. 1986. *Greek Insects*. London: Duckworth.

Deleuze, Gilles, and Félix Guattari. 1987. *A Thousand Plateaus*. Translated by Brian Massumi. Minneapolis: University of Minnesota Press.

Descartes, René. 1979. *Méditations Métaphysiques*. Paris: Flammarion.

Dexippus. 1990. *On Aristotle's "Categories."* Translated by John Dillon. Ithaca, N.Y.: Cornell University Press.

Diogenes Laertius. 1925. *Lives of Eminent Philosophers.* Vol. 1. Translated by R. D. Hicks. Cambridge, Mass.: Harvard University Press.

Dionysios Thrax. 1883. *Ars grammatica.* Leipzig: Teubner.

Dodds, E. R. 1951. *Greeks and the Irrational.* Berkeley: University of California Press.

Dumont, Jean-Paul. 1992. *Introduction à la méthode d'Aristote.* Paris: VRIN.

Eco, Umberto. 1994. *La Recherche de la langue parfait dans la culture européenne.* Paris: Seuil.

Euclid. 2007. *Elements.* Edited by J. L. Heiberg, translated by Richard Fitzpatrick. Austin, Tex.: Richard Fitzpatrick.

Euripides. 1994. *Cyclops, Alcestis, Medea.* Translated by David Kovacs. Cambridge, Mass.: Harvard University Press.

Evans, J. D. G. 1977. *Aristotle's Concept of Dialectic.* Cambridge: Cambridge University Press.

Everson, Stephen. 1997. *Aristotle on Perception.* Oxford: Clarendon.

Fagan. Patricia. 2013. *Plato and Tradition: The Poetic and Cultural Context of Philosophy.* Evanston, Ill.: Northwestern University Press.

Farabi. 1981. *Commentary and Short Treatise on Aristotle's "De Interpretatione."* Translated by F. W. Zimmermann. Oxford: Oxford University Press.

———. 2001. *L'Épître sur l'intellect.* Translated by Dyala Hamzah. Paris: L'Harmattan.

Fattal, Michel. 1988. *Pour un nouveau langage de la raison.* Paris: Beauchesne.

———. 2001. *Logos, pensée et vérité dans la philosophie grecque.* Paris: L'Harmattan.

Frede, Dorothea. 2004. "*On Generation and Corruption* I.10: On Mixture and Mixables." In *Aristotle: "On Generation and Corruption," Book I, Symposium Aristotelicum*, edited by Frans de Haas and Jaap Mansfield. 289–314. New York: Oxford University Press.

Frede, Michael. 1996. "Aristotle's Rationalism." In *Rationality in Greek Thought*, edited by Michael Frede and Gisela Striker, 157–73. Oxford: Oxford University Press.

Frisch, Karl von. 1993. *The Dance Language and Orientation of Bees.* Translated by Leigh Chadwick. Cambridge, Mass.: Harvard University Press.

Gadamer, Hans-Georg. 1976. *Philosophical Hermeneutics.* Translated by David E. Linge. Berkeley: University of California Press.

Gandt, François de, and Pierre Souffrin, eds. 1991. *La "Physique" d'Aristote et les conditions d'une science de la nature.* Paris: VRIN.

Gärdenfors, Peter. 2013. "The Evolution of Semantics: Sharing Conceptual Domains." In *The Evolutionary Emergence of Language: Evidence and Inference*, edited by Rudolf Botha and Martin Everaert, 139–59. Oxford: Oxford University Press.

Gibson, Kathleen R. 2013. "Talking about Apes, Birds, Bees, and Other Living Creatures: Language Evolution in Light of Comparative Animal Behavior." In *The Evolutionary Emergence of Language: Evidence and Inference*, edited by Rudolf Botha and Martin Everaert, 204–22. Oxford: Oxford University Press.

Gotthelf, Allan. 1999. "Darwin on Aristotle." *Journal of the History of Biology* 32, no. 1: 3–30.

Gould, James L., and Carol Grant Gould. 1994. *The Animal Mind.* New York: Scientific American Library.

Granger, Gilles-Gaston. 1976. *La Doctrine aristotélicienne de la science.* Paris: Aubier Montaigne.

Hamlyn, D. W. 1990. "Aristotle on Dialectic." *Philosophy* 65, no. 254: 465–76.
Heath, John. 2005. *The Talking Greeks*. Cambridge: Cambridge University Press.
Heidegger, Martin. 1958. *Essais et conferences*. Translated by André Préau. Paris: Gallimard.
———. 1959. *An Introduction to Metaphysics*. Translated by Ralph Menheim. New Haven, Conn.: Yale University Press.
———. 1984. *Early Greek Thinking*. Translated by David Farrell Krell and Frank A. Capuzzi. San Francisco: Harper and Row.
———. 1985. *History of the Concept of Time*. Translated by Theodore Kisiel. Indianapolis: Indiana University Press.
———. 1992. *Interprétations phénoménologiques d'Aristote*. Translated by Jean-François Courtine. Mauvezin: TER.
———. 1995. *Aristotle's Metaphysics Theta 1–3: On the Essence and Actuality of Force; Phainomenon and Logos in Aristotle (Marburg Winter Semester 1923/1924)*. Translated by Walter Brogan and Peter Warnek. Indianapolis: Indiana University Press.
———. 1996. *Being and Time*. Translated by Joan Stambaugh. New York: SUNY Press.
———. 1997. *Plato's Sophist*. Translated by Richard Rojcewicz and André Schuwer. Indianapolis: Indiana University Press.
———. 1998. *Pathmarks*. Translated by Thomas Sheehan. Cambridge: Cambridge University Press.
———. 2008. *Basic Concepts of Ancient Philosophy*. Translated by Richard Rojcewicz. Indianapolis: Indiana University Press.
Hermann, C. F. 1853. *Platonis Dialogi*. Vol. 6. Leipzig.
Herodotus. 1960. *Histories*. Translated by A. D. Godley. Cambridge, Mass.: Harvard University Press.
Hesiod. 1988. *Works and Days*. Translated by Richard Hamilton, Ellen Rainis, and Rebecca Ruttenberg. Pennsylvania: Bryn Mawr Commentaries.
Hicks, R. D. 1915. "On Doubtful Meanings of *Logos* in Aristotle." In *Proceedings of the Cambridge Philosophical Society* 100–102: 1–2.
Hobbes, Thomas. 1982. *Leviathan*. London: Penguin.
Höffe, Otfried, 2003. *Aristotle*. Translated by Christine Salazar. New York: SUNY Press.
Hoffmann, David. 2003. "Logos as Composition." *Rhetoric Society Quarterly* 33, no. 3: 27–53.
Hölderlin, Friedrich. 1984. *Hymns and Fragments*. Translated by Richard Sieburth. New Jersey: Princeton University Press.
Homer. 1995. *Odyssey*. Translated by A. T. Murray. Cambridge, Mass.: Harvard University Press.
———. 1998. *Iliad*. Translated by A. T. Murray. Cambridge, Mass.: Harvard University Press.
Hoy, Ronald R., and Daniel R. Robert. 1996. "Tympanal Hearing in Insects." *Annual Reviews of Entomology*, no. 41: 439–41.
———. 1998. "Acute as a Bug's Ear: An Informal Discussion of Hearing in Insects." In *Comparative Hearing: Insects*, 1–17. New York: Springer.
Irwin, Terence. 1982. "Aristotle's Concept of Signification." In *Language and Logos: Studies in Ancient Greek Philosophy, Presented to G.E.L. Owen*, edited by Malcolm Schofield and Martha Craven Nussbaum. Cambridge: Cambridge University Press.
———. 1988. *Aristotle's First Principles*. Oxford: Clarendon.

Jaeger, Werner. 1950. *Aristotle: Fundamentals of the History of His Development*. Translated by Richard Robinson. Oxford: Clarendon.

Jaulin, Annick. 1999. *Aristote: La métaphysique*. Paris: Presses Universitaires de France.

Judson, Lindsay. 1991. "Chance and 'Always or for the Most Part.'" In *Aristotle's "Physics": A Collection of Essays*, edited by Lindsay Judson, 73–99. Oxford: Clarendon.

Kerferd, G. B. 1981. *The Sophistic Movement*. Cambridge: Cambridge University Press.

Kirchner, W. H. 1993. "Acoustical Communication in Honeybees." *Apidologie* 24: 297–307.

Kirk, G. S., J. E. Raven, and M. Schofield, eds. 1993. *The Presocratic Philosophers*. Cambridge: Cambridge University Press.

Klein, Jacob. 1964. "Aristotle, An Introduction." In *Ancients and Moderns: Essays in Honor of Leo Strauss*, edited by Joseph Cropsey, 51–69. New York: Basic Books.

———. 1965. *A Commentary on Plato's "Meno."* North Carolina: University of North Carolina Press.

Kosman, Aryeh. 1967. "Aristotle's First Predicament." *The Review of Metaphysics* 20, no. 3: 483–506.

———. 1973. "Understanding, Explanation and Insight in Aristotle's *Posterior Analytics*." In *Exegesis and Argument*, edited by E. N. Lee, A. P. D. Mourelatos, and R. M. Rorty, 374–92. Van Gorcum: Assen.

Koyré, Alexandre. 1968. *From the Closed World to the Infinite Universe*. Baltimore: Johns Hopkins University Press.

Kraak, W. K. 1953. "First Attempts at Animal Ethology in Greek Biology (Theophrastus)." In *Actes du VIIe congrès international d'histoire des sciences*, 411–14. Jerusalem: Académie internationale d'histoire des sciences / Hermann.

Labarrière, Jean-Louis. 2004. *Langage, Vie politique et mouvement des animaux*. Paris: VRIN.

———. (Forthcoming.) "L'Homme apolitique: *Pessia*, *polis* et *apolis*."

Lallot, Jean. 1988. "Origines et développement de la théorie des parties du discours en Grèce." *Langages* 23, no. 92: 11–23.

Lang, Helen S. 1998. *The Order of Nature in Aristotle's "Physics": Places and Elements*. Cambridge: Cambridge University Press.

Langus, Alan, Jana Petri, Marina Nespor, and Constance Scharff. 2013. "FoxP2 and Deep Homology in the Evolution of Birdsong and Human Language." In *The Evolutionary Emergence of Language: Evidence and Inference*, edited by Rudolf Botha and Martin Everaert, 223–43. Oxford: Oxford University Press.

Lear, Jonathan. 1980. *Aristotle and Logical Theory*. Cambridge: Cambridge University Press.

———. 1988. *Aristotle: The Desire to Understand*. Cambridge: Cambridge University Press.

Leclerc, Ivor. 1972. *The Nature of Physical Existence*. London: Routledge.

Lee, Richard A., Jr., and Christopher P. Long. 2007. "*Nous* and *Logos* in Aristotle." *Freiburger Zeitschrift für Philosophie und Theologie* 54, no. 3: 348–67.

Lennox, James G. 1987. "Kinds, forms of kinds, and the more and the less in Aristotle's biology." In *Philosophical Issues in Aristotle's Biology*, edited by Allan Gotthelf & James G. Lennox. Cambridge: Cambrdige University Press.

———. 2001. *Aristotle's Philosophy of Biology*. Cambridge: Cambridge University Press.

Lloyd, G. E. R. 1983. *Science, Folklore and Ideology: Studies in the Life Sciences in Ancient Greece*. Cambridge: Cambridge University Press.

Long, Christopher P. 2011. *Aristotle on the Nature of Truth*. Cambridge: Cambridge University Press.

Loux, Michael. 1991. *Primary Ousia: An Essay on Aristotle's "Metaphysics" Z and H*. Ithaca, N.Y.: Cornell University Press.

Łukasiewicz, Jan. 1998. *Aristotle's Syllogistic*. Oxford: Oxford University Press.

MacIntyre, Alasdair. 2013. *After Virtue*. London: Bloomsbury.

Makin, Stephen. 2000. "How Many Ways Can a Capacity Be Exercised?" In *Proceedings of the Aristotelian Society, Supplementary Volumes*, vol. 74: 143–61.

Matthews, Gareth B. 1999. "The Normalization of Perplexity in Aristotle." In *From Puzzles to Principles? Essays on Aristotle's Dialectic*, edited by May Sim, 125–36. Lanham, Md.: Lexington Books.

———. 2003. "*De Anima* 2.2–4 and the Meaning of *Life*." In *Essays on Aristotle's "De Anima,"* edited by Martha C. Nussbaum and Amélie Oksenberg Rorty, 195–225. Oxford: Clarendon.

Merleau-Ponty, Maurice. 2013. *Phenomenology of Perception*. Translated by Donald Landes and Taylor Carman. London: Routledge.

Moreau, Joseph. 1962. *Aristote et son école*. Paris: Presses Universitaires de France.

Morel, Pierre-Marie. 2003. *Aristote*. Paris: Flammarion.

Mortley, Raoul. 1986. *The Rise and Fall of Logos*. Bonn: Hanstein.

Narcy, Michel. 1996. "Krisis et Aisthesis." In *Corps et âme—Sur le "De Anima" d'Aristote*. Edited by Cristina Viano. 239–256. Paris: VRIN, 1996.

Natali, Carlo. 1989. "Paradeigma: The Problems of Human Acting and the Use of Examples in Some Greek Authors of the 4th Century B.C." *Rhetoric Society Quarterly* 19, no. 2: 141–52.

———. 2013. *Aristotle: His Life and School*. Edited by D. S. Hutchinson. New Jersey: Princeton University Press.

Nietzsche, Friedrich. 1962. *Philosophy in the Tragic Age of the Greeks*. Translated by Marianne Cowan. Washington, D.C.: Regnery Gateway.

Nussbaum, Martha Craven. 1982. "Saving Aristotle's Appearances." In *Language and Logos: Studies in Ancient Greek Philosophy, Presented to G.E.L. Owen*, edited by Malcolm Schofield and Martha Craven Nussbaum. Cambridge: Cambridge University Press.

———. 1992. "The Text of Aristotle's *De Anima*." In *Essays on Aristotle's "De Anima,"* edited by Martha C. Nussbaum and Amélie Oksenberg Rorty. Oxford: Clarendon.

———. 1994. *The Therapy of Desire*. New Jersey: Princeton University Press.

———. 2001. *The Fragility of Goodness: Luck and Ethics in Greek Tragedy and Philosophy*. Rev. ed. Cambridge, U.K.: Cambridge University Press.

Oğuz, Burhan. 1988. "Aristote et le médrésé ottoman." In *Individu et société: L'influence d'Aristote dans le monde méditerranéen*. 213–35. Istanbul: Isis.

Owen, G. E. L. 1975. "Tithenai ta phainomena." In *Articles on Aristotle 1: Science*, edited by Jonathan Barnes, Malcolm Schofield, and Richard Sorabji, 113–26. London: Duckworth.

Pellegrin, Pierre. 1982. *La classification des animaux chez Aristote: Statut de la biologie et unite de l'aristotelisme*. Paris: Belles-Lettres.

———. 2009. *Le Vocabulaire d'Aristote*. Paris: Ellipses.

Pinker, Steven. 1999. *Words and Rules*. New York: Harper Collins.

Porphyry. 1992. *On Aristotle's "Categories."* Translated by Steven K. Strange. Ithaca, N.Y.: Cornell University Press.

Preston, Claire. 2006. *Bee*. London: Reaktion Books.

Rashed, Marwan. 2012. "Les définitions d'Aquilius." *Bulletin of the Institute of Classical Studies*, 55: 131–72.

Recco, Gregory. 2007. *Athens Victorious: Democracy in Plato's "Republic."* Lanham Md.: Lexington Books.

Rese, Friederike. 2005. "Praxis and Logos in Aristotle." *Epoché* 9, no. 2: 359–77.

Robberechts, Edouard. 1993. Review of *Pour un nouveau langage de la raison* by Michel Fattal. *Revue Philosophique de Louvain* 91, no. 90: 336–39.

Roochnik, David. 1990. *The Tragedy of Reason: Toward a Platonic Conception of Logos*. New York: Routledge

———. 2004. *Retrieving Aristotle in an Age of Crisis*. Massachusetts: Blackwell.

Rorty, Améile Oksenberg. 1992. "*De Anima* and Its Recent Interpretations." In *Essays on Aristotle's "De Anima,"* edited by Martha C. Nussbaum and Amélie Oksenberg Rorty. Oxford: Clarendon.

———. ed. 1980. *Essays in Aristotle's "Ethics."* Berkeley: University of California Press.

Ross, W. D. 1949. *Aristotle*. London: Methuen.

Rousseau, Theodore. 1962. "Aristotle Contemplating the Bust of Homer." *The Metropolitan Museum of Art Bulletin*, New Series, vol. 20, no. 5: 149–56.

Russon, John. 1995. "Aristotle's Animative Epistemology." *Idealistic Studies* 25, no. 3: 241–53.

Sallis, John. 1996. *Being and Logos: Reading the Platonic Dialogues*. Indianapolis: Indiana University Press.

Schmitt, Charles B. 1992. *Aristote et la Renaissance*. Translated by Luce Giard. Paris: Presses Universitaires de France.

Seaton, James. 1980. "Dialectics: Freedom of Speech and Thought." *Journal of the History of Ideas* 41, no. 2: 283–89.

Sheehan, Thomas. 1988. "*Hermeneia* and *Apophansis*: The Early Heidegger on Aristotle." In *Heidegger et idée de la phénoménologie*, edited by Franco Volpi et al., 67–80. Dordrecht: Kluwer.

Shields, Christopher. 1999. *Order in Multiplicity: Homonymy in the Philosophy of Aristotle*. Oxford: Clarendon.

Silverman, Allan. 1989. "Color and Color-Perception in Aristotle's *De Anima*." *Ancient Philosophy* 9: 271–92.

Sim, May, ed. 1999. *From Puzzles to Principles? Essays on Aristotle's Dialectic*. Lanham, Md.: Lexington Books.

Simplicius. 1992. *Corollaries on Place and Time*. Translated by J. O. Urmson London: Duckworth.

———. 1995. *On Aristotle's "On the Soul 1.1–2.4."* Translated by J. O. Urmson. Ithaca, N.Y.: Cornell University Press.

———. 2000. *On Aristotle's "On the Soul 3.1–5."* Translated by H. J. Blumenthal. Ithaca, N.Y.: Cornell University Press.

———. 2001. *On Aristotle's "Categories 5–6."* Translated by Frans A. J. De Haas and Barrie Fleet. Ithaca, N.Y.: Cornell University Press.

———. 2003. *On Aristotle's "Categories 1–4."* Translated by Michael Chase. Ithaca, N.Y.: Cornell University Press.

Sophocles. 1960. *Antigone*. In *Greek Tragedies*, vol. 1, edited by David Grene and Richmond Lattimore. Chicago: University of Chicago Press.

———. 1990. *Fabulae*. Edited by H. Lloyd-Jones and N. G. Wilson. New York: Oxford University Press.

———. 2002. *Œdipe roi*. Translated by Paul Mazon. Paris: Belles-Lettres.

Sorabji, Richard. 1993. *Animal Minds and Human Morals: The Origins of the Western Debate*. Ithaca, N.Y.: Cornell University Press.

———. 1996. "Rationality." In *Rationality in Greek Thought*, edited by Michael Frede and Gisela Striker, 157–73. Oxford: Oxford University Press.

Sparshott, Francis. 1994. *Taking Life Seriously: A Study of the Argument of the "Nicomachean Ethics."* Toronto: Toronto University Press.

Stocks, J. L. 1914. "On the Aristotelian Use of *Logos*." *The Classical Quarterly* 18: 9–12.

Thémistius. 1999. *Paraphrase de la métaphysique d'Aristote*. Translated by Rémi Brague. Paris: VRIN.

Theocritus. 1999. *A Selection*. Edited by Richard Hunter. Cambridge: Cambridge University Press.

———. 2002. *Idylls*. Translated by Anthony Verity. Oxford: Oxford University Press.

Theon of Smyrna. 1878. *Expositio Rerum Mathematicum ad Legendum Platonem Utilium*. Edited by E. Hiller. Leipzig: Teubner.

Thucydides. 1919–23. *History of the Peloponnesian War*. 4 vols. Translated by Charles Forster Smith. Cambridge, Mass.: Harvard University Press.

Viano, Cristina, ed. 1996. *Corps et âme—Sur le "De Anima" d'Aristote*. Paris: VRIN.

Vuillemin, Jacques. 1967. "Le Système des categories." In *De la logique à la théologie: Cinq études sur Aristote*. Paris: Flammarion.

Ward, Julie K. 2008. *Aristotle on Homonymy: Dialectic and Science*. Cambridge: Cambridge University Press.

Weigelt, Charlotta. 2002. "The Logic of Life: Heidegger's Retrieval of Aristotle's Concept of *Logos*." Ph.D. diss., Stockholm University.

Whitfield, B. G. 1958. "Aristotle and the Dance of Bees." *The Classical Review* 8, no. 1: 14–15.

Wildberg, Christian. 2004. "On Generation and Corruption I.7: Aristotle on Poiein and Paschein." In *Aristotle: "On Generation and Corruption," Book I, Symposium Aristotelicum*, edited by Frans de Haas and Jaap Mansfield. New York: Oxford University Press.

Winslow, Russell. 2006. "On the Nature of *Logos* in Aristotle." *Revue Philosophie Antique* 6 : 1–21.

———. 2007. *Aristotle and Rational Discovery*. New York: Continuum.

Zarcone, Thierry, ed. 1988. *Individu et société: L'influence d'Aristote dans le monde méditerranéen*. Istanbul: Isis.

Zirin, Ronald A. 1980. "Aristotle's Biology of Language." *Transactions of the American Philological Association* 110: 325–47.

GENERAL INDEX

action, 20, 58–60, 111, 116–17, 119, 125, 138, 143
actuality, 43–44, 48, 51–57, 59, 74, 75, 119; form and, 77; motion and, 72; sensation and, 94–96, 98; soul as, 78–80
affection, 91–95, 97
aition, 66, 69–70
akouein, 120, 124, 147–48, 150, 154, 155, 167, 238nn13–14
alteration, 132–33
ambiguity, 145, 162, 166–68, 238n12
anagkê, 59
Anaxagoras, 228n3, 232n66, 234n30
Anaximander, 32, 74
animals: learning and, 120; *logos* and, 64, 123–24; locomotion and, 101–9, 116, 119, 149, 152, 223n94; perception and, 101–3; sensation and, 90–102, 119, 120, 152, 169; study of, 81–82, 91. *See also* communication; motion
Antiphon, 73, 74
appetite. *See* desire
arguments, four kinds of, 183–84
Aristotle: ambiguity in, 5–6; dialectical method of, 6–14, 183–84, 217nn25–26, 219n41, 220n49, 221–22n76–77; exposition vs. research in, 11, 217n25, 220nn51–52; on the "fictitious," 33–34; Halley's comet and, 186, 245n120; on multivocity of being, 43–44, 49, 226n1; Plato's influence on, 14, 17, 34, 217n20, 217n24, 217n26, 222n77, 222n86; predecessors of, 220n46; Rembrandt's painting of, 141–42; supralunar vs. sublunar realms in, 12, 44, 69
arkhê, 70; *nous* and, 234n30
art and artisans, 72, 86, 105, 108, 114, 127–28, 131, 229n5; imitation and, 121, 140–41, 229n5; as knowledge, 166; poetic style, 246n5
articulation, 145, 159–66, 168
artifacts, 10, 62, 72, 227n7
"aspects," 26–28, 33, 37, 41, 45–46, 49–50; Descartes on, 28–30
Atomism, 68, 226n1
Aubenque, Pierre, 195, 220n57
autopsia, 169–70, 177, 205

Balme, D. M., 147
bees, xiii, 38, 41, 44–45, 48, 56–57, 73, 97, 123, 168, 177, 184–86, 192, 237n4, 239n24; aesthetic responses to, 240n34; buzz of, 151–55, 239n34; hearing and, 146–50, 152, 154–55, 240n39; recent research on, 237n11, 240n46
being. *See* "*logos* of being"; *ousia*
Benveniste, Émile, 211n1, 218n38, 241n46
Berti, Enrico, 218n31, 221–22nn76–77, 223n89, 225n15
Bodéüs, Richard, 235n5
bodily virtues, 133–35
Bolton, Robert, 219n41
Bonitz, Hermann, 5
buzzing. *See* voice production

Cassin, Barbara, 214n13, 234n20
causa, 28, 32, 37, 225nn26–27
causality and causation, 66–67, 68, 70–72
character, 113, 115, 125, 130–32, 134, 138, 140 42
children, 64, 86, 114–15, 122, 129, 140
choice, 136–37, 165, 172–73, 175
communication: animal, 145–55, 170, 177, 244–45nn106–7; human, 145–46, 155–77, 211n1, 244n106. *See also* sound; voice production

courage vs. cowardice, 20, 130–31, 135, 136, 142
Cyclopes and Cycloptic living, 194–206, 208

Darwin, Charles, 219n42
deduction. *See* induction and deduction
Deleuze, Gilles, and Félix Guattari, 211n1, 241n46
deliberation, 137–39, 165, 183, 196, 199
Democritus, 68
Descartes, René, 51, 69, 167, 169, 228n10, 230n30; matter in, 67; nature in, 73; *res cogitans* and *res extensa* in, 45–46, 51, 56, 67, 117; "somnolence" in, 38; wax example in, 28–30, 37–40, 44–46, 47–49, 57, 67, 73, 74, 97, 104. *See also* substance
desire, 86, 103–6, 107–9, 111, 113–16, 131, 165; *eukhê* and, 172; kinds of, 172–73, 175; *logos* and, 137–38, 143; voice and, 153
dialektos. *See* language
discrimination (*krisis*), 100, 102, 107; sensation and, 149

education, 11, 123, 124–25, 140; music and, 127, 129, 236n32
ekhein, 15, 20, 81, 113–14, 115, 117, 122–23, 126, 131–32
elenchus, 6, 7, 10, 14
Empedocles, 82, 84, 161
endoxa, 6, 8, 61–62, 216n15
ethics, 11, 113, 134, 137–39, 175; positive state and, 126
eukhê, 170–76, 185, 244n92; in Plato, 176
Euripides, 177, 192
excluded middle, principle of the, 3, 14, 21, 27, 54, 92, 147, 198; "included middles," 124, 236n27

firsthand vs. non-firsthand experiences, xiii–xiv, 4, 11, 21, 54, 59, 110–11, 125, 129–30, 139, 178–86, 192, 199; animals and, xiii, 155, 168, 177, 181; in art, 131; speech and, 145–46, 155, 169
form: *logos* and, 74, 80, 109; the soul as, 76–78
Frede, Dorothea, 230n19, 232n55
freedom, 127, 129–30
friendship, 138, 162, 223n98
Frisch, Karl von, 211n1, 240n46

Gadamer, Hans-Georg, 215n13
Gonzalez, Francisco J., 248n51
Gould, John L. and Carol Grant, 241n46
grammatical moods: imperative, 145, 154, 158, 164, 168, 170, 171–72, 174, 175, 182; indicative, 145, 168–70, 182, 185; optative, 145, 170–78, 182, 185, 244n96; subjunctive, 145, 153, 158, 168, 170, 171–72, 174, 182

habit, 113, 115, 118, 120–29, 138
happiness, 13, 175, 221n67
having. *See ekhein*
hearing, 115–16, 118, 120–21, 123–24, 130, 138, 149, 158, 168, 191, 235n5, 240n40, 240n44; ambiguity of term, 147–48; by animals, 95, 102, 120, 145, 146–55; breathing and, 151, 239n28; evaluations from others, 132, 139; Heidegger on, 233nn6–7; in Homer, 154; "rest" and, 164–65, 166. *See also akouein*
Heidegger, Martin, 211nn1–2, 212n7, 216n13, 229n5, 233nn6–7, 236n37, 243n89
Heraclitus, 27, 81–82, 91, 125, 223n99, 226n41; on *daimôn*, 125, 141; on *logos*, 3, 21, 35, 37–38, 40–41, 45–46, 48, 99; on nature, 63, 65, 87
Hesiod, 195, 223n97
hexis. *See* positive state
Hobbes, Thomas, 67, 117
Homer, 67, 154; on Cyclopes, 195–200, 203–5; Protagoras' criticism of, 171–72, 175
homonymy and synonymy, 9, 15–16, 18, 23–33, 36–41, 44, 162, 167, 179, 200, 207, 218n39, 224n10
Humboldt, Wilhelm von, 167
hylê and matter, 66, 67, 69, 73

hypokeimenon. *See* underlying thing

imagination, 104, 108, 165, 234n27, 244n103
imitation, 121–22, 127, 140–41, 194, 239n26
induction and deduction, 6, 13, 15, 17, 97, 222n79, 223n92
inherency, 43, 44, 48, 50–51, 56, 57–58, 62, 73, 75, 227n7

Jaeger, Werner, 222n86, 223n89
judgment, 29–30, 108, 128, 137

knowledge, 11, 15, 77, 78–79, 94, 127, 129, 166; sensation and, 104
kosmos and infinite space, 66, 69, 230n23

language, 8–9, 23, 157, 166–67, 215n13; dead languages, 79, 167; *dialektos*, 120, 150, 156, 159, 235n18, 239n25, 241n53; "linguistic defects" in the Other, 246n30. *See also* communication
laws and legislation, 64, 183–85, 194, 196–98
Lear, Jonathan, 216n13
learning, 120–22, 150, 181
letters, 156–61, 168
listening. *See* hearing
literacy, 158
locomotion, 19–20, 79–80, 101, 103–9, 116, 153; and motion, 66, 69
logic, 8–9, 24, 64, 75
logismos, 104–5, 109, 127, 165
logos: *alogos* vs., 61, 64, 116, 118, 198, 200, 207–8; claims enabled by, 178–85; destruction of, 234n20; etymology of, 3, 136, 211n1, 214n13; as health, 233n8; growth and, 64, 84, 98, 100, 190; in Hesiod, 223n97; human form of, 109; law and, 183; nature and, 64, 73–76, 213n10; non-human animals' lack of, 64, 111, 113, 124, 209; in Plato, 17, 222n83, 223n90, 243n72; nouns and verbs and, 163–64, 167; positive state and, 113, 129, 138; "potentialities with," 20, 60–63, 103, 110, 116, 165; as prayer (wish), 170–73, 175–76; range of meanings of, 5–6, 15–16, 21, 191, 211–16nn7–13, 224n3; as ratio (proportion), 5, 19–20, 63, 75, 82–84, 87, 89, 90, 99, 100, 107–8, 136, 209, 222n83; "rational potentiality" and, 137; as reason, 4–5, 20, 75, 116, 124, 165–66, 190, 209, 222nn83–84; as relation (inclusiveness), 3, 71, 89, 155, 191–92, 232n55, 248n49; sensation as, 97–100, 107, 108, 148–49, 190, 209; sophistry and, 183; soul and, 80, 82, 84, 123, 176; as speech, 4, 21, 75, 108, 145–46, 155–56, 166, 168–69, 177–78, 185–86, 190–91, 209; as standard, 5, 19, 20, 23, 34, 36, 40–41, 43, 46, 50, 51–52, 58, 59–60, 61–62, 73, 75, 83, 85, 87, 101, 129, 208, 209; Stoic, Gnostic, and Christian uses of term, 22, 191, 210, 212n8, 215n13; unreality and, 174; voice and, 159–60, 168–69
"*logos* of being," 16, 18, 19–21, 23, 24–26, 31–32, 34, 36–41, 44–46, 48, 50, 52, 73, 87, 101, 167, 178–79; artifacts and, 227n7; and being having *logos*, 187, 189–90, 208
Long, Christopher P., 248n49, 248n51
Lucretius, 68

MacIntyre, Alasdair, 217n25
maieutics, 7, 9, 10, 14
mean (middle path) vs. excess, 98, 100, 135–37, 195
mediation, 145, 156–59, 167
memory, 102–3, 108, 120, 127
Merleau-Ponty, Maurice, 91
motion, 19–20, 34, 36–37, 47, 65–68, 72, 86–87, 110, 137, 165; animal, 89–91; four kinds of, 68, 230n17; nature and, 65–66, 73–74, 86–87, 213n10; post- and anti-Aristotelian conceptions of, 66–70; potentiality and, 55–58, 62; sensation and, 91. *See also* locomotion
music, 45, 98–99, 129, 141, 235n18

Natali, Carlo, 218n33
natural scientist as "theorist," 64–65, 74, 86–87, 228n3
nature and natural phenomena, 9–10, 14, 63–66, 70, 72–76, 78, 86–87; Antiphon on, 73; art and, 72; *logos* and, 64, 73–76; motion and, 57–58; *physis* and, 229n5
necessitarianism, 53–55, 58–59, 228n18
Nietzsche, Friedrich, 40, 226n41
noise. *See* sound
non-contradiction, principle of, 3, 14, 21, 27, 30, 35–37, 40, 47, 49, 100–101, 147, 179; inclusion and, 34–35, 47, 169; rejection of, 101, 234n20
nouns, 158, 160–61, 163–68, 206–7
nous: desire and, 104–6; *logos* vs., 21, 138, 191, 208–10, 222n84, 248n49, 248n51
Nussbaum, Martha Craven, 217n24, 219n44
nutrition, 19–20, 63, 76, 78, 82–86, 90–91, 99, 100, 116–17, 122

organicity, 80–82
ousia, 28, 30, 65, 77, 179

Parmenides, 30, 68, 225n20
pebbles (for counting), 182–83
Pellegrin, Pierre, 134
perception, 101–4, 106, 107–8, 123, 148, 157, 216n15
physics, Aristotelian vs. modern, 66, 229n10, 230n19
place (*topos*), 68–69
Plato: ambiguity and, 167, 182; dialectic in, 7, 14, 99, 222n77, 223n90; *hypokeimenon* in, 225n23; influence on Aristotle, 14, 17, 34, 217n24, 217n26, 222n86; *logos* in, 17, 222n83, 223n90, 243n72; music and, 129; Socratic dialogue in, 6–7, 182–83
  WORKS: *Apology*, 58, 59; *Crito*, 47, 58; *Meno*, 223n90, 243n72; *Parmenides*, 217n20, 226n31; *Phaedo*, 14, 46–47, 58, 182–83, 228n9; *Phaedrus*, 221n74, 235n11; *Republic*, 7, 17, 34–35, 36, 45–46, 176, 226n31, 244n101; *Sophist*, 223n90; *Symposium*, 46; *Theaetetus*, 242n68; *Timaeus*, 235n11
pleasure and pain, 134–36, 165–66, 193, 198; voice and, 153, 158, 164, 181–82, 183
polis, 143, 162, 184, 196
politics, 11, 161, 176, 183, 195, 220n49; "political animals," 132, 138, 153, 176, 184
positive state (*hexis*), 113, 125–35, 137, 138, 141–43, 208, 236nn27–28
possibility. *See* potentiality
potentiality, 43–44, 51–62, 74, 75, 77, 79, 110–11, 119–20; Aristotle's definitions of, 56, 57; sensation and, 93–95
pragma, 65, 66, 225n27, 228n21
prayer. *See eukhê*
Protagoras, 171–72, 175, 179; dialectic and, 220n49, 221n71, 221n76, 225n15
prudence, 20, 83, 138–39, 158, 183, 185, 191, 194, 197, 208–9
Pythagoras, 99, 228n3

recognition, 49, 208, 247n47
Rembrandt, 141–42
representation, 24, 31, 40, 104, 121–22, 140–42, 179, 183, 224n6
reproduction, 19–20, 63, 84–86, 90–91, 99, 100, 114, 122, 153
respect, 123, 132
rhetoric, 58, 220n49

Sachs, Joe, 236n27
Sallis, John, 222n83
sensation, 4, 19–20, 29, 90–111, 126, 135–36; imitation vs., 122; locomotion and, 103; as *logos*, 97–100, 107, 108, 148–49, 190, 209; paradox of, 91–93, 95–96; *proaisthêsis* and, 234n23
shame, 131–32, 134

"simple bodies," 50–51
social knowledge, 10–11
Socrates, 6, 7, 14, 108, 121, 128, 228n9, 243n72; ambiguity and, 167; death of, 46–48, 50, 58–59, 61, 137, 165, 174–75, 182; dialectic and, 221n76. *See also* Plato
somnolence, 27–28, 30, 32–33, 38
Sophocles, 162, 167, 205–8, 247n47
soul, 11, 80–82, 84, 91, 116, 123; as actuality, 78–80; Descartes on, 47; as form, 76–78; three constituents of, 125–26; tripartite structure of, 116–19, 124, 143
sound (*psophos*), 148–50, 238n15, 238n17, 239n30; as noise, 147–50, 154. *See also akouein*; voice production
"spectacular" characteristic, 63, 64–65, 72, 74, 75, 85, 86–87, 232n64
speech. *See* communication; *logos*: as speech
stoikheia, 159–60
stretch (and stretching out), 34, 37, 40, 48, 64, 70, 71, 74–76, 80, 81–87, 89, 96–97, 99, 192; "back-stretched harmony," 3, 21, 35, 41, 48, 81, 99, 123; sensation and, 149; soul and, 118
sub specie aeternitatis viewpoint, 54–55, 59, 228n18
substance, 23, 28, 65; Cartesian *substantia*, 30, 37, 48, 50, 67, 73. *See also ousia*
syllables, 242n57, 242n62
syllogism, 6–7, 20, 71, 75, 104–9; locomotion as, 90, 109; memory as, 103; middle term in, 50, 71, 106–7, 116, 121; "practical," 104–7, 109, 116; *syllogismos*, 105, 106–7, 108, 165
symbolon, 161–62
synonymy. *See* homonymy and synonymy
synthêkê, 160, 224n12

temperance, 135
Thales, 221n59
Theocritus, 200–205

"underlying thing" (*hypokeimenon*), 25, 27–31, 36, 65, 225nn22–23
utopianism, 146, 176, 185

verbs, 160, 161, 163–64, 243n73
virtues and vices, 113, 133–39, 141; moral virtue defined, 137
voice production, 150–53, 156–58, 161, 164; buzzing and, 151–55

Wilkins, John, 167
wish. *See eukhê*

Zeno, 217n20, 221n71, 225n15

INDEX LOCORUM

APo.
I, 24: 106
I, 30
87b19–21: 13
II, 19
110b5–17: 209, 248n49
APr.
I, 1
24b19–21: 6
I, 24
41b7–8: 75
Cael.
II, 9
290b12ff.: 239n30
IV, 1
308a14ff.: 50
Cat.
1
1a1–13: 16, 18–19, 24, 31, 167, 179
2
1a20–b5: 25
4
1b25: 224n3
5
2b5–6: 28, 32
4a10–13: 28
4a23–4b11: 224n3
10
12b7–10: 224n3
12
14b15–20: 24
DA
I, 1
403b1–8: 227n7
I, 4
407b30–34: 84
408a9: 84
408a14–28: 84
II, 1
412a6–9: 76, 77
412a9–11: 77
412a11–20: 77
412a20–24: 77, 78
412a28–29: 80
412a29–412b1: 81
412b1–4: 81
412b11: 80
412b12–16: 227n7
412b20–22: 224n9
413a28–29: 82
II, 3
414b4–7: 103
II, 4
415a23–415b2: 85–86, 114
415b1–3: 104
415b28–416a9: 82
416a10–18: 19, 64, 76
416a19: 76
II, 5
416b35–417a1: 91
417a7–8: 93
417a8–10: 93
417a10–14: 94
417a23–25: 94
417a25–28: 94
417a29–30: 94
417a31–33: 94
417a33–b2: 94
417b3–5: 95
418a3–6: 95
418a14–16: 100
II, 8
419b9–12: 148
419b16–18: 148
419b22–24: 148
419b34–35: 148
420a5–6: 149
420a9–12: 149
420b6-8: 152m 235n18, 239n25
420b10: 150

DA, II, 8, *continued*
420b13–14: 152
420b14–17: 150
420b27–29: 150
420b31–421a1: 152
421a2–4: 151
II, 12
424a17–24: 96
424a25–28: 20, 97–98
424a29–32: 98
424a32–424b3: 98
424b2–3: 87
III, 2
426a8: 90
426a28ff.: 90
426b7–8: 20, 100
III, 5
430a14–17: 208–9
430a18–25: 209
III, 6
430b26–29: 209
III, 8
431b21–22: 91, 100, 110
432a3: 209
III, 9
432b5–6: 173
433a3–6: 104
III, 10
433a14–15: 104
433a20–21: 104
433a23–24: 104
433b26: 103
III, 11
434a6–16: 165
434a17–22: 20, 105
III, 12
434a26–30: 90
434a34–434b9: 103
434b15–16: 101
434b25–30: 103
III, 13
435a22–24: 100
435b24–26: 123
De Sensu
1
436b11–12: 91
437a10–11: 240n44
437a13–15: 164
7
448a9–13: 90
EE
1, 5
1216a11–14: 232n66
GA
I, 18
722b12: 161
II, 1
734b31–34: 51
III, 10
760b15–18: 154
V, 1
780a22–25: 238n18
V, 2
781a26–28: 239n26
GC
I, 2
315b14–15: 84, 232n64
316a5–12: 219n42
I, 4
319b6ff.: 48
I, 7
323b3–19: 91
323b32–34: 92
324a3–5: 92
II, 1
329b1: 78
II, 2
329b7ff.: 49
330a25–29: 50
330b3–8: 50
II, 3
330b31–33: 50
331a2–4: 51
HA
I, 1
488a7–10: 153
IV, 9
535a27–b5: 156–57, 159
535a29–31: 150
536a32–536b4: 156–57
535b3–12: 151
536a32–b4: 159
536b14–18: 120, 150, 155, 239n27
IX, 1
608a17–21: 157

IX, 40
623b27–34ff.: 38, 45, 56
625b9–10: 146, 150, 154
627a15–19: 147, 237n10
627a24–28: 146–47, 152
MA
1: 36
2: 36
7
701a6–13: 105, 106
701a13–19: 105
701a32–33: 20, 105
10
703a19–20: 103
Metaph.
I, 1
980a21: 86
980a27–981a28: 180
980a28–980b26: 120
980b23: 146, 148
980b26–981a13: 108–9, 127–28
981a27–981b5: 128
981b5–13: 166, 181
I, 10
993a17–19: 84
III, 1
995a29: 7
996b26–30: 27
IV, 3
1005b10, 13: 27
1005b19–20: 35, 226n31
1005b23–25: 27
1005b30–32: 27
IV, 4
1006a15: 100
1006a26: 234n20
1007a20–23: 39, 179
IV, 5
1009a32–35: 35
IV, 7
1011b26–27: 27
V, 2: 67
V, 3
1014a27–32: 159–60
V, 12: 56
VII, 10
1035b1–2: 24–25
VII, 17
1041b11–19: 160
VIII, 6
1045a14ff: 36
IX, 1
1046a11: 56
1046a24: 67
IX, 2: 110, 116
1046a36–1046b3: 61
1046b5–6: 61
1046b21–23: 137
IX, 5: 110, 116
1048a10–11: 165
IX, 8
1049b5–10: 57
1050a18–19: 74
XII, 3
1070a4–9: 71, 229n5
XIII, 7
1082b3: 34
XIV, 6
1092b32–33: 84
Mete.
I, 7
344b31–34: 245n120
I, 13
350a14–18: 169
II, 4
360a26: 161
IV, 9: 226n38
NE
I, 3
1094b28–1095a8: 11
I, 4
1095a14–21: 13
I, 7
1098a3–5: 13
1098a17–19: 13
1098a21–1098b8: 13
I, 10
1101a1–5: 127
I, 13
1102a33–1102b1: 117
1102b13–14: 117
1102b22–23: 118
1102b24: 130
1102b27–33: 118

NE, I, 13, *continued*
1102b29–1103a4: 11, 20, 114, 115, 116, 117, 130, 143, 191
II, 1
1103a21–23: 126
1103a27–31: 119
1103a31–1103b1: 120
1103b22–25: 122, 125
II, 2
1103b36–1104a11: 138
1104a18–27: 135
II, 3
1104b21–28: 136
1105a22–24: 158
II, 4
1105b9–18: 11
II, 5: 20
1105b20–28: 125
II, 6
1106a36–1106b5: 137
1106b36–1107a2: 137
III, 2
1111b12–13: 173
1111b20–31: 172–73
III, 5
1114a3ff.: 131
III, 10
1117b23–25: 131
V, 1
1129a29–31: 25
VI: 20
VI, 1
1138b25–29: 130
VI, 2
1139a36–1139b7: 111, 116, 223n95
VI, 3
1140a11: 130
VI, 4
1140b3–5: 105
VI, 8
1142a25–26: 209
VI, 7
1141b1–1141b3: 73
IX, 4
1166a32–b2: 138, 223n98
IX, 7
1167b34–1168a9: 86, 114
IX, 8
1169a12: 138
X, 9
1180a19–29: 183, 185, 194–95
1181b116ff.: 11
On Breath
9
485b7–10: 231n42
485b18: 19
On Int.
1
16qa3–4: 161
2
16a20–21: 160
16a21–22: 163
16a26–29: 160, 161
16a29–16b3: 163
3
16b9–10: 163
16b17–18: 163
16b19–25: 164
16b22–23: 164
4
16b26–28: 160, 168–69
16b33–17a2: 160
5
17a17–18: 160
6
17a25–26: 169
7: 75
9, 13: 110, 116
9: 19: 27
18b17–20: 54
18b20–25: 54
18b31–33: 58
19a7–11: 60, 116
19b1–4: 55
13: 19
22b18–23: 60
22b36–23a6: 60
23a1: 19
23a21–26: 52
23b7–13: 52
On Memory and Recollection
1
450a9–13: 102
453a10–14: 103

2
452b23–24: 102
On Respiration
9
474b31ff.: 152
On Sleep and Waking
2
456a11ff.: 152
3
456b17–18: 117
458a27–28: 117
PA
I, 1
641a1: 25
I, 5
645a14–22: 81–82
II, 1
647b18: 25
II, 10
656b16: 149
II, 16
660a3–4: 156
660a4–7: 156
II, 17
660a35–660b2: 120, 240n39
Ph.
I, 2
184b15ff.: 30
184b27–185a1: 30
185a5: 30
I, 4
187a12: 30
I, 5: 30
I, 6
189b12–22: 225n22
I, 7
190b33–191a2: 225n22
I, 8
191b27–29: 55–56
II, 1
192b8–23: 19, 36, 66, 69, 81
192b21–24: 57, 65, 73
192b33–34: 65
192b35–193a2: 65
193a2–3: 87
193a11–b19: 227n7
193a28–29: 73
193a30–31: 19, 64, 80
193b1–4: 73–74, 80
193b3: 64
193b18–19: 74
II, 3: 67
194b27–28: 74
III, 1
200b27–28: 110
200b33–34: 68
201a11–12: 72, 110
IV, 1
208b10–11: 70
IV, 14
223b21–22: 68
VII, 2
243a11: 68
244b12–15: 96
VII, 3
246a10–11: 133
246a11–17: 133
246a17–b3: 96
246b5–8: 133
246b21–247a2: 135
247a7–19: 135
246b18–20: 133
VIII, 4
255a5–10: 223n94
VIII, 7: 68
Po.
2
1448a1–7: 141, 194
1448a17: 194
4
1448b4–17: 121
16
1455a16–18: 247n47
19
1456b8–13: 171
1456b15–17: 171
20
1456b28–29: 156
1457a12–14: 163
1457a15: 163
1457a24–28: 163–64
24
1460a26–27: 248n47

Pol.
I, 1
1252b19–26: 198
1253a8–18: 15, 21, 64, 111, 145, 181–82
II, 1
1261a18–25: 184
II, 5
1269a7–8: 194
III, 6
1281a42–1281b10: 197
III, 11
1287b23–32: 196
IV, 7
1294a35: 161
VII, 6
1327b23–33: 247n42
1328a8–13: 247n42
VII, 12
1332a38–1132b11: 123–24
1332b6–8: 124
VII, 13
1334b15: 209
VII, 15
1336a34–39: 64
VIII, 5
1340a32–38: 140
Prob.
10
895a4–14: 156
11
903b34–36: 239n28
904b11–14: 239n28
Protrep.
12: 242n57
20–21: 228n18
22–23: 228n3
25: 122
26: 236n41
Rh.
I, 3
1357a: 58
1358b: 58
II, 6
1384a22–26: 131
1384a28–30: 131
1384a35–38: 132, 143
III, 1
1404b8–11: 245n5
III, 2
1405a16–18: 170–171
SE
1
165a6–10: 182
165a11–14: 167, 207
Top.
I, 1
100a25–27: 6
100a30–b21: 6
I, 2
101a35–101b4: 7
I, 12
105a13–19: 15
I, 15
106b6–10: 24
IV, 3
123a27: 25
VI, 2
139b34: 79
VI, 5
142b31: 158
VIII, 14
163a36–163b3: 221